MW00453416

Liaisons dangereuses

Liaisons dangereuses
SEX, LAW, AND DIPLOMACY IN THE
AGE OF FREDERICK THE GREAT

Mary Lindemann

THE JOHNS HOPKINS UNIVERSITY PRESS

BALTIMORE

© 2006 The Johns Hopkins University Press
All rights reserved. Published 2006
Printed in the United States of America on acid-free paper
2 4 6 8 9 7 5 3 1

The Johns Hopkins University Press
2715 North Charles Street
Baltimore, Maryland 21218-4363
www.press.jhu.edu

Library of Congress Cataloging-in-Publication Data
Lindemann, Mary.
Liaisons dangereuses : sex, law, and diplomacy in the age of Frederick the Great /
Mary Lindemann.
p. cm.
Includes bibliographical references and index.
ISBN 0-8018-8317-2 (hardcover : alk. paper)
1. Hamburg (Germany—History—18th century. 2. Trials (Murder)—
Germany—Hamburg—History—18th century. 3. Europe—Politics and
government—18th century. I. Title.
DD901.H27L56 2006
943'.515057—dc22   2005018224

A catalog record for this book is available from the British Library.

For Kate, Donna, Wendy, Caroline, and Judith
My incomparable colleagues of many years

Contents

Acknowledgments   ix
List of Maps and Illustrations   xiii
A Note on Names   xv

Prologue   1

PART ONE   *Events and Entanglements*

CHAPTER ONE   "Voilà—le spectacle!"   9
CHAPTER TWO   A Most Difficult Case   40
CHAPTER THREE   A Very Diplomatic Affair   77

PART TWO   *Dramatis personae*

Entr'acte   133

CHAPTER FOUR   A Brave and Upright Cavalier?   139
CHAPTER FIVE   A Woman of Pleasure   182
CHAPTER SIX   A Real Polish Prince, a Fake Italian Count,
and an Authentic Spanish Hidalgo   234

Retrospective   279

List of Abbreviations   285
Notes   289
Bibliography   323
Index   343

Acknowledgments

While researching and writing this book, I have accumulated an enormous number of professional and personal debts. Many people generously contributed their time and expertise. Pride of place must go to Andreas Kutschelis, a descendent of the von Kesslitz family. When I began work on this project, we met by fortunate accident (indirectly facilitated by one of Peter Albrecht's kaffeeklatsches). Since then he has been a fount of information about Joseph von Kesslitz, the entire Kesslitz clan, and Silesia in general. Although I might have been able to write the book without his help, it would have been a much shorter and poorer volume. Besides providing me with vital information on the Kesslitz family, he allowed me to use material from his private collection and family archives including several pictures. He also introduced me to the history of Silesia and, in particular, to that corner of Silesia—Grünberg and Glogau (now Zielona Gora and Głogów in Poland)—the Kesslitzes inhabited. I cannot thank him enough for his many kindnesses.

As I unraveled the story told in this book, I found myself venturing into areas of history about which I initially knew little. Several people facilitated my education. Larry Wolff of Boston College coached me in matters Polish and shared with me his superb familiarity with Casanova's memoirs. In addition, he read Chapters 5 and 6, corrected my facts, and set me straight on interpretations. While he is, of course, in no way responsible for remaining errors, the sections on Poland and Courland benefited immensely from his expert gaze. Jolanta Lion translated Polish biographical articles that allowed me to comprehend better the complexities of Polish politics in the 1760s and 1770s and the role the Poniatowski brothers played in them. Other people assisted me with Spanish materials. Hans Pohl offered suggestions about how I might discover more about Sanpelayo, while John Soluri and Richard Maddox, my former colleagues in the Department of History at Carnegie Mellon University, guided me through some Spanish labyrinths. Arleen Tuchman of the Department of History at Vanderbilt University located materials for me at the Annette and Irwin Eskind Biomedical Library and the Special Collections Librarian there, Mary H. Teloh, arranged for photocopies. Christopher Hanson of the University of Miami prepared the maps.

My old mentor and friend Guido Ruggiero has much to answer for. He first piqued my interest in "history from crime" and has suffered for it ever since. He read the entire manuscript and, as always, gave me plenty of advice—not all of which I have taken! Michael Miller (once again) read the whole work, not once but twice. He listened with spousal patience and nary a grimace (or perhaps only an occasional one) while dinner cooled or burned as I enthused about my sources and the story that has engrossed me for so long.

This book draws on archival and printed sources deposited in various countries and cities. I would first like to thank the staff at the Staatsarchiv Hamburg and especially Heino Rose, who has over the years, I think, grown accustomed to my bizarre requests. In addition, I would like to express my appreciation to the many archives where I worked or that provided microfilms or copies of materials that I needed: in Poland, the Archiwum Panstwowe we Wrocław, Archivum Panstwowe w Zielonej Gorze, Archivum Panstwowe w Zielonej Gorze, Oddzial w Wilkowie; in Germany, the Geheimes Staatsarchiv, Preußischer Kulturbesitz (Berlin), Sächsisches Haupt-Staatsarchiv Dresden, Stadtarchiv Dresden, Ratsarchiv Görlitz, Stadtarchiv Bautzen; the Haus-, Hof- und Staatsarchiv (Vienna); the Archives diplomatiques du Ministère des Affaires étrangères (Paris); and the Gemeentearchief Rotterdam. I also exploited the rich resources of several great libraries in the United States and in Europe including the Staats- und Universitätsbibliothek Hamburg, the British Library, the Bibliothèque nationale in Paris, the Special Collections of the Koninklijke Bibliotheek in the Hague, the Leopold von Ranke Collection, Special Collections at the E. S. Bird Library, Syracuse University, and the Library of Congress. In addition, the Interlibrary Loan Services at Syracuse University, Carnegie Mellon University, and my new home, the University of Miami, delivered books and microfilms to me with amazing rapidity and accuracy.

Several agencies provided time for research and writing, and I am deeply grateful to them all. These include a Deutscher Akademischer Austausch Dienst (DAAD) Study Grant (June–August 1996), during the course of which I first "encountered" Kesslitz. A National Endowment for the Humanities Fellowship for University Teachers in 1997–98 and a John Simon Guggenheim Fellowship in 1998–99 allowed me additional time for research. The Department of History, Carnegie Mellon University, made it possible for me to take advantage of these and other grants. Virtually the entire draft of the book was written while I was a fellow in residence at the Netherlands Institute for Advanced Study in the Humanities and Social Sciences (NIAS), in Wassenaar during the academic year 2002–3. I would like to thank the rector of NIAS, Wim Blockmans, the entire staff of NIAS, and my "fellow fellows" (and especially our particular friends, Ron Giere, Koen and Alison Kuiper, Esther-Miriam Sent, Jay Ginn, Heidi Keller, Gunhild Hagestad, and Rudy and Mineke Andeweg) for making that year as pleasant as it was productive. It was simply wonderful. My editor at the Johns Hopkins University Press, Jacqueline Wehmueller, believed in this book from the beginning and encouraged me throughout. An anonymous reader for the Press made a number of useful and pertinent suggestions that have improved the volume's style and argument.

Finally, this book is dedicated to my special colleagues at Carnegie Mellon University, Kate Lynch, Donna Harsch, Wendy Goldman, Caroline Acker, and Judith Schachter, who were far more than just good colleagues; they were—and are—dear friends, and their presence immeasurably enriched the seventeen happy years I spent in Pittsburgh.

Maps and Illustrations

Maps

Hamburg, c. 1775   14

Europe, c. 1770   80

Silesia, mid eighteenth century   142

Illustrations

Eimbeck'sches Haus, 1830   2

Neuer Wall, 1847   11

Rathaus and Niedergericht, c. 1700   61

Johann Julius von Hecht   94

Joseph von Kesslitz   140

Joseph von Kesslitz's parents   155

Rittergut Salisch   157

The Ritterakademie, Liegnitz   161

Unknown lady   184

Maria-Josepha, mother of three kings of France   202

Duc de Richelieu   211

View of Dresden   219

King August III of Poland   238

A Note on Names

Throughout the documentation, the spelling of proper names varies considerably. Romellini is often spelled with one l and her first name is frequently given as Antonina (hence the diminutive "Nina," with which she often signed her letters). The official documents, however, somewhat more frequently use Anna Maria Romellini and I have preferred to follow them here. Kesslitz is often rendered as Käselitz or Keßlitz, and Sanpelayo sometimes appears as San Pelayo or San Pelaÿo. Visconti's name, however, is always Visconti and, despite his Italian origin, his first name is invariably given as Joseph (rather than, say, Giuseppe). The English captain Barcker is presumably Barker, but he also appears as Bagger and Bagge. German names are always given here in their German forms (Friedrich Wilhelm, Georg, etc.) with the significant exception of Friedrich II (the "Great") who appears throughout this volume in the familiar English spelling of Frederick.

Liaisons dangereuses

Prologue

Hamburg, 19 October 1775, early morning

Few edifices in Hamburg impressed visitors more than the Eimbeck'sches Haus, which dominated the intersection where Dornbusch and the Kleine Johannisstraße met. The origins of the building lay in the Middle Ages; it took its name from the Einbeck brewers who tapped beer there. By the 1760s, it had fallen into such dilapidation that the city razed and rebuilt it. Like its predecessor, the new Eimbeck'sches Haus served multiple functions. The Ratsweinkeller occupied the basement, and the Gentleman's Hall on the first floor provided an elegant venue for private parties and public concerts. The city's magistrates confined important prisoners in its more modest second-floor chambers. It also housed the city's infrequently used anatomical theater.

On the morning of 19 October 1775, Friedrich Cropp and Joachim Friedrich Bolton, two physicians acting in the official capacity of medical examiners, set out on foot through the streets of Hamburg for the Eimbeck'sches Haus. As they approached the building in the early light, they perhaps first saw the Bacchus relief in front. The slightly ludicrous sight of the god of wine's crooked smile may have caused them to pause and exchange wry glances as they contemplated the task before them. Ascending one of two rather grand sets of stairs, they reached the large wooden doors, opened them, and went inside. It probably took a moment for their eyes to adjust to the dim light there, but they were soon able to proceed down the corridor to its end and then climb the stairs to the second floor. Finally, they stood before the low entryway to a small but well-appointed room directly under the roof. The windows provided good natural light, and the whitewashed walls brightened the mid-October gloom. Here lay a

Eimbeck'sches Haus, 1830.
Courtesy Museum für Hamburgische Geschichte, Hamburg.

body on trestles, the body they had come to inspect and autopsy: that of Count Visconti.

> On the orders of His Excellency the praetor [the investigating magistrate] Volckmann, we the undersigned *physici* of this city have examined [the corpse of] Count Visconti [who was] killed last night. He had the appearance of a man of about forty years of age, on whose well-formed body [we found] some twenty-three fresh cuts, slashes, and punctures . . . which had greatly disfigured him.[1]

Working deliberately, tilting the body first to one side, then the other, turning it over, and righting it again allowed Bolton and Cropp to locate a total of nine stab or puncture wounds, three on the right side of the body, four in the chest, and two on the left side. In addition, fourteen cuts of varying depth and extension covered his head, arms, and hands. They found the longest of these—almost six inches—on the left side of the face; it "reach[ed] from the ear to about the middle of the chin; the jaw[bone] was exposed." Even the superficial cuts had bled a great deal. Others were much worse, but would not in themselves have proved fatal.

The nine punctures were another matter, however, and the examiners considered at least four of them "very dangerous . . . and two of them assuredly mortal." Standard practice dictated that, after surveying the surface of the body, the physicians open the corpse to examine what eighteenth-century medicine referred to as "lethal lesions":

> [T]wo wounds on the right side had in fact penetrated the cavities of the lower body and chest, although [neither] had perforated the intestines. The seventh wound severed the cartilage of the eighth rib on the left side and had, despite missing both heart and liver, passed through the fleshy part of the diaphragm and made a hole about an inch and half in length in the pericardium. This [wound] must be judged absolutely fatal. The eighth wound, [found] between the sixth and seventh ribs, ripped a gash in the pericardium about two inches long . . . thus damaging it a second time. The left chamber of the heart, too, [displayed another wound] about one-and-a-half inches deep. [These injuries] opened the above-mentioned chamber in two [different] places. The slice into the left chamber of the heart caused the unavoidable exsanguination and rapid death of the count. [We observed] that all the [major] vessels, like the heart itself, were empty of blood.[2]

The twenty-three wounds they meticulously catalogued and described testified, beyond doubt it seemed, to a bloody murder. Although it was not their job to speculate, as they handled the stiffening corpse, the two physici could hardly avoid visualizing what must have happened: a stab here and a thrust there. Cuts on the hands suggested a fierce struggle to ward off an attacker. The face, frozen in a grimace and horribly mutilated, silently yet eloquently gave evidence of frenzied action. After completing their autopsy, they drew up their findings, which they delivered to the magistrates in charge of the case that same day. It is here that the story of the man in the anatomy chamber begins to unfold as the magistrates painstakingly collected testimony to discover the sequence of events that led to the death of Count Visconti on the night of 18/19 October 1775.

Four people performed the drama this grisly scene has introduced: a Silesian Prussian nobleman and erstwhile officer, Joseph, baron von Kesslitz; the Spanish consul in Hamburg, Antoine Ventura de Sanpelayo; an

Italian-French-Polish courtesan, Anna Maria (Antonina or "Nina") Romellini; and a self-styled Milanese count, Joseph Visconti. Several broader historical currents had swept them together and to Hamburg, a city whose international, diplomatic, and economic relationships would all be profoundly affected by their fateful meeting. The incidents as they occurred on the night of 18/19 October provoke us to consider how the various strands of the narrative came into being—who constructed them, how, and why. Visconti's demise produced tangled legalities that were as hard for the magistrates to uncoil then as they are for us today. Were the events of that evening murder or self-defense? Was this a heinous plot to dispose of a troublesome intruder, the unfortunate result of a duel, or the act of an honorable man forced to defend himself and his friends from the unprovoked attack of a savage brute? All Hamburg buzzed with rumors. Few people remained impartial or indifferent, and virtually everyone had an opinion. The results of the affray reverberated through all layers of Hamburg's community, not only agitating its citizens but also disturbing the numerous foreigners within its walls. The consequences of this cause célèbre reached far beyond Hamburg. Visconti's death, Kesslitz's role in it, Sanpelayo's painfully embarrassing involvement, Romellini's lurid past, and the fact that all were foreigners made this a "very diplomatic affair." Reported in the newspapers, circulated as gossip in the streets, and whispered about at soirées, it also stoked the indignation of crowned heads and government officials in at least four countries: Prussia, Spain, France, and Austria.

But above all this is a story of people. Kesslitz, Romellini, Sanpelayo, and Visconti were not merely eighteenth-century types but individuals. Retired and furloughed military men and nobles loosed from their moorings cast up in many European cities. Few places were more accessible and enticing than Hamburg for an aristocrat of modest means. Few places offered a businessman like Sanpelayo more scope. Many who lived by their wits, and sometimes by selling their bodies (for sex or soldiering), found employment in Hamburg as well. Visconti was one such eighteenth-century bird-of-passage. The celebrated Giovanni Giacomo Casanova was perhaps the pick of the litter, but scruffier adventurers and swindlers were found everywhere, surviving by skill or guile, sponging off others or testing their nerve in preposterous impostures. Like all his ilk, Visconti lived a drama that interspersed moments of plentitude or even luxury with periods of penury and utter desperation. European history pullulates with such characters, but perhaps they became commoner than usual in the fluid social circumstances of the mid to late eighteenth century. Petty noblemen pretended to greatness, and barbers' sons like Visconti claimed the blood of their social betters, whose names they also assumed. Bonded together by history, choice, and chance, their lives intersected with the larger political figures who shaped their world. For them and for those who encountered them, these were *liaisons dangereuses* indeed.

PART ONE

Events and Entanglements

CHAPTER ONE

"Voilà—le spectacle!"

Only three—or perhaps four—people knew what had really happened that night, and by early morning one of them was dead. Over the next days, weeks, and months, several versions of the incident circulated and competed for legitimacy and credibility. Witnesses told their stories, rumor spread others, and the legal system generated yet another. There were few eyewitnesses, and none of them were disinterested. The testimony collected was voluminous, because the investigating magistrates cast their nets widely, trawling in anyone who possessed the tiniest scrap of knowledge or who had had even the most perfunctory contact with any of the principals. This testimony produced mountains of material. Some of it was worthless. Yet crucial information lay buried in it. Taken as a whole, it was a pastiche of the important, the titillating, the irrelevant, and the misleading. Garbled or inaccurate versions appeared within weeks in several widely circulating newspapers.[1] Equally prolix—if harder to pin down and evaluate as a form of historical evidence—were the many rumors that flew about. Only echoes of these have survived as off-hand remarks in meetings of the Senat (Hamburg's city council and highest governing organ), hints obscured in diplomatic dispatches, and innuendoes that enlivened private correspondence. Rarely did anyone attempt to gather all this together into a coherent narrative. One person did so: the syndic of the Senat, Garlieb Sillem, a well-respected lawyer and valued civil servant.[2]

Sillem was one of four municipal syndics and, as such, legal advisor to Hamburg's government. His narrative must be the starting point, not because it offered the correct, most accurate, or even best written version, but precisely because it arranged the various stories, testimonies, and observations into a coherent whole. This smooth narrative not only ordered the course of events but also considered the motivations of the people involved, laid out the legal implications, and weighed the potential public and international repercussions of the case.

Sillem composed his "Historical Narrative" primarily as a summary and as a working document for his senatorial colleagues.[3] His evaluation could also act as a plan for Hamburg's governors to follow, and it thus detailed the legal and diplomatic complexities of the case. Yet despite its undeniably official character, it is striking how lively, even literary, the document is in its combination of history and dramaturgy. Sillem saw the events unfold as a stage play, and much of his language, and even the structure of the report, bears a pronounced theatricality. Some of this is hardly surprising, because the characters and action are the stuff of the drama, comedy, and farce of the late eighteenth century. Thus, Sillem incorporated into the precisely numbered paragraphs of a legal document the swirling motifs of nobility and baseness, love and cabal, pretension and reality.

The physical layout of the report reflects these narrative choices. On the right-hand side of the folio sheets, Sillem laid out his account in flowing paragraphs. On the left, in the margins, appeared the stage directions and the actors' cues: "Arrival of Visconti, Romellini's situation, and Visconti's first visit to her"; "First scene between Visconti and Romellini, and the preparations of Kesslitz and Sanpelayo"; "Sanpelayo and Kesslitz on the way to Romellini and their arrival there"; and so forth. Sillem described his entire presentation as a *Factum,* but meant thereby not so much "a true account" as rather a plausible assemblage of information into a narrative designed to offer the basis for decision-making within the Senat. At sundry places in the document itself, he directly assessed the probability of the events as portrayed and the possibility of competing explanations or other temporal sequences. Besides the "facts" and the historical recitation of the proceedings in the order he perceived them, his narrative also speculated on the "Circumstances and the character of the persons involved in the history" and "doubts about what happened"; it concluded with "comments concerning the truth or falsity of the account."

The action as it proceeded on the night of 18/19 October 1775 by no means advanced as seamlessly as Sillem presented it in this "historical re-telling." Rather, he created a homogenous narrative by selecting, excising, and accentuating. Legal requirements sometimes flattened idiosyncratic language or occasionally twisted the prose into legalese, but as a whole the document retains its immediacy. It must have been as gripping for its contemporary audience as it is for the historian who encounters it today between the dusty blue covers of an eighteenth-century file folder. Sillem's struggle to make sense of the material before him also helped marshal

Neuer Wall, 1847. Courtesy Museum für Hamburgische Geschichte, Hamburg.

rambling statements into a more compact form. Some of this planing is consistent with the document's legal character, but other parts arose from Sillem's own interpretation of events.

"The facts are the following," Sillem began.[4] On the 18th of October, about 5:30 in the afternoon, Joseph, Count Visconti "having been released from arrest in Bergamo . . . [and after journeying first] from Augsburg and most recently from Braunschweig," reached Hamburg. Shortly after his arrival, he secured lodgings at an inn called the Stadt Copenhagen, and immediately sent a valet to a house on the fashionable Neuer Wall where one Anna Maria Romellini resided. He instructed his messenger to en-quire if Romellini was home, but not to reveal his identity or mission. Romellini's cook, a woman named Maria Anna Engauen, told him that her mistress was indeed at home. The valet then asked the cook to say nothing about his visit to her mistress or anyone else. As soon as Visconti had confirmed where Romellini lived, he "wrapped [himself] in a white coat" and set off to see her. He was, the man remembered, "in a near frenzy." It was about 7 P.M. When he entered the house, he muffled his face in his broad coat collar. He appeared to be "very agitated." The cook, who had opened the door, asked for his name to announce him. He refused to answer, pushed her aside, stormed up the stairs, and burst into Romellini's parlor.

As soon as Visconti entered the room where Romellini was sitting, he demanded that she pack everything up and depart with him immediately. When she replied that nothing in the house was hers, however, and that it all belonged to Sanpelayo, he became furious, showed her a knife he carried with him, and threatened "to slit open her belly." Romellini sought to quiet him down by assuring him that she would go with him if he insisted. When he refused to be reassured, she became alarmed and se-cretly sent her servant out of the house to locate Sanpelayo. The maidser-vant left the house about 8 P.M., carrying with her the message that San-pelayo should attend Romellini as soon as possible, "for Visconti was using her badly." The cook came across Sanpelayo at dinner with the French minister in his residence and gave him the message. She also warned him to be on his guard. On returning, she found Romellini in a distraught state, "trembling all over." When Sanpelayo did not appear promptly, Romellini dispatched the cook again, this time to find Kesslitz and to request his immediate assistance.

In the meantime, and unbeknownst to Romellini, Sanpelayo had left the French minister's house to see if he could quickly—and surreptitiously—ascertain what was happening at Romellini's. When the cook cracked open the door, Sanpelayo asked whether Visconti was still there and if he intended to stay. She told him that Romellini had failed to cajole Visconti into leaving. Without entering the house, Sanpelayo turned away and walked over to Dreyer's coffeehouse, where he knew that his friend Joseph, baron von Kesslitz, often spent his evenings. There, he found Kesslitz playing cards with friends and told him that Visconti intended some mischief and was perhaps planning to abduct Romellini and steal every-thing moveable in the house. He prevailed upon Kesslitz to accompany him to his mistress's, where he would endeavor to persuade Visconti "in a friendly fashion" to abandon such ideas. Kesslitz hesitated. First, he proposed letting the whole affair wait until the next day, pointing out to Sanpelayo that the watch had already closed the city gates, and that Visconti would thus not be able to exit. But Sanpelayo insisted, and Kesslitz gave in, agreeing to go with him to Romellini's. His consent was conditional, however. He would accompany Sanpelayo only if the consul pledged that he would refrain from saying anything rude or coarse to Visconti and not give him reason to feel insulted. He urged Sanpelayo to try gentle persuasion with Visconti to ease him out of the house. Sanpelayo did not tell Kesslitz that Visconti had a knife with him or that Visconti had already exchanged angry words with Romellini.

Having achieved Kesslitz's reluctant cooperation, Sanpelayo went home and changed out of the formal attire he had been wearing at the French minister's *souper*. Kesslitz went back upstairs in the coffeehouse to finish his rubber of whist. One of his partners, the young Baron (Lieutenant) von Schlabrendorff, later testified that when Kesslitz sat down at the table again, he seemed "very irritated," grumbling that "this is a most irksome matter. I very much dislike getting involved in other people's affairs, and now I must interfere in something that is really none of my business at all." In the meantime, Sanpelayo had reached home and changed his clothes, setting aside the decorative sword he had worn at dinner. Carrying only his cane, he walked back to the coffeehouse. He met Kesslitz on the street, and von Schlabrendorff watched the two of them disappear down the Große Johannisstraße in the direction of the Neuer Wall. As usual, Kesslitz wore a sword. On the short walk to the Neuer Wall, Kesslitz once again pressed Sanpelayo to let the matter lie until the following day. The consul refused, adding that "he was very worried about his furniture." Kesslitz replied that he ought to alert the watch and ask to have a man positioned outside the house to assure that Visconti and Romellini removed nothing. Kesslitz's logic failed to sway Sanpelayo, and they were still debating the matter when they arrived at Romellini's door. It was about half past ten.

Just as they were crossing the threshold, Romellini hurried up and whispered to Sanpelayo that Visconti had a knife. Only later did she warn Kesslitz. The two friends ascended the staircase and entered the room in which Visconti and Romellini had been drinking tea. At first the conversation was calm and polite, even banal. The three men exchanged the usual compliments and engaged in some small talk. Sanpelayo inquired of Visconti where he was staying. To which he responded: "Here, in this house, where my wife is." Somewhat taken aback and a bit annoyed, Sanpelayo countered that the house and everything in it were his. Kesslitz and Sanpelayo then made several "reasonable" suggestions about how to resolve the delicate situation, proposing for instance that Visconti pass the night

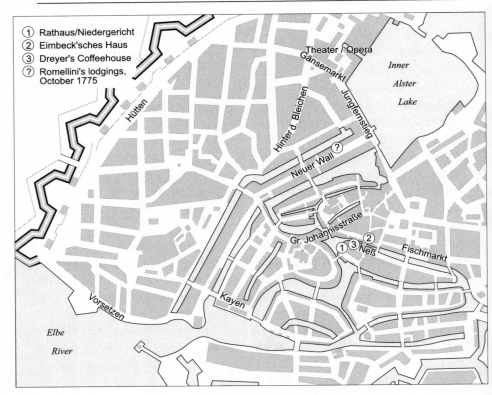

1. Rathaus/Niedergericht
2. Eimbeck'sches Haus
3. Dreyer's Coffeehouse
?. Romellini's lodgings, October 1775

Hamburg, c. 1775

either with Sanpelayo or Kesslitz and then the next day all could be arranged to everyone's satisfaction. Sanpelayo offered Visconti a 100 louis d'or note as a guarantee that Romellini would still be there the next morning, as she promised. Kesslitz and Sanpelayo suggested that if Romellini was really his wife, then she could leave with him that evening and come back in the morning to collect her clothing, jewelry, and papers. After some discussion, Visconti agreed to this last plan and asked the cook to call a coach, which she did. According to Kesslitz and Sanpelayo, Visconti then began to do "all sorts of silly things," calling Romellini "his dear little wife"—which, however, she repeatedly and emphatically denied being. About midnight, the coach pulled up in front of the house. During the entire sequence of events, Kesslitz spoke in very friendly terms to Visconti, clapped him on the shoulder, called him "my esteemed friend," and asked him to be patient only until daybreak. Sanpelayo said little. At this point, everything seemed to be settled, at least for the evening, but this calm in fact preceded the storm.

As the coachman waited impatiently below, Visconti seized Romellini by the hand and tried to force her down the stairs. When she hung back, he grew incensed, grabbed a small scissors off the table, and stabbed her in the hand with it, wounding her palm and fingers. He twisted her arms, "almost dislocating them," and tore the trim of her dress, put his arms around her as though trying to carry her off bodily, and whispered to her fiercely in Italian: "Before long you will be hanged, and another will be hanged as well." He tossed a "furious glance" at Sanpelayo, elbowed Romellini toward the window, and once more threatened to rip her open if she did not depart with him immediately. He turned to Kesslitz and asked him to leave him alone with Sanpelayo so that they could work out their differences in private, but Kesslitz refused. Visconti continued to tussle with Romellini and, while doing so, reached into his trouser pocket as if to pull out his knife. Romellini cried: "Oh, Jesus! he's drawing [*il tire*] [a knife]!" Apparently, however, Visconti had not actually gone for a weapon, and neither Sanpelayo nor Kesslitz recollected seeing a blade at this point. Kesslitz went over to the struggling couple, freed Romellini from Visconti's grasp, and advised her to leave the room. Kesslitz continued to reassure Visconti that no one was trying to elude him or escape; Sanpelayo threatened to call the watch. Several times during these minutes, the cook came in to announce that the coach was waiting below; finally, it pulled away without its passengers.

Now Romellini tried to bolt from the room, but Visconti spun round to pursue her, unsheathing his knife as he moved. In the meantime, Kesslitz had bent over to retrieve his hat from a chair, and he thus failed to notice the weapon in Visconti's hand. As Visconti passed Kesslitz on his way to catch Romellini, he stabbed Kesslitz in the face, slicing "into the left nostril, from just under the left side of the nasal bone into the right cheekbone." Blood gushed out. Kesslitz staggered back, completely stunned by the blow. He grabbed at the frame of the door and clung to it. Having disabled Kesslitz at least temporarily, Visconti swiftly lunged at Sanpelayo, stabbing at his throat. Sanpelayo desperately parried the blow with his cane. Visconti resumed the attack and, this time, Sanpelayo threw away his stick and grabbed at Visconti's knife hand in a desperate attempt to save himself. Instead of cutting Sanpelayo's neck, Visconti's blow slid into the collar of his coat, rending it in several places. The two men scuffled, and Sanpelayo ended up on the floor, with Visconti sitting on top of him, the blade of the knife held to the nape of his neck, pressing into the flesh. Sanpelayo called out "Jesus! He's killing me!" and begged Kesslitz to save him.

Aroused from his stupor by Sanpelayo's cries, Kesslitz pulled himself together, drew his sword, and struck Visconti with the flat side as he rolled around on the floor with Sanpelayo. Visconti turned, raised himself halfway up, and thrust at Kesslitz. Kesslitz bent over Visconti, seizing the blade of the knife in an attempt to twist it out of Visconti's hand. Visconti pulled the knife back, dragging it through the palm of Kesslitz's hand, badly lacerating the left index finger. Visconti slashed out once more, striking Kesslitz in the cloth of his coat and ripping through it. To prevent Visconti from hitting him again, Kesslitz slammed the hilt of his sword into Visconti's face, causing him to topple backwards.

But the blow deterred Visconti for only a moment; he sprang up and "in a rage" threw himself at Kesslitz once again. Diving under Kesslitz's guard, he laid hold of the sword blade. Later, Kesslitz said that he remembered almost nothing more of the fight until it was over, except that he had struck at Visconti repeatedly in trying to fend him off. He also recalled that Visconti had grasped the blade of the sword several times and held on so tenaciously that Kesslitz had to exert all his might to retain his weapon. Visconti seemed mad with fury. During the entire confrontation, Sanpelayo neither did anything to assist Kesslitz nor attacked Visconti. Finally, Visconti collapsed on the floor in a pool of blood, falling completely still—almost certainly dead—a few minutes later. According to Romellini, who had reentered the room just as the fighting ceased, as Visconti expired, he breathed his last words to her: "Avenge me!"

For Sillem, almost as crucial as the action itself was what happened immediately after the struggle ended: the "First movements of the implicated persons after the event."[5] Once Visconti lay still, Kesslitz hurled away his sword, ran out of the room, and shouted for the watch, "without realizing what he did." Sanpelayo followed and continued to lament and whine, sobbing to Kesslitz, "I have you to thank for my life."

After leaving the room where the combat was about to occur, Romellini had dashed upstairs, flung open a window, and screamed for help. When no one appeared, she ran down the stairs to the front door and cried out again for the watch. As she descended, she noticed Visconti lying in a pool of blood through the glass door that separated the room from the corridor. During the fight between Kesslitz and Visconti, the cook had abandoned her original place by the parlor door. At about 1 A.M., she left the house, crossed the Neuwalls-Brücke, and requested two soldiers to return with her.

Alerted by Romellini's screams, four night-watchmen now arrived. Going up the steps to the house, they saw Sanpelayo standing in front of the door and Kesslitz leaning on the balustrade. The latter asked them to call for "Dr. Wördenhoff" (that is, the lawyer Dr. Johann Hinrich Detenhof;[6] the shock and the pain of his wound caused Kesslitz to slur his speech). The night-watchmen then departed, having observed "nothing exceptional." Just as they were leaving, two soldiers arrived and the cook returned, reporting that she had gone to get the doctor, who lived nearby. Apparently, she had misconstrued her instructions and had gone, not to Detenhof, but to a physician, Dr. Grund (an understandable mistake in the circumstances).

Events had shredded any composure the cook possessed. When speaking to the military watch on the Neuwalls-Brücke, she was in such a hurry and so unnerved that the officer who returned with her had little idea of what she had actually said and why she had summoned him. Her garbled report let him think that Sanpelayo "had stabbed to death a stranger, a Frenchman." The soldiers were taken upstairs to Romellini's lodgings, but from where they stood they could not see the body, because Visconti lay in a corner of the room, tucked out of the line of sight. Kesslitz showed them his wounds and told them that he had been attacked. The soldiers first assumed that he and Sanpelayo had fought. However, as the two men now looked to be on friendly terms, they concluded that "the fight was over," and that nothing official thus remained to be done. Detenhof, who had arrived by then, allowed them to think so. Satisfied at least for the moment, they left.

In the meantime, Romellini and her cook had gone to fetch a surgeon named Regiment, and he arrived about then, as did Dr. Grund. Grund escorted Kesslitz into the room where Visconti lay. and there Kesslitz gave him a brief version of the entire chain of circumstances. Regiment and Grund called Detenhof at about 2 A.M. Detenhof took a short history of events from those present and then dismissed the watch (who were still hanging around), saying "that he would himself report everything the following morning to the presiding magistrate."

Yet by then the machinery of the law was already grinding away. The auxiliary watch stationed on the Neuwalls-Brücke reported the affair to the main watch, whose commander passed the information on to the *Prätor*, or praetor, the magistrate responsible for criminal investigations and for maintaining order on the streets. Although now it was about 3 A.M., Praetor Volkmann immediately dispatched three officers to the scene. These officials arranged for Visconti's body to be carried to the Eimbeck'sches Haus, where, as we have seen, it rested until the physicians autopsied it the following morning. They detained Kesslitz and removed him to the same place. Guards were stationed in Romellini's lodgings. Such were the events of the night of 18/19 October 1775 as Sillem summarized them in his report. This was what Kesslitz referred to as "le spectacle."

The Judicial Narrative

Sillem presented a full accounting of the results of the investigation to the Senat on Monday, December 4th, some six and a half weeks after Visconti's demise. As one of Hamburg's four syndics, his usual duties included foreign affairs as well as advising the Senat on all legal matters. Like his three colleagues in office, he was a trained jurist and, also like them, a member of the Senat, ranking directly below the four *Bürgermeister* and above the other council members (*Ratsherren*).[7] Although Sillem only rarely dealt directly with criminal matters, important cases like Visconti's violent death warranted his participation. The Senat considered his involvement a sensible precaution for other reasons as well. The principals in the case were either too important or too controversial to overlook, and the affair had both agitated the public imagination and attracted the interested attention of the Prussian, Austrian, French, and Spanish courts. (The syndics functioned virtually as Hamburg's foreign ministers.) These foreign entanglements and the extreme diplomatic delicacy of the matter meant that Sillem and the Senat had to satisfy several audiences at once. Dealing with the case thus perhaps called for an astute legal mind and a strong figure at the helm.

Toward the end of November, when Sillem composed his history, all the evidence had been accumulated, all the witnesses heard, and all the principals interrogated. Sitting down to draft (or rather to dictate) his presentation of the facts, Sillem had before him the findings of the investigation he and his colleagues had carried out over the previous six weeks.

One thing was seemingly beyond doubt. No one, least of all Kesslitz, denied that Visconti had died by his hand. Everything else, however, was murky and raised more questions than could be quickly or irrefutably answered: Was this murder or self-defense? Was Visconti the aggressor or the victim? What role had Sanpelayo played? What was the relationship of all three men—Kesslitz, Sanpelayo, and Visconti—to the woman, Romellini, and to each other? How had a diplomatic consul, an honorable officer, a notorious loose woman, and a make-believe count become involved in an affair that had terminated disastrously for them all? And what had brought a Prussian, a Spaniard, a Milanese, and a Venetian together in Hamburg on that fateful night in late October? None of this was clear, and all of it prickled with legal, political, and diplomatic thorns. Few homicide cases in Hamburg's legal annals would prove more difficult to sort out, and none would be more fraught with international implications.

Hamburg's legal system was basically inquisitorial, although it retained some aspects of an older accusatory (or adversarial) process. The word "inquisitorial" has a nasty ring to it, imparted by a long-standing (and exaggerated) distaste for the purported injustices of the Spanish and Roman Inquisitions and the integral role torture supposedly played in their methods of obtaining evidence. In late medieval and early modern times, however, the introduction of Roman law and inquisitorial procedures formed part of a movement to reform the legal system by discouraging private justice, feuds, trial by ordeal, and the payment of blood money. In many places, accusatory aspects lingered, however, reflecting Germanic traditions, and these became especially obvious in criminal procedures. (In Hamburg, the criminal procedure was known as the *Fiskalisches Prozeß*, fiscal process.)[8] The most important early modern legal formulation in the German Empire, the *Constitutio Criminalis Carolina* promulgated in 1532, embodied both conventions.

Legal historians typically compare and contrast the accusatorial and inquisitorial processes. The major difference lies in how procedures are initiated. Roughly defined, "[t]he essential difference between pure accusatorial and inquisitorial procedure consists in this, that in the former the injured party pursues his rights. . . . In inquisitorial procedure, on the other hand, the state prosecutes crime."[9] The *Carolina* was, it should be remembered, a reform document that, while retaining some elements of the older accusatory process, also deterred it and tried to balance the need to deal effectively with crime and the wish to shield individuals from legal excesses (as well as, of course, against arbitrary justice). The *Carolina*, unlike its many Germanic predecessors, advanced "the view that the object of criminal procedure is to permit a judgment to be made about the authorship of criminal acts, based on a rational inquiry into the facts and circumstances." Officers of the state, either a judge or an investigating magistrate (in Hamburg, one of the two praetors), conducted that inquiry. The *Carolina*, like all the legal codes derived from it or based on its principles (and this includes the general and specific provisions of Hamburg's legal codes), set out detailed guidelines for taking and evaluating the testimony of eye- and character witnesses; determining when torture should be applied; and testing the veracity of information (especially confessions) obtained under duress.[10]

Constitutional forms and local customs thus shaped legal procedures in Hamburg as elsewhere in early modern Europe. Hamburg law was derived mostly from Roman statute law, but retained remnants of Germanic traditional law as well.[11] While the major legal statutes of 1605 and 1622 set up basic rules, a hundred years of strife between the Senat and the collegial bodies (made up of citizens of lesser rank) produced precedents, compromises, and usages that substantially modified practice. The whole edifice was tremendously ramified and, although clear procedural formulas existed, sharp disagreements arose over what should be done in particular instances. During the whole period from 1622 to 1811, conflict characterized the exercise of justice in Hamburg. Above all, the citizen members of the major court of first instance—the Niedergericht—vigorously defended their authority. They jealously watched over and championed the rights of citizens against interference from the Senat that, in their eyes, threatened to encroach on, limit, or even destroy civic freedoms (*bürgerliche Freiheiten*). The members of the Niedergericht included the two praetors (praetors were senators and, as such, members of the city council) as presiding judges and nine citizen judges (of whom two had to be trained in law and served as president and vice-president of the court). Additional members included six court procurators, of whom one, the procurator fiscal, roughly approximated a prosecuting attorney.[12]

The Niedergericht formed the court of first instance in criminal cases and the members of the court jealously guarded this right. Although the Senat never openly denied the Niedergericht's legal authority, the line separating its jurisdiction from that of the Obergericht, the highest court, which was identical to the Senat, was never clearly and firmly drawn. And there existed multiple ways to maneuver around the Niedergericht. During the course of the eighteenth century, more cases came to be judged extrajudicially (by the Senat) or summarily (by the praetors). Especially after midcentury, the number of cases heard in the Niedergericht shrank appreciably. With that decline, however, the "vigilance and the pugnacity" of the members of the Niedergericht waxed as they struggled to ensure that nothing infracted their jurisdiction or eviscerated their legal prerogatives. The Niedergericht's "secret protocol," now lost, registered repeated complaints over this slow but steady strangulation. The whole process was, at least in the court's eyes, notorious and nefarious.[13] The judges of the Niedergericht considered their positions "a civic office of the greatest importance and political significance" and fiercely defended what they regarded as their traditional and hard-won rights to ensure that no one and nothing trespassed on them. Only the Niedergericht, for instance, could sentence a citizen to a penalty that dishonored, that is, only it could condemn a citizen to be beaten, imprisoned, or executed. The Niedergericht thus served as "a bulwark of civic tradition," and most citizens regarded it as one of the city's "most critical republican institutions." Not too surprisingly, the Niedergericht's sensitivity to slights and anything it perceived as a usurpation or even the least impairment of its position led to tussles between the Senat and the Niedergericht. Any infringement—real or supposed—was viewed as a direct threat to the republican freedom of the citizenry and was not to be countenanced. Virtually all these battles arose over single incidents.[14]

The Niedergericht (as well the city's other collegial bodies, that is, governing organs such as the Treasury that were staffed by citizens selected from parish members) defended traditional legal forms as the embodiments of the liberties and rights of Hamburg citizens. Thus, violations of forms were not trivial incidents, but serious matters. In the late sixteenth and early seventeenth centuries, decades of unrest and outright civil strife had finally produced judicial methods guaranteeing that citizen delegates, rather than members of the Senat, would exercise justice. Several recesses that ended such upheavals, as well as the legal codes of 1605 and 1622, institutionalized these compromises.

What, then, were these all-important conventions?[15] Those governing investigative and court procedures were paramount among them. Having ascertained to his satisfaction that a crime had actually taken place, the senior praetor initiated an investigation. If the crime involved a death (whether deliberate or accidental), he arranged for physicians to examine the body and, according to their report, determined if a homicide had occurred. The praetor's first, general (or summary) investigation, on which he kept "a special copy and protocol of the facts brought into evidence," began once it was determined that a crime had indeed occurred; the corpus delicti—in this case, the body of Visconti—proved the existence of a crime.[16] Praetors not only concerned themselves with verifying the actuality of a crime but also with discovering its "features." The praetor then interrogated witnesses on his own authority. Such witnesses had to have "attained their majority . . . be responsible, of good name and reputation, disinterested and not a known enemy of the suspect." They must possess actual knowledge of the affair; that is, their testimony must not rely on hearsay. Above all, they had to swear to their statements.[17] Over the course of the seventeenth and eighteenth centuries, praetors in Hamburg had devised a set of rules, or rather practices, guiding investigations and communicated them to their successors in office either by word of mouth or as handwritten instructions. Much care was taken to obtain untainted testimony. Yet the very character of the preliminary interrogations (as well as the more detailed special investigation held later) significantly shaped the story that emerged. Praetors took considerable pains not to put words into witnesses' mouths and to maintain their impartiality. One should not, for instance, ask "At what time did you see Hans Caspar break into the house of Johann Schmidt?" but rather "What did you observe on the street at 9 P.M. on the 22nd of this month? Whom did you see? What was he doing?"

Once the praetor decided that a crime had been committed and identified a suspect, he placed him or her under arrest. Noncitizens were confined in the Watch, but "if a person of rank" was involved, the prisoner was held in the Eimbeck'sches Haus. The latter policy, of course, pertained to Kesslitz. Hamburg's citizens were held elsewhere, usually in the Winserbaum. At this point, the praetor arranged for his actuary to obtain evidence from "all persons who could contribute anything to the clarification of the circumstances." In Kesslitz's case, these statements—the *Abhörungen*—ranged extensively and included the depositions of an array of people in addition to the three surviving principals: the innkeeper and his servants; the man who had driven Visconti to Romellini's house on the Neuer Wall; the neighbors; all of Romellini's previous landlords and landladies; and even fleeting acquaintances.[18]

Almost simultaneously with the taking of first statements in the case, other formalities had to be completed (besides arranging for an autopsy and burial). In case of a death, the *Gassen-Recht*—a term for which there is no good English equivalent—had to be held. This was a formal ceremony, presided over by the senior praetor and his clerk and involving the jailer-executioner and bailiff, which took place where the murder had occurred or where the body had been found. The suspect, if available, was led through the streets to the location of the crime by the bailiff and formally queried as to whether he admitted the deed. The holding of the *Gassen-Recht* publicly announced that a crime had been committed, but it also functioned as a purgation ritual.[19]

If the praetor judged the case a serious one, he then presented the evidence from the general investigation to the Senat, which decided whether the suspect should be charged in court or if it could reach a verdict outside of court, that is, extrajudicially. The latter, however, generally pertained only to minor crimes. More serious cases went to the Niedergericht forthwith, one of whose members framed the indictment. Any punishment decided extrajudicially could not be a defamatory one; to safeguard citizens' honor, only the Niedergericht could impose such punishments.

The next step was the special investigation (*inquistio specialis*). This was, properly speaking, the real criminal investigation and the moment at which the praetor began to make his case. In order to "instruct the judges properly," this second round of interrogations was an "examination on articles," that is, the suspect was "questioned in particular."[20] The crucial phrase here is "questioned in particular." The material for forming pertinent questions came directly from the information the general investigation had produced. The clerk of the court, closely supervised by the syndic in important cases, drew up a set of "unambiguous" questions. In Kesslitz's case, Sillem prepared forty-seven specific points of interrogation.[21] Proceeding to the special investigation was a serious, and virtually irrevocable, step in the criminal process. Public and learned opinion generally agreed that "the examination on articles bears the stigma of infamy" because it prepared the ground for an indictment "that by itself dishonors the suspect." Yet this particular form of infamy or dishonor was "only conditional," because it was washed away when or if the suspect was exonerated.[22]

At this point in the process, the role of the praetor as investigating magistrate moved to the fore. According to the law code of 1622, he was to note "everything that is in any way useful either to the prosecution or to the defense."[23] Once again, customary practice dictated that the praetor (or his clerk) transcribe the details "as accurately as possible." He should not be content with simple admissions or denials, but should diligently pursue all leads, demanding full details from the witnesses or suspect(s). For example, if a thief volunteered, "I stole from there or there," he should be asked to specify: "How did you break into the house?" "When did you commit the crime?" "What did you obtain for the [stolen] goods?" "Where are the goods now?" and so on. Investigating magistrates, moreover, should conduct more than one examination and require the suspect to repeat his story at different times, while punctiliously noting both discrepancies and the suspect's general demeanor: was he or she credible, frightened, confused, reticent? After interrogating the suspect(s) along these lines, the praetor then turned to the others involved—bystanders, accomplices, or witnesses—and examined them likewise. When contradictions arose, the praetor could confront witnesses face-to-face to resolve disparities. Magistrates sometimes resorted to torture, but almost never in a case involving a person of rank. One applied judicial torture not to gain a confession per se but to obtain confirmation of facts or the names of accomplices.[24] Historically, the use of torture had provoked the sharpest controversies between the Niedergericht and the Senat. The Niedergericht only very infrequently ordered a suspect under its jurisdiction tortured, and it always insisted on its right to have representatives present during any "sharp questioning." Several times during the eighteenth century, the Niedergericht asserted its position vigorously, protesting against what it perceived as the high-handed and illegal behavior of the Senat.[25] No one, of course, dared even whisper "torture" in the Kesslitz case.

Once the examination on articles was concluded, the praetor returned all the documents to the Senat. If cause warranted, the Senat charged the most junior of the four syndics with presenting the case to the Niedergericht. The president of the court then requested the senior praetor to arrange for the suspect to be *vorgeführt*, that is, to appear in person before the judges of the court. Minutely detailed rules preserved differences in rank and legal status at this stage as well. Citizens, for instance, wore their distinctive black coats, were unfettered, and were escorted to the courtroom by the bailiff. For a suspect who had not been sent to the common cells (*Frohnerei*), generally a foreign person of quality, like Kesslitz, a lower court official accompanied him or her; such a suspect also appeared unshackled. Those confined to the *Frohnerei*, appeared bound, led in by the jailer-executioner (the *Frohn*) or his man, both of whom counted as "dishonorable people." Contact with either was instantly polluting. In front of the judges' bank, the prosecutor, known in Hamburg as the *Fiskal*, pronounced the formal charge. In serious criminal cases, the court forwarded all relevant documents to a defender, who had six weeks in which to devise his defense. Defenses were presented in writing. When the defense was read into the record in court, the suspect appeared once more. The court then deliberated and reached its decision, the *Findung*, which the president announced in court; again, the suspect had to be physically present. Thus, personal appearance in court usually occurred three (and sometimes four) times. Once a judgment in important cases had been reached, it was automatically appealed to the Obergericht, that is, to the Senat, which could approve, revise, moderate, or exacerbate a sentence, or even set it aside entirely. On his or her final appearance in the Niedergericht and after appeal to the Senat, the suspect received the sentence. The condemned enjoyed no further right of appeal, either to the imperial courts or to any other jurisdiction.[26]

A cat's cradle of rules, conventions, and traditions thus closely bound together the steps in the legal procedure. Whether a rule was trivial or not, whether a form served to obscure the facts or not, whether a convention retarded proceedings, subverted justice, or protected vital rights, depended very much on one's position and point of view. Citizen judges regarded every attempt to circumvent conventional practice, or modify even the tiniest detail of ceremony, as the first fatal step on a slippery slope that would send the city careening into chaos. They struggled mightily—and competently—to maintain firm control over the legal process in its entirety. While the Senat rarely disputed the Niedergericht's right to jurisdiction in criminal cases, it often sought to bend the rules. And one cannot deny that at times the elaborate, festive, and formal procedures of the Niedergericht could easily degenerate into form for form's sake. The Niedergericht and Senat often squabbled over petty points that seemed a complete waste of time, as the Senat and legal reformers maintained. Judicial delays caused considerable disgruntlement in the eighteenth century and topped every list of the alleged abuses that fed a desire to improve the criminal system and court practices. If the legal reformers of the eighteenth century (waving the banner of enlightenment and humanitarianism) focused on the abolition of torture, just as important to many of them was the streamlining of justice, which could only be achieved by hacking away tangles of those "many caviling little" practices that clogged judicial paths. The two imperial courts—the Reichskammergericht (Imperial Cameral Tribunal) and the Reichshofrat (Aulic Council)—presented major targets for such charges. Still, the pace of judicial decision-making in many places had often slowed to the point of paralysis, and many bemoaned the retention of forms that, in their eyes, did little but frustrate justice. Achieving judicial reforms that would accelerate the course of justice, however, stirred up the opposition of those who saw in these forms the best way to protect their rights. In Hamburg, the collegial bodies (and the Niedergericht was one of the most important of them) feared that such initiatives would cut into or even slash their powers, and that their civic freedoms would vanish with them.

For all these reasons, Hamburg's entire process of investigation and its variation on the inquisitorial process produced different narratives about a crime than did the accusatory process associated with English common law and jury trials. Yet inquisitorial proceedings proved no less dramatic than the accusatory ones that played out in front of a jury. Although the proceedings were held in camera, the investigations and trials were nonetheless public events in other ways. Exchanges were written, rather than oral and often circulated after the fact in pirated or leaked editions. Even if no heated give-and-take between prosecutor and defender occurred, still a public drama unfolded and was reported in the rumors that circulated everywhere. The representatives of other governments (in this case, Prussia, France, Spain, and the Empire) eagerly consumed such gossip and then disseminated it throughout Europe in official reports and personal correspondence. Much of the drama of the Kesslitz case derived from its local and international notoriety. Public interest peaked as the case drew in more and more influential citizens and government officials.

The character of the inquisitorial process, with its emphasis on the role of the investigating magistracy, also limited, or rather shaped, the presentation of the drama in particular ways. The document prepared by Sillem for the Senat's consideration had, for instance, to fulfill certain legal and customary requirements. For all its legalese, however, it was hardly dull reading. It was Sillem's task to take the variety and volume of testimony and mill it into a smooth history and a working document that would present the case to the Senat in a manner allowing those who had not read all the materials or been present at the interrogations to make an informed decision on how to proceed further. Moreover, while composing his narrative, Sillem had to think about the requirements of the Senat and to keep in mind that his audience was mixed.

Hamburg's constitution required that a certain percentage of members of the Senat be trained in law. According to the *Haupt-Rezeß* (principal recess) of 1712 (the foundation for the government in Hamburg in the eighteenth century and until 1860), of the twenty-four men who made up the city council (*Senators*), eleven were to have legal degrees (doctorate or licentiate); of the four *Bürgermeister*, three had to be legally trained; and, of course, all four syndics had legal degrees. The remaining members were merchants.[27] Thus, the legal reserve pooled in the Senat was broad and deep. Moreover, each senator held the praetorship in rotation, and each thus garnered at least some familiarity with Hamburg's legal forms. Those merchants who spent years in the Senat (and co-option was for life) must eventually have come to know a good deal about legal matters, while those educated as legalists understood mercantile desiderata. The typical Hamburg merchant family, with its alternating generations or sibling patterns of merchants and jurists, laid down a thick layer of judicial and administrative expertise as well. A good example here—and a pertinent one—was the Anckelmann family. Almost all of its male members were active in civic politics, although the family also remained deeply involved in business. In the seventeenth and eighteenth centuries, five Anckelmanns became senators. One, Paridom Friedrich Anckelmann, was a syndic during the Kesslitz affair and he, as well as Sillem, participated directly in its unfolding.[28] These men constituted Sillem's immediate audience, but hardly his only one.

Sillem sought to reconcile the various testimonies extracted from witnesses at differing times and in differing circumstances. The number of those who gave statements and the amounts of paper generated were quite enormous. The investigating magistrates not only collected testimony from the principals in the case (Romellini, Kesslitz, and Sanpelayo) and from those present in the house during the incident (Romellini's small daughter and her cook), as well as those who arrived afterwards (the surgeon Regiment, the physician Grund, the lawyer Detenhof, and various members of the night watch and militia), but also from a whole range of people who had come to know Kesslitz, Sanpelayo, Visconti, and Romellini over the weeks and months that preceded the night of 18/19 October. The first two sets of testimony—on the course of the event itself—will concern us here; the next set and the extended testimony of Romellini, Kesslitz, and Sanpelayo on their pasts forms the basis for the second part of this book, "Dramatis personae."

"Facts"

On one vital point, the facts of the case seemed crystal clear: Kesslitz had killed Visconti. The testimony taken immediately after the event and that gathered at great length some time later concurred. Romellini, Sanpelayo, Kesslitz, and the others related how Visconti had first attacked Kesslitz with his knife, forcing Kesslitz to defend himself. Sillem and the Senat seemed inclined to believe Kesslitz and Sanpelayo, or rather not disinclined to take their version at face value, except that there *were* a few disquieting details bothersome enough to throw the whole matter into doubt and confusion. First, the autopsy report was disturbing. Visconti had suffered not merely one or two or even three major wounds, but *twenty-three* wounds, of which the physicians considered two "absolutely mortal" and nine "very serious." The many stab wounds and deep slashing cuts and the mutilation of the body that resulted suggested a fury, and perhaps a hatred, that far exceeded the requirements of simple self-defense. Second, only Kesslitz and Sanpelayo really knew what had happened behind the closed door of the room. Although the door had a glass panel and opened onto the corridor, none of the women in the house had evidently looked through it and into the room during the fray. Or, if they had, they steadfastly denied it. Sanpelayo had certainly had reason to harbor feelings of hostility toward Visconti, who had threatened to purloin his woman as well as his property. And Kesslitz's motives, too, seemed unclear. Why had he agreed to accompany Sanpelayo if he knew Visconti to be a villain (as his own testimony soon revealed)? When things began to heat up, why hadn't he left or called for the watch? And what exactly was *his* relationship with Romellini? Was it possible that he, too, had had an affair with her? Or that he and Sanpelayo (and perhaps even Romellini as well) had conspired to get rid of Visconti as a troublesome intruder? Finally, had the fight been fair? Had only Kesslitz battled with Visconti or had Sanpelayo been involved as well, thus pitting two (or even three, with Romellini) against one?

The Senat had good reason to accept Kesslitz's story. The whole situation deeply embarrassed the city and threatened to involve it in awkward and possibly even dangerous exchanges with Prussia and Spain. Moreover, Kesslitz and Sanpelayo were noblemen who had resided in Hamburg for some time and had mingled on friendly terms with the upper crust of merchants and the foreign, diplomatic, and political elites. Neither had been involved in any serious trouble, although several peccadilloes sullied Sanpelayo's record, including a sizzling paternity case a few years previously. Sanpelayo's liaison with Romellini was disagreeable, but, at least until the night of 18/19 October, he had conducted himself with reasonable restraint, if not perfect discretion. He had maintained her as his mistress, paid her bills, and appeared in public with her, but apparently had neither flaunted her nor expected anyone to receive her as a respectable woman. Many worthy citizens viewed the affair as at best unfortunate. Sanpelayo's lechery was distasteful, but libertinage was hardly unknown among the foreign communities in Hamburg. One suspects that his friends simply ignored her. Kesslitz had also conducted himself well. He had no reputation as a troublemaker; he had not attempted to seduce the young daughters of wealthy citizens, nor was he a drunkard, hothead, gambler, or obvious adventurer. He traveled in some of the best circles and counted members of the nobility and merchants in the city among his friends. Visconti, on the other hand, appeared worse than a nobody; a roughneck and a brute, a man who lived off a woman's body, a cheat, an imposter, and a crook. Romellini was negligible; just another one of the many women who made their living on their backs. So why the fuss? Why not simply bury Visconti quietly and hustle Romellini out of the city on one pretext or another?

The answer has much to do with the position of Hamburg as a free imperial city and its constant need to assert its independence and its sovereignty. The investigating magistrates and the members of the Senat had their doubts, of course. Through the Senat meetings and in subsequent negotiations trickles the sense that Kesslitz and Sanpelayo had acted neither properly nor prudently. Sanpelayo had a position that brought him into contact with the high and mighty of Hamburg, and his several indiscretions could not but besmirch them all to some extent. He had not always acted with the gravity and decorum expected of a person who represented the considerable mercantile interests of Spain in Hamburg. If some could turn a blind eye to his infatuation with Romellini, they were only willing to do so as long as the affair aroused no public scandal. Once blood had flowed, understanding came to an end. Throughout these months, therefore, there surfaces more than a bit of pique with Sanpelayo, which is also observed in dealings with Kesslitz, because they had put the city in such an uncomfortable position.

Yet the governors of Hamburg were also quite honestly concerned about a murder in the city. Visconti may not have been a great loss, but the Senat reacted vigorously to incidents in which people took the law into their own hands, and it was not about to allow a foreign nobleman to flout the law, despite its fervent wish to avoid diplomatic imbroglios. Visconti had died a beastly death, and that sort of violence could not be ignored, even if the diplomatic and political repercussions of a legal case against men like Sanpelayo and Kesslitz might result in considerable unpleasantness or worse.

Those involved in the investigation thus scrutinized testimonies carefully, hunting for inconsistencies, for hints that perhaps the real story deviated from the straightforward one of self-defense that Kesslitz and Sanpelayo steadfastly maintained. Despite its general congruity on major points, the accumulated testimony provided much grist for the mills of skeptics and rumormongers. Obviously, the framework of testifying shaped each telling to a large degree, but to a surprising extent, the personalities and the motives of participants colored their words. All related their stories as fairly complete and continuous narratives, albeit with prompting. The second set of interrogations—those done in November 1775, about a month after Visconti's death—provided the most detail. They not only addressed the events of the night but also deeply probed each person's background. Although the responsible magistrates determined the framework of the investigation and encouraged the witnesses and suspects to present their stories in a coherent and chronological form, they also allowed the men and women they had before them to speak at considerable length and contribute whatever they considered relevant. One of the reasons we are able to reconstruct anything of the lives of Romellini and Visconti, for example, in addition to those of Kesslitz and Sanpelayo, is that Romellini babbled quite freely to her interrogators, revealing much about her previous relationships, as Kesslitz and Sanpelayo also did, if to a lesser degree. The principals molded their own stories, perhaps only half-consciously, not merely to play to the audience of investigators or to excuse suspicious actions but also to make sense of it themselves. The act of relating caused them to organize their stories into smooth historical accounts, when the actual remembrance of what had happened may well have been nonsequential or even spasmodic. In this way, a kaleidoscope of memory flashes clicked into a narrative. By retelling the story according to the situation of the investigation, they simultaneously imprinted it in their own minds, perhaps constructing a narrative as such for the very first time. Articulation does as much to construct memories as it does to relate existing ones.

So what, then, were the variances in the stories and why did they matter? The stories differed little in terms of the facts but rather more significantly in terms of the style and situation of the teller. If Kesslitz's story was a tragedy, Romellini's was melodrama, and Sanpelayo's, farce. Obviously, the entire tale ended tragically—or maybe the word is calamitously—for all and especially for Visconti. Tragedy, melodrama, and farce. Kesslitz's tragedy stemmed from his inability to cope with unforeseen circumstances. Romellini's story spilled over with the mannered emotions, absurd coincidences, intense interpersonal conflicts, and stereotypical responses of two lovers characteristic of eighteenth-century melodrama. At least to the point when Visconti attacked him, Sanpelayo perceived only a farce of improbable situations and exaggerated characters.

Tragedy, Melodrama, and Farce

The words Kesslitz uttered when Dr. Grund arrived on the scene early on the morning of 19 October—"Voilà, le spectacle!"—convey much of the sense of tragedy and much of the dismay he must already have been feeling.[29] Throughout his months of confinement, and in each of his statements, he emphasized his regret about the whole mess and expressed his distaste for having had to deal in any way with a scoundrel like Visconti, who "because of his bad reputation I would not like to have anywhere around me for very long." Only Sanpelayo's persistence had overcome his misgivings on that fateful night, and he had protested throughout (which other people corroborated). He had repeatedly asked Sanpelayo to wait until morning and repeatedly told him that he would accompany him only if Sanpelayo promised to offer Visconti "no insult," keep his temper, and endeavor to arrange everything amicably.[30] Throughout the evening, Kesslitz tried to mollify Visconti and, according to his version, did his utmost to forestall violence or uproar. When Visconti became agitated and made threatening gestures and his speech became incoherent and unbalanced, Kesslitz wanted to leave and even suggested to Sanpelayo that they should do so together, because "I wearied of having to witness such unpleasantness" any longer. He fully believed that once they had gone, "these two [Visconti and Romellini] would . . . make up." In the end, he had stayed at Sanpelayo's request and because he had feared that Visconti would harm Sanpelayo or Romellini or both. Finally, and after further (albeit futile) attempts to persuade Visconti to leave, he had proposed to Sanpelayo that they go. But just as he reached for his hat, "I received the blow from Visconti who was standing next to me." Not until Sanpelayo cried out for help did he rouse himself to ward off "that murderous assassin . . . [and] the great and immediate danger in which my unarmed friend was as he sought with all his strength to defend himself against his attacker." Only then did Kesslitz act. Later, he remembered little about the fight until the moment when Visconti lay dead or dying on the ground.

This initial statement hardly changed at all in subsequent tellings, although Kesslitz added things. Kesslitz portrayed himself as having been a reluctant observer and an almost involuntary participant. The intensity of the fight had robbed him of all accurate remembrance, although he was quite sure that Sanpelayo had taken no part. He saw himself, not Visconti, as the victim of a series of highly unfortunate circumstances.[31] In all his subsequent testimony, Kesslitz stressed ever more vigorously how much he had disliked getting involved, a leitmotif of his original statement. Everything he knew about Visconti repelled him and made him loath to embroil himself with the man in any way. Since he was not a nobleman, a gentleman, or an officer, any quarrel with him was bound to be debasing, even defiling. Visconti was by repute "a coward and a base fellow . . . who would not even have the courage to draw his sword." In the summary examination, the magistrates conducted on the morning of 20 October, Kesslitz strongly protested "all such procedures," that is, from his arrest to his detention, and the criminal investigation, "in that the death of the Count Visconti [should be considered] not as a premeditated murder but rather a *moderamen inculpatae tutelae,* a true form of self-defense," for he had only sought to preserve his own life and that of his friend.[32]

Kesslitz's accounts repeated his aversion to the whole matter. He had had to be implored by a friend—not once but several times—and he had repeatedly maneuvered to extricate himself and sedulously sought to avoid any confrontation. When first Romellini's maid and then Sanpelayo tried to persuade him to help, he had proffered various excuses. To the maid, he said that "Herr Sanpelayo was not at the coffeehouse and that she would have to search for him herself." If Sanpelayo did, however, turn up there, Kesslitz would pass on the message. He had categorically refused to hunt for Sanpelayo himself. Sanpelayo was more successful in the end, but Kesslitz had also put him off. Sanpelayo had eventually won him over, but when the consul returned to fetch him, Kesslitz had stalled: Wouldn't it be best to wait until morning "for [he] . . . was very tired . . . and really only wanted to go home." (And Sanpelayo verified a good deal of this, pointing out that Kesslitz had tried to beg off, saying that "it was already quite late, the weather was bad, and he . . . was a little worn out and rather untidily dressed.")[33] Kesslitz still held back, but eventually, if grudgingly, agreed to go, especially as Sanpelayo seemed distraught with worry about his possessions and as Sanpelayo had expressed no distaste for nor any animosity toward Visconti. Besides, he wore no weapon.[34]

The best intentions had motivated Kesslitz—to mediate and make peace —even after he entered Romellini's lodgings and saw her almost hysterical with fright: "he believed that she was practically numb with fear."[35] He could hardly have abandoned any woman, even one of her notoriety, to the mercies of such a monster. From the very beginning Kesslitz had worked to prevent violence; the words he most frequently used to describe his initial conversations with Visconti were "friendly" and "amiable." He and Sanpelayo had engaged in some small talk, exchanging the normal greetings and compliments, although Visconti had answered Sanpelayo only very coldly. He was warmer to Kesslitz, asking him how things were with him and about his health. Kesslitz responded in kind, inquiring about Visconti's travels in Italy and if he had passed through the Tyrol on his way back to Germany. However, the situation had become worrying when Sanpelayo asked Visconti where he was staying, and the latter replied, "Here, where my wife is." As tensions escalated and as Visconti insisted ever more vehemently that he would remain in the house with Romellini overnight, Kesslitz had continued to try to avoid conflict by offering Visconti a way to save face. Walking up and down in the room with Visconti in a "friendly manner," he had suggested that "if Romellini really was his wife, she should go with him." Kesslitz swore on his honor that Sanpelayo had rented the house and often spent the night there. "Wouldn't it be better," Kesslitz had proposed, "to take Romellini away with you now rather than staying overnight in the house of a stranger, which would only give a wrong impression" about Romellini—that she was a woman of ill repute. If, however, she left with Visconti in the morning, everyone would assume that he had merely entrusted her to a friend's (Sanpelayo's) care while he was away, and that that friend had arranged lodgings for her on Visconti's commission. It was perhaps a fine plan, but Romellini refused to cooperate. Visconti had pleaded with her and, falling at her feet, caressed her and spoke to her sweetly. Kesslitz had found this all rather amusing, and he had still suspected no villainy: "he had observed the entire scene from the very beginning until that moment as a kind of comedy."

Things were now reaching the point where Kesslitz's attempts to save the situation became unworkable; events soon spun out of control, although Kesslitz insisted that he had had no inkling that bloodshed was inevitable. The decisive moment came when Romellini refused to enter the coach with Visconti, and he started struggling with her. Visconti asked Kesslitz to leave him alone with Sanpelayo to sort the whole mess out, but at this point Kesslitz was loathe to go, particularly as he now realized that Visconti was very angry with Sanpelayo. Kesslitz remembered the "fierce look" with which Visconti had greeted Sanpelayo, and he replied that "he had come with Sanpelayo and would not leave without him." When Visconti continued to remonstrate with Romellini and began to use force, Kesslitz had interfered to the extent of grabbing Visconti's wrists, thus allowing Romellini to escape. He then spoke to Visconti "in all earnestness" warning him not "to attempt violence in another man's house or it would be necessary to call out the watch."

Romellini fled the room. Kesslitz bent down to retrieve his hat from a chair, saying to Sanpelayo as he did: "Let's go now as well." At that point, Visconti's assault left him "completely stunned and bloody." He did not rouse himself again until Sanpelayo cried out to him in desperation: "He's killing me!" Only then did Kesslitz draw his sword, "because he now regarded Visconti . . . as a mad dog." He remembered trying to wring the knife out of Visconti's hand and smashing Visconti in the face with the hilt of his sword, but after that point, as the fight grew more desperate, he recalled little, reacting—as he later suggested—as a berserker, unaware of his surroundings, of the other people in the room, and even of what he was doing in the fury of the moment, "for he had lost all feelings and memory." He recalled only "that Visconti had a couple of times grasped the blade of his sword," and that he had had to use all his might to wrench it away from him. Moreover, throughout the fight "Visconti never once beseeched him for mercy . . . but rather only gave out great groans such as those coming from people who carry heavy burdens." Visconti was an animal. Not until Visconti fell to the ground did Kesslitz regain his senses. Kesslitz nonetheless believed "in all good conscience" that he had "never exceeded the bounds of self-defense" in his desperate fight with Visconti. One could not possibly view Visconti in these circumstances as anything but "a murderer and a madman." Kesslitz had never intended "to run Visconti through, but . . . merely to keep Visconti from harming him."[36]

Romellini told a very similar story, at least in its outlines, but her tale was more melodramatic. It began earlier in the evening and portrayed a woman caught between lovers, desperately trying to be rid of the inconvenient one, for whom she nonetheless still felt some affection. Moreover, whereas Kesslitz's story understandably focused on the fight and the events leading up to it, Romellini's centered on the time she had spent alone with Visconti, for (at least in her version) she had never witnessed the conflict at all. Thus, the various strands of the complete tale were woven with story threads thicker in some places than in others: Kesslitz concentrated on his attempts to conciliate Visconti and his failure to do so, while Romellini's version was denser at the beginning than in the middle, when events had allegedly proceeded in her absence.

The magistrates took an initial statement from Romellini on the morning after Visconti's death and then interrogated her formally over a period of four days in late October and early November. Whereas Kesslitz's interrogations and his statements returned again and again to the events of 18/19 October, Romellini's statements—significantly shaped, of course, by exploratory questions—offered more information on her previous life and her acquaintances. Her interrogators were, of course, interested in the course of events, yet Romellini and they together forged a longer tale that located the critical action in places far removed from the house on Neuer Wall.

She commenced her story with a short account of her background— "her father was an officer of noble birth"—and then she described her relationship to Visconti, with whom she had concluded a *mariage de conscience* in Hamburg some eighteen months previously. When Visconti abandoned her with his unpaid debts, she had taken up with Sanpelayo and had "lived with him as a good friend or rather as his mistress." When Visconti had unexpectedly reappeared and commanded her to pack up everything in the house and leave with him, she had refused; "while she might be a libertine, she was not a crook."[37]

In the more extensive evidence she gave at the beginning of November, Romellini described in far greater detail the events that occurred during her tête-à-tête with Visconti. Other than the statement of her cook, who was not always present, hers is the only information we have about the crucial period of early evening, 18 October. About fifteen minutes after the valet's inquiry, she had been sitting in her boudoir, trimming a dress, when "a man completely concealed in a white coat entered the room." At first, she had thought it was Sanpelayo and so addressed him. When he revealed himself to be Visconti, she had felt "completely at a loss." Visconti had asked her, "What [do you mean] Sanpelayo, doesn't your heart tell you that it is I, Visconti?" He then stalked about the room, admired the fine furnishings, and inquired if she had any good silver plate. When she answered that, yes, she had, he took out his purse and showed her its meager contents: two louis d'or and a few groschen. She noted that he was poorly dressed and asked him how he fared. To which he replied that she had enough for him to live quite well. Moreover, he intended to remain with her and regarded "everything there as in fact his." When she countered that it was not her property and she could not so crassly deceive her lover, Visconti became "extremely agitated" and threatened to retaliate against Sanpelayo. He then took a knife out of his pocket and demanded that she sleep with him or "he would slit open her belly," as he had done, he reminded her, to another faithless woman in Italy. One more death meant little, because "he had wearied of life and would anyway not live much longer." Before he died, however, he wanted revenge. Frightened, Romellini sought to distract him. She served him tea and rusks, but her attempts to divert him only worked for a short while. He soon returned to his demands that she take everything and leave with him, while expressing great animosity toward Sanpelayo. Espying the portrait of Sanpelayo that hung in the room, he became very agitated and "wanted to slash it to shreds." She prevented him from doing so by speaking softly to him. Yet she was badly frightened and terrified of remaining alone with him any longer. On a pretext, she left the room and sent the cook out to find Sanpelayo. Curiously, at this point, Visconti asked Romellini to send for Kesslitz, saying "he wanted to talk to [him] and to see if he was still his true friend." He warned her, however, to remain completely silent; otherwise, he would "take revenge on her." Between the time she sent the cook to locate Sanpelayo and his arrival, Visconti apparently told her about his recent adventures in Italy (a story he repeated differently to Kesslitz and Sanpelayo). During a stay in Venice, he had become the lover of a singer in the opera buffa. When she took another lover and played him for a fool, he "beat her with his riding whip and threw ink on her."

Just then, Kesslitz and Sanpelayo had arrived, and Romellini's account of the interactions among the three men, and with her, corresponds almost entirely with Kesslitz's and Sanpelayo's versions, although the tone and emphasis differ. Her telling has another ring and rhythm to it, stressing Visconti's repeated insistence that she was his wife and her own denial of this and adamant refusal to leave with him. He had continually implored her—in Italian—to come away with him: "Nina, take the silver and pack everything you can and come with me. Let me take care of everything [from now on]." When she refused, he had twisted her arm to the point of breaking it, stabbed her in the hand with a scissors, and attempted to force her to leave. All this agreed with Kesslitz's story. When Kesslitz pulled her away from Visconti, Visconti had "attempted to stab her [with the knife]," but he missed and "struck Herr Baron von Kesslitz in the face with the blade." In other words, she believed that Visconti had really wanted to kill her and had only hit Kesslitz by mistake. When she fled the room, Kesslitz had not yet drawn his sword, and she never saw him do so. She had locked herself in her bedroom, opened the window and yelled "Fire! Murder!" and called for the watch. When no one came, she left the room again, and as she was passing the sitting room in which the fight occurred, "through the glass door . . . she observed Baron Kesslitz [sitting] on one chair and Sanpelayo on another, their heads drooping." As she came nearer, she espied Visconti "lying on the ground in his blood with his head on a chair cushion." She opened the door and went into the room and asked, "What terrible thing has happened here?" Kesslitz could not speak because of the blood pouring into his mouth, and Sanpelayo was sitting on the chair almost unconscious. Visconti still had a knife in his hand and kept stabbing into the ground with it, as if trying to strike someone. He also struck out with one leg until he was finally exhausted and [then] let the weapon drop [from his hand]." His last words to her were "Avenge me," which he said twice, in a "weak voice." Then he lay still.

For Romellini, her relationship with Visconti—a man of passionate and even violent temper—was a love affair gone terribly wrong. Nonetheless, her tale portrayed Visconti as deeply attached to her, and she to him, at least at some point during their long acquaintance. He had loved her; he had wished to take care of her and wanted her to go away with him. As we shall see later, when we examine the lives of these two unhappy people in more detail, her connections with him were complex. Old ties, if not exactly affectionate, and perhaps only those of desperation and mutual need, bound them together. She and he had concluded a (legally invalid) *mariage de conscience*. But Visconti was unreliable. Besides being violent and impetuous, he also repeatedly stole money and clothes from her and left her holding the bag, or he lived on the money her lovers gave her. When he had abandoned her eighteen months earlier, Sanpelayo must have seemed a godsend to her: a wealthy man, willing to set her up in her own establishment, pay her and Visconti's debts, include her in his entertainments, and introduce her to his friends, including respectable men like Kesslitz. Part of her shock in seeing Visconti reappear must have been, not only because she feared what he might do (having been well acquainted in the past with his tendency to turn nasty), but also because he threatened to rock the boat. Her understanding with Sanpelayo had been clear and simple: he would keep her "under the sole condition that she share him with no one else and that she had no other relationships. [A bargain] she kept to the letter." Visconti could thus only have been a very unwanted guest that night, and she must have been truly frightened to send for Sanpelayo, who could easily have (mis)interpreted the situation as a betrayal of trust.

How did Sanpelayo view the events of 18/19 October?[38] If Kesslitz approached the meeting with Visconti with reluctance and a distaste bordering on revulsion at having to involve himself in such an unseemly affair, Sanpelayo assumed a less somber attitude. Although not exactly lighthearted as he and Kesslitz walked through the dark streets down the Große Johannisstraße and along the canals to the Neuer Wall, he was not overly concerned about Visconti's reappearance, although he was worried enough—or cautious enough—not to go alone. One gathers that he feared more for his possessions than for the loss of Romellini. He probably seriously doubted that she would abandon him for the returned adventurer. His superior social background may well have made him confident of his ability to manage a man like Visconti, and he foolishly let his contempt show. Sanpelayo corroborated Kesslitz's insistence that he curb his temper and try to work out things in a calm and amiable way. He told Kesslitz that that was entirely his intention and that he had with him "neither a sword nor other weapon." Both men felt that, despite his rather distasteful reputation and occasional brutish behavior (Sanpelayo admitted that he knew Visconti to be "a wicked and a nasty man," and that Romellini had warned him to be wary of Visconti and to bring a friend along with him for protection), Visconti was a rather pathetic rapscallion, who could be easily managed with pretty words. "We flattered ourselves," Sanpelayo related, into thinking that Visconti would be easily placated and that the two of them together would be able to ease him out of the house "with no further alarm." Sanpelayo repeated very closely the words Kesslitz used in describing their initial dealings with Visconti in Romellini's lodgings: both of them had spoken "in a very companionable way" to Visconti.[39]

Sanpelayo regarded Visconti's entire demeanor and the man himself as somewhat amusing or even preposterous, if also vexing. Visconti was not a serious rival, but someone to be gotten rid of as quickly and quietly as possible. He observed the interplay between Romellini and Visconti with a perhaps poorly concealed expression of bemused contempt (or was it wry bemusement?). When Visconti implored Romellini to leave with him, Sanpelayo (and perhaps Kesslitz as well?) considered the scene comical. Visconti down on his knees, fondling Romellini, calling her by pet names, addressing her as "his soul, his life, his best little wife"; it was all too ridiculous. The whole interlude between Visconti and Romellini appeared truly absurd in Sanpelayo's eyes, like the melodramatic gestures of buffoons and giddy women with whom one associated for only one purpose. It was low comedy. Indeed, when Visconti began tugging and twisting at Romellini, the comedy degenerated into slapstick, and Sanpelayo observed it virtually unmoved (except perhaps for amusement). He leaned on his cane, "saying not a word either to Visconti about stopping or to her." He and Kesslitz were almost detached observers, although not for long. One wonders to what extent Sanpelayo's almost derisive attitude stoked Visconti's fury.

When Kesslitz had had enough, his words expressed a sense of distaste for Visconti's improper behavior, if less detachment, finally saying to him as he scuffled with Romellini: "Count, let the lady go, I beg you! What kind of behavior is this, to attack a woman. . . . Aren't you ashamed of your-self?" Kesslitz warned Visconti that he was just asking for the watch to be called to end all this.

A few minutes later, Visconti attacked Kesslitz, and the farce became serious drama. Having wounded Kesslitz, Visconti turned on Sanpelayo, who feared for his life and cried out for Kesslitz to rescue him. While Sanpelayo sat or lay there, "completely taken aback," Kesslitz fought des-perately with the count, who "parried, stabbed, and cut like the very devil," until he fell dead to the ground. Sanpelayo had done nothing more in his defense except yell repeatedly: "Drop the knife! Drop the knife!" He had no doubt that Kesslitz had saved his life.

What Visconti thought is written only in blood.

Conclusion: Facts, Fictions, and Narratives

After reading these several stories, and after listening to the many testi-monies, one is tempted to try to figure out what the facts were (as Sillem did) or, at least, to determine which story, which sequence of events, and which narrative came closest to the truth. That the stories coincided con-sistently lent them an air of verisimilitude, as Sillem admitted, but even then it seemed that some vital parts were missing and nothing really explained why the quarrel had terminated so bloodily. We may feel some sort of empathy with everyone in Romellini's lodgings. Visconti died, and the lives of the others were about to be turned upside-down for months on end.

Earlier, I suggested that the act of telling the story, whether as a rather open-ended statement or in response to questioning, actually constituted each person's remembrance of the event. Recently, scholars in several fields (among them, history, cultural studies, and anthropology) have agreed on this constructive function of narrating. Many of these have been interested in how people construct their social identities and, at the same time, understand their own actions and make sense of the world about them. We shall return to this more technical sense of what is called narrativity in the second part of this book, which examines the lives of our protagonists as historical types. Obviously, they were all individuals too, and one should not expunge their uniqueness. Yet the stories they and others told about their lives reflected social, political, and cultural expectations. Here we also need concern ourselves—albeit briefly—with another strand of the narrativity argument. The important thing is not to look for "lies" or "verities" or "truth" or "fiction" but to understand how people con-structed the stories that they did and what they sought (often quite unconsciously) to achieve thereby. When Natalie Zemon Davis examined the "pardon tales" of sixteenth-century France, she looked for fictions. "Pardon tales" were supplications for remission of punishment. In such stories, people were certainly trying to excuse their actions and obtain a pardon, but they also "accounted for motive, and . . . made sense of the unexpected and built coherence into immediate experience."[40]

Thus the stories told by Romellini, Kesslitz, and Sanpelayo were, in this sense, all true, as was the narrative Sillem crafted for the Senat. In examining the construction and function of these narratives, we are not seeking to discover "what really happened," for in a very real sense we can never know and "what really happened" was multiple; it happened differently for everyone involved. Even the sequence of events and the cadence of action moved to different rhythms: sometimes largo and pianissimo, sometimes with a sharp, staccato suddenness that surprised everyone. More important here is how these stories were told. Each incorporated parts of eighteenth-century culture, but each also reflected that culture. It may be trite to say so, but these texts need to be unraveled, each thread followed back to its origin, either in the lives of the individuals involved or in their historical context. This chapter literally—and figuratively—has done nothing more than set the stage by introducing the stories that formed the events of that night and the people involved in them. How Hamburg's government and the wider world reacted to these circumstances depended largely on which story each person or group preferred. For everyone involved, it was a most difficult case, one that upset domestic politics and drew down upon the city the unwanted attention of greater political animals.

CHAPTER TWO

A Most Difficult Case

Practically no one disputed that Kesslitz had killed Visconti. But had he committed a murder? Although testimony gathered during the course of the investigation shaped a plausible case for self-defense, other indications suggested a darker, more complicated story. Most damning were the twenty-three wounds Visconti had suffered. The medical examiners had judged at least two "absolutely mortal" and nine others "very serious." Moreover, the circumstances of the fight—it had taken place in a closed room, no uninvolved witnesses were present, and two men had perhaps fought one—raised serious doubts about whether the plea of self-defense was as transparent as it at first seemed. Should the fight between Kesslitz and Visconti be considered a duel? Finally, immediately after the killing, all the principal actors had done some very peculiar things, which fed the quite reasonable suspicion that perhaps someone, or several people, had been trying to obscure the facts or even conceal the death entirely. Clearly, the ambiguity of the events themselves, the identities of the people involved, and the lack of impartial onlookers complicated the investigation enormously. In addition, both the dispute smoldering between the Niedergericht and the Senat and the tensions over the position of nobles and foreigners in the city retarded the criminal and legal proceedings. The fact that all those involved in the case were aliens, and that Kesslitz was the noble subject of a powerful ruler, Frederick the Great of Prussia, generated a series of foreign entanglements that made this much more than an ordinary murder investigation. It became a diplomatic crisis and a cause célèbre that astonished at least three European capitals: Berlin, Madrid, and Paris.

The Varieties of Killing

The meanings of "kill" or "strike dead" in eighteenth-century legal theory and practice were multiple, as they are today.[1] The various definitions existed not only as arcane legal conventions; they corresponded as well to a broader understanding of the difference between culpable and nonculpable deaths. Certainly, jurists evaluated both intentions and actions in deciding whether a death was premeditated, accidental, or justified, and thus, respectively, homicide, misadventure, or self-defense. In addition, they generally agreed that several conditions reduced culpability: insanity, inebriation, extreme youth, senility, and femaleness. Still, there was considerable disagreement about how to evaluate mitigating circumstances. Thus, although no one doubted that Kesslitz had killed Visconti (i.e., committed a *Niederschlag, Totschlag,* or *Entleibung*), had he committed a homicide?

In early modern Europe, legal and popular thinking about causing a death—about *Totschlag*—rested on a long historical evolution of customary and Roman law. The legal codes of the late eighteenth century perpetuated the tension between custom and legal statute. Barely submerged beneath the surface of legal precepts lay the remnants of older mental structures. Law not only set definitions of criminal behavior and specified rules for punishing offenders; it served as an instrument of state power and a way to define boundaries separating private action from public responsibility. Nowhere does this become clearer than in the knotted issues surrounding the multiple interpretations of "killing" in medieval and early modern times. Such definitions incorporated issues of honor, social rank, military and civilian status, private and public spheres, and the boundaries separating civil and criminal actions. By the last quarter of the century, the battle between the right to private retribution and recourse to public justice had been settled, at least in theory. The legitimate exercise of violence had devolved almost exclusively onto the state. Only a handful of precisely defined and narrowly circumscribed situations, such as the authority of masters over apprentices, parents over their children, and husbands over their wives, allowed the private use of duress. If all admitted the general principle, much quarreling occurred along the boundaries. Questions of honor and responsibility could assume explosive dimensions when an individual's actions transgressed the touchy sense of sovereignty a polity maintained against the rest of the world. In some respects, Hamburg acted just like every other state in forbidding duels as an unacceptable form of private justice, for instance. In other ways, Hamburg reacted even more nervously, simply because it saw itself as a republic in a monarchical world and because mightier powers, such as Denmark, had repeatedly and forcefully challenged its sovereignty and endangered its independence.

The distant German past acknowledged the division between private and public forms of justice but allowed a far greater range to the exercise of private justice and private accommodation than the legalists of the eighteenth century were willing to countenance. Still, these very ancient customs reveal some distinctions—in the attention placed on intent, for instance—that continued to shape legal thinking about killing into the eighteenth century. A deadly blow struck in rage or "in the heat of the moment" seldom merited capital punishment. In such instances, law allowed private revenge or sought to reconcile the victim's relatives with the perpetrator. A duel or a judicially constituted ordeal could resolve the matter, just as the payment of blood money might expiate the death; either provided adequate compensation.[2] Eighteenth-century legal observers (following the Roman Tacitus) developed a basically sociological interpretation for why such arrangements had sufficed for the ancient Germans. Murder appeared to have been uncommon in a putatively simpler and less corrupt world where the Germanic tribes held property in common, and where "avarice for gold or money did not drive them." Thus the tribal Germans had felt little need, it was argued, to smite or rob their neighbors.

Tacitus's explanation for the customs of private revenge, ordeal, duel, and blood money linked these practices to deeply held ideas of friendship, hatred, and feud. For these ur-Germans, both good will and enmity were inherited, or rather passed down through the generations, from father to son and ultimately to all males of the lineage. Thus, they chose to deal with murder or "killings" in as conciliatory a manner as possible, preferring compromise to violence precisely to avoid the perpetuation and escalation of malice and bloodshed that a system of inherited guilt and obligation could so easily nourish. If unable to achieve a compromise, the parties settled the matter by a Zweikampf—which should not be understand in the more modern sense of dueling, but rather as a customary procedure that healed rifts in the community rather than sowing the seeds of future dissension or raising a thirst for revenge.[3]

The introduction of Christianity and the influence of the Romans on the Germans as the supposed purity and isolation of the old tribal organization diminished nurtured a growing sense of the difference between killing "done with deliberation and malice aforethought" and killing that was the result of "negligence or an accident that occurred without intent or volition." Only the former merited the death penalty, and then only after due legal process. Yet eighteenth-century legalists recognized that not until the fifteenth century had the older customs of reconciliation and payment of blood money fallen into abeyance as valid legal procedures.[4]

The *Constitutio Criminalis Carolina* formed the basis for most criminal codes in central Europe at least until the end of the eighteenth century.[5] Article 137 differentiated between homicide and manslaughter, as well as between intentional and unintentional crimes. The penalty generally prescribed was death, unless there existed a "legal justification" (self-defense, or if the perpetrator was an executioner). The form capital punishment took also distinguished between varieties of killing and killers. Decapitation befell those who murdered in anger and precipitously. Premeditated murder, and especially the murder of near relatives (that is, all parricides, fratricides, and infanticides), of masters, or of "very distinguished persons" mandated a more severe penalty: breaking on or with the wheel or tearing the flesh with hot pincers before execution, as well as imposing other dishonoring circumstances such as being "dragged on a sledge" or an ox hide to the place of execution, being denied burial in consecrated ground, or left to rot on the gallows.[6] Thus the penalty for varying degrees of killing reflected not only society's, or at least the legal system's, estimation of the heinousness of the crime but also motive and social rank.

Thus, not all murderers seemed equally culpable, and various reasons could excuse or exonerate them. For example, the *Carolina*—like most legal codes based on it—recognized self-defense as an absolving circumstance. The *Carolina* explained:

> Whosoever defends his own life and person, and kills the one who forced him to defend himself, is guilty of no crime. Thus, anyone who is attacked, threatened, or hit with a deadly weapon or with [deadly] force, and [who] cannot flee or avoid [his assailant] without sacrificing [his life] or [without suffering] harm to his body, life, honor, and good reputation, is also allowed to defend himself. If he kills his attacker, he is guilty of no crime. Moreover, he is not required to stay his hand until he is actually struck.[7]

The Duel

In Kesslitz's case, however, the issue was, not only whether the law could regard the killing of Visconti as "a proper self-defense," but also whether it should be considered as the outcome of a duel and therefore punishable as a crime. Roman law made no specific mention of dueling. The tribal Germans had, however, recognized feuds and retaliation. Such satisfaction was in fact "obligatory in certain cases in order to save innocence and honor." Dueling—or rather private satisfaction—became a matter of personal honor and good reputation in the Renaissance. Legal commentators glossed dueling as a form of self-defense for anyone "who cannot escape a duel without losing his honor and good name." This provision particularly pertained to persons of rank or officers who could neither flee nor refuse a challenge if insulted, let alone if physically attacked.[8] Even in the eighteenth century, a nobleman was obliged to accept a challenge and expunge an insult with his weapon and, if necessary, his lifeblood. Casanova, who fought five duels, explained how impossible it was for a "man of honor" to ignore an affront. "If he were to act in the Platonic way"—that is, "put up with grave injuries rather than to inflict them"—he might be regarded as "a good Christian and a fine philosopher," but society would view him "no less dishonoured and despised . . . and perhaps [he would be driven] from the Court and excluded from noble assemblies with great opprobrium."[9]

Only a duel could preserve personal reputation or a sense of honor (*Ehrgefühl*) once a *point d'honneur* was touched. One might duel as well to defend the honor of one's social group, or *Stand*. An insult to a nobleman or an officer effectively insulted his brethren, his family, and his lineage. An unwillingness to defend the estate's honor was reason enough to ostracize the defaulter, and such conditions weighed most heavily on nobles and officers. When someone in the group—or the group as a whole—suffered an insult or a blow, only a duel or an abject apology could annul the damage done.[10]

Dueling had its heyday in Europe in the sixteenth century, when monarchs had not yet successfully curbed or harnessed their nobilities.[11] It served as the means by which "social elites . . . asserted their right to be above the law." Or, more simply, one who (properly) wore a sword was his own avenger. Laws passed in the sixteenth century to control dueling and other forms of private and vigilante justice proved ineffectual. In fact, dueling probably became more attractive precisely when it was linked ever more firmly to a set of aristocratic sensibilities circling around honor.[12]

Most historians agree that dueling in the Germanies was a fashionable import from France in the seventeenth century (especially during the Thirty Years' War), where duels had become "deregulated," that is, where the duel had become "extrajudicial," in that it had become "private, or concerned a point of honor, and where the combatants had no spectators or judges but themselves." The language of dueling always remained French: *rencontre, touché, secondieren,* and, of course, *satisfaction*. The hybrid French-German term *Satisfaktionsfähig* described someone capable of giving satisfaction, that is, a proper opponent in a duel.[13] Curiously one of the earliest records of a German killed in a duel involved a nineteen-year-old man in Hamburg. The Hamburg anti-dueling edict of 1660 refers to the numerous instances where "people of ordinary ranks, following the example of the upper classes, sent out challenges and fought duels,"[14] although such comments should not be taken as prima facie evidence of either the frequency of dueling or its popularity among non-nobles.

Dueling as a type of private justice fit poorly with the growing attempts of states to gather into their own hands all legitimate forms of force. The sixteenth and seventeenth centuries witnessed two other developments that joined to make dueling a crime or at least worked to hinder its occurrence. First, territorial states, in the Germanies as elsewhere, tried to domesticate their nobles, to render them more manageable, and to make them more useful to the state. In some ways, this endeavor emasculated the nobility, or at least restrained nobles and channeled their energies into the military or into budding bureaucracies. At the same time, and consequently, nobles became acknowledged social superiors possessing special rights and privileges. The second development propped up the first and amplified the endeavors of almost all states to build standing armies and to exercise greater centralized control over those forces in staffing and running them. Of course, some of these initiatives crossed each other. By making nobles into officers and gentlemen whose position codes of conduct defined as much as birth and martial prowess, the state also had to offer them a special social and cultural status in the form of a particular kind of honor. Noblemen and, by definition, military officers were *Satisfaktionsfähig*, whereas merchants, peasants, and artisans generally were not. Attempts to wean the nobility away from the private feuds and warfare they had once viewed as their privileged domain, and that had, for instance, ripped France apart during the religious wars of the sixteenth century, set into motion a countervailing tendency: a need to define nobility in terms of a special kind of honor (usually military) and to allow nobles de facto to seek satisfaction for defilement of honor, while forbidding them to do so de jure. By the seventeenth century, almost all German rulers had made dueling a *delictum publicum* and thus a punishable offense.[15]

What happened in Prussia illustrates the awkward issues involved as social and political circumstances, as well as the proclivities and emotions of individual monarchs, combined either to rein in dueling or tacitly encourage it. The first anti-dueling law in Prussia appeared in 1652 during the reign of Friedrich Wilhelm, the Great Elector, but the courts showed little zest for enforcing it. Friedrich I exacerbated punishments for dueling by mandating that duelists be dispatched by hanging, rather than being granted a more honorable death by ax or sword, and that their corpses allowed to decay without burial. Yet even he equivocated and dismissed officers who ignored a challenge. King Friedrich Wilhelm I of Prussia "was more forgiving, thus adumbrating the fundamental connections between dueling and militarism that would mature in the Second Empire." His son, Frederick the Great, was even more sympathetic to the nobility in general and, while he abhorred the principle of dueling as a brutish residuum unfitting to an age of enlightenment, tolerated it among his officers and expressed contempt for a man who balked at defending his honor with his blood.[16]

Thus, dueling created inconsonances. While Frederick the Great, under the influence of the French philosophes like Montesquieu, could ridicule the duel as "a point of honor badly placed" ("ce point d'honneur mal placé") and regard it as a barbarous custom, he also recognized the inherent ambivalence and the need for an "expedient" that would "uphold individual honor while allowing the law its full rigor." This was trying to square the circle. Moreover, while theory and law condemned dueling, courts (and especially military courts) punished it only reluctantly. An officer who declined to fight when challenged or insulted might well find himself a social outcast.[17] Immanuel Kant at the very end of the century observed that dueling "receives leniency from the government, and it is made a matter of so-called honor in the army to take action against insults into one's own hands." Even citizens of merchant republics like Hamburg, who generally sneered at military and aristocratic pretensions, could nonetheless accept that a nobleman once insulted found himself in a very difficult position. If he did not fight, he forfeited his honor.[18]

Dueling may seem a problem unique to states with a military or a resident nobility and less of an issue for merchant emporia like Hamburg. Hamburg lacked, of course, both an indigenous nobility and a legally defined patriciate (as a sort of quasi-nobility). Although Hamburg engaged a certain number of soldiers for its garrison, few were nobles and thus *Satisfaktionsfähig*. During the course of the seventeenth and eighteenth centuries, however, dueling was to some extent democratized, because it became a custom among the middle classes as well as among university students (although the latter development only peaked in the dueling corps of the Kaiserreich and the Dual Monarchy). How many native Hamburgers engaged in duels is not very clear; the city executed no one for dueling, although some forms of fighting might have been judged spontaneous duels—*rencontres*—and punished as such.

Hamburg prohibited dueling in ways that built quite consciously on the models the Empire and other German territories had initiated. First in 1660 and then again in 1699, Hamburg promulgated anti-dueling edicts.

The former remarked on the need for such an edict because "duels . . . have become so common."[19] This and similar phrases indicating "recent increases" of undesirable behaviors or crimes formulaically preceded the enactment of almost every eighteenth-century edict or ordinance, and they in no way prove that more duels were being fought in the city. Outrageous incidents, whether frequent or seldom, elevated perceptions as much as did actual numbers. The affair of the comte de Montmorency-Bouteville, whom Cardinal Richelieu had executed in 1627, marked a milestone in the slow extinction of dueling in France. The comte fought some twenty-two duels in about thirteen years. He and his cousin (and frequent second) were tried by the royal court and decapitated by the public executioner, to the horror and chagrin of bluebloods throughout Europe. The Klettenburg case in Frankfurt in 1709 was similarly renowned, although here it seemed that the result of a duel between a new and an old noble actually strengthened alliances between the two groups. Both causes célèbres became part of dueling lore. Both, perhaps paradoxically, contributed to dueling's fame and notoriety and to its allure, while simultaneously feeding a growing aversion to it.[20]

The timing of the prohibition against dueling in Hamburg must be set into the larger historical context. A condition of almost civil war that reigned in Hamburg from the 1690s and through the early 1700s was finally halted by an imperial commission and the establishment of a new municipal order in the constitution of 1712, which "provided the foundation for stability over the next 150 years."[21] While this civic peace proved by no means illusory—the number of riotous incidents in subsequent decades was tiny—nonetheless it took some time for Hamburgers to develop new political and social modi vivendi. The principal goal in the late 1710s and 1720s was to heal the still festering civic wounds and to forestall further outbreaks of violence, while forging new ideals of civic culture and defining private and public behavior suitable for a merchant republic. The dueling edict of 1720 can be seen as part of this larger project.

The wording of the 1720 prohibition closely followed that of edicts against dueling promulgated in other states and threatened duelists with similarly draconian punishments: seizure of property; abrogation of the right of the duelist's family to inherit his estate; summary condemnation to death by decapitation; and denial of "all Christian [funerary] ceremonies," "burial in a common grave or in unconsecrated ground," or forfeiture of burial entirely.[22] This edict, which remained in force throughout the eighteenth century, prescribed penalties for dueling that sought to arrest its spread by reversing the polarities of its purpose. If dueling was an integral part of the "code of honour which gave it its *raison d'étre*,"[23] then one way to combat it was to transform it into a polluting or dishonoring process. Polities tried to do so by punishing offenders not only in "body and property" but also in their honor.

Honor was critical yet ineffable. Honor—or rather the attributes of honor—varied with each social grouping. Although some occupations during the course of the seventeenth and eighteenth centuries came to be defined more rigorously as "dishonorable" and "polluting," each social group valued its own honor. Honor was protean and appeared in many guises: knightly and bourgeois honor, male and female honor, artisan and military honor. Definitions of honor paralleled the definitions of virtues each group saw itself as possessing and that each group used to distinguish itself from others.[24]

If dueling were to be made dishonorable, then perhaps it could be extinguished. Hamburg law specified that those who died in duels were to be buried either without Christian ceremonies or in unhallowed ground (if buried at all). Scholars have often remarked how polities used the threat of a dishonorable burial or even a pauper's funeral to inculcate desirable behaviors and prevent undesirable ones. The *sepulcrum asininum* (*Eselbegräbnis*), or burial in unhallowed ground without a religious ceremony, awaited a range of criminals (especially parricides), as well as a number of people regarded as dishonorable because of their occupations (executioners, skinners, and the like).[25] With the edict of 1699, and even more unambiguously in the 1720 statute, Hamburg condemned duelists in body, soul, and honor. Yet public and even governmental opinion divided here, and the meliorating phrases in the edict "as thought proper" or "according to the circumstances" allowed room for face-saving compromises. And indeed, few who died in duels were denied burial in consecrated ground. Usually, the city permitted their relatives to claim the bodies and make their own funeral arrangements; these were often only discreet rather than dishonorable.[26]

It was, moreover, difficult to prove that a fight was indeed a duel. In all edicts proscribing dueling, clauses accorded people the right to defend themselves against an "unprovoked attack." Could Kesslitz's killing of Visconti be seen as a legitimate form of self-defense, then, and was he thus legally "answerable for nothing to anyone"?

Murder or Self-Defense?

Kesslitz was clear in his own mind about what he had intended and about how he regarded his behavior on the night of Visconti's death: "that it was never his design to run Visconti through, rather he only . . . used the point of his sword to keep Visconti from injuring him."[27] Legally, everything hinged on whether Kesslitz had defended himself as he claimed or not. If one could interpret Kesslitz's actions as self-defense and nothing more, then he was, as his lawyer and legal phraseology put it, "answerable to no one" and not subject to punishment.[28] One can trace the legal debate as it twisted through the days and weeks of the investigation, turning on just this point. Several knowledgeable observers evaluated Kesslitz's culpability differently. These disparate views lie scattered throughout the vast documentation the case generated, but three documents encapsulate the various positions: the history of the case Sillem composed (already discussed in Chapter 1); Detenhof's written defense of Kesslitz; and the report of the Fiscal, or prosecutor.[29] Each author crafted his narrative for a different purpose—as an explanation of the legal position to the Senat that also served as court of final appeal (Sillem), as a defense (Detenhof), and as an official court document, a *Libellus* (the Fiscal). All developed their arguments around the deeds and the supposed intentions that had emerged during the investigation. Each meticulously reviewed the specific elements of the case, as well as carefully weighing Kesslitz's actions against the letter of the law. The situation presented immense difficulties. Even the description of the circumstances to the French court—from a sympathetic point of view—admitted that "the legal case is very thorny," and that many of the facts could be stacked up to condemn Kesslitz and Sanpelayo as easily as to exculpate them. "For it is not easy to ascertain if Monsieur Kesslitz remained at all times within the [proper] boundaries of self-defense [*une juste defense*]. As there were two [of them], one armed with a strong sword and the other carrying a cane, against Visconti alone, who had only a simple knife, it seems surprising [*étonnant*] that two men were not able to deal with an ugly situation without having to kill [Visconti] in such a dreadful [*effrayant*] manner."[30]

On Monday morning, 4 December 1775, the Senat received two documents.[31] The first was the "Historical Narrative" Garlieb Sillem had composed as legal advisor to the Senat; it was based on documents gathered in the general investigation. As syndic, Sillem advised the members of the Senat on the legal procedures. Yet he functioned as more than just a legal pundit. As a member of the Senat, he understood the broader issues involved and was especially sensitive to its diplomatic ramifications (addressed more fully in Chapter 3). His opinion thus never stood simply for that of the government. Moreover, his was only one voice in the debate, albeit an important one, especially as he controlled communications with the Niedergericht and foreign powers. He was neither an impartial nor fully disengaged expert, but rather worked behind the scenes to manipulate the outcome of the case. The second critical document was Detenhof's 108-page preliminary defense, arranged in 124 paragraphs. Here, Detenhof reviewed the major events of the case, measured the occurrences against legal writings and precedents, and ended by demanding that "Baron von Kesslitz be declared completely innocent" and be released forthwith.[32]

Sillem's conclusions were equally clear. In respect to the law, he opined that "Kesslitz had committed no actual *homicidium dolosum,* and [had] indeed not [even fought] real duel; nor had a *rencontre* taken place." What the law and Sillem understood as a *rencontre* was an act perched uncomfortably between a formal duel and a spontaneous eruption of violence, that is, where "two persons who had argued, without any premeditation, grabbed weapons and fought with one another."[33] Sillem's reasoning and the logic of his arguments must be compared to the other voices in the debate and especially to that of Kesslitz's defender, Detenhof. Both agreed on relevant points of law, but they varied in their interpretation of the actual incident, its consequences, and the repercussions for Kesslitz. Detenhof, for example, argued that neither a duel nor a homicide had taken place on the night of 18/19 October 1775. What had happened was neither premeditated nor culpable, but rather only a necessity (*homicidium necessarium*), if a manifestly ill-fated one.[34]

The entire case revolved around the simple conundrum: "If and to what extent Baron von Kesslitz had observed the *moderamen inculpatae tutelae* [that is, the proper limits of self-defense] or if and in how far he had violated them?" For "an irreproachable self-defense," the letter of the law specified three requirements: (1) the attack must be unwarranted, dangerous, and precipitate; moreover, the survivor must not have been the aggressor; (2) the danger must be apparent and the force used to combat it appropriate and not exaggerated; and (3) the victim must have had no other way to save himself, or any opportunity to avoid the fight. Detenhof insisted that even among jurists considerable controversy existed as to what counted as a reasonable reaction. "How much less can one expect a person untrained in law, and especially a soldier, to be able to shape his [self-]defense in response to *offensioni vilentae* along the lines of a disputed and not very consistent set of rules in order not to exceed their limits," Detenhof thus argued. "To do so would require not only a complete command of the law and a *rectum iudicium,* but also a free and unclouded mind, which in such cases . . . [one] cannot possibly attain."[35] In short, Detenhof pointed out that one could hardly expect a man confronted with a brutal attacker to take the time to weigh dispassionately vague and obscure legal restrictions about what he might legitimately do to defend himself.

Everyone possessed the right of self-defense; of that there was no dispute. The fundamental understanding of self-defense was equally clear: "One is allowed to defend himself against an illegal attack, [for] one cannot be expected to sacrifice life and limb to an opponent without protecting himself." The antagonist, moreover, had to "accept the consequences of his assault," even if he died as a result. Self-defense formed the sole exception to the rule that only the state had the right to punish a crime. By the end of the eighteenth century, the Prussian General Law Code (*Allgemeine Landrecht*) allowed each individual the right to protect himself, his family, or his fellow citizens from the threat of illegal harm "through a means appropriate to the situation." So much, however, depended on that ambiguous phrase: "through a means appropriate to the situation."[36]

In addition, almost no one denied that a man might mount a defense of himself, his family, and his friends. He might even be morally *obligated* to reply with lethal force to lethal force in such circumstances. Less clear was his right to preserve property or honor with such vigor. But another question remained open: whether the person so assailed should be *required* to try to flee or avoid the attacker *first* before deploying force against him? According to the *Carolina*, the victim did not have to prove that he had attempted to elude the attacker or use less than deadly force, "unless this was possible without harming his honor." Many legalists, however, reasoned that someone who had the opportunity to retreat and did not could not claim self-defense. Honor, or the possible loss of honor if one refused to defend oneself, vastly complicated the situation. Once again, opinion divided on whether the right to self-defense also pertained when one's honor, rather than life and limb, was threatened. Was a duel fought in the name of honor a legitimate form of self-defense, for instance? Most German law throughout the seventeenth and eighteenth centuries remained imprecise on that point, and court decisions thus varied with particular incidents.[37]

Detenhof shaped his plea on just these ambiguities: "[First] the law of nature and, second, statute law endow each person with the right to defend himself against an apparent danger to life and limb. . . . This [right] extends to any dangerous offensive even if it does not threaten life and limb but rather honor and good reputation, and [those rights] extend as well to relatives, friends, and [indeed] any one illegally imperiled.[38]

Detenhof thus asserted that honor could and must be defended as ardently as life and limb. However, the argument failed to convince everyone. Many felt that self-defense hardly extended that far. Johann Klefeker, one of Hamburg's most prominent jurists (and a syndic until his death in early 1775), pointed out that people believed "erroneously" that one could "strike down a foe" to salvage honor. Rather, the victim should flee if flight was possible and was culpable if he did not do so. Klefeker spoke strongly for civil peace and considered dying in a duel as a cloaked form of suicide. He quickly lost patience with pretensions of honor or any putative need to defend it in blood.[39]

Whether an attack was or was not regarded as just depended furthermore, as Sillem instructed the Senat, upon whether the aggressor enjoyed a legal and legitimate right to use force, even deadly force, against another person. Only a few people or corporate bodies embodied such legitimacy: magistrates and their delegates; a husband who discovered his wife in the act of adultery; or a father who punished an insubordinate child. Visconti stood in no such relationship to Kesslitz and thus enjoyed no such authority. The danger of the assault was equally evident. Visconti had wielded a "large Parisian knife," an instrument fully capable of inflicting lethal damage. Before he could draw his sword, Kesslitz had received physical proof of the "sharpness" of that knife's edge. Despite having a weapon, Kesslitz was in serious danger from Visconti. "It is said," Sillem observed, "that it is difficult even for the most capable fencers to defend themselves against such a weapon. Especially the Italians have been taught to allow their opponents to run under their blade, and when that maneuver succeeds there is no defense. Thus, it has often been forbidden to carry such a knife if it has a [sharp] point." One could not, Sillem argued, hold it against Kesslitz that he had availed himself of the only weapon available, a good strong sword, even if "objectively" it might be considered a mightier weapon than a knife. The mental and physical condition of the aggressor were as important as the weapon, because "even the bare fist can kill if the assailant is a strong man and the victim is weak." Such circumstances perfectly justified the use of a weapon against an unarmed foe to fend off an attack. Hardly surprisingly, Detenhof's defense deployed much the same wording.[40]

Detenhof offered an extended commentary on the dangers knife fighters posed, especially Italian knife fighters. Swords were barely equal to the task of self-defense against them. Even if "many people consider an attack with a knife or a stiletto not very serious . . . one must remember how an Italian bandit with a knife or stiletto [once] fought three men in a room. Another famous recent case in Rome involved a berserker with a knife against eight men with swords; he slew five of them before . . . being cut down himself. . . . In addition, these bandits, when they suspect they will be involved in serious combat, habitually fortify themselves with opium mixed in a powder. [They take it] to fire up their spirits and courage and [in this condition] can shrug off light wounds and are not quick to fall to the ground."

Visconti's pocket had contained a "small packet, folded in the way an apothecary wraps up his powders." "Who would not suspect," Detenhof opined, "that a vagabond and cheap adventurer like Visconti would not have opium in such a paper," and that he had swallowed it before the fight?[41]

No one doubted that Visconti had flung himself at Kesslitz with little or no warning. Moreover, Visconti had no rights over Romellini, let alone to property found in her lodgings. No legal marriage or even a *mariage de conscience* had taken place between the two, so no adultery could possibly exist. If one admitted that Kesslitz had done no wrong in using a sword to defend himself against an expert Italian knife fighter, nonetheless, in order to sustain the justification of self-defense, the danger he found himself in had to be obvious and his response measured. Certainly, Detenhof insisted, "everything must turn on the [real or perceived] danger to life and limb" that confronted the victim, and not "on the size and numbers of wounds" the dead man had received. After having been bloodied by Visconti's first blow, Kesslitz had every reason to believe that when Visconti had finished with Sanpelayo, he would turn against him, and thus "he drew his sword to defend himself and his friend and struck Visconti with it." Kesslitz had intended nothing more than "to drive Visconti away from Sanpelayo" or to stun him so that he could disarm him more easily.[42]

If Kesslitz had really desired to slay Visconti, here was his chance: he could have run him through instead of simply smacking him with the flat of his blade. Visconti's first wound was in fact self-inflicted. By trying to wrench the sword out of Kesslitz's hand, he had hurt his own finger. Kesslitz then rammed the hilt of his sword into Visconti's jaw; again using less than deadly force to fend off his opponent. Sillem, too, could only conclude that Kesslitz had "initially sought to use mild force, exactly as legalists require." Nothing daunted, Visconti returned to the attack again and again, stopping only when killed. While Kesslitz could not remember exactly what had happened after the first few passes, Sanpelayo testified that Kesslitz "could not have otherwise saved his life," for Visconti kept "jabbing at Kesslitz with his knife, first from one side and then from the other."[43]

One still wondered, Sillem conceded, how someone could continue to battle with such vehemence when already severely injured. Both Kesslitz and Sanpelayo insisted that Visconti had never halted his aggression until he lay dead on the ground. The physicians who examined the body implied that this might have been true: "there is no doubt that a man in a rage can endure many large and serious wounds . . . even on the head" and yet barely feel them. He could fight on for some time and even "press a vicious attack as long as his limbs . . . were not disabled and his bones remained unbroken." Only massive loss of blood finally diminished Visconti's fury. None of his wounds had disabled his extremities, and the physicians thus believed it quite possible for Visconti to have continued his onslaught until the bitter end. "Even in death his face seemed to reveal something evil and defiant," they observed. It seemed probable to them that "not the number of wounds but only death stopped him from carrying out his intent to kill."[44]

The question then turned to whether Visconti was such "a vengeful, sly, and desperate man" that one could reasonably expect such rabidity. Sillem tallied up Visconti's qualities, or rather lack of them: all pointed to a savage and perfidious nature. He was a cheat, an imposter, "a godless gambler, a rascal, possibly branded, a pimp, a quarreler," and, finally, he lived "in utmost poverty." Detenhof presented Visconti in as unfavorable a light. He was notorious everywhere as a "rootless vagabond and a bad 'un." The lawyer argued that Visconti could have had only "evil intentions" in demanding that Romellini leave with him. Visconti's actions must be regarded "as a breach of domestic peace . . . and a crime."[45]

Despite the fury of Visconti's assault, his malice, and his treachery, Kesslitz had responded with restraint, at least initially. Visconti could very well have inflicted the two "completely fatal wounds" that eventually killed him on himself "by running onto the sword." Nonetheless, it seemed equally difficult to deny that in the latter stages of the fight, Kesslitz had showed "some agitation." Sillem believed some excess excusable, for Kesslitz had been seeking to make peace when he had been struck in a cowardly fashion. He had had good reason to believe that his friend might be murdered, and he had no way of ascertaining whether Visconti might have other weapons concealed on his person, such as the small pocket pistols (*Terzerolen*) Italians were "known to carry." All these circumstances could sufficiently explain a certain degree of anger or even justified fury on Kesslitz's part. Detenhof emphasized that one could hardly have expected a cool assessment of danger in an environment of bloody acrimony.[46]

Finally, in order to satisfy the final requirement of legitimate self-defense, the fight had to have been inescapable, and the survivor had to have exhausted all reasonable means to avoid it. It did seem that Kesslitz could simply have left Romellini's lodgings when Visconti turned violent. One had to remember, however, that when Visconti first wounded Kesslitz, the latter was actually reaching for his hat in order to leave. Once the fight was joined it might have been more dangerous for Kesslitz to flee than to stand his ground, since his only avenue of escape was a narrow stairwell. He would also have had to abandon Sanpelayo—and Romellini—to Visconti's mercy. Kesslitz, moreover, could not have been expected to retreat, because "he was a nobleman and a soldier [and] according to the unanimous opinion of criminal legalists could not be required to flee" to avoid danger. Honor prevented Kesslitz from "slinking off" to save himself and from abandoning Sanpelayo to be "ignominiously" slaughtered.[47]

If Kesslitz somehow bore culpability for what had happened, he was not solely answerable for the unhappy outcome of the encounter. After all, Sanpelayo could have prevented the whole fiasco by appealing to the magistrates in a timely manner. The edict of 1720 forbidding dueling specified that every person was required, if he or she suspected that a duel or even a *rencontre* had occurred, to inform the magistrates and to send for the watch. Neither Sanpelayo nor Kesslitz had had much reason to anticipate any violence when they went to Romellini's lodgings that night. Sanpelayo, of course, knew Visconti to be "an unpleasant [and] spiteful man." Still, he had bought him off successfully before and had no reason to suspect that money would not work again. Sanpelayo had, after all, a legitimate right to protect his property (the furniture, not Romellini!). Everyone in the city knew that Sanpelayo was "not exactly a brave soul." Had he contemplated any real trouble, it seemed unlikely that he would have returned to Romellini's at all that evening, or else he would have gone better armed than with just a walking stick or taken more than a single companion with him. His lack of preparedness suggested that he had had no fight in mind.

Kesslitz, too, was aware of Visconti's shady past. He had become acquainted with him years earlier in Breslau and knew him to be a swindler and a con man. He thought him "a cowardly and base fellow" who "lacked even the courage to draw his sword." Kesslitz did not realize that Visconti had struggled with Romellini earlier in the evening, and that he carried a knife hidden in his pocket. Kesslitz could not have believed that his meeting with Visconti would go so terribly wrong. The circumstances as Sillem painted them cast Kesslitz in a favorable light: "he had accompanied [Sanpelayo] merely as [an act of] friendship" and in order to make sure that any conflict would be settled "à l'amicale." As events progressed, however, was there any moment when Kesslitz and Sanpelayo should have reasonably expected extreme violence to result? It was not clear that this had been the case. Even while Visconti grappled with Romellini, neither Kesslitz nor Sanpelayo had felt much would happen, for Kesslitz was actually preparing to leave at this point. Detenhof's defense pictured Kesslitz as a man at pains to spare Visconti's life, at least in the opening stages of the struggle. Visconti had never given him a chance, however, and flew at Kesslitz with "such furor" that he punctured the latter's coat and vest several times. Visconti, moreover, virtually skewered himself on Kesslitz's sword in his mindless charges. Kesslitz was a peacemaker, although one who had failed, and Visconti had never been anything less than an envenomed aggressor. The temperamental difference mattered greatly.[48]

Sillem ventured the opinion that in deciding whether or not self-defense had occurred, one needed to examine closely not only the circumstances but also the personae of victim and survivor. In this case, a huge social difference separated the two: "Visconti [was] a real villain and a bandit, and only his [untimely] death saved him from the gallows. Kesslitz [is] an honorable man. Thus, his testimony, as much as is possible in his own affair, well deserves our credence. The one man [was] an irascible, sneaky, and desperate fellow, while for Kesslitz there is no evidence that he ever sought a fight or quarreled with anyone." Kesslitz had profited in no way from Visconti's death; rather, he could only reap "thousands of misfortunes" from it. He might have been guilty of poor judgment, but not of murder or even manslaughter. "Merely a somewhat ill-considered friendship" had drawn him into an unfortunate encounter. The "catastrophe" that resulted had come from the "mortal danger" that surrounded him and from a "deficit in perfect judgment" that had itself perhaps resulted from the painful wound he had suffered. His anger appeared not "unjustified," although it had perhaps been "too heated." In his summation, Sillem concluded that Kesslitz's self-defense had been neither "disproportionate nor extreme." One could accuse him of an excess of force only in that he had had sufficient opportunity to alert the watch and had failed to do so. This last, however, was not a particularly grievous charge.

Sillem believed, therefore, that one could spare Kesslitz the special investigation normally required. If the Senat and Niedergericht refused to take this step, however, then it was best to apply an "extraordinary punishment." "Extraordinary" meant neither "harsh" nor "exemplary," but rather quite the opposite: lenient. Above all, one should select a solution that would not create a flap. Sillem also recommended that the Senat not force Kesslitz to submit to a fiscal procedure (a prosecution), for such would by itself constitute "a severe punishment for a nobleman and soldier of otherwise unblemished reputation . . . because it carries with it the suspicion of guilt," even if it could never be proven. The Senat, however, set aside Sillem's recommendations. On December 6th, just two days after receiving Sillem's report and Detenhof's written brief, the Senat denied Detenhof's supplication for Kesslitz's immediate release and authorized the lower court to proceed "with the fiscal procedure in the normal manner."[49] This fateful decision on the part of the Senat and Niedergericht gave the Prussian government strong reason to intervene and effectively transformed a (possible) crime into a (certain) cause célèbre.

If so much evidence indicated that Kesslitz had only acted in self-defense—the conclusion of the Senat's own syndic—why continue the case? Why allow a legal process to mortify Kesslitz? Why was he only released five months later under conditions that left his honor forever suspect? One answer is that all the events presented above could be, and were, interpreted in a different light by those for whom Kesslitz's role in the affair seemed far less innocent.

The investigation connected with the fiscal procedure produced a *Libellus* (literally, "little book," but here meaning a formal legal communication) composed by the fiscal. This document offered a more damning analysis of Kesslitz's actions.[50] Whereas Detenhof and Sillem accepted as basically accurate the testimonies presented by Kesslitz, Sanpelayo, and Romellini, the *Libellus* expressed considerably more skepticism about the integrity of their statements, "for the facts as told rely mostly on the testimony of people [themselves] involved." Even if the inconsistencies were few and there had been little opportunity for the principals to coordinate or even cook up their stories, nonetheless plausibility could "never be turned into judicial verity." The *Libellus* proceeded to evaluate the case for self-defense more critically than either Sillem or Detenhof had done. Here, Kesslitz did not appear as the unoffending victim of a vicious attack, because he had been cognizant of "the nature of the imbroglio" from the outset, and he also knew Visconti and his character. "Kesslitz himself," the *Libellus* went on, had "realized that it would have been greatly preferential to have avoided the turmoil" by calling in the authorities, "but he disregarded his own good counsel." Even late in the evening, he might have halted the course of events. Instead, he had spurned the opportunity to flee and failed to call the watch, as he might have done, for example, when the cook sent for the coach.

Most of all, the *Libellus* questioned whether "so ferocious a counterattack . . . proved really necessary." The fiscal was far less convinced than Detenhof or even Sillem that a knife (and "not a very sharp one" to boot), even in the hands of a "desperate Italian," quite equaled a strong sword in reach or effectiveness. Nothing in the investigation had revealed "any superiority of one [man] over the other in strength or skill in fencing." The argument that Visconti had simply not let up, charging Kesslitz again and again in a sort of bestial rage, the fiscal also found less than persuasive. "[It] is . . . hard to imagine how a man even in a great fury could press an attack with such force [after receiving] so many wounds." Besides, Kesslitz had suffered no serious hurt before the real fight commenced. The document referred to the two light injuries Visconti had inflicted: a cut on the hand, another on the face. Even more incriminating, Kesslitz had received no other wound during the entire fight, whereas he had pierced Visconti's body a total of *twenty-three* times. "All these circumstances," when taken together, cast doubt on the "real danger" Kesslitz found himself in, the *Libellus* commented. It was also "very odd" (and, thus, hardly believable) that two people, one armed with a sword and the other with a stout walking stick, could not have subdued Visconti without butchering him. This, and especially "the number and severity of the wounds [Visconti] received . . . provoke the thought that the [self-]defense was itself far more vigorous and relentless" than the original attack, and that it had quickly degenerated into a sheer "lust for revenge." Moreover, Kesslitz had pursued the offensive "past the point where any further counterforce could be thought warranted." What Kesslitz and Sanpelayo had done immediately after Visconti's death appeared equally enigmatic. Instead of turning to the authorities, they called in Detenhof, who had attempted to conceal what had taken place. Yet despite the harshness of these phrases, the fiscal expressed a certain understanding of Kesslitz's dilemma and had little good to say about his opponent, who had led "[a] loathsome life." The differences between the two men, one noble, upright, honest, a retired solder, perhaps even a hero, and the other, an adventurer and ne'er-do-well (if not worse) only strengthened Kesslitz's position. Their very divergent lifestyles and backgrounds lent credibility to Kesslitz's story. The fiscal allowed as well that a person "of a military condition" had some right to "go further" in self-defense than did civilians.

Despite its occasionally sympathetic words, the document hardly whitewashed Kesslitz, although clearly the fiscal regarded Visconti's death as no great loss. The fiscal's findings therefore portrayed a drama dissimilar to the one retrospectively choreographed by Detenhof and accepted by Sillem. If many people in Hamburg conceived of the affair as "Kesslitz's tragedy," others were less credulous and believed a different version altogether: "Visconti's murder." The truth is, of course, obscure, but—as we shall soon see—after the case was officially closed (and after Kesslitz left Hamburg), Romellini offered up a darker and spicier tale than the one she had originally broached in her testimony, one that reversed all the polarities of "victim" and "aggressor." Yet it was not only that the facts of the case could suggest that Kesslitz was not as innocent as he might at first have seemed. Other important reasons for why he languished under arrest in Hamburg for another five months lie in the circumstances of Hamburg and, as we shall see in the following chapter, even farther afield, in Berlin, Madrid, and Paris.

Violence and Civil Society

The violence that erupted on the night of 18/19 October 1775 arose from a peculiar set of circumstances, but violence was hardly unusual in a city like Hamburg. Contemporaries viewed the potential for it as deeply embedded in human disposition. Behind every reckless act lay a story linked to individual personality and origins. Yet these never existed in isolation from each other. And, moreover, typecasting was rife. There is little variation in how the different narratives portrayed Visconti, for example: he was a cowardly, false, and brutal fellow from whom one could expect nothing but trouble. Observers found Sanpelayo and Romellini, too, relatively simple to emplot. If Visconti was a rogue, Sanpelayo was a lascivious and perhaps foolish Latin lover, and Romellini a frivolous libertine. Kesslitz's nature attracted more debate, however, partly because he embodied all the ambiguities of nobility. Some accounts portrayed him as an honest broker, a man at pains to avoid conflict and yet one willing to risk his life to save that of a friend (and, of course, his own). Less sympathetic observers figured him to be Sanpelayo's dupe, but that image, too, could coincide with a nobility viewed as slightly (or more than slightly) gullible. Nobility itself was complex. One meaning derived from a nobility of soul that adjectives like "brave," "honorable," and "self-sacrificing" convey. In the late eighteenth century, however, a second, less attractive sense of nobility competed with the first. Of the many characteristics of nobility that appealed less, none was so troublesome, and none so obvious, as nobles' propensity (real and imagined) for violent behavior. Added to the perceived lawlessness of nobles like Kesslitz was his "foreignness." He was a Prussian. Sanpelayo was Spanish; the fake count, Italian, and Romellini, Italian-French. Citizens of cities like Hamburg felt themselves different from nobles in heart and marrow (and that often meant that they also felt superior to them). Nobles and foreigners together were a volatile combination, and one that repeatedly brewed disorder.

All societies must, of course, deal with violence. Although force can undermine or even destroy a society, no polity can maintain its integrity, ward off internal and external enemies, or continue to exist without applying force. In early modern societies, civil authorities eventually succeeded in monopolizing all legitimate violence. They banned feuds and vendettas and forbade vigilante justice. The nobility were one major target of this domestication, but the process applied to other social classes as well, and in cities as well as in territories. This is such a well-known historical phenomenon that it would hardly deserve mention here except for two points that bear directly on the story of Joseph von Kesslitz. First, self-defense remained the one form of force or violence allowed individuals. Second, he killed Visconti in the republican city-state of Hamburg, in which citizens governed citizens, and in which there were, if one is to believe contemporary boosters, "no nobles, no patricians, no slaves, no, not even subjects." Accordingly, all members of the civic community stood equal before the law. Obviously, this estimation ignores the significant social, political, and economic inequalities Hamburg's inhabitants experienced. The myth also masks the worth different groups placed on honor and noble birth. Did some people enjoy more "right to be violent" than others, for example? Were some perceived as more likely to disrupt the peace by virtue of their origins? And to what extent did violence result from—or reveal—a clash of noble and *bürgerliche* values in the context of Hamburg? To understand Kesslitz's dilemma fully and how it entwined with issues of self-defense, rank, and foreignness, we need to appreciate the ambiguous position nobles had in Hamburg during the last third of the eighteenth century.

Few cities were more proudly and defiantly *bürgerlich* than Hamburg. The political muteness of economically puissant middle classes in many German territories in the eighteenth century never applied there. Hamburg was a merchant-republic par excellence, in which the burghers controlled the government. The political clout of the great mercantile families matched their economic power. Splits between wealthy but disenfranchised merchants and entrenched patriciates that disturbed other cities, such as Nuremburg and Frankfurt, did not exist in eighteenth-century Hamburg. Hamburg's political elite was composed of merchants and of the sons and brothers of merchants who had studied law and thus doubly enjoyed eligibility for crucial governmental ranks. Half of Senat seats were reserved for jurists (and three of the four *Bürgermeister* posts), as were the pivotal positions of syndics and secretaries.

Hamburg's elite was also in an important sense an open one. No "noble-like" patriciate defined by law, and to which admission was closely guarded, restricted, or perhaps even impossible, existed. The composition of Hamburg's merchant elite was itself extremely fluid. Admittedly, political power could (at least for a time) cluster in certain families whose members filled multiple roles in government at its pinnacle (in the Senat) but also in the many other municipal offices, and especially in collegial bodies and courts such as the Niedergericht. Nonetheless, despite ties of intermarriage and common interest, these families never consolidated into a clique inaccessi-

Rathaus and Niedergericht, c. 1700.
Courtesy Museum für Hamburgische Geschichte, Hamburg.

ble to outsiders. Hamburg's economic fortunes during the eighteenth century—a dizzying sequence of gigantic booms and titanic busts—ensured that few families held on to wealth and power for more than a few generations. New families, men of talent and nerve, ambitious and daring entrepreneurs moved in and up, often with astonishing speed. Many powerful men had originally come from outside Hamburg. While, as we have seen, conflicts between the Senat and the collegial bodies continued to perturb civic harmony throughout the eighteenth century, those conflicts rarely disrupted the more general sense of being Hambourgeois to which all (or almost all) citizens professed. Indeed, the very tough battles fought between the Senat and the collegial bodies revolved around who was thought best able to uphold that tradition.

Openness, however, had its limits. Religious minorities, not only Jews but also Mennonites and Catholics, found little toleration and less sympathy until late in the eighteenth century, although some wealthy Sephardic Jews and merchants of Reformed backgrounds struck agreements with the city that guaranteed them the right to reside there and pursue their business (and sometimes even their religion) under restricted conditions. The city's strident pride in its *Bürgerlichkeit* fostered a certain disdain for foreigners and for social groups other than burghers, and, in particular, for nobles. Even at the very end of the century, one knowledgeable witness observed that sociability in Hamburg still split into two groups: the "rich and well-educated *négoçiants*" and the circles around the *corps diplomatique*. Others remarked that "the two groups did not particularly care for each other."[51] In fact, sharp legal differences divided Hamburg's citizens from the nobility. Like the Jews and some other religious minorities living in Hamburg, those of noble birth were ineligible to become citizens or to own property. To exercise political rights in the city—to assume a civic office—one had to own property. Inability to do so thus effectively excluded nobles from office, and any citizen who accepted a title of nobility could not use it if he wished to retain his property and position. Whereas the ennoblement of citizens often happened in other parts of Germany, it occurred only rarely in the northwest and in Hamburg. There were only nine cases of intermarriage joining Hamburg citizens with noble families in the seventeenth and eighteenth centuries. Likewise, only a handful of Hamburg citizens in the long period from the sixteenth century until 1806 accepted patents of nobility. Yet change was in the air. One historian counted no cases of ennoblement from 1670 to 1740, but thereafter the number increased. Most of these men, however, were ennobled either before they came to Hamburg or after they left. Apparently, Hamburg merchants found titles unappealing. As the imperial finance minister reported in 1798 to his master, "their great wealth makes monetary rewards useless, and in Hamburg it is not usual for bankers and merchants to strive for patents of nobility." He accordingly suggested that a prominent Hamburger be rewarded with flasks of Tokay wine instead. When Caspar Voght accepted the title of *Freiherr* in 1801, the citywide consternation was great, and the enlightened journal *Hamburg und Altona* could only put a good face on it by assuring its readers that, despite his new title, "the Freiherr von Voght will always remain the admirable free imperial citizen" he had once been. Voght was one of few Hamburg citizens who actually enjoyed and valued the company of the nobility and who moved comfortably in its circles at the European level.[52]

Legal strictures and traditions did much to cool and distance the relationships between resident nobles and the rest of Hamburg's society. The majority of nobles in the city for most of the eighteenth century (at least until the French Revolution sent streams of émigrés and refugees flooding northwards) were the diplomatic and consular representatives of other states. Representatives to the Lower Saxon *Reichskreis*, or Imperial Circle, or to the Hanse cities often resided in Hamburg. Among these, in the mid 1770s, were Baron [*Freiherr*] Anton Binder von Kriegelstein, the imperial emissary; Baron de la Houze, the French minister plenipotentiary; Baron von Hecht, the representative of the Prussian crown; and, of course, Sanpelayo, the Spanish consul. All preferred Hamburg to, say, Lübeck or Bremen.[53] For much of the century, these nobles formed their own circle, isolated from the leading social and political elites of the city, with whom they had only formal, diplomatic contact. How deep that isolation truly was can be debated, of course. Many people moved across the divide easily.

Diplomats and members of their suites who were not nobles certainly also played an important role in the cultural life of the city. In the first half of the eighteenth century, for example, the eminent musicologist, author, and poet Johannes Mattheson (1681–1764), although born a Hamburger, served as secretary first to the British representative and then to the grand duke of Holstein. Mattheson authored *Der Vernünfftler* (The Reasoner), the first "moral weekly" in German, a publication closely modeled on the British *The Tatler* and *The Spectator;* indeed, he translated and reprinted entire sections of his models. Thomas Lediard, secretary first to the Danish and then to the British representative in Hamburg, directed the Hamburg opera from 1727 to 1732. Interactions between diplomatic communities, foreigners, and Hamburg citizens ensued in other ways as well. For example, the merchant Francesco Brentano, who had been born in 1713 in Como and become a citizen of Hamburg in 1737, served as the Saxon resident in Hamburg from 1766 until his death in 1782.[54]

Such connections underscore the significance of the diplomatic corps to Hamburg's cultural and social life. Informal contacts between diplomats, their secretaries, and the nobles who wintered over in Hamburg meant that the lives of Hamburgers and foreigners, citizens and nobles were never totally separated from one another. Contact between nobles and commoners certainly occurred elsewhere and in other forums during the eighteenth century. For example, in the spa town of Bad Pyrmont, nobles and the well-educated, upper levels of the *Bürgertum* associated freely with one another, brought together not only by the charm of the place but also by a shared interest in the progressive ideas of the day.[55]

In the middle of the century, Thomas Lediard noted that in Hamburg, "Gentlemen or Nobility they have, properly speaking, none." Yet the city was not without its "Gentlemen and Persons of Distinction," who were, according to Lediard, "either foreign Ministers (of which there are from almost all the Potentates of Europe) and the Nobility of the neighbouring Countries of Denmark, Holstein, Lunenbeurg, and Brandenburg, for whom this City is a Sort of Fair or Assembly, chiefly in Winter; and many of them have Houses here."[56] Mattheson is perhaps not the best example (he was born in Hamburg and educated there), but he, like a handful of others, linked diplomatic and governmental and native and foreign societies. For instance, his schoolmate Barthold Heinrich Brockes (a significant figure in Hamburg's early Enlightenment) was a senator. Mattheson had as students men who later held important positions as Senat syndics and secretaries.[57] And this was in the period of the 1720s to 1740s, at a time when the principal German moral weeklies produced biting critiques of nobility.

Lediard's "familiar letters" written in the late 1730s painted a less stuffy portrait of Hamburg merchants and Hamburg's social life than other commentators sketched. Even if much of what he wrote was tongue-in-cheek and sometimes even barbed, his observations pictured the life of indigenous Hamburgers. In public houses outside Hamburg, "and in particular [those] that we stopp'd at," he noted, for example, "Music, Dancing, Nine-pins and all manner of Diversions, insomuch that the whole Place had the Appearance of a Fair."[58]

Thus, ascertaining the true position of the nobility in Hamburg and judging the relative degree of warmth or coolness felt toward bluebloods are not simple matters. To see this quintessentially *bürgerliche* city as perpetually and unanimously disdainful of the pretensions of nobility and immune to the lure of the courtly world tells only half the story. The distance the law placed between Hamburg citizens and nobles was only imperfectly reflected in the actual social relationships between the two. Moreover, those contacts altered over the course of time as both groups— Hamburg's good, solid burghers and the nobility with whom they came in contact—changed. Neither group was the same in the 1770s and 1780s as it had been in the opening decades of the century. Many things had conspired to move the two groups closer to each other and to roll back old prejudices and suspicions. Some of these factors were felt throughout Europe or Germany, others were unique to Hamburg. The growth of religious toleration (the French and imperial diplomats were Catholic, of course), the continued expansion of world trade, in which Hamburg played a crucial part, the ineffable but certain effect of enlightened ideas of humanitarian solidarity, all helped to produce what James Sheehan has called a "cosmopolitan provincialism" in cities like Hamburg: an openness and flexibility in social and religious issues that reflected and accompanied the economic realities of the times, even if they were not a direct result of such realities.[59]

In the early years of the eighteenth century, merchants, even in a major center of trade like Hamburg, suffered agonies of doubt about their social and cultural position. Hamburg's premier moral weekly, *Der Patriot* (The Patriot), which appeared from 1724 to 1726, took on the task of constructing a positive and distinctive bourgeois identity. In doing so, *Der Patriot* and its imitators sought to separate the burghers from the nobility, but also insisted that burghers were superior in moral terms, especially to court nobles. The goal was to wean burghers away from noble pretensions and to educate and refine them at the same time. Most of the moral weeklies turned a decidedly cold shoulder toward court culture; it wallowed in immorality, prized appearance over reality, and encouraged a conspicuous consumption that often ruined nobles and their families. It was a world of shallow climbers and careerists, where men and women pushed and shoved for vain advantage and for the glitz of power (but rarely the reality) that came with it. Outward splendor masked inner decay. Such were not the true measures of humanity.[60]

As reprehensible as were the attributes that passed for virtues at court, the inherent falsity of the setting was much worse. People were not what they seemed; rather, they went about "masked."[61] Imposture was what court life was all about, and such imposture was anathema to a mercantile culture where (at least in the rhetoric of the day) deals should be transparent, open to the scrutinizing gaze of the community. The virtuous merchant should be honest and fair, hard-working and modest, satisfied with a moderate lifestyle and too respectable to enter into the get-rich-quick schemes that speculators and stockjobbers preferred. Here the aftershocks of the massive upheavals caused by the early speculative ventures in stocks—the Mississippi and South Sea bubbles—hung all too freshly in the minds of merchants. Stockjobbers were in many ways like nobles—pushers, dissemblers, and adventurers, men like John Law and, on a more diminutive scale, the soi-disant "Comte" Visconti. Good citizens, of course, rarely exhibited a full suit of mercantile and civic virtues.

All too often, moreover, nobles acted on their violent propensities. As one historian observed, "nobles' amusements and their social ideologies . . . helped to form individuals who were competitive, edgy individuals who adapted readily to violence as a mode of life."[62] Their luxurious and often lascivious lifestyles and their very concepts of honor led them into ferocity and criminality. They dueled, brawled, and rode roughshod over their social inferiors. In place of the basically feudal ideals of honor nobles clung to, *Der Patriot* set *bürgerliche* virtues. Reason, goodwill, honesty, piety, diligence, transparency, and frugality, these virtues were the same for all humanity, but the merchant seemed to demonstrate them most frequently. Merchants and "enlightened burghers" were, moreover, peaceable and peace-loving. The exercise of these qualities was what constituted true honor. *Der Patriot,* other moral periodicals, and the enlightened journals of the mid to late eighteenth century accordingly decried the idiocy of dueling, insisting that words alone could neither harm nor defame a virtuous man. True honor could only be lost or besmirched by one's own villainous conduct, never by another's words or implications.[63]

Nobles were also predatory, especially poor nobles and army officers (especially ci-devant officers), and they stalked their prey among the offspring of respectable parents. Nobles played cards and caroused, often inducing the sons of merchants to do the same, sapping their strength in drinking bouts and whoring expeditions and draining their purses at cards and in other games of chance or skill like billiards. Even more susceptible were daughters. Young women of the lower classes often yielded to the blandishments, promises, and trinkets noblemen dangled before them, eventually producing bastards that fell to public care and shamed their mothers. Daughters of good families were less likely to sacrifice their virginity to the seductive words of a nobleman, but they were often induced to flee with them and marry without their parents' consent. Abduction or rape easily blurred into seduction and elopement.

Article 118 of the *Carolina* defined abduction or kidnapping (*Entführung*) and seduction (*Verführung*), "when a wife of maiden of good reputation is abducted against the will of her husband or father, even if she herself acquiesces," as sex crimes. Marriages performed without parental consent were to be declared invalid, whether or not the woman had agreed to the match. Hamburg's laws on the subject were based on the *Carolina*.[64] The famous exploits of the devilish chevalier de Morsan and the notorious marquise de Brinvilliers turned on seductions with frighteningly unhappy endings. The virtuous young maiden of good family who was swept off her feet and into the arms of an often poor, but invariably handsome and noble, army officer was a common eighteenth-century literary trope; the noble abductor was a stock character. Even at the very end of the century, one of the most popular plays to be seen on stage in Hamburg was Johann Friedrich Jünger's *Die Entführung* (The Abduction).[65]

Abduction was also a very real and not infrequent occurrence in Hamburg, where Danish, Swedish, and Prussian officers resided when furloughed, retired, or on active duty as recruiters. Such incidents evoked considerable concern and resulted in specific regulations being passed to deal with them. Of course, in many and perhaps in the majority of cases, maidens of good reputation were not ripped kicking and screaming from their fathers' homes. Many girls colluded with their abductors and staged abductions in order to pressure their parents into accepting undesirable suitors or force their fathers to release inheritances and dowries after they had entered into unsanctioned unions. Either way, parents had good reason to be wary of the young officer, perhaps the new friend of the son of the family, who was invited to tea. But welcomed into their houses such men and officers were. In fact, breaches of hospitality elicited almost as much parental rage as abduction itself.

Again, as in the case of dueling, individual incidents often inflamed public opinion and constituted causes célèbres that stuck in public consciousness and shaped attitudes for quite a while afterwards. By the time our anonymous "patriot" was writing in the mid 1720s, surely no one had forgotten the Wentzhardt scandal of 1718, when the Swedish lieutenant Jonas van Biorenberg had abducted the daughter of a prominent Hamburg citizen, Johann Heinrich Wentzhardt? The young woman was apparently a completely willing victim; the couple later wed. According to Wentzhardt's lawyer, however, Biorenberg acted "like all his pack"—that is, like all nobles—running off to fill the ears of "the crowned heads [of Europe] with untruths . . . and to incite them to anger and displeasure against Hamburg."[66] While such cases were hardly everyday happenings, they created much stir in the city's rumor mills, in the law courts, and farther afield as well, drawing down on Hamburg the exceedingly disagreeable attention of foreign courts (as the Biorenberg case did). The 1740s raised a rash of episodes, including the kidnapping of the daughter of a wealthy sugar refiner named Pingel by a Danish lieutenant. The very next year, the Hamburg authorities apprehended a Prussian corporal, "who posed as a lieutenant," in the act of a similar abduction (he was "sharply whipped" and sentenced to twenty-five years imprisonment). Two other cases loomed in recent memory, having occurred in 1771 and in 1775. The first involved the abduction (or elopement) of the daughter of a merchant named Mauen with Baron von Kottwitz, a lieutenant in the Prussian army. The couple subsequently married in Altona. The second was even more disconcerting: Baron Krohn, at the time resident minister of the duke of Saxony-Hilburghausen, ran off with a young woman named Anna Maria Schnittler. She and her father had apparently disagreed about his suitability as a suitor, and she solved the problem by eloping with him.[67] There was thus good reason for Hamburgers to associate nobles with the kind of trouble that could set diplomatic pots aboil.

All these factors greatly complicated the relations between nobles and commoners. It is certainly far too simple to imagine an unbridgeable cultural and social gulf yawning between nobles and merchants in Hamburg for most of the century, despite the rhetoric of moralists and the apprehensions of parents. The relationships between nobles and burghers in Hamburg presented a variation on a European theme present since the sixteenth century: "double-sided penetration" (although in Hamburg neither the typical "feudalization of the upper bourgeoisie" nor the "embourgeoisement of the rural aristocracy" pertained).[68] The standards of conduct adhered to by bourgeois traders and the nobility in the eighteenth century also incrementally merged into one almost universal code. Jonathan Dewald and others have suggested that what we see here is the gradual development of the "idea of the gentleman as a social model: that is, a social idea that stressed achievement, ability, and personal appeal, and made lineage merely a pleasing adjunct to these personal qualities." This, Dewald notes, helps us understand a society that "was at once aristocratic and fiercely anti-aristocratic."[69]

Additionally, the staid, rigidly orthodox (Lutheran) merchant of the early 1700s (if indeed he ever existed except as paragon and exemplar) had changed his spots considerably by the last third of the century. Economically, it was a brave new world. The safe, solid business deals of the family firm slowly lost their attraction in the faster-moving world of the 1770s. Admittedly, the middle of the century had been an economic rollercoaster, with Hamburg benefiting from the Seven Years' War and then suffering after its conclusion and especially under Frederick the Great's newly introduced protectionist policies. Still, by the 1770s, recovery had made headway. More firms entered briskly into world trade, more merchants engaged in practices they had once condemned as stockjobbing and speculation, and more suddenly found themselves the possessors of enormous wealth. Lifestyles, too, adapted. Houses were roomier, meals longer and more luxurious, coaches rolled more frequently through streets once busy only with the hustle and bustle of commerce. Hamburg merchants did not, as patricians of smaller cities within territorial states often did, enter the service of a prince to seek and attain nobility. Nonetheless, their lives became more elaborate and sumptuous. The press of the day roundly decried luxury, but leisure and pleasure soon became perfectly acceptable parts of a good citizen's lifestyle. Luxury, some pointed out, also fueled industry and amplified Hamburg's prosperity. Hamburg's merchants began to educate their sons differently as well. More studied at universities. Fewer rich men's sons were thought properly raised when they had learned only accounting and how to run a business. Mercantile skills were prized but were no longer uniquely regarded as the sole proper education for a young man of good family in Hamburg. At the same time, more came into contact with nobles and delighted in the experience. In short, Hamburg's merchants were simply more worldly and more inclined not only to seek the pleasures of the here-and-now but to see in those pleasures a positive good. In this, they partook of the greater tendency toward the pursuit of happiness that was the hallmark of eighteenth-century life in Europe.[70]

If citizens, even businesslike ones, were more likely to build villas outside the city, raise their children otherwise than their parents and grandparents had done, enjoy new pleasures and pastimes—play cards, attend operas and plays, while away time in a coffeehouse—theirs was not the only social group that participated in such diversions. Although salon culture attained most prominence in France and England, nobles and bourgeoisie met and interacted in salons in the Italian capitals and in Berlin as well. If Hamburg's salons paled in comparison to the brighter lights of Paris and Berlin, nonetheless many other venues mixed nobles, foreigners, and citizens: coffeehouses, pleasure gardens, opera, theater, and promenades. The progressive amalgamation of the two cultures mirrored the new patterns of sociability that embraced nobles and nonnobles alike in Hamburg. Kesslitz himself frequented garden parties in Hamburg, visiting the factor Wolterstorff to enjoy his villa outside the city's walls.[71]

As citizens changed over time, so, too, did the nobility. Norbert Elias's documentation of the "process of civilization" began with the gradual taming of the feudal nobility. The speed with which a warrior nobility became a courtly nobility and a service nobility varied in states throughout Europe. In the Germanies, too, some states housebroke their nobles more effectively and rapidly than others. The rococo court culture—an alloy of deceit and frivolity—that *Der Patriot* had lampooned in the 1720s had not expired by the 1770s, but it was dying. Maria-Theresa's court in Vienna was formal and by no means frivolous. Frederick's court in Potsdam was a virtual men's club. Some rustic nobles remained the hard-drinking, basically illiterate boors vividly portrayed in eighteenth-century fiction, and who people the pages of Casanova's memoirs. Increasingly over the course of the century, the German nobility as a whole became better-educated, economically more savvy, and more like the very parvenu groups—rich merchants and influential bureaucrats—they had once scorned. Uneducated nobles were a rare breed in the eighteenth century. Ever since the sixteenth century, the nobility had recognized the necessity of education for sheer survival. Toward 1600, one German noble observed: "Studies are a necessity for the nobility" and "neglecting them . . . means decline of the nobility."[72] More and more nobles received university-style educations at the numerous academies (*Ritterakademien*) or at institutions like the famous Karl's School in Ludwigsburg (Württemberg), where nobles and sons of the middle classes studied side by side. Kesslitz was the product of such an education, at the renowned Liegnitz Academy in Silesia.[73]

By the 1720s, *Der Patriot*'s vision of the nobility was thus in many ways already a caricature. It formed part of a program of enlightenment that, in its attack on social injustice, lampooned the nobility, and especially the lower nobility, often mercilessly, but it hardly reflected a sociological reality. Popular writers like Goethe in his *The Sorrows of Young Werther* (1774) and Voltaire in *Candide* (1759) "offered exaggerated depictions of the lesser nobles' poverty, ignorance, and pride." The types parodied therein still existed in the last quarter of the eighteenth century, but they were becoming less common as real figures. These portrayals corresponded little to the more successful nobles, who themselves often converted early to the program of the Enlightenment.[74] The vision broadcast in *Der Patriot* might therefore best be seen as an attempt to define *Bürgerlichkeit* more closely than to mirror the real failings of nobility. Obviously, of course, one could point to examples of carousing, immorality, brutality, riotous behavior, spendthrift habits, and sheer lawlessness among the nobility throughout the eighteenth century. Prodigious consumption of alcoholic beverages often marked noble army officers. The Hessian captain Carl von Dalwigk-Hof was "very fond of brandy and is therefore poor in managing his finances." The brothers Gottlob and Carl von Buttler-Elberberg in 1813 ran up enormous bar bills in Kassel while in the city for four weeks to negotiate the sale of a heavily encumbered estate. The size of gambling debts was proverbial and often gargantuan. Individual cases were frequent enough to give nobles a bad name, but such vices were hardly limited to the nobility.[75] Moreover, counterexamples of prudence, shrewd management, sobriety, and erudition were as effortlessly found, if less likely to arouse attention. Wolf Helmhards von Hohberg presented a fine example of a seventeenth-century aristocrat who was an agriculturist, poet, and scholar. The Silesian von Reichenbach family flourished on a grand scale. In the 1730s and 1740s, Leopold Freiherr von Reichenbach managed his estates with an impressive degree of financial and economic acumen. By applying new forms of husbandry, buying advantageously, and investing shrewdly, he created enormous wealth for himself and his family. If the magnitude of his affluence was unusual, economic success stories were not.[76]

Clearly, the authors of *Der Patriot* felt the need to warn their readers—the good burghers of Hamburg—away from a *fainéant* and wasteful lifestyle they regarded as the antithesis of the active and prudent behavior of the merchant, which also best sustained the city's prosperity and political life. The ignorance, pride, and sense of entitlement by reason of birth they so effectively castigated were less likely to be found among the diplomats who lived in Hamburg, possibly because they themselves had often been recently ennobled. The Prussian resident Johann Julius von Hecht, for example, had only received the title of *Freiherr* and the valued particle *von* in 1762, ten years after first being credentialed to the city.[77] More than in real nobles, the posturing haughtiness *Der Patriot* mocked was found in those, like Visconti, who passed themselves off as nobles, adopting a contrived, exaggerated, and, for that matter, outdated style. They were astonishingly successful with their assumed titles, swagger, and bluster. The "false prince of Albania" in the early 1770s found it child's play to obtain credit and swindle thousands from bankers and merchants in such sophisticated merchant centers as Amsterdam and Venice, leaving them holding worthless letters of exchange not once but many times in succession. In Naples, Casanova reports, this sham prince "duped the Cavaliere Morosini . . . by persuading him to put up a surety of six thousand ducats for him." Drawing on those funds, he moved on to Florence "in a fine carriage, with his mistress, two tall lackeys, and a valet . . . took splendid lodgings . . . engaged a fine coach . . . took a box at the opera . . . hired a cook . . . [and] gave his beautiful mistress a lady-in-waiting."[78] Visconti was a less successful version of the faux prince. His tricks worked on a reduced scale, and his ambitions seem to have been more limited, yet, he, too, posed as a nobleman and an officer, and such impostures certainly opened doors for him.

Merchants and burghers clearly found the allure of nobility and association with aristocrats hard to resist. Noblemen added charm and a dash of excitement to prim bourgeois existences. Burghers welcomed into their homes not only nobles whose lifestyles approximated those of their hosts but also those who were a bit *scandaleux,* valuing them (if that is the correct verb) for the whiff of danger that clung to them and for the splash of color they imparted. In more concrete terms, the attraction of titles and landed estates for commoners who had "made good"—either in public service, the military, or trade—is part of the history of early modern Europe. The movement of many of the middle class into the ranks of the nobility was a well-known phenomenon. Erstwhile traders and bankers went on to live off their investments and the proceeds of their estates. Moral weeklies, like *Der Patriot* and others like them in mercantile societies, felt that such defection contributed to the decline of urban prosperity and civic virtues in equal measure.

If the picture painted by *Der Patriot* was not an accurate representation of "the nobility," even in the 1720s, what were the relationships between the Hambourgeoisie and resident nobles and other foreigners like, then, both in terms of general perceptions and prejudices and (more important for our purposes here) daily social interactions? Where did they meet? The answer is: in Hamburg's high society.

High Society

Hamburg's high society is elusive and had at least three sites: the group of Hamburg's prosperous merchants, bankers, lawyers, and magistrates; its intellectual high society; and its "fast" or flashy world. Members of the first two groups overlapped frequently, but the denizens of the third also (and increasingly in the last half of the century) moved among the others. Charlotte Sophie, countess von Bentinck, the estranged wife of the duke of Portland's brother, presided over the leading salon. In the 1760 and 1770s, diplomats, foreigners, and nobles congregated at her house. In the 1780s, and informally even earlier, a number of small groups that brought together intellectuals, lawyers, and merchants constituted the sociable basis for the Enlightenment in Hamburg. It is not clear, however, to what extent foreigners of noble birth appeared in these circles, or whether they ever were able—or wanted—to penetrate them.[79] The interaction between foreigners of rank (whether that rank derived from intelligence, money, political affiliation, or birth) and Hamburgers was not hard to find and enough evidence suggests that contact between the high society of the rest of Europe—including the noble part of it—and Hamburgers was common.

Caspar Voght, admittedly by no means a typical Hamburg burgher, was the son of a senator and a merchant of the same name. Voght always felt less enthusiasm for the life of a trader or politician than his father did. Even as a youth, he inclined more to an aristocratic lifestyle than many others in Hamburg. A charming story portrays him picking his sister up at Madame Calvet's French *pensionat* in the Johannisstraße and bending over the hand of the old lady to kiss it, the very picture of a young *gentilhomme* with his curled and powdered hair.[80] In later life, he traveled extensively, restlessly, almost obsessively. He thus avoided the major civic offices that otherwise seemed his birthright. Unlike many Hamburgers, he felt at home with the nobility and at court. He loved the shimmer of high society, even though he also spent much time organizing and administering philanthropic projects in Hamburg. Interesting here is the story of the three-year grand tour he made in his early twenties. His father planned to have his son visit various businesses and branches throughout Europe: he sketched out a trip to Amsterdam, London, Lisbon, and Oporto. His father's diplomatic links proved equally important, and Voght journeyed with impressive letters of recommendation in hand. He had the inestimable advantage of being his father's son. Caspar Voght père had helped King Gustav III achieve the Swedish throne, and the king recommended his son to the Swedish ambassador in Paris. Also involved in the behind-the-scenes political maneuvering that led to Gustav's accession was the count de Vergennes, then the French representative to the Swedish court. By 1775, Vergennes was France's foreign minister and, as such, involved in the Kesslitz affair. Caspar Voght fils had close ties to him too. During his journey, the young Voght found "the circle of my acquaintances who were merchants" all too "narrow and serious." Life at court intrigued him, not only because of its beautiful women, grace, and style, but also because of its lively intellectual environment. In Paris, he moved in very good company and often dined at midday with Vergennes in Versailles, where among others, he met Benjamin Franklin. From Paris, he traveled to Cadiz with Vergennes's letters of recommendation to the marquis d'Ossin, the French ambassador to Spain, in his portmanteau. The latter arranged for Voght to be presented to the royal family. In Venice, he lived with Count Algarotti; in Bergamo, he moved in the society around Count Suardo; and in Vienna he associated with Count von Fries. He was not blind to the frivolity and immorality of high society, but he regarded its flaws as relatively innocuous and found young noblemen "pleasant roués" and "very gallant." The many smaller courts of Italy he described as "very cosmopolitan and usually highly cultivated" places that prized music and poetry. In Potsdam, he saw "old Fritz" and was enraptured: "His life has remained a permanent lesson for me." He felt Frederick to be greater than Napoleon. Unlike Napoleon, Frederick was not only admirable in victory; he was greatest in adversity. What really elevated Frederick above Napoleon in Voght's eyes was his genuine veneration of art and science. Few Hamburgers would have spoken quite so warmly of Frederick in those years of economic competition exacerbated by Prussia's mercantilistic policies after the end of the Seven Years' War.[81]

Voght and his father, and, one assumes, many others as well, had a rather close knowledge—and far more than a passing acquaintance—with the *corps diplomatique* in Hamburg. When Voght returned from his grand tour in 1775, he found those positions "exquisitely occupied." Diplomats lived in "great opulence." Among these, he singled out for special mention the Danish minister, Baron von Schimmelmann (a social and political climber par excellence); the Russian Pushkin; the Empire's minister plenipotentiary, Binder von Kriegelstein; and France's "Monsieur de la Houze and his very lovely wife." Binder von Kriegelstein and de la Houze played important roles in the Kesslitz affair and were obviously well acquainted with the best Hamburg families and its most powerful men. Clearly, too, Vergennes was quite familiar with Hamburg's affairs and maintained personal contacts with some of its most influential citizens. This diplomatic circle, according to Voght, "embraced me wholeheartedly," as did Countess von Bentinck. All the other aristocrats who lived in Hamburg opened their houses to him as well. He noted that "well-educated *Réfugiés*" (that is, men of Huguenot background), merchants like Pierre His, Albert Ochs and his son Peter (one of Voght's closest friends as a youth), and Pierre Boué acted as mediators between nobles and merchants because of their education and their fluency in French. The firms of His & Ochs and Boué were among the very richest in Hamburg.[82]

Nobles and citizens met elsewhere as well: at the opera, at the theater, on the city's streets and promenades, and, especially, in the city's many coffeehouses. On the night of October 18, Kesslitz was in one of the most fashionable of Hamburg's coffeehouses, Dreyer's, when Sanpelayo came to fetch him. Kesslitz had also occasionally met Visconti at Dreyer's as well. Kesslitz's whist partners indicate the kind of social mixing that occurred there. Sitting down with him were an old friend and one-time comrade-in-arms, Friedrich, baron von Schlabrendorff (a lieutenant in the Prussian army), Dr. Jürgensen, and the merchant Frantzen. Also present was the gentleman-in-waiting von Blücher. According to testimony given by the owner, Hans Andreas Dreyer, Kesslitz was an "honest and upright cavalier" who frequented his coffeehouse to play billiards and engage in other *jeux de commerce*. He never saw him wager high stakes and did not believe him to be a cardsharp or a professional gambler. Dreyer also knew Visconti, although not very well, from visits he had made a year or so earlier.[83]

Coffeehouses functioned as centers of sociability during the late seventeenth and throughout the eighteenth century. Hamburg in the eighteenth century had a rich and well-developed coffeehouse culture that dated from the late 1600s. A contemporary chronicler noted that first an Englishman and then a Dutchman had sold coffee and tea there, and that thereafter the two beverages "became so popular that anyone who could afford it began to drink [them]." From that time onward, the coffeehouses were full and there were many of them in Hamburg, especially near the Exchange and the Rathaus: im Neß, Bohnenstraße, an der Alster, auf dem Großneumarkt, and auf der Kayen. Throughout the century, the number of coffeehouses grew, as did their clientele. In 1700, there were six; 1710, nine; 1740, eleven; 1750, fourteen; and in 1780, just five years after the Kesslitz affair, twenty. In the eighteenth century, coffeehouses in Hamburg thronged with customers for the two hours after the Exchange closed at noon. Here merchants, but also diplomatic representatives, met to exchange small talk and things of much greater value: "news," political gossip, and economic information. Whereas in the first half of the century, perhaps the most popular coffeehouse in Hamburg was that of the Italian Galli, located in the Kleine Johannisstraße, by the middle of the century, Dreyer's Coffee-house im Neß had assumed pride of place. Not only much of Hamburg's high society but also the circle of intellectuals and publicists around Friedrich von Hagedorn met there. "Nightlife" in Hamburg began in coffee-houses. An English traveler in the 1760s observed that "at Dreyer's coffee-house; they have five billiard-tables, and several rooms where they play at ombre and whist; the latter being now a fashionable game in this country. The company play pretty deep, are well attended, with wax-lights, silver candlesticks, and other articles of excellence." To assist in the game of billiards, Dreyer employed a *marqueur,* who acted like a croupier, keeping track of bets and settling up at the end. Dreyer's croupier was one of the witnesses examined in the Kesslitz affair.[84]

Stakes were often large and games of chance varied from the mild and pleasant whist and ombre to various forms of hazard, including the infamous—and frequently proscribed—Royal Oake. "The multitude of people that frequent the coffee-houses for the sake of play is surprising," our English commentator noted; "numbers of them are sharpers, under the titles of counts and barons, who lye in wait for strangers, to seek whom they may devour."[85] Not surprisingly, high-stakes play often frayed tempers. Hotly exchanged words sometimes led to fisticuffs and even duels.[86] Foreigners, businessmen traveling on affairs, and officers gravitated naturally to the coffeehouses. Many of them lodged in inns—often for long periods of time, like Johann Gottfried Bruchbach, a man who had been doing business in Hamburg for four years and lived during that time in the Stadt Copenhagen—and spent their evenings in coffeehouses, enjoying the sociability and the chance to while away the hours in pleasant companionship over drinks and games of chance. Bruchbach, too, had known them all: Kesslitz, Sanpelayo, Visconti, and Romellini.[87]

Other public places, like theater stalls and opera boxes, drew together the same social groups, and frequently added women. The first permanent theater in Hamburg opened in 1686. Sporadically during the eighteenth century, the opera played three days a week (Mondays, Wednesdays, and Thursdays). "Well-to-do citizens and the numerous nobles, who spend their time here to amuse themselves, are the most dedicated opera-goers." Romellini went to the Comèdie with Sanpelayo and perhaps attended the opera with him. She certainly accompanied him on walks along the city's promenades. The most famous and popular of these, a few steps from Romellini's lodgings in Neuer Wall, was the Jungfernstieg, a fine, wide avenue along the inner Alster lake dating from 1665. Shaded with trees, and offering an exquisite panorama of the city, the Jungfernstieg was a marvelous place to see and be seen. Its spaciousness attracted the city's foreigners in large numbers, as well as nearly all of Hamburg's fashionable —and not-so-fashionable—society. Crowds thronged there from midday through the night and into the early morning hours. Strollers enjoyed the air, the views, the opportunity to flaunt new clothes and fancy hats, while consuming the pastries, fruits, and refreshing drinks nearby stands sold.[88]

Among those who could afford it (and Sanpelayo was one of them, of course), riding and coaching parties were common. Romellini, Sanpelayo, and Kesslitz had at least occasionally made up such pleasure groups with other nobles and friends. One acquaintance of Romellini's testified, for instance, that the latter "was much seen in the company . . . of the Spanish consul. [She] went riding and driving with him [and appeared with him] at the Comèdie" and other places of amusement. "[And such] was common knowledge in the city."[89]

Romellini, Sanpelayo, Kesslitz, and Visconti were not so strange a mix, then. Libertines, nobles, merchants, and adventurers associated freely with one another in Hamburg. If their mingling sometimes produced sparks, it was not inherently volatile nor even unusual. They lived cheek-by-jowl, they frequented the same amusements, they had similar interests, and they shared each other's company and occasionally each other's beds. That the successful merchant and consul should befriend the economically embarrassed Prussian nobleman, that his mistress should be involved with an adventurer, and that all of them should have come together in Hamburg was not remarkable. Notwithstanding that they were all familiar types in the city, the native Hambourgeoisie could still, however, regard them with suspicion and even thinly veiled hostility. Yet Hamburg could only survive as an open society. Economic prosperity and political necessity made it home to rich and poor, foreign and native, honest and unscrupulous, republican citizens and monarchical subjects alike. That civic harmony sometimes suffered, as it did in 1775, was the inevitable price to be paid.

CHAPTER THREE

A Very Diplomatic Affair

Spain's foreign minister, Marquis Jerónimo Grimaldi, called the Visconti case "malheureuse," "scabreuse," and "facheuse." France's minister to Hamburg, Mattheu de Basquiat, baron de la Houze, found it "grave," "très mauvaise," and "compliqué." The imperial resident in Hamburg, Freiherr Anton Binder von Kriegelstein, regarded it as "distasteful" and the stuff of "public scandal." But no matter what the expression or the language, the "sanglante catastrophe de Visconti" had become a very diplomatic affair. The record of virtually every session of Hamburg's Senat from October 1775 through June 1776 (the Senat met thrice weekly) mentions it. During the weeks directly following the incident, most discussion admittedly revolved around the criminal investigation, but even while legal inquiries continued, troubles with the Prussian, Austrian, Spanish, and French courts had begun. Over the subsequent months, diplomacy was king. Daily maneuvering in local settings may seem paltry or even silly, but the complex and involuted world of baroque statecraft frequently pivoted on such happenings.

For these reasons, one should resist the temptation to bifurcate early modern diplomacy into two separate processes: the "big" diplomacy of wars, peace negotiations, and the forging of alliances and a "little" diplomacy of occasions and diplomats on mission, elevating the importance of the former over the irrelevance of the latter. From the minutiae and grinding boredom of quotidian diplomacy, we learn how states struggled with one another and how successful or not each was in asserting its will. Seemingly inconsequential incidents did not, therefore, merely function as excuses or pretexts; rather, they created diplomatic and political situations or shifted existing ones, sometimes radically. Thus, one should envision eighteenth-century diplomacy as a tapestry woven from fibers of varying colors, thicknesses, types, and strengths, resulting in a textured cloth that was lumpy, uneven, and often unattractive, threadbare in places and overly bulky in others, but that nonetheless covered the nakedness of power politics. Integrated into its patterns were all sorts of ambitions and agents, secret and overt, talented and bumbling. Within its interstices could be located virtually the entire pageant of eighteenth-century society: nobles, commoners, spies, ministers, adventurers, imposters, crooks, and even cross-dressing men and women. To accept some of these as legitimate diplomats and discard others as dilettantes rends whole cloth into meaningless scraps. Ordinary persons and apparently evanescent circumstances often initiated diplomatic affairs and the steps taken in such instances had momentous political and diplomatic repercussions and were pregnant with symbolic and propagandistic value.[1]

One striking characteristic of European diplomacy after the Seven Years' War (1756–63) was a general military stalemate. Thus, from 1763 until 1792 when France set to war on all Europe, the continent remained relatively quiescent. Diplomacy hardly ceased, of course, with the coming of peace. A rudimentary if unarticulated sense of a balance of power dominated the diplomatic sphere and exerted a restraining effect on the ambitions of governments in foreign affairs. In these years, the three eastern European powers—Prussia, Austria, and Russia—sought to avert new clashes that would ruin them financially. This policy, particularly associated with the Russian foreign minister, Nikita Panin, became known as the Northern System and had as its primary goal the preservation of peace in the area. In this arena, Poland played a key role, particularly as a place to allow the three states to aggrandize their territories without having to fight for what they intensely coveted.[2]

The entire edifice of diplomacy rested on the assumption "that the game of international politics, even if pursued competitively for individual state interests, was supposed to promote an overall general interest, the independence and security of individual states, or of at least the most important ones."[3] Within this larger framework, daily politicking and daily diplomatic maneuvering assumed greater importance. In a world of relative international stability, the footprints left behind by residents, ambassadors, consuls, and their agents as they trod the often narrow and sinuous pathways of routine diplomacy reveal how states guarded their sovereignty and protected their interests. The very real diplomatic issues involved did not only concern the retention or acquisition of territory and population or even attempts to secure economic resources. Just as fundamental was determining "which political entities were to enjoy the right to participate, if not as equals, then at least as recognised members" of a group of sovereign states.[4] Such basic factors underlay and contoured the Kesslitz affair.

Hamburg, Germany, and Europe

Hamburgers were commercial creatures through and through, and economic ties linked the city-state to most European polities. But if Hamburg lived from business, it was not an economic animal *tout court*. Other issues—especially religion and justice—equally determined Hamburg's relationship to the rest of Europe.

Until well into the eighteenth century, Hamburg's trade with the Netherlands, Spain, and Portugal, as with Spain's colonies, remained impressive, and Antoine de Sanpelayo was only one of many Spanish merchants who prospered in it.[5] The groundwork for the flourishing commercial and diplomatic relations with Spain had already been laid in the late sixteenth century, and they were strengthened by a series of trade agreements that benefited Spanish and Hanseatic merchants equally. These lucrative economic links had political dimensions and diplomatic repercussions, among them the right of the Hanse to name consuls in Spain and, from 1607 onwards, to maintain a permanent mission in Madrid. In the seventeenth century, Hanseatic or Hamburg consuls took up residence in major Spanish centers: Hanseatic consuls in Cádiz, San Sebastián, Málaga, Seville, and Coruña; Hamburg consuls in Alicante, Sanlúcar, and the Canary Islands. As trade with Spain waned in the second half of the century, the number of consulates shrank. Most Hanseatic consuls in Spain and Portugal belonged to prominent commercial houses and received only small honoraria for their work.[6] This arrangement probably profited Hamburg more than Spain, for the Spanish crown explicitly acknowledged Hanseatic consuls and extended legal protection to Hanse merchants living in Spain. Spanish merchants and consuls did not, however, enjoy reciprocal rights in Hamburg and this disparity would eventually prove an embarrassment to Sanpelayo, whose legal status remained ambivalent.

Hamburg transshipped Spanish products throughout northern Europe and European products to Spain, and through Spain to its colonies. In return, Spain rained a veritable cornucopia of goods down on Hamburg, including iron, wine, olives, and oils, while the colonies provided products such as indigo, tropical woods, hides, gold, and silver. Metals (tin, iron, steel, copper), wax, lumber, glass, and, most important of all, linen cloth, largely woven in Silesia, passed through Hamburg on the way to Spain and

Europe, c. 1770

thence to the New World. Linen accounted for almost 50 percent of this stream of goods, which flowed through ports like Cádiz, Málaga, Seville, Barcelona, and—Sanpelayo's home—Bilbao.

During the War of the Spanish Succession (1701–1714) and the Great Northern War (1700–1721), Hamburg's relations with Spain appreciably deteriorated.[7] The two trading partners renewed their old attachments just before the middle of the century as economic power substantially shifted to northwestern Europe. Geographical realities led to expanded commercial, diplomatic, and political connections. By 1740, a consul represented Spain in Hamburg; by the end of the century, both a Spanish minister plenipotentiary and a consul general resided there. The number of Hanseatic/Hamburg consuls and agents in Spain had also grown. Their duties included protecting merchants in Spanish ports; removing obstacles to mutual trade; executing shipping formalities; and reporting on all matters relevant to commerce. This last chore inevitably touched on political and diplomatic issues. Experienced merchants represented the Hanse and Hamburg in Spanish ports. Franz Riecke, for example, had done business in Cádiz for a decade before being appointed consul. Von der Horst served as Hamburg's consul in Oporto for almost half a century. Finding a skilled and reliable agent for the court in Madrid proved somewhat more difficult, although from 1739 to 1795, two non-Hanseatics, the French factor Antoine de Conty and the Antwerp merchant Johann Franz van der Lepe, spoke ably for north German *commerçants*. Van der Lepe conducted the often tense negotiations between Spain and Hamburg over Sanpelayo's role in the Kesslitz affair. While consuls served chiefly as commercial agents, one must not draw too firm a line between diplomatic and commercial duties, especially when considering a mercantile polity like Hamburg. The official appointment of Hamburg's agent in Madrid, van der Lepe, was to His Catholic Majesty, the king of Spain, and his brief was mostly political and diplomatic. Nonetheless, the Senat specifically charged him to observe and report on "everything that concerns our commerce."[8]

The Spanish consular presence in Hamburg was less regular and more contentious. Not until 1732, when Spain named an agent to Copenhagen, did the kingdom maintain a regular diplomatic or consular mission in northern Europe. In 1740, Giacomo Poniso became "Consul de España en Hamburgo," thus opening a period of Spanish consular representation in Hamburg that proved neither continuous nor unchallenged. From the very beginning, Hamburg refused to regularize the situation; a year of wrangling went by before the Senat officially accepted Poniso as consul.[9] When Poniso died in 1758, no one replaced him until Madrid designated a young Bilbao merchant, Antoine de Sanpelayo, as consul in 1768. The Senat contested the official character of that appointment, and this somewhat irregular situation proved singularly distressful to Sanpelayo (and to Spain) when things went wrong in 1775.[10]

At midcentury, two issues repeatedly agitated the understanding between Spain and Hamburg, almost destroying a mutually advantageous economic liaison: the protection agreement Hamburg had concluded with the Barbary pirates to safeguard its shipping in the Levant and the bitter, protracted struggles over the right of the Spanish military to recruit in Hamburg. Both situations touched on diplomacy and economics, and in both instances, Spain trod hard on the very tender toes of Hamburg's sovereignty.[11]

Throughout the seventeenth century, the raids of the Barbary pirates repeatedly threatened to sever Hamburg's Mediterranean trade. To protect its ships, Hamburg concluded a treaty with the dey of Algiers. The corsairs wanted more from Hamburg, however, seeking supplies of weapons and ammunition. In 1751, the Senat agreed, although the city's Commerce Deputation demurred, fearing that Hamburg would reap "greater disadvantages" from offending Spain "than peace with the Algerians would offer benefits."[12] The Spanish crown reacted rapidly and forcefully to thwart the agreement by interdicting all trade between Spain and Hamburg and then demanded that Hamburg abrogate its treaty with the dey. The vigor of Spain's reaction surprised Hamburg and greatly dismayed government and merchants alike. The conflict dragged on for months, until Hamburg agreed to break its treaty with Algiers and allow the embarkation in Hamburg of "some recruits" for the Spanish army from German territories. (This second point stoked new troubles between Hamburg and Spain, in which Sanpelayo played a central role.) Commerce with Spain was reestablished and thus, economically, the outcome was a good one, for Hamburg's trade with Spain far outweighed its losses to the pirates. Yet the city had undeniably suffered a diplomatic setback. In agreeing to the shipping of "some [German] recruits," the city moreover plunged into other diplomatically treacherous waters. Although the city carefully specified that this recruitment "would not be prejudicial to the German Empire, nor to its august head, His Majesty, the emperor,"[13] nothing could forestall the emperor's wrath for long.

Over the next fifteen years, as Spanish officers repeatedly appealed to the Senat for permission to deliver recruits to Spain from Hamburg, the Senat found its position an increasingly uncomfortable one. Hamburg wanted to placate the Empire (by not allowing recruiting) but also wanted to do nothing to jeopardize its commercial connections to Spain. Hamburg's attempt to steer a middle course pleased no one, however, and in 1768, the Spanish king, through his foreign minister, Grimaldi (still in office in 1775–76), ordered Sanpelayo to inform the Senat of the importance with which the Spanish crown regarded this privilege. The king of Prussia, through his representative in Hamburg, Johann Julius Hecht (from 1762 on, *von* Hecht), now weighed in against Spanish recruitment.

In fall 1769, the emperor proscribed recruitment in stronger terms than before, although he simultaneously expressed sympathy for Hamburg's delicate position vis-à-vis Spain by acknowledging the value of Hamburg's commercial contacts with the Iberian peninsula. Here things stood, seemingly deadlocked. Only the strenuous efforts of the new consul, Sanpelayo, and of Hamburg's agent in Madrid, van der Lepe, finally broke the impasse. The two managed to convince the Spanish state that it had backed Hamburg into a corner, and their joint efforts resulted in the cessation of Spanish recruitment there.[14]

Trade with Spain was important, but in the world of larger European connections, relations with the Empire were paramount. Economic competition between the two states should not be underestimated, but in the eighteenth century, the critical points of dispute arose from religious and political differences.[15] Hamburg's ties to the Holy Roman Empire were old and venerable ones. The Empire had actively intervened in Hamburg's affairs on several occasions. In the seventeenth and early eighteenth centuries, the emperor had dispatched commissions to mediate disputes and calm the civil unrest that repeatedly erupted between the citizenry and the Senat.[16] Hamburg's chronic inability to order its own house, therefore, opened the door to imperial intrusions upon its sovereignty. Internal instability always signaled to other powers the chance to renew their hardly benign attention in Hamburg. The very mediation of the Empire that ended civic strife also inevitably infringed on Hamburg's sovereignty. Powers competed over Hamburg, not to conquer it or even control it, but to stake out their spheres of influence, while reducing the rights of competitors. Obviously, Hamburg was not merely a pawn in this great game. Although militarily weak, the city could deploy its own diplomatic expertise to pit one state against another to its advantage. Moreover, it frequently tapped its deep coffers to buy off enemies.

Hamburg's stance toward the Empire rested on two pillars: self-government and neutrality. During the eighteenth century, independence for Hamburg meant having the sovereign states of Europe acknowledge it as a free imperial city. Although the Reichskammergericht affirmed Hamburg's status as a free imperial city in 1618, not every European power respected that finding. The Danish crown, for instance, refused to accept it and repeatedly tried to exert jurisdiction over Hamburg. Not until 1768, in the famous Gottorper Agreement, did Denmark recognize Hamburg as sovereign and answerable only to the Empire. Most European polities likewise considered Hamburg an independent "city-state" (*Stadtstaat*) that enjoyed all the privileges the Peace of Westphalia had granted sovereign territories, which included the right to maintain unrestricted ties to other states and administer civil and criminal jurisdictions free from outside interference.[17]

The Empire often stepped in to protect Hamburg's sovereignty and independence of action, and Hamburg reciprocated economically. As the largest German port, Hamburg served as the Empire's entrepôt. Hamburg coordinated the massive trade linking northern and eastern Europe to its western and southern regions. The river Elbe and the Elbe-Oder canal allowed Hamburg to exploit an enormous hinterland, and the city's economic tentacles stretched well into the south of Germany, into central Austrian lands, and even into Hungary. Hamburg literally opened a gateway to the broader world for Austria. Particularly valuable in the trade from Austrian lands to the west was Silesian cloth, especially linen.[18]

After the Seven Years' War, greater freedom of action characterized Hamburg's political, diplomatic, and commercial position relative to the Empire, and the city grew more closely linked to Prussia. Simply put, Hamburg no longer relied preponderantly on the Empire for the maintenance of its independence. In general, although the "partnership of (self)interest" between Hamburg and the Empire persisted, it was nonetheless inevitably attenuated as other political powers rose and the Europe-wide system of power politics was reconfigured. This was also true economically. Austria's loss of Silesia to the Prussians meant that one of Hamburg's major sources of export textiles was no longer under imperial control.

Thus, all in all, in the late 1760s and early 1770s, Austria and the Empire were becoming less vital to Hamburg, while Prussia, despite the mercantilistic policies Frederick the Great pursued in these years, was becoming more central. Prussia did not, however, merely replace Austria and the Empire in the calculations of Hamburg's leaders. Nor was the shift complete. Although the balance of affinity tilted toward Prussia after 1763, Austria and the Empire hardly vanished off Hamburg's diplomatic horizon. Complete harmony did not characterize Hamburg's relationship with Prussia either, although no question of total estrangement ever arose. The cordiality of the bond waxed and waned but exchanges between Prussia and Hamburg became more frequent and the ties between them firmed.[19]

An informal group of powerful men in Hamburg nonetheless ensured the continued strength of the Austrian connection.[20] Before and especially during the Seven Years' War, a circle of Senat members clustered around the Hamburg syndic Johann Klefeker and the wealthy merchant Philipp Hinrich Stenglin held sway in the Senat, making it pro-Prussian in its sympathies. After the Seven Years' War, the economic crisis that radiated outward from Berlin was often analyzed in Hamburg as resulting from the anti-free-trade policies of Frederician Prussia. This perception combined with (or perhaps fed) a growing republican animosity toward the Prussian monarchy or tyranny (depending on your point of view). The Klefeker-Stenglin clique lost power; Stenglin had died, and Klefeker grew old and feeble. As the pro-Prussian faction weakened, a pro-Austrian cadre crystallized around Johannes Schuback and Martin Dorner, two merchants who traded extensively with Austria and who wielded considerable political clout. Schuback's brother Jacob was syndic from 1760 to 1784 and deeply involved in the Kesslitz case. Hans Jacob Faber, who became senior syndic in 1775, was already strongly pro-Austrian in his sentiments. The two imperial residents in the city, first Count Karl Josef Raab zu Rauenheim and then Binder von Kriegelstein, had done much to cultivate him.

Legally, too, Hamburg was bound into the constitution of the Empire, and issues of sovereignty and independence thus always played out within the scope of that connection. The Empire's jurisdiction over its members was embedded in its legal system, especially in the two imperial courts, the Reichskammergericht and the Reichshofrat. Major polities within the Empire enjoyed the *privilegium de non appellando* (privilege of not appealing) that "prohibited subjects of the territorial ruler to whom this privilege was granted from appealing to the imperial courts beyond the verdicts of the highest territorial courts." Hamburg, however, possessed only a limited *privilegium*, and the imperial courts repeatedly accepted appeals from Hamburg, despite the protests of the Senat. Each such appeal, no matter what the decision, chipped away another little piece of Hamburg's independence.[21]

Besides politics, law, and economics, religion, too, complicated Hamburg's generally good understanding with the Empire. The continued poor treatment of Catholics in a city famed as "the [Lutheran] orthodox lion of the north" particularly galled imperial sensibilities. In the first quarter of the century, resentment of Catholics struck popular as well as theological chords. This "combination of confessional politics with high diplomacy was potentially explosive" and detonated several times.[22]

Since the end of the seventeenth century, the emperor had stretched a protecting hand out over the Catholics. Still, anti-Catholic incidents repeatedly troubled civic peace, and the tinder usually flashed into flame over the imperial resident in or, more concretely, over his chapel. The theory and practice of international law as it had developed in the seventeenth century made diplomatic representatives immune from both criminal and civil jurisdictions and also recognized an envoy's right to freedom of religious exercise for himself, his family, and his suite. Other co-religionists generally enjoyed freedom to attend these services as well.[23] Still, controversies over the children of mixed marriages, for instance, provoked the ire of Hamburg's strictly orthodox Lutheran clergy and excited much popular animosity as well. The minister plenipotentiary sat at the center of it all when the storm broke in 1719 and "a full-scale attack was launched" on his chapel and residence, destroying both. In order to avoid crippling political and diplomatic reprisals, the Senat agreed to rebuild the edifices at its own expense and to pay a fine of 200,000 Reichsthaler. Members of the Senat undertook a humiliating journey to Vienna to apologize to the emperor in person, literally on their knees. Although religious tensions relaxed over the next decades, enough flare-ups occurred to make the issue of residents' chapels a continued bone of contention between the more leniently inclined Senat, on the one side, and the less forbearing Lutheran clergy and Bürgerschaft (Assembly of Propertied Citizens), on the other. The damage Hamburg suffered was not only monetary; "equally if not more important was the question of sovereignty and urban pride." Moments like these—and like the Kesslitz affair decades later—contested sovereignty, and such causes célèbres, therefore, formed the building blocks of eighteenth-century diplomacy. By the time Kesslitz (a Catholic and an erstwhile Habsburg subject) killed Visconti, the prickliness of Lutherans over the Catholic presence in the city had sensibly diminished. Yet it was not until 1785 that Catholics (and the Calvinists) received the right to worship there openly. The sense of belonging to a beleaguered Catholic minority probably remained quite strong in the 1770s, and in a request for help made to the imperial resident, Binder von Kriegelstein, Romellini presented herself as "an unfortunate co-religionist."[24]

Prussia often stood by Hamburg as its good friend and stalwart defender, but the city's relationship with Prussia was not untroubled either. Again, religious issues (the position of Calvinists in Hamburg) grated on both states. Hamburg's strained neutrality during the Seven Years' War also nettled the Prussians. Later, tempers ignited over the mercantilist policies Frederick the Great pursued with greater vigor after 1763 as he attempted to rebuild his shattered state.[25]

Prussia's defense of Hamburg was not disinterested. The kingdom's access to the sea (like Austria's) lay down the Elbe, and Hamburg facilitated the transshipment of Silesian products, especially linen cloth. If these economic interests dovetailed neatly in the late seventeenth and early eighteenth centuries, such accordance was often conspicuously less obvious in other areas. The continued unsatisfactory treatment of the Calvinists in Hamburg particularly irked the Hohenzollerns. Whereas the Catholic minority in Hamburg remained economically insignificant, there were many wealthy merchants among the Calvinists, who exerted considerable economic clout. In this conflict, as in that over religious worship for Catholics, the Senat—concerned as always about securing Hamburg's sovereign rights and stimulating trade—tried several times to ease religious restrictions on Calvinists. Nonetheless, religious toleration for both groups increased only slowly and the continued intransigence of the Lutheran ministry, the Bürgerschaft, and popular opposition repeatedly thwarted the Senat's efforts.[26]

Prussian residents, too, fueled religious fires. Jean (or Johann) Destinon, the Prussian resident in Hamburg from 1724 to 1752, decided in 1739 to build a venue for Calvinist worship in secret. This clandestine attempt touched off an affray that stopped just short of blowing up into a major diplomatic incident. Soon thereafter, the Calvinists worked out an agreement with the city, and in 1785, they were granted freedom of worship, although, like other religious minorities, they did not gain full political rights until after 1814.[27]

In economic terms, Hamburg's association with Prussia experienced a series of ups and downs in the eighteenth century. After 1745, the mercantilist policies of Frederick the Great cut into Hamburg's markets in the Elbian hinterlands. If Hamburg tended to move in the direction of free trade, while Prussia drifted toward a more mercantilist pole, their economic self-interests meant that neither thought it prudent to snap the connection joining them. During the Seven Years' War, Hamburg profited enormously from its neutrality, selling grain and matériel to all the belligerent parties. During the conflict itself, several incidents—how Hamburg's newspapers reported the course of the war; unofficial victory celebrations for one side or another; attempts by sympathizers to support either the Prussians or the Austrians; and, above all, the entwined issues of recruitment and deserters—caused trouble with Prussia, the Empire, and France.[28]

When the war ended, the financial crisis that broke in Berlin swiftly affected all of northern Europe and hit Hamburg broadside. The decade after 1763 ushered in a period of depression and nervousness in the city's economy, which Frederician anti-free-trade policies exacerbated. Through the 1760s and 1770s, there was often friction between Hamburg and Prussia, although it never reached the point of enmity. In incidents like the one the Kesslitz affair touched off, each state sought to assert its own agenda, whether economic, diplomatic, or political. Hamburg grew very cranky about Prussian infringements on its sovereignty, whether real or imagined.[29] Frederick the Great, for his part, reacted with hypersensitivity to real or perceived snubs. In the 1760s, Sir Andrew Mitchell remarked that Frederick "laughs at all formalities," but also observed that "no man is more tenacious of them in whatever he thinks touches his rank, dignity and consideration." Thus, one might understand part of the tension between Hamburg and Prussia over the Kesslitz case, not only in terms of concerns over sovereignty, but also in terms of Frederick's fastidiousness over slights to Prussian rank, honor, and power.[30]

That Hamburg did not founder in these turbulent waters can be at least partly attributed to the good offices of Johann Julius von Hecht, the Prussian resident in the city since 1742. Although Hecht always aggressively represented the interests of Prussian royalty, he nonetheless sympathized with the knotty problems Hamburg encountered living in the shadow of an evolving German dualism. Repeatedly, Hecht attempted to moderate the Prussian response to incidents in Hamburg that seemed about to slide out of control. For instance, during the Seven Years' War, he mediated a dispute over alleged "partisanship," that is, pro-Prussian reporting in Hamburg's newspapers, that had infuriated the Russians and Austrians. Hecht's feeling for Hamburg's difficulties and his effectiveness in dealing with his master and the city both may well be attributed to his kinship with the Hamburg magistracy. Hecht had wed the daughter of a Hamburg *Bürgermeister*, and another *Bürgermeister* was his brother-in-law.[31]

Notwithstanding Hecht's skill, however, many episodes occasioned the raucous and undignified diplomatic wrangling that long characterized Hamburg-Prussian relations. In 1720, when a Swedish lieutenant protested a legal decision against him to the Reichshofrat, he also petitioned the Prussian king and, according to the Senat's brief in the legal matter, "succeeded so well [there] with his libels that Prussia raised him to the rank of colonel and also demanded that Hamburg . . . allow him to recruit [in the city]" for the Prussian army.[32] Friedrich Wilhelm I exploited the opportunity to press for Hamburg's consent to a recruitment that the city had often and vigorously rejected as incompatible with its republican nature, its sovereignty, and its neutrality.[33] The Senat indignantly refused to accept Biorenberg as a recruiter. In response, the king demanded a *Satisfaktion* from the city in the form of 100,000 Reichsthaler and threatened to confiscate all goods belonging to Hamburgers in Prussian and Brandenburg lands if Hamburg refused to endorse Biorenberg's patent as recruiter. The Senat reiterated its position that "in exercising its legal duties according to local usages and the acknowledged constitution of the Empire, the city need bow to no foreign jurisdiction" in administering criminal justice.[34]

It is easy to dismiss such cases as blips that had little or no impact or that represented inconsequential moves on a larger chessboard of power. Clearly, one cannot claim that these affairs assumed the importance of war and peace (although occasionally they triggered the former). Still, in a period of relative diplomatic quiet, where exchanges between the two states must be judged as generally good, such instances of day-to-day haggling were the ways polities did politics. Incidents, routine politicking, and subtle movements were the individual skeins knitted together to form complex diplomatic designs.

Hamburg's ties—economic, political, and diplomatic—to another great power, France, evolved more slowly, and the occasional brouhahas tended to be more muted. Throughout the seventeenth century, France's economic contribution to Hamburg's prosperity remained modest. By the middle of the next century, however, it had been transformed. French business soon outweighed Dutch trade, because France's access to overseas markets and the colonial products that came from them had grown substantially, while Dutch ones shrank. Later in the eighteenth century, France became Hamburg's foremost trading partner, acting as a middleman for French exports to central Europe and a conduit for the export of central European products (including linen from Silesia) to markets in France and its colonies. All in all, however, one might characterize the French connection (at least until the French Revolution) as low-key and generally free of major perturbations, despite some religious problems with the Huguenots in Hamburg and with the French resident, who, like his diplomatic colleagues, used his position to facilitate Catholic worship. Nothing approached the dimensions of the major upset with the Empire in 1719 over the destruction of its residence. In the Kesslitz affair, France's role proved more purely diplomatic and personal. The French minister plenipotentiary, Baron de la Houze, intervened for Kesslitz as a nobleman and perhaps also as a friend, or the friend of a friend. Still, much of the diplomatic discussion between Spain and Hamburg went through de la Houze and through Paris, and the French therefore acted as crucial intermediaries. Indeed, the entire affair occupied the time and energies of virtually every important diplomatic representative and raised eyebrows at virtually every European court.

The Diplomatic Structure of Old Regime Europe

Old regime diplomacy reached its zenith in the latter half of the eighteenth century. Already early in the century, the several parts of the European diplomatic system had been codified: they remained virtually unchanged until the French Revolution transformed everything. Most striking of the alterations since the days of "Renaissance diplomacy" was the development of more rigorously defined duties and more professionally staffed foreign offices. During the course of the eighteenth century, the handling of foreign affairs in Spain, France, Prussia, and the Empire became more organized and increasingly separated from the administration of internal affairs. No polity at the time, however, unambiguously divided domestic business, finances, and foreign affairs.

Moreover, one should not overvalue the professionalism of eighteenth-century diplomacy and diplomats. In many cases, only diplomats' longevity in office, rather than official structures or training, provided for continuity of policy. While few ministers and diplomats could rival the perenniality of Prince Wenzel Anton von Kaunitz-Rietberg (who served as imperial court and state chancellor from 1753 to 1792), others, such as Vergennes and Choiseul in France, Grimaldi in Spain, and, especially, Karl Wilhelm Finck von Finckenstein and Ewald Friedrich von Hertzberg in Prussia directed foreign affairs over many years and (at least for a time) enjoyed the considerable favor and trust of their respective monarchs.[35] Just as many (probably far more) diplomat-adventurers served a multitude of masters and mistresses or conspired to carve out spheres of influence and erect their own little kingdoms. The Dutch baron Jan Willem van Ripperda served the Spanish, the Dutch, and the Austrians, before dying in Morocco. Casanova, too, sometimes functioned as a secret agent and quasi-diplomat. And, in France, Louis XV maintained a whole system of secret diplomacy, independent of, and unbeknownst to, his foreign office. Thus, throughout the eighteenth century, the diplomatic world possessed its own large share of adventurers, imposters, and amateurs, whose machinations were never unimportant and often exerted considerable influence on the greater European world. For every diplomatic scrivener, there was a gunslinger.[36]

A dense network of resident diplomats glued the system together. Republican polities like Hamburg (or, for that matter, the Dutch) maintained their own consuls and agents in European capitals and economic entrepôts but kept the number of diplomats low and preferred to dispatch delegations of highly placed officials, such as senators and syndics, to conduct important business. As this example suggests, therefore, the separation of foreign and domestic affairs in Hamburg was virtually nonexistent. In many ways, the syndics functioned as Hamburg's foreign ministers, and the convergence of their two roles—as legal experts and diplomatic officials—made their position pivotal in the Kesslitz affair.[37]

Each of the major European powers maintained its own representative —minister plenipotentiary, resident, consul, or agent—in Hamburg.[38] By the eighteenth century, the function of the resident diplomat was neither any longer what Abraham Wicquefort in the mid seventeenth century designated "an honest spy" nor a Machiavellian manipulator spreading bribes, concocting plots, and trying to topple crowns from monarchial heads. Envoys had become mediators in the task of reconciling "conflict-ing ambitions and help[ing] different states to coexist, at least for consid-erable periods, in a reasonable degree of amity."[39] None of that, of course, stopped polities from jostling for power, but it did enhance the impor-tance of the resident in the eighteenth-century diplomatic milieu.

Diplomatic residents in Hamburg, like Hamburg's agents and consuls in other places, were critical players in the negotiations that arose out of the Kesslitz affair.[40] The diplomatic community to a good extent comprised its own (albeit not closed) society in Hamburg, but diplomats socialized not only with one another but also with members of the government, affluent merchants, other foreigners (and especially the nobles among them, like Kesslitz), and often with denizens of the demimonde like Romellini and Visconti. Certainly, the diplomatic representatives and their secretaries knew one another, and all were equally well acquainted with the syndics, with whom they conducted official business on a daily basis.

As consul, Sanpelayo enjoyed less prestige than the ministers plenipo-tentiary who represented France and the Empire. De la Houze, France's minister plenipotentiary in Hamburg from 1772 until his recall in Novem-ber 1779, took a keen interest in all the diplomacy surrounding the Kesslitz affair. He staunchly advocated the rights of the nobility and Catholics in Hamburg in general and was a powerful supporter of Kesslitz in particular. Moreover, many of Hamburg's official communications with the court of Spain passed through his hands. Remember, too, that in the early evening of 18 October, Sanpelayo had dined with him.

Binder von Kriegelstein, de la Houze's imperial counterpart, had ar-rived in Hamburg only about three months before the Kesslitz incident broke. He remained resident (with a short hiatus from April to December 1785, when he was in Copenhagen as chargé d'affaires) until his death in 1794. The careers of de la Houze and Binder von Kriegelstein advanced along parallel lines. As ministers to Hamburg, they were also the represen-tatives of their governments to the Lower Saxon Circle, to Lübeck and Bremen, and to various smaller northern European states. De la Houze, for instance, was France's minister plenipotentiary to Braunschweig-Wolfenbüttel and Mecklenburg-Schwerin. Binder von Kriegelstein served as the imperial representative to Mecklenburg-Schwerin, Mecklenburg-Strelitz, and Oldenburg, as well as being *Hamburg's* representative to Paderborn from 1790 until his death. Both were experienced diplomats who had previously served in Italian states (de la Houze as plenipotentiary to Parma and Binder von Kriegelstein to the kingdom of the Two Sicilies) in the late 1760s and knew each other from those sojourns.[41]

Prussia's resident in Hamburg, Hecht, had a rather different position and career trajectory. De la Houze lived in Hamburg for about seven years, and Binder von Kriegelstein spent almost twenty years of his life there, although most of them after the Kesslitz affair. Neither record rivaled the long-term presence of Hecht, who arrived in January 1752 and was Prussia's man in Hamburg until his death in March 1792. For more than forty years he, like de la Houze and Binder von Kriegelstein, represented his government as delegate to the Lower Saxon Circle and Lübeck. Whereas de la Houze and Binder von Kriegelstein were ministers plenipotentiary— that is, men fully authorized to represent their governments and negotiate —Hecht's powers as resident were more circumscribed. He was obliged to consult more frequently with his superiors in Berlin.

Sanpelayo was a diplomat cut from an entirely different cloth. Although like the other three, he, too, was noble, or at least a member of the gentry-like hidalgo class, unlike them he was not a professional emissary. As a consul—and one of disputed status, moreover—he ranked below the ministers plenipotentiary and the residents. Still, as the question of recruitment for the king of Spain's armies amply demonstrated, he could exert considerable weight in Hamburg's internal politics (as well as its foreign affairs), and his intervention could benefit the city. Nonetheless, the Kesslitz affair revealed his more controversial position with painful clarity. He possessed no other diplomatic title or responsibilities than that of Spanish consul, and he actively engaged in trade and commerce.[42]

In the Kesslitz affair, de la Houze, Binder von Kriegelstein, and Hecht served as the conduits through which negotiations between their governments and the Hamburg Senat flowed. Other agents were also active, including the functionaries of Hamburg in Berlin, Paris, Vienna, and Madrid, as well as the French envoy to Spain and the imperial representatives in Paris and in Madrid. The information that passed between these men spun dense diplomatic webs across western Europe.

In Vienna, Hamburg's agent was Joachim Gottlieb Fabrice, while Jacob Wever occupied that post in Berlin. In France, Lucien Courchetet functioned as Hamburg's longtime agent. He had been appointed in 1730 and served until his death in 1776. Apparently, however, in his last years, his assistant d'Hugier did most of the work, and the latter dealt with all Kesslitz issues at the French court. Finally, van der Lepe represented the Hanse cities (and thus also Hamburg) in Madrid from 1765 until his dismissal in 1796. Like the ministers plenipotentiary and residents in Hamburg, these men typically labored for several masters. Wever, for instance, represented Anhalt-Berenburg at the court of Frederick the Great. Not one was a native Hamburger. None of these men on the spot had the right to make policies or decisions, yet they surely had much to say about how policies were implemented and positions represented. Distance and initiative often allowed them to craft policies de facto to a greater extent than one might assume, and this may not always have pleased their superiors.[43]

Johann Julius von Hecht: The Prussian Resident

No one involved diplomatically in the Kesslitz affair was more important and more active than Hecht, Prussia's resident minister, who is thus central to our story. His activities as resident minister in Hamburg before 1775 both excellently illustrate the dimensions of contemporary diplomacy and convey a sense of the man and his personality. What Hecht did on a daily basis, the positions he defended, how he interacted with Hamburg's magistrates, and what claims he and his government pressed on behalf of their subjects exemplify the many troublesome incidents that bedeviled relationships between the two polities.

The normal run of Hecht's duties spanned a broad, almost limitless range of activities (that, of course, differed little in their outlines from those of his diplomatic counterparts). He might be asked, for instance, to probe why the Hamburg Insurance Company had delayed payment to a Prussian policyholder; to expedite the distribution of the estate of a recently deceased Prussian trader; to protect Prussian subjects from "rapacious" recruitment by other states; to facilitate *Prussian* recruitment in Hamburg; to pursue bankrupts whose creditors were Prussians; to assist Calvinists; and to forward reports on epidemics and epizootics, such as the hoof-and-mouth disease that raged in Hamburg's rural territories in the early 1770s. This list is illustrative, not exhaustive, for almost nothing constrained what a resident might be called upon to do in the service of his country, its rulers, and its people.[44]

Still, several recurrent issues typified and disturbed the relationship of Hamburg with Prussia: the rights of Calvinists; trade with the Elbian hinterlands; and, especially, recruitment. Even seemingly frivolous occurrences fueled long exchanges between the two polities. Issues of sovereignty characterized almost all individual cases, raising intricate questions about the range of authority each exercised. Chief among these was the question of what rights a Prussian subject possessed while living in Hamburg. No one doubted the immediate subjection of such persons to Hamburg law, and yet room for maneuver, and thus room for controversy, never disappeared. Two cases from the 1770s perhaps best demonstrate how personal affairs became affairs of state and simultaneously provide immediate background to the Kesslitz incident.

Johann Julius von Hecht.
Courtesy Museum für Hamburgische Geschichte, Hamburg.

Army officers enormously complicated the lives of residents and local officials. Dealing with their misdeeds—duels, elopements, and debts—inevitably raised substantive issues of jurisdiction, propriety, and sovereignty; these were exactly the questions that aggravated the Kesslitz case. Repeatedly, criminal cases—such as the Guyard incest trial (in which a daughter accused her father, a Hamburg citizen and Prussian postmaster, of molesting her) and scandals regarding Prussian officers who dueled, gambled, or ran up fabulously large debts—were bargaining chips in negotiations between Hamburg and the Prussian court. The conflicts assumed economic dimensions as well, but always at base lay the issue of Hamburg's right to make legal decisions regarding Prussian subjects. Precedent favored Hamburg. Nonetheless, and especially when Prussian officers were implicated, Hamburg's governors acted with caution, while Prussian officials and the Prussian court expressed a "deep concern" that sometimes masked diplomatic bullying, as the earlier affray over Biorenberg shows. Two relationships proved especially fraught: romantic liaisons between nobles and bourgeoises, and the often violent confrontations between foreign recruiters in Hamburg.

The proximity of nobles and well-to-do bourgeois in the city—with nobles often finding a warm (or at least not a chilly) reception in the homes of merchants with far-flung interests or cosmopolitan tastes— could spring the lid on a Pandora's box of troubles. Each misadventure provoked a series of political and diplomatic problems and renewed discussions about justice and the constitution of the city's civil society. Such cases were commonest in the first half of the century and declined in frequency as the rise of sentimentality perhaps diluted older standards of parental authority; still, they never entirely stopped.

By the time Kesslitz killed Visconti in 1775, no one had forgotten the scandal of a few years earlier when the young daughter of a reputable merchant had eloped with a Prussian lieutenant.[45] On 5 December 1772, a distraught father—the merchant Georg Mauen—appealed to the Senat for help in recovering his daughter, who had been "kidnapped" by a Baron von Kottwitz (another Silesian, Herr zu Cammelwitz near Glogau) with her connivance.[46] The Senat ordered both detained; Kottwitz in his lodgings and the young woman at an inn. Kottwitz and Elisabeth Engel Mauen explained their predicament to the Senat. They had chosen this extreme measure because their parents stubbornly sought to prevent them from marrying. For three years, they had waited in vain for parental approval. Only when their hopes seemed irretrievably dashed did they resolve on desperate tactics.

Three days after the supposed rape, however, Mauen was beginning to accept the situation, and, fearing the ruin of his daughter's good name if he did not, he consented to the marriage, appealing to the Senat for permission to set the nuptials in motion. Hecht now stepped in and informed the Senat that although Elisabeth's father had agreed to the union, it was not that simple: as a Prussian officer, Kottwitz could not marry without royal approval. Although the couple's daring ruse had wrung assent from her father, "no Prussian officer may wed without the king's permission." By now, both Kottwitz and Mauen were united in their wish for a speedy ceremony.

In March 1772, Kottwitz married his Elisabeth clandestinely in Altona and in doing so touched off yet another round of legal problems, thereby snarling an already complicated external diplomatic and internal political situation even further. Citizens and citizens' children were not allowed to marry outside Hamburg, except with the special, previously obtained permission of the Wedde—the government agency responsible for citizenship issues, as well as for dispensing the license to wed.[47] The marriage had taken place in the French Reformed church in Altona. Mauen had not objected, in order to salvage "the honor of his daughter and his family." The Senat intervened with the Wedde, asking for its indulgence in this case. Here the Senat had to tread gingerly to avoid undercutting the prerogatives of the Wedde, an important collegial body, whose rights its citizen members jealously guarded against any "tyrannical" encroachment by the Senat. Thus the Senat carefully, even meekly, thanked the Wedde for its acquiescence "considering the circumstances." The Senat further assured the Wedde that although such an exemption theoretically infringed "on local law and practice" and indeed on the very authority of the Wedde, it would do everything in its power to avoid such requests in the future, and it emphasized that it did not consider this "generous assistance" either in any way a reduction of the Wedde's proper role or a precedent for subsequent cases.[48]

And so the matter ended. It demonstrates the almost inevitable overlap of internal and external policies such cases produced. Such diplomacy in little things could, therefore, brew up nasty confrontations, but it could also smooth out the bumps between two powers and prevent major upsets. The method gave each party scope to push its interests. Once Elisabeth had spent the night with Kottwitz (whether sexual intercourse had occurred or not; it may well not have), the result seemed preordained. Had Mauen continued to withhold his consent, however; had the Prussian court not eventually granted Kottwitz permission to wed; or had the Wedde been more intransigent, the outcome might have been very different.

Crimes menaced good diplomatic relations more seriously, for they raised major jurisdictional issues. These proved particularly intractable when the person in question was an army officer or noble. One striking example in the second half of the eighteenth century was the Rolff case. Carl Rolff, like Kesslitz, was a Prussian soldier, although a sergeant rather than a lieutenant. His case overlapped with the Kesslitz affair and interposed itself into the very fabric of that more exciting scandal. In December 1775, two months and some days after Kesslitz had killed Visconti, Rolff struck down his Danish opposite number, the recruiting sergeant Christian Jensen, so badly slashing the large veins and arteries of Jensen's pancreas and stomach that, according to the medical report, "he must have bled to death rapidly."[49] The fight (or duel?) stemmed from a misunderstanding arising from an illicit trade in recruits. Another Prussian recruiter had promised Jensen ten Reichsthaler for each sturdy recruit he provided, but when Jensen produced one, he was offered only a ducat, on grounds that the man was "already rather old." Rolff was the go-between in the deal. Feeling misled and cheated, Jensen indignantly refused the lesser amount. Apparently, an exchange of hard words took place, and Jensen called out to Rolff, "Dog's cunt, draw [your weapon]!" To which, Rolff replied "I'm ready!" Before Jenssen could use his sword, Rolff had run him through. Literally, dead for a ducat![50]

The murder involved Prussian and Danish interests, and important figures quickly weighed in on both sides. On 5 January 1775, for example, General von Koschenbahr wrote to Hecht from Berlin pressing him to intercede on Rolff's behalf, especially because "the whole affair can at its very worst only be viewed as a duel" and could, moreover, be just as easily presented as self-defense or a *rencontre*. The Senat, for its part, felt unable to dismiss the matter as harmless. Syndic Faber confided to Wever in Berlin: "the guilt of Rolff . . . becomes more and more obvious" with each passing day.[51] By the middle of January—with the Kesslitz case still going strong—the cabinet in Berlin officially requested Rolff's extradition. Frederick explicitly warned that "the sergeant Rolff cannot be judged" in Hamburg. The Senat vigorously avouched its own jurisdictional rights in support of sovereignty. While the Senat was willing to release recruiters to their home jurisdictions in most instances (especially when the duelists were both foreigners), this case differed: Rolff had, in the Senat's opinion, committed "an obvious public murder." The response from Berlin—this time appearing over the king's signature—just as firmly asserted royal prerogatives and scolded the Senat for its impertinence. Instead of proffering "proper respect," the Senat had had the "nerve" to arrogate to itself "improper dominion" over Rolff.

By this time the Senat had begun to believe that extradition was the best or at least the safest policy, but the decision was not its alone to make. Jurisdictional issues belonged to the competence of the various collegial bodies, including, of course, the Niedergericht. And not only the courts were affected. The Senat, acting on the advice of its syndic, refused to release Rolff without first consulting the Oberalten (Council of Elders), another important collegial body, which represented the parishes, "because the case involves the *Salus publici.*" It was a prudent move, for the Elders proved compliant and raised no major objections. To judge by several previous cases, however, the reaction might have been considerably more vehement if the Senat had released Rolff on its own. While the Elders conceded that extradition was "the best possible expedient," they urged the Senat to do everything possible to ensure that "our legal rights" remained inviolate.[52]

Things did not move rapidly enough for the Prussians or for Copenhagen. While the Danes did not dispute Hamburg's jurisdiction, they bowed to it only as long as "other courts are [not] accorded privileged treatment," and if Hamburg would "promise that in identical circumstances Denmark will enjoy the same consideration."[53] If the Danes were restive, the Prussians were virtually apoplectic. On March 20, Syndic Anckelmann read at the Senat's meeting a very distressing letter from their agent in Berlin. Wever's endeavors to present the Senat's case "in as favorable as light as possible" had earned a sharp rebuff, expressed by royal hand: "I cannot allow a foreign power to punish my subjects." At the same time, Frederick promised that the military court would inflict on Rolff "the very same punishment . . . as he would have received in Hamburg." The case dragged on through May and thus was not concluded until after the Kesslitz decision in mid April. Once extradited to Prussia, Rolff was court-martialed and sentenced to eight years' hard labor and loss of rank; a cabinet order, however, transmuted the sentence into a year's hard labor with no diminution of rank.[54] The Senat could not have been pleased, and it is hard not to see the outcome as a deliberate slap in the face for Hamburg.

In the Senat protocols, the Rolff case and the Kesslitz case are interleaved, and following one inevitably leads to the other. Many of the issues were identical, and their diplomatic implications cannot be understood without cross-referencing them, especially as no one in either Hamburg or Potsdam viewed them as separate. The counterpoint of one against the other exacerbated tensions between Hamburg and Berlin throughout early 1776. Dueling and other violence among and between recruiters reached epidemic proportions in the spring and summer of that otherwise eventful year. Kesslitz's friend Lieutenant von Schlabrendorff, the man who had first encouraged Kesslitz to come to Hamburg and who was the son of Kesslitz's patron, General von Schlabrendorff, himself had the misfortune to kill a fellow Prussian officer, Captain von Borck, in a duel over an insult at cards. Schlabrendorff fled the city and eluded the authorities' attempts to lay hold of him. The Senat quickly seized the opportunity to lament the many recurrent problems recruiters caused and to comment on the apparent inability of the Prussians to control their people. The Senat emphasized the bad example and the unfortunate precedent the Rolff case had set in causing the magistracy "not inconsiderable embarrassment" vis-à-vis other powers in the city. Hamburg wanted to subpoena Schlabrendorff (a judicial action that asserted in its very execution the right of the city to judge him), and Berlin once again challenged Hamburg's "presumption." Foreign Minister von Hertzberg expressed his dismay over an event he termed "regrettable" and "distressful," but refused to concede Hamburg any jurisdiction over Schlabrendorff and, more generally, denied the magistracy any legal authority whatsoever over Prussian recruiters. Nonetheless, the Prussians were chagrined: three of their officers had been involved in lethal violence in Hamburg in a period of less than nine months.[55]

All these cases clearly demonstrate that the presence of foreign noblemen and recruiting contingents always created problems. The diplomatic wrangling that resulted was by no means unique to republican city-states or the autocratic Prussian monarchy. Jurisdictional issues involving those accused of having committed crimes troubled the relations between virtually all European states and occupied a goodly percentage of the time ministers plenipotentiary and residents spent in negotiations. Such jurisdictional hassles inevitably had implications for each state's sovereignty (and its perceptions of that sovereignty). The difference in the case of Hamburg was not only one of degree, however. Hamburg was a small state, militarily weak, and dependent on the goodwill of its mightier neighbors to survive. Still, the impotence of the city should not be overstated. Wealth, political savvy, diplomatic acumen, and the competing jealousies of larger states gave Hamburg a protection not easily breached. However, Hamburg's problems in asserting its sovereignty and maintaining its independence did not only arise from its size and relative weakness. Hamburg saw itself as a republican island in a monarchical ocean. Internally, sovereignty was also contested. Disputes with outside powers could quickly inflame internal quarrels and vice versa. The Senat and the collegial bodies struggled for mastery, and the additional, internal fractures that causes célèbres effected freighted them with broader implications. Although tussles between various internal groups characterized all states, Hamburg proved more vulnerable to them than most because of the continuing (if admittedly somewhat muted) feud between the Senat and the bürgerliche elements in government. These were not battles to be lost.

For all these reasons, as the Kesslitz affair became a sensation, it not only disrupted Hamburg's relationships with other powers and called into question the city's sovereignty vis-à-vis those states but also threatened to rub open the barely scabbed-over wounds of civil strife. The conflict between the city-state and the monarchs was at one and the same time a conflict over authority and power in the city. The former became, in the end, the more threatening (as the collegial bodies agreed to cooperate with the Senat to prevent greater diplomatic disasters), but the nerve ends of internal conflict lay not far beneath the surface, and the Kesslitz scandal thus rapidly assumed political and civic as well as legal and diplomatic dimensions.

Kesslitz's Honor and the Sovereignty of States

Kesslitz waited six months for the court to determine his fate. Only on 12 April did he finally learn what the Niedergericht had concluded:

> Although the investigative documents clearly indicate that the deceased had attacked the Herr Arrestant without all cause. . . . [Nonetheless] . . . he failed to [act appropriately], neither calling out the watch nor requesting aid from the proper authorities. Also that he in the heat of the moment and in an enraged state exceeded the boundaries of a proper self-defense and [moreover] that a strong and well-based suspicion [still] remains against him. Yet, in consideration of the six-months' arrest he has already endured, [it has been decided] to request no further punishment. However, he is condemned to cover all the court costs and all other expenses. After paying the same and after swearing the cleansing oath [*Urfehde*] usual [in such cases], he is to be freed from detention.[56]

Half a year had gone by. What had taken so long? Part of the answer lay in the deliberateness of the investigative and legal procedure in Hamburg. But contributing far more to the dilatory resolution of the Kesslitz affair was the diplomacy it involved. As the plot thickened, it clogged official channels, while simultaneously activating behind-the-scenes exertions. The state of play in one place influenced negotiations elsewhere, accelerating, retarding, or even derailing them completely. The legal actions ran on for some seven months between mid October 1775 and May 1776. During that time, the Prussian and Spanish courts frequently, and often forcefully, intervened with the Senat, while the French and the Austrians played secondary but hardly unimportant roles. Few meetings of the Senat passed without recording or responding to a Prussian memorandum, and the correspondence with Madrid became almost as dense as the weeks stretched into months.[57] The diplomatic maneuvering between Hamburg and Berlin, Madrid, Paris, and Vienna went on concurrently. It also played out on several levels. The residents and ministers plenipotentiary were intimately involved in facilitating the official flow of information. In addition, letters passed between Sillem and the Foreign Office in Berlin; between Sillem and Hamburg's agent, Jakob Wever; and between Hecht and his superiors, von Finckenstein and von Hertzberg. Furthermore, Wever

haunted the corridors of power, informally sounding out cabinet ministers and other persons of quality (including Prince Heinrich, the king's
brother), and Hecht did likewise among his many acquaintances and
family in Hamburg. Sillem and Hecht, for example, carried on a series of
private discussions parallel to more open ones. In addition, Detenhof
traveled to Berlin to rally support for Kesslitz and connived whenever
possible to shape the outcome of the case. These several levels of action
entwined. The official channels of late eighteenth-century diplomacy were
porous and permeable as well as malleable.

The negotiations that slowed the resolution of the case to a crawl and
that preoccupied the energies of the Senat and the syndics for months
pivoted on three salient points: sovereignty, jurisdiction, and honor. All
three appeared in some form or another in almost every discussion held,
every note sent, and every petition that passed between Hamburg and the
greater powers, no matter who wrote, sent, or said it. Quickly the battle
lines hardened. The Senat defended the inviolability of the legal process,
arguing that a binding set of legal rules and regulations restricted its
ambit. These were constitutionally determined and impossible to circumvent. Such prerogatives belonged exclusively to the Niedergericht, and its
citizen members vigorously defended them as sacrosanct safeguards
against senatorial tyranny. Early on, Sillem had alerted Hecht that "the
Senat can make no decisions summarily and the case must be more fully
clarified through the detailed interrogation of all parties" before any conclusions could be reached.[58] The following conditions were not negotiable,
the Senat insisted: the necessity of adhering to the correct legal procedures
even in their details; the inability of the Senat to decide the case extrajudicially; and the legality of Hamburg's jurisdiction over Kesslitz. The
last, in particular, simultaneously asserted Hamburg's sovereignty and the
legal powers it enjoyed as a free imperial city.

The entire diplomatic back-and-forth between Hamburg and the other
powers involved in the Kesslitz case can be reduced to just these aspects,
although differing forms and languages twisted them into many outland-
ish shapes. Kesslitz's honor and how the proceedings and the results of
those proceedings might affect him, his superiors, and Prussian or Spanish
dignity quickly became hotly contested. Honor—hard to define, easy to
lose, and impossible to describe—existed, of course, very much in the eye
of the beholder. Everyone agreed that involvement in a criminal case
seriously diminished or even despoiled personal honor entirely. Where
one was imprisoned, with whom one associated while there, how one was
punished, all these imprinted indelible marks of dishonor that persisted
even in commercially dynamic, modern republics like Hamburg. If honor

was important to republican citizens, it had even greater significance for nobles like Kesslitz and in European kingdoms. In a world where nobility, despite its undeniable political and social resilience, no longer counted as the unambiguous seal of superiority, honor had to be even more aggressively asserted and protected.

Illustrative of the many issues that cut so painfully across cultural, legal, and honorific lines was the *Gassen-Recht*, which the praetor was obliged by Hamburg law to order performed when any violent death occurred. And performance neatly depicts what took place at the scene of the crime. The *Gassen-Recht* commenced the criminal process (fiscal procedure) and possessed the double significance of a public proclamation of the city's jurisdictional right and a rite of purgation. It literally "called out murder" and represented a public admission that violence had broken the sanctity of the community. The language of the rite was formal and anachronistic. It solemnly intoned the events, identified the victim, and called on the suspect to deny or admit his guilt.[59]

Being cited to appear as the accused at a *Gassen-Recht* was a dangerous legal and cultural eventuality, for it was not merely a ceremony; it verified that a crime had been committed for which the death penalty *might* be applied. If not actually dishonoring, it nonetheless tarnished one's reputation. By announcing the existence of a fiscal procedure, it named a suspect and pulled him or her into the machinery of a series of events that could step by step strip honor bare. In terms of honor besmirched, whether the person was or was not exonerated mattered little; contact with the process and the people involved—such as the bailiff and the jailer-executioner—was popularly accepted as dishonoring. Magistrates and judges insisted that these cultural disadvantages did not, in fact, exist, and that the fiscal procedure by no means dishonored; only conviction was ignoble. To little avail. Those who spoke for Kesslitz stood unanimously behind the desire to avoid this "formality."[60] Despite its protestations that the *Gassen-Recht* did not defame, the Senat, too, resisted putting a nobleman through the public humiliation of having to account for his deeds under the gaze of curious bystanders. The debate over the holding of the *Gassen-Recht* pointed up the differing interpretations of the "empty ceremonies" and "meaningful parts of the criminal process" that encumbered the process from beginning to end. Repeatedly, the Prussian court and officials in Berlin requested (or "required") the suspension of one or another of what they referred to as "mere conventions" or "empty ceremonies" (Frederick favored the latter expression). The Senat countered that far from being meaningless or inconsequential, such forms constituted integral parts of the criminal investigation and were, moreover, matters over which it possessed scant control. Pleading impotence was only partly a ploy to shift responsibility. The decision to launch the fiscal procedure belonged to the Niedergericht, which quickly bristled when any action trespassed on its traditional rights. Thus, the Kesslitz affair raised important issues within the framework of Hamburg's political culture. It not only aroused the barely slumbering suspicion of the *Bürgerschaft* that the Senat too readily cozied up to monarchs but conjured up the specter of a resurgence of senatorial tyranny, which the burghers had been trying to suppress for more than a century.

Another normal part of the fiscal procedure was the *Vorführung*—or personal appearance of the accused—before the court, which was equally regarded as injurious to one's honor, if not actually dishonoring.[61] Precedent existed for ignoring the *Vorführung*, and such exceptions had occurred relatively frequently in the recent past when an appearance in public might harm the good name and reputation of a prominent citizen (or a member of his family). When Engelborg Singelmann, the daughter of Elder Jacob Singelmann, was suspected of infanticide in 1750, the Senat and Niedergericht agreed, out of respect for her father, to excuse her both the *Gassen-Recht* and personal appearance in court.[62] Although the Niedergericht eventually acquiesced in sparing Kesslitz the *Vorführung*, allowed the *Gassen-Recht* to be conducted in his absence, and agreed to "use moderate language as much as is congruent with law and accepted practice," it nonetheless did not surrender abjectly.[63]

The considerable delay in reaching these decisions did much to heighten Kesslitz's anxiety. The Senat learned from one of his visitors that "Herr von Kesslitz is extremely agitated, fearful that a criminal charge will be leveled at him, [especially] because such would utterly destroy his current and future prospects," especially as his means were very modest. Just a week later the Senat justified his fears by deciding to initiate the fiscal procedure.[64]

Obviously, this step could only cause trouble with Prussia by raising tricky questions of honor and jurisdiction that turned on the king's right to intercede in favor of his vassal. In Hamburg, it threatened to reanimate the rancorous old battle with the collegial bodies. The Niedergericht would surely stand up for its rights, thus forcing the Senat to take a harder position toward Berlin than it might have wished. Unanimity hardly reigned in the Senat itself on the best manner of proceeding. Clues as to how different positions developed are to be found in several places, but particularly in Sillem's off-the-record notes to Wever in Berlin and van der

Lepe in Madrid. These official communications, layered with personal interventions and with subtle attempts to sway opinions and undermine other positions, are thus excellent places to observe diplomacy at work.

In this correspondence, Sillem named no names, of course—he would hardly have been so indiscreet—but he broadly hinted that he was coaxing some members to come round to his position and maneuvering cautiously around others whom he could not sway. As the case dragged on, Sillem became convinced, convinced himself, or found it prudent to be convinced that Kesslitz was guilty of nothing more than excessive self-defense. Pragmatically, of course, his position as syndic conditioned him to worry rather more about external relations than internal ones. He certainly wished to retain good ties with Prussia, albeit not at *all* costs. He admitted that the whole affair was distasteful in the extreme and believed that Kesslitz had acted imprudently and probably rashly. Sillem evinced far less sympathy for Sanpelayo and none at all with Romellini or Visconti (or Detenhof, for that matter, whom he regarded as a dangerous troublemaker). Yet not everyone in the Senat felt the same way. Another syndic, Paridom Friedrich Anckelmann, was friendlier to Kesslitz. Other senators found Kesslitz's innocence less believable and doubted that the events had taken place as the principals described them. None mourned Visconti or worried much about Romellini's fate. For them, Sanpelayo's role assumed greater moment, and his actions smacked of culpability. Others thought Kesslitz guiltier than he seemed. Some, like Sillem, were willing to wink at the events (even if they found them contemptible) in order to preserve commercial and political ties with the powers involved. Some were clearly furious with Sanpelayo for so unnecessarily bringing about the whole disaster. Others may have actually relished the chance to twist Frederick's tail.

Trouble from the Niedergericht and from Berlin came swiftly. Almost reflexively, the Niedergericht complained that the Senat had ignored the proper form in requesting that the *Vorführung* be set aside. More disturbing to the Senat, however, was the "intercessionary letter" from Berlin, signed by Finckenstein and Hertzberg, that it received on 8 January 1776:

> Von Kaeselitz [*sic*], a subject of Our Gracious King and a former officer in His army, had the misfortune to kill in your city a certain adventurer who called himself Comte Visconti. He has been arrested and indited for that action. All circumstances demonstrate, however, that this unfortunate man [Kesslitz] found himself in a situation where he had to defend himself. He did not [moreover] even exceed the [proper] limits of self-defense. He deserves, therefore [your] sympathy and mercy. His Majesty has charged us to intercede . . . for him, asking that the fiscal process be halted, that he be exonerated and set free.[65]

The Senat hardly blinked: "one cannot reverse the fiscal procedure [once initiated]."[66] It softened the blow, however, by promising "to employ all possible *ménagement*" in how the case would be treated. *Ménagement* meant "moderation" and "respectful consideration," and the word was vague enough for both sides to use it at completely cross purposes. One side's *ménagement* appeared as arrogance or even deliberate provocation to the other. Over the next few weeks, the Senat tried to hasten the process toward a mutually satisfying conclusion, an acceleration that it defined as *ménagement* and that the Prussians perceived as procrastination. Despite what seems to have been a sincere hope on the part of the Senat to get the whole thing over as quickly and as painlessly as possible, the case continued for five additional months.

If the legally prescribed investigative process generated vast amounts of paper, just as many quills scraped on Kesslitz's behalf in Hamburg and Berlin. Detenhof was nothing if not tenacious. He was also pertinacious, pushy, and "sudden and quick to quarrel." His initial attempts to have the process against Kesslitz dismissed out of hand had failed. In the closing days of November or in early December, Detenhof approached Nicolaus Matsen, an acquaintance of his then practicing law in Hamburg. Shortly thereafter, the Senat selected Matsen as its secretary. In 1784, he became syndic and a powerful figure in the enlightened circles in the city and a voice of reform in the Senat. Detenhof solicited his advice: Was it more prudent to accept the inevitability of the fiscal procedure "without further fuss," or should he renew his efforts to have it curtailed? Matsen strongly advised him to pursue the second course. "Remember, dear Dr.," Matsen reminded Detenhof, "how very many long-winded forms burden our criminal process, how much time they consume, and how little one can control the outcome." His advice? Persevere. Detenhof should make "another . . . [and] ardent appeal" to the Senat. In particular, "everything possible should be tried," and he should especially encourage Hecht to "exert himself more strenuously" on Kesslitz's behalf than he had previously done. He further urged Detenhof to obtain a copy of the royal Prussian patent stating that "anyone who is involved in a criminal process, even if he is fully exonerated, is hereby declared ineligible for civil or military service in the future." Most fascinating are the two sentences that close the letter. Matsen expressed his sincere hopes that a second run at the Senat would be successful, for in that case "you [Detenhof] can count on the support of the entire public [here in Hamburg] that greeted the decision to begin the fiscal procedure with almost unanimous disapproval. More when I see you. . . ." Matsen sent this to Detenhof on 8 December. Did he perhaps become Detenhof's spy in the Senat, feeding him confidential information? Detenhof appeared to be peculiarly well informed about what happened in the Senat's supposedly confidential meetings. He sometimes anticipated the Senat's decisions and actions with uncanny skill, but perhaps he benefited from insider information.[67] And Detenhof followed Matsen's advice in carrying the battle directly to Berlin, traveling there in February 1776.

Within three weeks of the Senat's decision to continue the case, indeed, to advance to the fiscal procedure, the Prussians had come to regard the Senat's attempts at conciliation as totally unsatisfactory and its assurances as nugatory.[68] Months of increasingly terse, even angry, exchanges ensued. In Hamburg, during the early weeks of 1776, the criminal investigation continued and the fiscal procedure against Kesslitz ground forward. At the same time, Detenhof's protestations began to affect how the court in Berlin saw the case. Detenhof's calculated tone of outrage and his bulldog tenacity soon bore fruit. He managed to excite considerable discontent about the way the magistrates in Hamburg had dared to treat a Prussian nobleman and a war veteran. Especially in the circles around Prince Heinrich, disapproval (even indignation) waxed. The prince had commanded Kesslitz's battalion during the closing stages of the Seven Years' War, and like many commanding officers, he retained a sense of responsibility and noblesse oblige toward his subalterns. General von Koschenbahr, an intimate of the Prince Heinrich circle, intervened in Rolff's case almost at the same time, and it must have seemed to these high-ranking officers that Hamburg's audacity and presumption had reached previously unheard-of heights by late 1775. If Detenhof had failed to persuade the Senat to abort the proceedings, his intimations had assuredly embittered relations between the two polities. First, he charged that the Senat had deliberately, perhaps even maliciously, misrepresented the legal details to Berlin. According to Detenhof, there was scarcely enough evidence to warrant a criminal indictment of Kesslitz, especially inasmuch as he had only drawn his sword to save his life. Moreover, Visconti was "no count, but merely a vagabond," who had attacked Kesslitz and Sanpelayo with "a brigand's dagger" and totally "without warning." Here, Detenhof repeated the self-defense mantra that thus "Baron von Kaselitz [sic] . . . is responsible for nothing to anyone" and should be immediately released and fully absolved. Second, the Senat's contention that it could not interfere in the normal exercise of justice or judge the case summarily was simply false. According to Detenhof, the Senat enjoyed complete and perfect liberty to act extrajudicially, order Kesslitz released out of hand, or clear his name entirely. Third, and tellingly, Detenhof stressed that avoiding the criminal process was absolutely essential to spare Kesslitz's honor, for not only did the criminal process in and of itself blemish, it was bound up with "many very unpleasant and vilifying formalities" in Hamburg. Such stigmas engendered special problems for Kesslitz, precisely because "if the opportunity [again] presents itself, [he wishes] to engage once more in military service," a pathway that would be closed to him if stripped of his honor. In conclusion, Detenhof loosed the sharpest bolt: "The Senat has often freed [suspects] or decided a case extrajudicially, [even] against many evil fellows . . . guilty of infamous crimes." Detenhof cited the instance of a Polish subject whose case the Senat had settled without trial when the king of Poland interceded. This situation clearly implied that Hamburg had willingly accommodated the Polish monarch but refused to extend the same courtesy to Frederick. Touchy questions of prestige and sovereignty thus bubbled out into the open.[69]

Over the next months, Detenhof kept up the pressure both in Hamburg and in Berlin. At the same time, the Senat and Sillem labored just as furiously to defuse the situation and to reestablish a spirit of cooperation with the Prussian court. To counter Detenhof's obviously effective machinations, the Senat called on Jacob Wever. Wever, Hamburg's agent in Berlin since 1771, had experience, but he proved over time not to be the most tactful or perhaps even the most reliable or skilled of agents. He tended to boast of his own successes or imputed ones and was temperamentally a bit too fiery, or perhaps too opinionated. He sometimes failed to preserve the calm demeanor needed to mediate successfully. Later in the case, for instance, the Senat began to suspect that his reports were less trustworthy than they should be and even that his interventions might have done rather more harm than good.[70]

By the end of January, as Wever worked hard in Berlin to turn circumstances to Hamburg's advantage, Hecht was being forced to remonstrate more vigorously with the Senat and in harsher terms. In a note of 26 January, Hecht brought up the annoying incident involving the Polish subject that Detenhof had fed to Berlin. "We have learned," he began, "that on the insistence of the Polish minister, a fiscal procedure initiated against a certain Massani [sic] was terminated. This incident demonstrates that such a determination lies well within the power of the magistrates."[71] Surely, he queried rhetorically, the Senat did not want to convey the impression that it was more inclined to oblige the Polish crown than the Prussian one? This touched off a lengthy response in which the Senat argued that "Massani's" case in no way compared. Massani, "or, as his name properly was, Marsani, alias Bresnowsky," had not committed murder or any crime for which the death penalty could have been applied. Marsani was a simple fraud. He had taken jewelry entrusted to him by a lady and kept it. The Senat had not abrogated the fiscal procedure in that case, because it had never begun. Rather, "on the request of the king of Poland," the Senat had arrested Marsani "for a *crimen falsi* committed elsewhere" and extradited him to Warsaw.[72]

The Prussians, however, chose to see this all as a rather simple matter in which the magistrates were denying them the same consideration they had unquestioningly accorded the pusillanimous king of Poland. Their prestige in the halls of Europe was at stake. The dimensions sovereignty, status, and exercise of power assumed in the case are very clear in the extensive correspondence that flew back and forth between Berlin and Hamburg in these months. Convinced at least partially by Detenhof's arguments, the Prussians believed that Hamburg had failed to handle Kesslitz with the consideration due him as a nobleman and, far more important, as Prussian subject for whom the king himself had interceded. The tug-of-war over the fiscal procedure scarcely veiled these more vital issues of state.

On 6 February, Hertzberg and Finckenstein emphasized to Hecht that although "we in no way desire to limit the Senat's exercise of its legal prerogatives" or to determine outcomes, they continued to believe that the Senat indeed possessed the power to set aside the fiscal procedure or even a sentence once pronounced. In a memo Sillem handed to Hecht, the Senat claimed otherwise. Certainly, in the case of "minor crimes and especially those where the legal statutes allow an arbitrary punishment" to be imposed, it often reached decisions summarily. When the criminal code specified capital punishment, and especially when a death had occurred, the legal situation took on an entirely different aspect, however. In such instances, "the Senat never makes a definitive finding, as we, in our extrajudicial powers, do not possess the *jus vitae et neces.*" Such cases, the Senat emphasized, had to be brought before the Niedergericht. Whether the killing proved to have been intentional or accidental, a matter of self-defense or premeditated murder, or even what extenuating circumstances existed, was basically irrelevant. Hamburg's constitution required the judges of the Niedergericht to initiate the special investigation in order to determine the facts of a case, and "once the special investigation is launched, the 'socalled' fiscal procedure is its inevitable outcome." As both the general and special investigations had already concluded when Detenhof appealed to Berlin, the time had passed, the Senat insisted, to halt the process.[73]

There was, in short, no retreat. The Senat lacked the power to do so. Besides, good reasons existed to let things go on. This particular incident presented extreme difficulties in terms of the evidence already at hand. All the eyewitnesses were involved and thus had reasons to prevaricate or cloak their actual roles. Moreover, experience taught that it was wise to make haste slowly, for "accidental [or] totally unsuspected events can often bring long-concealed truths to light." One could hardly blame the judges for wishing to prolong the process in order to learn everything there was to be revealed. Here, the Senat half-admitted that it had not hurried to close the case and had quite contentedly let Romellini, Kesslitz, and Sanpelayo "stew" for while to see if they might "break" and give up one of the others.[74]

Berlin remained unimpressed. Finckenstein and Hertzberg now argued that the fiscal procedure, in fact, formed no integral part of Hamburg law but rather was merely a "ceremony" much like the personal appearance; both rested solely on customary, not statute, law. They cited the massive twelve-volume work of Johann Klefeker, Hamburg's much respected and recently deceased syndic, back to the Senat. In volumes 3 and 5, they noted, Klefeker described the fiscal procedure as "nothing more than an unimportant and meaningless ceremony." If, however, the Senat insisted on this "unimportant and meaningless" observance, then Berlin wanted several conditions met: that the Niedergericht waive the formal appearance in court; that the process avoid all "ignominious formalities"; and that the authorities completely exonerate Kesslitz. If, however, the investigation disclosed that Kesslitz had overstepped the bounds of "justified self-defense" and that "an extrajudicially determined punishment cannot be avoided," this should be as mild as possible and Berlin should be notified in advance to prepare the option of a pardon. Although the fiscal procedure would continue, it would do so "in a modified form." The Senat agreed—and induced the Niedergericht to agree—to dispense with "these ignoble customs" and purge what Berlin termed "objectionable language" in the charge itself. This was encouraging but not fully satisfactory to Berlin, and the ministers reminded the Senat of their other, more important demand: "to absolve Kesslitz entirely."[75]

Throughout the winter of 1775 and into spring 1776, issues of honor, but also of prestige, jurisdiction, and sovereignty remained sticking points in the debate between Hamburg and Berlin. Was the *Gassen-Recht* dishonoring? What about the fiscal procedure itself? Detenhof insisted that both were, Kesslitz feared they were, Berlin readily believed they were, and the Senat worked hard to show they were not. Detenhof adroitly exploited this extreme testiness over honor, using it to foil any compromise between Hamburg and Berlin. While in Berlin in early February 1776, Detenhof poured his accusations into every ready ear and went as far as to accuse the Senat of willingly sacrificing Kesslitz to keep the peace within the municipal family, that is, to avoid ruffling the feathers of a Niedergericht inclined to preen. More than just a grain of truth rested in that charge, although the

Senat and especially Sillem wanted every bit as much to avoid provoking Prussia.

Detenhof insisted that the Senat had determined to implement the fiscal procedure against Kesslitz, despite its dubious legality. Citing legal precedents, Detenhof maintained that neither "a normal criminal punishment" nor a "dishonorable criminal charge" against Kesslitz "had and could have any basis." Both were "unlawful." Just as shocking as the illegality of the proceedings, according to Detenhof, was the Senat's persistence in rejecting "all benevolent royal intercessions" on Kesslitz's behalf. The Senat had chosen the wrong path at the start and now was doing everything in its power to justify its mistakes by proving a crime. Immediately before Detenhof's departure for Berlin, the Senat had initiated new interrogations of several witnesses who had already made their statements; all this could do was muddle them—render them "confus." The Senat intended to continue questioning witnesses, moreover, until a criminal verdict was actually returned. The result would be "such evils ... as the obscuring of facts and the unnecessary inflation of costs." The Senat would balk at nothing, Detenhof charged, even subterfuge. It had, for instance, forwarded only the physicians' *visum repertum* to Berlin, "maliciously" holding back the revealing appendix to that report "that spoke for Kesslitz" in showing that the victim's attack had been "ferocious," that he had continued to struggle "until the ultimate moment," and that Kesslitz had reacted "with great restraint" (*ménagement* again) and in a manner intended "to preserve [Visconti's] life."[76]

What could one possibly think, Detenhof concluded, except that the Senat had deliberately withheld evidence that favored Kesslitz while feeding Berlin everything that suggested Kesslitz's greater guilt? Such obfuscation, such deception, stemmed from the Senat's deep-seated *Animositas* to Kesslitz and, Detenhof cleverly hinted, toward Berlin as well. Wasn't it suspicious that instead of the above exculpatory evidence, the Senat had preferred to present a statement from one of Kesslitz's guards, indicating his "perfect satisfaction" with the conditions of his arrest? Well, what else did one expect from a man like Kesslitz? Clearly, he was too noble a soul to complain about the officers assigned to guard him, who were, after all, only doing their duty. The costs of the whole "unnecessarily protracted" investigation deeply unsettled Kesslitz, "under which crushing fear his spirit suffers so much that it is impossible for him to enjoy good health." One should keep in mind, Detenhof insisted, that Kesslitz's whole reason for being in Hamburg was to promote the interests of his fatherland. He had, according to Detenhof, left Glogau (in Silesia) and journeyed to Hamburg solely "in the real service" of Frederick's Silesian subjects. He had nurtured the "present florescence" of the Silesian linen trade with Spain (not very likely), and he intended to benefit his Silesian countrymen even more by setting up a trading center in Landeshut to facilitate the direct export of linen to the Iberian peninsula. Wasn't that, Detenhof intimated, perhaps the real reason the Senat had set itself so firmly against Kesslitz? Wasn't it jealously guarding the city's economic interests by sacrificing him and then disposing of Sanpelayo into the bargain? In an affair laden with so many hidden machinations, neither he nor his client could place much trust in the Senat's impartial administration of justice.[77]

If Detenhof was busy, the Senat was hardly idle, and it did its best to counter the advocate's baneful effect. Sillem wrote directly to Finckenstein and Hertzberg to assure them that the Senat was doing everything in its power to show Kesslitz "all possible leniency and mildness." Sillem also complained to Hecht about the attempts of some people "in a most unseeming manner" and "at the highest levels" to blacken Hamburg's name by presenting an utterly false picture of the legal process in the city.[78] But Sillem—typically—did more: he exhorted Wever in Berlin to exercise the "greatest vigilance" and to monitor each step Detenhof took closely. He should, moreover, do his best "to stand in his way and checkmate" the lawyer's every move. Most important, Wever must convince the heir to the throne that the fiscal procedure was "not a vile thing" and that "no violent resistance" to it was called for.[79]

While Sillem dictated his letters and Wever cooled his heels in the antechambers of powerful men in Berlin, Detenhof busily lined up supporters. He persuaded Kesslitz's sister, abbess of the Poor Clares' Cloister in Glogau, to petition Cabinet Minister Friedrich Wilhelm von Sellentin on her brother's behalf. According to Wever, she filled her letter with "calumnies and untruths." Fortunately, Wever described Sellentin as "a good friend of mine," who would laugh off these specious accusations. Others proved more sympathetically inclined to Kesslitz, including such powerful figures as the cabinet minister Hofmann, Captain Boullet (Prince Heinrich's private secretary), and Prince Heinrich himself. Yet, Wever reassured the Senat that none of these, with the possible exception of Prince Heinrich, would much benefit Detenhof or Kesslitz. Sellentin, for instance, "would only try to extract as much money as possible [from Detenhof] and promise for it what he cannot deliver." Wever believed that Sanpelayo's money was bankrolling Detenhof, referring to the "many Spanish doubloons in cash" Detenhof had in his purse, but that, Wever insisted, would be wasted. Wever launched his own counteroperation on 5 February. The timing was good, because "on that day at 10 A.M. the normal audience in the home of Minister von Finckenstein takes place." With a properly humble demeanor,

Wever delivered the Senat's letter to the two ministers. Unfortunately, his exertions failed to avert the dispatch of yet another strongly worded complaint to Hamburg, although in an attached note to Hecht, the two ministers advised him to "spare the Senat" as much as possible. In the conclusion to his dispatch, Wever communicated his deep contempt for Detenhof, who cut such a poor figure that Wever could hardly believe that anyone would take him seriously. Hecht, too, came in for some harsh criticism, for Wever regarded both Hecht and Detenhof as cynical careerists and busybodies:

> It is possible that in the beginning Herr Hecht had good intentions. Since then, however, he has changed and placed himself entirely and unjustly on Detenhof's side. Still what else can one expect of such men? Years of experience have convinced me that their zeal is only intended to stir up as much trouble as possible in the smaller states of [the Empire] and thereby puff themselves up to seem twice as important as they are. If one believes exactly the opposite of what they say, then at least one will be less frequently deceived by them.[80]

Wever's disdain for Detenhof's abilities was perhaps misplaced, for the lawyer had effectively stirred up a hornet's nest in Berlin. His not-so-subtle hints had apparently done their job. The Prussians protested to Hamburg that they "knew" of several other instances where Hamburg had treated other powers with more courtesy and respect. Marsani was just one such example. Two generals had complained to the Foreign Office, insisting that Kesslitz and Prussia receive not a jot less than what the Senat had—supposedly—accorded the Poles. Wever immediately recognized this as a dangerous situation that profoundly affected Prussian conceptions of honor and power. Any thought that Hamburg might more willingly accommodate the Poles than the Prussians could only infuriate. Wever advised approaching the Foreign Office directly, but also inquired whether the Senat might not be agreeable to altering the legal procedures somewhat, for "the devil must always be allowed to play his games." Virtually at the same moment, back in Hamburg, Sillem had gone to see Hecht, who told Sillem "in confidence" that if the Senat refused to stop the fiscal procedure, he had already received instructions from Berlin "to accept [that decision] under certain conditions." Sillem was relieved, but his relief lasted only minutes, perhaps only seconds. As they stood chatting, another post from Berlin arrived and "turned everything around again." Clearly, Detenhof had once again made headway. Hecht immediately showed Sillem the message. His heart must have dropped as he read: "that with the next post, His Majesty himself will dispatch a letter to the local magistracy in which He will demand the cessation [of the fiscal procedure]: Thus we wanted to inform you first . . . that you should not bow to the Senat's will [in this matter]." One wonders if Hecht had not perhaps choreographed the whole scene?

So what could be done at this point to preserve municipal dignity and freedom of action, without allowing the case to jeopardize Hamburg's relationship with Prussia? Sillem tendered a compromise. He proposed that the Senat yield to the king's wishes in canceling all the remaining formalities (at least if the court determined Kesslitz to be guilty of nothing more than having defended himself too vigorously). One could thus represent the compromise as a courtesy to Frederick. Sillem argued that the Senat need only "consult with a deputation [of members] of the Niedergericht." He strongly advised against presenting the plan to any other collegial body, such as the Bürgerschaft or the Elders, primarily because they had no power in criminal cases, but also because "it will be very troublesome to make everything clear to them and, if they raise objections, [the whole matter] will fall into an impossible tangle and utter confusion, which as a result will not only elicit [more] ill will from the interested courts but cause damage and [increase] costs."

If the Senat felt his proposal allowed too much, Sillem suggested a middle road: omit some objectionable formalities, unless, of course, the Niedergericht found Kesslitz guilty of a crime (which self-defense was not, of course). He preferred the first solution as by far the most expedient and least alarming. Sillem conceded that many prescribed steps in the fiscal procedure possessed "trifling significance" in themselves. What the king really wanted, Sillem assumed, was for the case to be wrapped up extrajudicially. By retaining all the traditional forms, the city would only embroil itself in a line-by-line dispute with Berlin. Everything would be blown out of proportion, even more than it already was. Finally, worst of all, "as Herr Hecht has confided [to me], the king will be moved to [demand] Kesslitz's extradition." And if the king sought Kesslitz's return to Prussia for trial, Hamburg would be hard put to refuse unless it was willing to clash diplomatically or sever ties with Berlin. The economic and political consequences of such a step did not even bear thinking about. Moreover, Sillem admitted that "the wish of the king [is] not even by any means wrong." "All legal experts," he continued, "agree that in cases involving people of rank, despite [the normal forms of the investigative process], one must eschew all ignoble usages." At least according to Sillem, the king's demands therefore represented no attempt to interfere in the exercise of justice in Hamburg; he rather merely wished to sweep nonessential formalities out of the way. Finally, Sillem reassured the Senat: such a decision created no prejudice for the future. In these special and always rare instances, one "could proceed in a similar manner."[81]

The action the Senat took on the 28th conformed partly to Sillem's specifications. The Senat dispensed with most of the objectionable formalities but also "insisted strenuously" that the arrangement retained its validity *only* if Kesslitz were found to have defended himself legitimately. If the Niedergericht and Senat concluded that he had violated the proper limits of self-defense, even if only in using excessive force, then the compromise would collapse.[82] Although Sillem may have won over his colleagues in the Senat (or at least convinced them that his proposal offered the lesser of two evils), the Niedergericht still had to approve the details. The delicate task of obtaining its consent was Sillem's job. As the obliging counterproposal traveled in the postbag to Berlin, the action shifted back to Hamburg, where the Senat now had to sell its decision to its fellow citizens.[83]

The dynamics of political life in a republican city-state can perhaps be understood no better than by observing the backdoor politicking that now took place. One week after receiving the Senat's appeal, the Niedergericht petitioned for a conference. Literally, this meant that the Senat would send one or more delegates to the Niedergericht building, immediately next door, to meet face-to-face. Dressed in the sartorial splendor of their senatorial robes, with their pearly white ruffs framing their faces, the deputies trudged over to meet the praetor in the foyer. He informed the Senat's delegate that the Niedergericht was willing to dispense with the *Vorführung* and grant Kesslitz the right to be examined in his room (rather than in court). The Niedergericht, however, "could not consent" to the other points. The deputation returned to the Senat chamber with this not totally satisfactory report; the Senat asked them to try again. So back they went, this time charged with "emphasizing verbally" the necessity of a "more compliant answer." The Niedergericht stood firm, and when the deputation returned a second time (the Senat was still in session), it could only report that "the [court's] members have declared that they cannot modify their previous decision" without affronting their "duty and their consciences." Stalemated by the Niedergericht, the Senat decided, reluctantly, to solicit the Elders' intercession. (Although throughout the eighteenth century, foreign affairs remained almost exclusively the business of the Senat, nonetheless, in serious instances or those with far-ranging consequences, the Senat was compelled to seek the consent of the Elders as the representatives of the Bürgerschaft.)[84] On 8 March, the Elders acceded to the Senat's proposal "in all points." The acquiescence of the Elders swayed the Niedergericht, and on the following Monday, it, too, came round.

Having gotten what it wanted, the Senat quickly moved to mend fences by promising the Niedergericht that the methods employed here "shall infringe in no way in the future on the rights" of the citizens' court. Two weeks later, more formally, the Senat thanked the Niedergericht for its "patriotic declaration" and again reassured its members that this "irregular procedure . . . in no way limited their legal prerogatives." The care the Senat took to placate the Niedergericht testifies to the seriousness of the issues involved. Often rebuked for its "tyrannical overlordship," the Senat trod as gingerly as possible in the minefields of internal politics. But the Senat was resolute—and persistent—in its demands and one does not get the feeling that the Niedergericht could have successfully withstood the pressure. That it gave in to the Senat did not mean, however, that it viewed as any less grave the implications such decisions bore. If the protest was only rhetorical, it nonetheless came from the heart, and words meant much in the discursive arena of Hamburg's political culture. The Niedergericht had not, it should be emphasized, gone down without a fight; its very protestations, and its ability to make them, testified to the continued strength of the collegial bodies that represented citizens' issues in Hamburg's political world, even if their power was often only obstructive.[85]

A palatable compromise slowly emerged, but one thing in the program remained a sticking point, and it was again over the question of honor that new troubles erupted. The agreement hammered out among the various parties—the sentence—had a catch: the *Urfehde*.

The *Urfehde*, a practice derived from older common law, ritually restored peace between litigating opponents or between the magistracy and an individual. In it a person acknowledged, under oath, the legality of his imprisonment (or torture) and renounced his right to revenge or retribution. Would swearing the *Urfehde* taint Kesslitz's honor? Detenhof and Kesslitz certainly believed so, and they were hardly alone in this. By taking the oath, Kesslitz would admit that the Senat and city had had the right to conduct the legal investigation and to detain him. He would likewise forfeit recourse to further appeals.[86]

The *Urfehde* was an outrage, or at least Kesslitz perceived it as such. Detenhof promised not to give up until it was retracted, and he knew just where to jab this sharp new weapon for the best result. The *Urfehde*, he protested, not only besmirched Kesslitz's honor; it also impugned Prussia's. Additionally, he petitioned Berlin to require the Niedergericht to absolve Kesslitz unconditionally and to unburden Kesslitz of the need to pay the costs, which should—"by all rights," he emphasized—be Sanpelayo's responsibility. With some sense of here we go again, Sillem wrote to Wever, once more asking him to do his best to ascertain how the court in Berlin and the cabinet would react and to forestall Detenhof's inter-ference. Sillem admitted—at least to Wever—that the swearing of the Ur-fehde "carried with it ill-repute," yet really meant nothing more than that an individual openly renounced his rights of vengeance or claims to dam-ages, and "even those completely exonerated . . . swear it."[87] On the final disposition of the case, he could not yet comment: "If the superior court [Senat] will confirm, revise, meliorate, or exacerbate the finding of the Niedergericht, I cannot say."[88]

In fact, this time, Detenhof was finished. His plea evoked a vigorous response but hardly the one he had anticipated. In a dispatch to Hecht, Berlin expressed its complete contentment with the finding. Berlin now admitted that Kesslitz had "far exceeded . . . the limits of self-defense." Such an excess merited perhaps an even more serious punishment. Thus, "he should count himself fortunate." Moreover, he should not balk at swearing the Urfehde, because "it in no way damages his honor." The suggestion that Sanpelayo bear the court costs Berlin dismissed as "truly absurd." Berlin ordered Kesslitz "to calm down." Detenhof earned harsher words. "This person," the note read, "carries his impertinence and pre-sumption to such extremes as to misuse Our protection for Kesslitz to insult and defy the Hamburg magistracy." Hecht was therefore commis-sioned to tell Detenhof that such chicanery must immediately cease, and that he should reprimand the lawyer in the strongest terms for his audacity and overweening pride. When Wever learned of the dressing down Deten-hof had received, he commented: "I have to admit that I have not enjoyed anything as much as this in a long time."[89]

Although the case was now almost finished, some loose ends were still flapping around. The king's displeasure with Detenhof had a salutary effect; Kesslitz blew up at Detenhof and dismissed him as his advocate. Wever crowed: "and so is Detenhof paid for his boastfulness!" Kesslitz did not, however, get off scot-free. Hecht was instructed to order Kesslitz back to Silesia immediately upon his release. Some rumors (false in the end) circulated that Frederick intended to confine Kesslitz in the fortress at Spandau.[90]

For Kesslitz, however, bitter pills remained to be swallowed before he could depart from Hamburg. The superior court confirmed the decision of the Niedergericht on 24 May. On Saturday the 25th, Kesslitz swore the Urfehde and promised "on his word of honor" to cover the expenses; he was then released. He had spent over seven months in the Eimbeck'sches Haus. The costs were considerable, amounting to at least 5,778 mark cou-rant. On 14 June, he paid 300 Reichsthaler, and the praetors covered the rest out of their treasury. If for Kesslitz the case was almost over, the sensation it had created smoldered for a while among his patrons and friends in Berlin, where the swearing of the *Urfehde* had "stirred up quite a ruckus." Several of his supporters told Wever, "Potsdam was not happy with this" at all. Their dissatisfaction may have been intense, but it could not go very far, for the deed was done, and the king and the Foreign Office had approved the final resolution of the case. As far as official Berlin was concerned, Kesslitz's Hamburg adventure was over.

The Kesslitz Affair and His Catholic, His Most Christian, and His Imperial Majesties

Understandably, the Kesslitz affair upset the relations between Prussia and Hamburg profoundly and immediately. But the diplomatic uproar hardly ceased there. Sanpelayo sought—and found—support in Madrid. The appeal to His Catholic Majesty (the king of Spain) then drew in His Most Christian Majesty (the king of France). Paris mediated between Hamburg and Madrid because Spain had no minister plenipotentiary in Hamburg. Thus not only Hecht but also the French minister in Hamburg, Baron de la Houze, took Kesslitz's and Sanpelayo's part and pulled their courts into the orbit of Hamburg's external affairs and internal politics. Involved, too, if rather more peripherally, was Binder von Kriegelstein as the representative of His Imperial Majesty. The mechanics of these negotiations worked much as they did with Berlin. Issues of honor were equally pronounced, although, and especially in the exchanges between Spain and Hamburg, it was not the honor of an individual officer that was at stake but the honor of Spain's official representative in Hamburg. And Sanpelayo's honor entwined with economics as much as it did with jurisdictions and sovereignty.

For its part, the Senat dreaded the negative repercussions on its relationship with Spain and acted quickly to provide the court in Madrid with its version of the situation.[91] It involved a few basic yet vital points. Madrid (and Paris, too, for that matter) defended the diplomatic position of the consul and took considerable pains to ensure that Hamburg neither charged Sanpelayo with any crime nor inflicted on him the indignity of a criminal investigation. As with Prussia, perceptions and performances of sovereignty proved decisive. Once Hamburg had sufficiently reassured the Bourbon courts that the Senat had no intention (or, for that matter, any real evidence) to pursue a criminal case against Sanpelayo, the debate shifted to discussions of Sanpelayo's position and his prestige as consul. Both courts equally strove to have Romellini banished forthwith from Hamburg as a troublesome element, whose presence only aggravated Sanpelayo's discomfort. As Hamburg got bogged down in lengthy negotiations with Berlin, however, legal proceedings slowed to a crawl, first annoying, then infuriating the court in Madrid, which desired nothing more than a speedy resolution to the whole distasteful affair. The Senat, despite its sincere wish to preserve good feelings with Spain, was just as clearly peeved with Sanpelayo, not least because of his continued scandalous conduct with his mistress. Now, the old desire to be rid of a Spanish consul resurfaced as well, and the incident seemed a golden opportunity to insist on Sanpelayo's recall, with the added benefit of thereby avoiding the naming of a successor. The Kesslitz affair, despite its seeming concentration on the fates of four luckless individuals, quickly inflamed older antagonisms and became integral to larger political goals.

On the morning of 19 October, Sanpelayo, "as the publicly credentialed representative" of his government, placed Kesslitz under his protection. Kesslitz had, he insisted, saved his life and committed no crime in doing so but rather fulfilled a moral duty to defend himself and his friend. Sanpelayo assumed the costs of a Catholic burial for Visconti in Altona and agreed to support Romellini and her daughter for the duration of the investigation. The Senat claimed a deposit of 1,000 marks and extracted a promise from him on his word of honor not to leave town.[92] The costs thus incurred (and they mounted alarmingly) caused considerable agitation in Madrid and Paris, and the size of the sum alone was not the sole grievance.

Baron de la Houze, who had protested in early December against the decision to launch the fiscal procedure against Kesslitz, soon was seeking out members of the Senat at their homes, "vigorously taking the part" of Kesslitz and Sanpelayo. De la Houze expressed his support in many ways, for instance, asking permission to see Kesslitz at his discretion. He emphasized how much sympathy existed in the city for Kesslitz. Far from snubbing him, the entire nobility then resident in the city had "taken Kesslitz's side," and as evidence of their esteem, they had all sent their cards to him at New Year's as customary.[93] As time passed, de la Houze became more deeply involved, ratcheting up the intensity of his protests and multiplying the number of his demands. By the beginning of February, some three and a half months after the event, de la Houze had lost all patience. He requested an audience with members of the Senat, asking, significantly, for a deputation to wait on him at his house at 11 A.M. The Senat avoided sending an official delegation, instead dispatching two of its colleagues to meet with de la Houze in a less ceremonial, even casual, way. When Syndic Schuback and the Senator Caspar Voght returned to the Senat from their visit, they related the details of an unpleasant encounter. De la Houze had brusquely informed them that "he had received commissions from both crowns. . . . to take Sanpelayo's part with all possible earnestness." He maintained that the city possessed no legal jurisdiction over Sanpelayo as Spanish consul. The French court championed Sanpelayo to protect the position of its own consul in Hamburg: "There are here in Hamburg only two foreign consuls, that is, the French naval consul and Monsieur Sanpelayo. My court would never permit the city to arrogate to itself any form of control over the former. And that is just as true of the latter." He hardly minced words. Nothing could be clearer; the French court viewed the intimidation of Sanpelayo as a similar threat to its own representative. Through de la Houze, the Spanish court "expressly required" that all actions against Sanpelayo immediately cease, and that those already undertaken be declared null and void. Furthermore, he dictated the exact words the Senat was to use in composing a binding statement to Spain: "that there will be no criminal process whatsoever [initiated] against Sanpelayo, either directly or indirectly." The Senat must guarantee that the "Romellini affair" be closed as quickly and quietly as possible. De la Houze's foremost complaint was that Romellini had been living for so long—"so unnecessarily long"—in Sanpelayo's house and had run up exorbitant expenses, which the consul had to pay. He related an annoying incident in which one of her guards had said "very inappropriately" to Romellini: "Just eat up—Sanpelayo will have to pay for it all in the end anyway!" After all, de la Houze continued, "one really should have driven her out of the city as a common whore [putain]." The city had seized Sanpelayo's property and many of his private papers, and the praetor refused to return them. De la Houze was not through. He warned the Senat of the evil results its "presumption" could cause; "there are already secret plans under way to transfer the Spanish consulate to Altona," a move that would, he cautioned, have a "very negative effect" on Hamburg's commerce and might prompt other countries to do likewise. The deputation had no trouble discerning the greater danger lying behind this admonition: if the Spanish consul left Hamburg because the city had failed to respect his immunity, the French consul would not be far behind. The Senat, after receiving these bad tidings, admitted that the intervention of de la Houze had completely altered the situation. The case was now irremediably diplomatic.

Things were moving swiftly, however, and what happened in Berlin, in Romellini's boudoir, in Kesslitz's cell, and on the streets could very quickly give the affair a whole new complexion, first tightening the screws on the Senat, then relaxing them again. The sequence repeated itself several times. On the same day de la Houze's protests reached it, the Senat learned with dismay of Detenhof's departure for Berlin. Abruptly, however, Sanpelayo's missteps alleviated the Senat's problems with de la Houze and Spain, allowing a brief breathing space. As Detenhof traveled to Berlin, the Senat received a report from the watch posted at Romellini's door: Sanpelayo had forced his way into her lodgings and "impertinently" harangued the guards. The Senat quickly took this ammunition and loaded its diplomatic guns. A memorandum sent to its agent in Spain, van der Lepe, related these events to him. To chasten de la Houze, and perhaps shut him up for a time, the Senat had Schuback (who was de la Houze's neighbor and apparently a good acquaintance) try to persuade de la Houze to prevent Sanpelayo from making any more such "indecent" visits to Romellini. The Senat rather cleverly shifted the responsibility to de la Houze, while at the same time informing the officers of the watch that they should *not* stop Sanpelayo from seeing Romellini. Sanpelayo was to be trapped by his lust. The Senat carefully kept track of each visit and rather gleefully ground de la Houze's nose in it, while speaking to the court in Madrid (through van der Lepe) in injured tones of its "distress."[94]

Van der Lepe was kept abreast in Madrid of the latest developments by the memorandum that he received, which also allowed him to shine a favorable light on the Senat's side of the story. In late October, van der Lepe had received a résumé of the facts that explained how at first everything had gone smoothly; the interrogations had presented no difficulties and the procurator was ready to indict. Then Kesslitz's advocate had "staged a *coup de main,* [by] addressing himself [directly] to the court in Berlin." Detenhof had thereby forced the Senat into time-consuming, exhausting exchanges that "interrupted the course of justice" for some months. Thus, an affair that should have been easily decided and quickly resolved had become positively byzantine. While Sanpelayo had not been charged with either killing or wounding Visconti, still, "one could hardly regard him as totally innocent," the Senat argued, for "he occasioned all the excesses by his frivolous behavior [and] his scandalous libertinage with a person of Romellini's caliber. He took the inconsiderate step of involving Monsieur Kesslitz in a villainous affair and compromised himself and his friend with [the plots of] a nasty adventurer like the soi-disant Visconti." Under these circumstances, having to assume the costs seemed a not terribly unfair burden for the consul. Moreover, the Senat expressed itself "a little unhappy" about Sanpelayo's conduct since the incident. Not only had he initiated this *affaire scabreuse,* but he had consistently failed to act as one would expect of a consul and, despite having no claim or entitlement to the privileges and prerogatives of a minister, he "often put on the airs" of one. He categorically refused to appear before the praetor to answer questions and yet at the same time "presumed to offer his protection" to Kesslitz. Moreover, "forgetting himself," he addressed "rather heated" letters to the Senat, of which the Senat enclosed "a small sample" so that van der Lepe could extract instances of Sanpelayo's inappropriate conduct to counter (or even forestall) the complaints the Spanish court raised.

Especially offensive (and especially useful as a way to damage Sanpelayo's character with his superiors) was his conduct with Romellini. In order to see "this debauched woman," he "sank to [the trick of] disguising himself in a guardsman's coat." Sanpelayo had taken the opportunity "to pursue a liaison that completely dishonors him in the eyes of all the world." The Senat specifically instructed van der Lepe to raise this particular issue with the foreign minister, Grimaldi. At the same time, van der Lepe was to assure Grimaldi of the Senat's commitment to impartial justice on a matter that had "greatly intrigued the public." The Senat would be "mortified" if, by his own "irregular conduct," Sanpelayo obliged it to treat him in the future with "less esteem for his person." The Senat meant exactly the opposite, of course. Van der Lepe should use the opportunity of an audience with Grimaldi to "slip in [*glisser*] a little word" about the possible revocation of Sanpelayo's patent as consul. It was not possible, the Senat insisted, "that he should still remain here in an official capacity after the affair is concluded." Obviously, as the Senat confided to van der Lepe, one could not write this sort of thing to Grimaldi or present it to the Spanish king directly. Rather, he should handle it discreetly, "under four eyes."[95]

On the very same day, de la Houze's demands spurred the Senat to post another note to van der Lepe, explaining its position on consular representation and on the rights and immunities a consul in Hamburg possessed. The Senat referred to the consular situation of Hamburg's agents in Cádiz and Málaga who lived under Spanish authority and pronounced it obvious "that Monsieur Sanpelayo must be similarly subject to the jurisdiction of Hamburg, especially as he does much business here." The Senat had treated Sanpelayo with great tact: he had not been detained; Romellini remained in her lodgings on the Neuer Wall; and the Senat had even ignored "those indecent visits that he continues to make" to her. Quite frankly, the Senat had tired of Sanpelayo's blustering threats to leave Hamburg in favor of either Altona, Harburg, or Stade. Expressing some indignation of its own, the Senat deemed these actions "a radical attack on this good city, against the Hanseatic understanding [with Spain]" and, moreover, "contrary to long-term observances."[96]

In the same month (March), the Senat felt compelled to detail why the case languished. It was a "most ticklish" situation. Kesslitz's claim of self-defense had always been shaky, and the Senat quickly pointed out that "it is perplexing" that two relatively young and healthy men—Kesslitz and Sanpelayo—had not been able to "get rid of [*débarrasser*] a nasty villain" like Visconti without having to kill him "in such an alarming manner." The Senat found it hard to comprehend how Visconti had continued to attack while so badly wounded. And, finally, condemningly: "It is inconceivable that Monsieur de Sanpelayo, once Monsieur Kesslitz had drawn his sword in order to separate [the two other men] would do nothing, standing by with arms crossed, [remaining] a passive spectator, and that Monsieur Kesslitz, without receiving a single wound [in the fight], was able to inflict so many on his attacker." The conditions were "rather peculiar and often contradictory." Still, despite mystifying circumstances that appeared to condemn both men more than they exonerated them, the Senat had neither moved against Sanpelayo legally nor interfered with his business. On the contrary, "not a single day passes that he has not appeared in public at the Exchange, in the circles [of his acquaintances], and, in short, anywhere and everywhere he pleases." Despite all the respect and forbearance shown him, however, Sanpelayo never ceased to protest, arguing that the members of the Senat "planned to let the full burden" of costs fall on him and him alone and schemed to employ this occasion as a pretext to ruin his business, a business that the city regarded as, in his words, "odious." Besides, the Senat charged, the whole affair had emanated from Sanpelayo's own faults. He had consistently failed to demonstrate the traits reasonably desired in one who represented an esteemed court. Indeed, he brought upon himself and the city "all these unfortunate consequences" by giving in to a "wild passion for an outright libertine, who had already been passed through several hands."[97]

In February, problems with de la Houze over Sanpelayo continued, although de la Houze, too, was beginning to perceive the untenability of the consul's position. Moderation slowly returned to his language. On 10 February, Schuback held a private meeting with de la Houze in which the minister plenipotentiary promised to wait and see "if the Senat lashed out at Sanpelayo or handled him with proper regard." The first would evoke a vigorous defense on de la Houze's part; the second, his gratitude and his assistance in dealing with Paris and Madrid.[98]

De la Houze was painfully aware of just how damaging Sanpelayo's continued "lascivious visits" to Romellini were and he found it increasingly difficult to excuse or defend his friend. Grimaldi's patience had just about run out, however, and the Spanish minister was both a far more important man and a greater potential foe. When van der Lepe waited on

Grimaldi, the latter made the audience a painful half-hour for Hamburg's representative. Van der Lepe had barely finished presenting the usual compliments from the Senat and was just expressing the desire "to cultivate harmony and royal favor," when Grimaldi abruptly broke in: "But let's get down to business here. Surely you have come to discuss with me the affair of Sanpelayo? And just when will it be over? Voilà—it's been dragging on for four months now!" Van der Lepe carefully explained the attendant complications and emphasized the problems with the Prussian court Detenhof's meddling had caused. All to no avail. Grimaldi: "But Monsieur! How does all that concern our consul and the Romellini [woman]? Neither the one nor the other struck or killed that adventurer. I deeply deplore their lechery and his scandalous behavior with that loose woman, but she has committed no crime other than to be a debauchee, in a word, a whore [*putain*]." She deserved nothing more than banishment, surely? So what was holding things up? Grimaldi could only conclude that something else, altogether more diabolic, was afoot, and that by retarding the process, the Senat hoped to ruin Sanpelayo and drive him out of business. That impression, of course, was exactly what the Senat wished to avoid at all costs. While no evidence suggests that the Senat deliberately set out to bankrupt Sanpelayo, it definitely desired to be rid of him as consul.[99]

Van der Lepe's vivid description of this meeting caused great consternation in Hamburg. All too obviously, Sanpelayo enjoyed "much support at court" and a "huge storm" threatened the city. The Spanish king himself learned "to his great displeasure" that the Senat and the investigating praetor had failed to extend to Sanpelayo "all the respect . . . due a man in his position. [The city] had observed his business jealously and was using this opportunity . . . to destroy him utterly." Did the city want such treatment to "become the rule" for how Spain dealt with Hamburg's citizens?[100] A chilling thought, that, because the kingdom's many ports bustled with Hamburg merchants.

The Senat tried to refute these claims, explaining—yet again—that the reasons for the delay derived from no desire to break Sanpelayo, but rather from the problems either created by Berlin or arising from the normal judicial process. The case involving Sanpelayo and Kesslitz was moving no more slowly through legal channels than others, if one discounted the admittedly unfortunate delays Prussian intervention and Detenhof's machinations had occasioned. To derail Grimaldi's persistence, the Senat fed van der Lepe damning information on Sanpelayo, further instructing him to paint the consul's actions "as black as possible." The Senat reiterated its heartfelt desire to keep relations with Spain sweet, especially where commerce was concerned, but also insisted that no one could absolve

Sanpelayo entirely, and that he himself had done much to bring the Spanish crown into disrepute.

In Madrid, van der Lepe was to repeat the gossip that many in Berlin and Vienna believed Romellini and Sanpelayo to be hardly as innocent as they at first appeared. "The authors of these rumors insist that Monsieur Kesslitz after having struck the first blow against Visconti, dropped his sword, whereupon Sanpelayo and Romellini flung themselves on Visconti and slaughtered him." Sanpelayo and Romellini allowed Kesslitz to take the blame (or induced him to do so by offering him money) because he—as a nobleman and a Prussian—would either escape prosecution entirely or be protected by Berlin. The Senat passed this story on to Madrid, not so much because its members believed it (although some were convinced), as merely to indicate the complications involved and the almost impenetrable murkiness of the facts. Now, however, as the troubles with Berlin had been resolved, the main obstacles to a swift conclusion had also been removed.[101]

In March and April, the Spanish court continued to protest the speed (or lack of it) with which the case advanced and continued to charge that Hamburg aimed to destroy Sanpelayo. Yet gradually, the tone moderated. The mediation of Binder von Kriegelstein in Hamburg, of the imperial representative in Spain, and of Vergennes in Paris eventually lessened tensions between Spain and Hamburg. Reports flowing back to Hamburg from van der Lepe soon became less disconcerting and then even heartening. By mid March, the news from Paris, too, had become mildly encouraging. Hamburg's agent there, d'Hugier, described a conversation he had had with Vergennes in which the latter had noted that France's close political and dynastic ties to Spain and the lack of a Spanish minister plenipotentiary in Hamburg meant that France could not remain uninvolved. Nonetheless, Vergennes declared that he and his court saw no reason to complain about how the city had treated Sanpelayo, and "that he never intended contesting the jurisdiction of the city over the consul." The Senat moved to conciliate de la Houze as well, dispatching Schuback to see if one could prevent the French representative from spoiling the outcome at this late date. Schuback told de la Houze—in confidence—to leak the news to Sanpelayo that Senat had already assured the Spanish court that he would only bear responsibility for costs already incurred; no further claims would be levied.[102]

By mid March, the Senat could breathe a little more easily. The Prussians and the French seemed satisfied, and Spain was happy, even though van der Lepe still had to listen to Grimaldi grumble, "sometimes using very hard words," about the length of Romellini's detention and what it was costing Sanpelayo. By now, however, the complaints had lost steam and become almost pro forma. By now, too, the Senat worried less about Grimaldi's ire. Even somewhat earlier, at the beginning of March, when Sillem received one such complaint from Madrid, it had signified little. When he showed it to Binder von Kriegelstein, for instance, the minister only laughed and said: "It doesn't mean anything; don't worry about it." And he was right. By the end of March, Grimaldi fell silent, except to express satisfaction with the outcome to van der Lepe "in the most gracious terms" imaginable. Some weeks later, Vergennes did the same. Yet Sanpelayo, like Kesslitz, had not emerged from the ordeal unscathed. Madrid reprimanded him sharply and reminded him that only the influence of his friends had allowed him to keep his post as consul.[103] At this point, the Senat could relax (at least for the moment), having successfully pacified three mighty courts without sacrificing any sovereignty, or rather any part of it that seemed particularly crucial.

Unresolved, however, was the issue of Sanpelayo as consul, of Spanish consuls, and of consuls more generally in Hamburg. Jurisdiction lingered as one sticking point closely linked to the weightier matters of reciprocal commercial relationships. Throughout the case, but most obviously in the dealings with Spain and France, the two issues entwined. In February, de la Houze protested against "the entire procedure" in all its details as it affected the Spanish consul and went on to argue that the exercise of local justice over a consul violated "international law . . . no matter what contrary customs one claims to have established in Hamburg." In explaining the situation to Hamburg's agent in Paris, Sillem presented a rather different perspective. "There is," he maintained, "quite a difference between a Spanish consul who has already appeared several times in court on civil matters and a *commissaire* of France; between simple jurisdiction and jurisdiction over crimes and misdemeanors; and between a consul who is also a businessman [Sanpelayo] and a *commissaire* who is not." If queried on this matter, van der Lepe could counter that "Hamburg's consuls in Cádiz and Málaga are subject to the jurisdiction of His Catholic Majesty." Thus it followed that Hamburg could exert jurisdiction over Sanpelayo, especially when one took into account the substantial dimensions of his business in the city. That stipulation did not, the Senat assured the Spanish crown, mean that Spanish subjects having legitimate business in Hamburg lived at risk. Rather, "all foreigners, and especially the subjects of His Catholic Majesty, are welcome in Hamburg" and equally enjoyed all the rights and privileges that they had claim to; the same pertained to Sanpelayo.[104]

The demands of commerce and the desire to preserve good commercial ties with Spain and France clearly ranked at, or very near, the top of the Senat's agenda, but not at the expense of surrendering legal jurisdiction or diminishing sovereignty. These sometimes conflicting political and economic factors could embroil the Senat and Hamburg's merchant community in internal bickering (despite the fact that about half of senators were themselves merchants). The bargaining over the abortive treaty with the Barbary pirates earlier in the century had caused the Senat and the Chamber of Commerce to clash. Certainly, the Senat appealed time and again to the clemency and benevolence of His Catholic Majesty (and His Most Christian Majesty) to preserve the good feelings that existed between Hamburg and Spain, "as His glorious predecessors had previously done over the centuries." The Senat registered distress at how "a simple matter of law could [have] become an affair of state" and come to endanger Hamburg and Hanseatic privileges. Even after the satisfactory conclusion of the Sanpelayo-Kesslitz affair, the Senat continued to urge van der Lepe to exploit every possible occasion "to retain the protection of His Majesty" and do everything in his power to "revive, enliven, and enlarge [*ranimer, vivifier et agrandir*] our joint commerce."[105]

Perhaps the clearest indication of how commerce and sovereignty interlaced in the Kesslitz affair came after its end. Kesslitz had left Hamburg in July; Romellini had been banished; and Sanpelayo was no longer consul (the Senat had sought and achieved his dismissal). Of the three principal actors still alive after 19 October, Sanpelayo alone remained in Hamburg, and he was packing, planning to settle elsewhere. A civil suit his one-time landlady, the widow Amberg, brought against him for unpaid rent delayed his departure, however. The Senat refused to intervene, at least officially, arguing that this was a legal matter over which they could bring no influence to bear. Sanpelayo's successor in office, Manuel d'Urqullu took up the cudgels on his behalf, however, claiming his right to do so as the current consul and because Sanpelayo's diplomatic immunity had been violated.[106] From the very beginning of his intervention, Urqullu adopted an arrogant and impertinent tone, and his partisanship provoked yet another tussle over the putative and real rights of Spanish (and other) consuls in Hamburg. Clearly, the legacy of the Sanpelayo affair had sensitized the court in Madrid and the Senat in Hamburg to these vital matters of prestige, power, and protection.

Each party wanted to avoid a major blowup; none of them, however, would cede any more ground. In May 1777, Urqullu complained to the Senat about "the falsity of the pretexts" under which the widow Amberg had "dared inconvenience" the court. He called for an immediate end to proceedings and branded her claims as preposterous. "It is something I do not consent to and would never consent to, even if Monsieur Sanpelayo were [only an ordinary] subject of His Majesty." Quickly the Senat appealed again to van der Lepe for some clarification on the reciprocal rights of Spanish and Hamburg consuls. Although Sillem preferred to "let this pass in silence, for as with other true bagatelles, it is best ignored," the problem rankled, because it raised more serious issues. Moreover, the new consul to Hamburg presented little improvement over Sanpelayo. Like his predecessor, Urqullu quickly overstepped his position. Despite being only a "simple consul," he had assumed "the airs of an ambassador and a tone haughtier than that which would be permitted an ambassador." Urqullu's demands were inadmissible, for Sanpelayo's was a civil case that in no way fell under a consul's purview.[107]

Urqullu continued to press. Exactly one week after his first letter to the Senat, he shot off a second one, using much stronger language. "I am surprised," he wrote, "that you presume to assert . . . that this dispute has nothing at all to do with the functions of a consul." Everything that touched on the interests of the subjects of the king of Spain he considered his "proper business." He found the pretensions of the widow Amberg absurd and suggested that if her advocate dragged out the case in the hopes that they would wear down Sanpelayo's resolve, then "he deceives himself." With an indignant flourish, he ended: "I shall never allow it." His intention was not, he insisted, to divert the course of justice, but merely to attain a swift resolution to a "disagreeable . . . and ridiculous" public spectacle.[108]

The Senat punctured his temerity: "The Senat does not recognize your patent as consul." It further stressed Amberg's civil case against Sanpelayo had "nothing to do with consular duties." The case was a simple one, relating to "the lease of a house, [involving a contract] made between a female citizen of Hamburg and Monsieur de Sanpelayo, one-time consul, who now does business here." The courts alone could decide the matter. The letter ended with a clear rebuff: "The only thing I [Sillem] expect of you is that you calm down and rest assured that the Senat is doing nothing to impede the case; justice will be served out with complete impartiality." What happened in the end is unclear, although it may be that Sanpelayo's death (in November 1778) terminated the matter.[109]

Finally, one should take a moment to observe the roles others played in the long drama. If theirs were often small parts, like all bit players, they occasionally performed valuable services in moving the plot along. Binder von Kriegelstein, the imperial resident minister, generally cooperated with the Senat to alleviate tensions. The Senat frequently solicited his advice or requested—privately—that he contact one of Vienna's representatives in either Madrid or Paris to help maneuver around some bumpy stretch on the diplomatic road.[110] As one traces Binder von Kriegelstein's appearances through the Senat's protocol, it is clear that he did not always approve of the Senat's actions, and that his contact with the case was not only incidental.[111] During the course of the investigation, and at least until the beginning of 1776, Binder von Kriegelstein and the Viennese court seem to have been little inclined to interfere. Murder was, moreover, not appealable to either of the imperial courts, and none of the principals still alive was an imperial subject. As the difficulties with other powers mounted, however, Binder von Kriegelstein became more active, both on his own initiative and when solicited by the Senat.

As Detenhof worked his evil magic in Berlin, Sillem sought Binder von Kriegelstein's help: Could he speak to the imperial representative in Berlin to parry any blows due to misunderstandings? Binder von Kriegelstein's good offices were, of course, partisan. Austrian-Prussian rivalry and the dualism it engendered were new facts of life in late eighteenth-century diplomacy. True, the Austrian defeat in the Seven Years' War lay twelve years in the past, but it still smarted, and Prussia had, after all, snatched away and then held on to the very rich prize of Silesia. Maria-Theresa's chancellor, Wenzel Anton von Kaunitz-Rietberg, remained an inveterate and implacable enemy of Frederick the Great and Prussia. Relations between Austria and Prussia had admittedly grown less tense since 1763. Yet if Austria and Prussia could cooperate to their mutual benefit (as partners, for example, in the first partitioning of Polish territory in 1772), the competition nonetheless continued. So, if Binder von Kriegelstein assisted Hamburg at various points, some of that aid was directed against Prussia, while it also expressed the Empire's old interest in the city. Likewise, when de la Houze had gotten very huffy with the Senat in late January and early February 1776, Binder von Kriegelstein quickly wrote to his counterpart, the comte de Mercy in Paris, to ensure the "preservation of the city's legal prerogatives." The Empire viewed safeguarding Hamburg's legal sovereignty not only as useful in battles with other powers but as continuing proof of its overlordship. Yet Vienna also pointedly reminded Hamburg how advantageous its protection was and that it expected reciprocation. The Senat's decision to treat Binder von Kriegelstein to a dinner indicates that he accomplished these tasks tactfully, and that the Senat appreciated his help. A good meal may seem either too little or too obvious a bribe, but such were the elements of eighteenth-century diplomacy.[112]

Binder von Kriegelstein's advice and intervention were, however, less welcome on other occasions. Although he generally remained supportive of Hamburg in the Kesslitz case, not everything the Senat did pleased him or his superiors. Sanpelayo's lickerishness especially vexed him. By April, he was livid and complained strongly to the Senat about Sanpelayo's visits to Romellini and about the Senat's apparent inability (or unwillingness) to halt them. The consul's conduct was "offensive in the extreme." Recently, Sanpelayo had gone to see her "on Good Friday in broad daylight, causing a public scandal." How could the Senat allow this to go on? Why hadn't de la Houze been told to stop Sanpelayo? The Senat had tried—without success—to get the French minister to remonstrate with Sanpelayo. But the Senat also deliberately allowed the visits to continue in order to build a stronger case against the Spanish consul.[113]

The decision of the Niedergericht on 12 April also exacerbated tensions between Binder von Kriegelstein and the Senat. Binder von Kriegelstein professed little sympathy for Sanpelayo's complaints, but his attitude toward Kesslitz differed. He had always been gravely concerned about Kesslitz's honor. When Syndic Schuback informed Binder von Kriegelstein in person of the final disposition of the case, he was shocked to learn that the minister "already knew it all." And, in a rather surprising turn of events, he expressed deep dissatisfaction about the entire procedure and especially with the decision of the Niedergericht. The requirement that Kesslitz swear the *Urfehde* deeply offended him. The finding had "appalled everyone." Only with difficulty was Schuback able to restore calm.[114]

Binder von Kriegelstein presented one face to the Senat officially—that of a sympathetic supporter, if also one occasionally annoyed by the Senat's pusillanimity in not reining in Sanpelayo, refusing to punish Romellini appropriately, and maltreating the true victim in the case, Kesslitz—but his reports to Vienna reveal another Binder von Kriegelstein entirely. This man was a consummate purveyor of what we might consider gossip. In the diplomatic world of the eighteenth century, however, salacious tidbits were not (or at least not always) mere chitchat but vital information, upon which government ministers sometimes acted. Binder von Kriegelstein's dispatches, as we shall later see, repeated the delicious and disturbing rumor that Sanpelayo and Romellini were the true killers and Kesslitz their dupe. Thus, although he could accomplish little, and although Sanpelayo's conduct, Romellini's lifestyle, and Kesslitz's dishonor offended and annoyed him, they were useful tools. But the case was over and only the epilogue of Sanpelayo's quarrel with Amberg tottered on.[115] The diplomatic incident was finished, as was the "malheureuse, scabreuse, compliqué, plus épineux, très mauvaise, . . . mais importante affaire" of Joseph, baron von Kesslitz.

PART TWO

Dramatis personae

Entr'acte

Four protagonists performed in the drama of 18 October 1775: Joseph von Kesslitz, Antoine de Sanpelayo, "Comte" Joseph Visconti, and Anna Maria Romellini. By the early hours of the next day, only three still lived to repeat their tales, and two of them did so extensively. How much of what they told can we believe? What form did their narratives take, and how can the historian use them to reconstruct the lives of four people dead for over two hundred years? Richest, if perhaps most problematic of these sources, are the investigations the magistrates conducted into the incidents of the night of 18/19 October as they struggled to unravel the course of events, evaluate motives, weigh evidence, and, ultimately, assign blame. To understand what these inquiries revealed and how contemporaries understood it, we must resituate these narratives in the historical background from which they came and to which their creators belonged.

The process of taking testimony was inherently dialogic (between an interrogator and the interrogated) and dialectic (questions not only required answers, but provoked particular responses, and responses then triggered further questions). The magistrates who collected testimony by no means accepted everything they heard as true. Nor should we. Like us, they remained skeptical, for example, of testimony given under torture, but they also recognized that the interrogative process itself often generated set answers. Like us, they asked, To whose advantage? Who benefits? They perceived that no witness was totally impartial, and that few in fact were neutral. They recognized that testifying was a creative act involving two or more participants. Any question shaped the answer it received. Even when, as frequently happened in the Kesslitz case, the magistrates posed open-ended questions and speakers went on at length, seemingly unable to stop, it is naive to think that neither influenced the other.

If we accept that each testimony was a creative experience, then what can we believe? Or can we believe anything? The answer is yes and no, for much turns on what we mean by "believe." Obviously, each of the protagonists in relating his or her story endeavored to present him- or herself in a favorable light, perhaps even seeking to "get off." Such "fiction in the archives" is commonplace.[1] The magistrates were as aware of this as we are, for they were experienced in dealing with crimes and fastidious about the collection and evaluation of evidence. They rarely satisfied themselves with one person's account and diligently brought other testimony to bear in order to corroborate or refute it. Contemporaries gathered as much ancillary information as possible and relied on acquired wisdom. For instance, they wanted to know from the Habsburg administration whether Visconti was or was not a member of the famous family of the same name; they consulted the Catholic betrothal registers to see if either Sanpelayo or Visconti had married Romellini; they wrote to authorities in other cities seeking to learn more about the previous lives of their suspects. They did in their time what historians have done ever since: research to verify "facts." Can we find baptismal records of Romellini or her children? Was the duke of Courland actually in Venice when Romellini said he met her there? Had her father served the Polish king? Some of these points can be authenticated with reasonable plausibility. Others, of course, cannot, because the historical tissue has long since disintegrated into virtual nothingness. Yet these realities are not chimerical, even if our knowledge of them is always imperfect.

Over the past few decades, and under the influence of other disciplines, historians have become extremely wary about "truth," even to the point of accepting that truth is always subjective, that it is always constructed or is more textual than real. Recently, scholars in several fields—history, cultural studies, and anthropology—have come to agree on the constructive function of narrating. Anthropologists like Sherry Ortner "posit that it is through narrativity that we come to know, understand, and make sense of the social world, and . . . that we constitute our social identities." Indeed "social life is itself *storied*." Still, "social actors are [not] free to fabricate narratives at will." Historians engaged in writing the "new" biography recognize similar principles in pointing out that "every social location offers a limited number of possibilities from which individuals can create a possible self." Such techniques can help us further analyze the social, cultural, and political worlds Kesslitz, Romellini, and their audience(s) peopled and constructed.[2] Equally useful for the historian, if in a different way, are the paired concepts of "listening *with*" storytellers (rather than listening *to* them) and "thinking *with*" stories (rather than thinking *about* them).

134

Arthur Frank elaborated this method for medical ethics. "Thinking about a story," he wrote, "is to reduce it to content and then analyze that content. Thinking with a story is to experience it affecting one's own life and to find in that effect a certain truth of one's life." Thus, actors and those portraying the actions of others not only recount or summarize but also plait in "other, larger cultural stories" as they style their individual ones.[3] Frank presents this as a method by which health care providers might become more sensitive to their patients, but the concept of "thinking with" is also quite fruitful for historians. Kesslitz, Sanpelayo, and Romellini and those who "told their stories" thought about them—looking for "truth" or "lies"—but they also thought *with* them.

The real-time constitution of these stories is still more involved. Literary theorists and psychologists have argued that the act of narrating actually creates identities. Usually, this perception refers to written autobiographies, "for the selves we display in autobiographies are doubly constructed, not only in the act of writing a life story but also in a lifelong process of identity formation."[4] One could go further and insist that events only become real to people (even events in their own lives) when they have to marshal incidents into cohesive narratives; when they speak them aloud or write them down. Obviously, such fabrications are neither inherently genuine nor inherently false. In a similar vein, Hayden White has argued that when events are narrated in written form, such as in a history or as reported in newspapers, such forms take "chaotic experience" and transform it into a "meaningful moral drama."[5] One should, therefore, accept the creative attributes of such compositions rather than stress their deliberately guileful or devious purposes. Such structures are always multilayered. Even when the author has purposefully cast his or her story as an apologia, the text never works exclusively in that manner. These insights help us comprehend how Kesslitz, Romellini, and the others assembled and arranged the many elements of their stories. Accepting such perspectives does not, however, deny that real things happen.

But to what extent can we regard the information produced mostly through interrogations, or written with a particular purpose in mind (a *Factum*, a brief life history, or a letter), as some kind of autobiographical reflection? The stories or narratives that Kesslitz, Sanpelayo, and Romellini told about themselves are a type of autobiographical writing (or narration) that functions as an "I-document," or what historians refer to as "egodocuments." When the historian Jacques Presser first defined the topic (and created the word) in the 1950s, he "proposed to use his neologism for diaries, memoirs, personal letters and other forms of autobiographical writing."[6] Recently, scholars have differentiated these forms from formal autobiography or memoirs, mostly (although not inevitably) because they are ephemeral, not intended for publication, or perhaps only conceived of as messages to be passed to friends or family members. Such egodocuments have been analyzed in a variety of ways and used to study reading practices, family relationships, popular culture, attitudes, and so on. In these egodocuments, as in more formal autobiography, one can detect the elements of "self-fashioning" and identity construction discussed above, for such egodocuments also have as their purpose "not primarily the reconstruction of the life of the author, but the construction of an identity." Their very "textual ambivalence" reflects "the flexible, shifting and chameleonic character of personal identities."[7] The stories Kesslitz, Romellini, and Sanpelayo told were attempts to create identities, sometimes consciously (as, for instance, when Kesslitz portrayed himself as a zealous soldier of the king of Prussia or when Romellini cast herself in the role of the hapless victim of scheming men) and sometimes unwittingly.

Yet can the fragments our protagonists provide be legitimately characterized as egodocuments? Most students of the subject would willingly accept that egodocuments can be partial, slight, and even unintentionally authored. Of course, such a position raises the perfectly valid objection that if one defines egodocuments so broadly, what cannot be slotted into the category? We need not concern ourselves too much with this problem or, for that matter, with the lengthy and complex discussions over how to analyze such texts.[8] A little common sense and a good dash of historical expertise make it possible to accept these accounts as narratives, to uncover what their authors were trying to achieve (in terms of their audience[s] and their internal, psychological needs), and to let them guide us as we trace people's movements over unique historical landscapes.

The shape of these narratives, the language (words, phrases, expressions), and the forms are neither random nor unique; little is very original here. Still, one of the great values of such unoriginal stories is that they represent how people thought and reflect the influence of the models they used to think with. True crime stories and novels gave to narrators and their audiences alike important frameworks of understanding and representation, although few slavishly followed a single plot line (even if one can sometimes identify deliberate emplotments). Novels and true crime stories were essential elements of the culture in which our narrators lived. For this reason it is unnecessary (and also impossible) to prove that either the recounters or their audiences ever read any of these works. Just as important to remember is that neither accounts of true crime nor novels were entirely imaginary. They drew upon eighteenth-century types and actual occurrences. Novelists like Restif de la Bretonne based fictional creations on incidents from their own somewhat scandalous lives. Likewise, they emphasized both the contemporaneity (*histoire récente*) of their tales and their authenticity—for instance, proclaiming their sources to be "real letters" or "discovered papers."[9]

Few books in the eighteenth century sold better than the romances of real life. Such were the best sellers of eighteenth-century Europe, whether true crime stories that titillated and thrilled, parables of love gone wrong, or the adventures of scoundrels, cheats, and spies. François Gayot de Pitaval's twenty-four volumes of *Causes célèbres et intéressantes avec les jugements qui les ont decidées* (Celebrated and Interesting Cases and the Judgments That Decided Them) was the most famous and quickly found imitators, translators, and editors. If the stories, according to Pitaval, were "instructive" (morally, for a broad public, and legally, for neophyte jurists), far more people read them because they "perfectly satisfy our curiosity"—far more perfectly, Pitaval insisted, than novels did. Among the causes célèbres that most frequently found their way into these collections were the well-known tales of "The Pretended Martin Guerre," "The Chevalier de Morsan," "The Deserted Daughter," "The Contested Marriage," and "The Married Nun." These accounts of love and betrayal, of great evil and equally great innocence became hardy literary perennials, repeated and retold with different characters and set in different times and places. Though true, their details often surpassed the most fevered imaginings of novelists and exceeded the skills of the finest raconteurs. They validated the old adage that truth is stranger than fiction, and the audience seemed virtually insatiable. They rivaled the fiction of the day in another way as well: women were often protagonists.[10] Besides these almost universally known tales, each city had its own informal Pitavals in both published forms and in the rumors and tales that circulated spatially and chronologically. Perhaps people in Hamburg in 1775 and 1776 had forgotten the story of "Maiden Heinrich"—the cross-dressing murderess executed in 1701—but they certainly remembered Engelborg Singelmann, the Elder's daughter, thought to have killed her newborn infant in 1750, and, even more vividly, Charlotte Guyard, née Martin, who accused her father of incest in 1766, recanted, ruined her husband with the case, and, in general, caused a furor that reached to Paris and Berlin. It would be absurd to suggest that Kesslitz or Romellini deliberately or knowingly drew on such examples to construct their stories and self-fashion their lives. Still, these tropes, plot lines, and especially character types were available in versions widely disseminated among the public. It is hardly surprising that they should appear in the narratives Kesslitz and Romellini told, as well as immediately striking responsive chords in their audiences.

The following chapters, therefore, do two things at once. First, they reconstruct the lives of the main characters, following them as far back and as far forward in time from 1775 as sources allow. At the same time, they analyze the stories the protagonists told as versions of the other experiences that animated the eighteenth-century imagination and that seemed completely real to their contemporaries. Yet there is no substitute for context, and each of the following chapters places its characters in the circumstances of their times, paying close attention to specific locales, social standing, cultural milieus, family circumstances, and upbringing. This is an eclectic approach, but one well suited to capturing and portraying the richness of these lives.

CHAPTER FOUR

A Brave and Upright Cavalier?

Joseph von Kesslitz baffled some of his contemporaries and embarrassed far more. His presence in Hamburg was something of a mystery to the Prussians. Like us, they wanted to know why he had left Silesia, where he had gone, how he had lived in the interim, and what had drawn him to the city. If the Hamburg authorities lacked definitive answers to these questions, they had at their fingertips a series of possible explanations. They had known many ex-officers down on their luck who sought their fortunes in Hamburg. Noble birds of passage roosted there, as did less flighty men of affairs. Kesslitz's friendship with Sanpelayo and his occasional association with de la Houze made him a recognizable figure in urban society. Certainly, his was a familiar face among the denizens of Dreyer's coffeehouse. His type was frequent and, at least on the surface, Kesslitz was unexceptional. Still, the individual man remained obscure and his origins and activities were not immediately transparent.

If the Prussian court and the Hamburg magistrates wanted to know more about Kesslitz—to track his life story from its beginning, to discover his motives, to evaluate his ambitions, and to plumb his character—so, too, does the historian. We desire to comprehend what shaped the man. Obviously, all people are products of their environments. One's early years years, upbringing, education, experiences as one matures, and the broader cultural and intellectual milieus that surround one all play their part. Huge impersonal forces shaped Kesslitz as much as they shape anyone, then or now. Still, he was also an individual who made choices. Kesslitz never found himself completely at the mercy of powers he could neither understand nor control. Much he could not escape: his birth, for instance. But that alone hardly predicted how circumstances affected him.

Context is crucial in reconstructing Kesslitz's life (and, in subsequent

Joseph, Freiherr von Kesslitz, 1763–65.
Courtesy Andreas Kutschelis, private collection, Northeim.

chapters, the lives of the other principals): the conditions of his birth (as eldest son); his home and its history (Silesia during the turbulent midcentury decades); his religion (Catholic); the class to which he belonged (an established but impoverished rural nobility); the occurrences of his youth (as a student and an officer); and the disappointments he encountered (losing both his estate and his career). Just as important is how he responded to each of these events. His reactions were sometimes typical but often unusual and even inventive. Uncovering the motives of individuals is perhaps the most arduous historical task and, inevitably, the one for which we generally have the least information. During the course of the investigation into Visconti's death, Kesslitz composed a short life history (about eight folio pages in length) that illuminates the darker corners of his life, but it must be read with great care. Its purpose was obvious: to win the support of the Prussian crown. In it, he related a tale of loyal service, of fealty to and admiration for, Frederick the Great. Still, it is an immediate and revealing document. Before turning to this small and incomplete autobiography, however, we shall want to examine the larger circumstances of his life. Silesia exerted the first great influence on him, and there we must begin.

Silesia

Until the middle of the eighteenth century, Silesia was something of a European backwater. For centuries, it was often portrayed as little more than a still life. The fame and deeds of "its princes, politicians, and intellectuals rarely reached beyond the narrow confines" of their home.[1] In 1740, however, all this abruptly changed, and for the next quarter century at least, Silesia lay at the very heart of European affairs. After the Holy Roman Emperor Karl VI died in October 1740, Frederick the Great swooped down on Silesia in the most daring Machiavellian coup of the century. Invoking the old familial link between the Hohenzollerns and the hereditary princes of Silesia, the defunct Piastens, to justify his action, he invaded Silesia and thus launched the first of two Silesian wars in the early 1740s that rapidly drew in the greater powers of France and England. Treaties in 1742 made Silesia a permanent part of the Prussian state. In 1756, war broke out again over Silesian territory, and this new conflict quickly escalated into the Seven Years' War, a Europe-wide conflagration that pitted new coalitions of powers against each other: the Habsburg monarchy and France on one side, and Prussia and Britain on the other. It was also the first global conflict in history involving Europe's colonial possessions from Asia to the North American continent. During the years when Silesia was becoming Prussian, as battles were joined, finances reorganized, and administrators recommissioned, Joseph von Kesslitz grew up, went to school, quarreled with his father, and fought in the Prussian army.

To be born in Silesia in 1733, as Kesslitz was, was to be born into a world greatly dissimilar to Hamburg. Hamburg was urbane and urban, hustling and bustling, cosmopolitan and bourgeois: an epicenter of mercantile life and the Enlightenment. In Silesia, Joseph and his compatriots drew on an entirely different heritage. Silesia harbored a vigorous aristocratic culture. Castles and manors peppered its landscape, and the nobility farmed their estates and dominated their peasants. Sixty to seventy percent of the land in Silesia remained in the hands of the nobility, far more than in Braunschweig (7.9%), Austria (18.8%), East Prussia (30%), or even in Pomerania (40–50%).[2] To be born in Silesia was also to be born into a world of smoldering religious tensions and into a social system where many family trees branched into Protestant and Catholic limbs, although Joseph's family was one that had not so split. Protestants enjoyed greater strength in the area of Lower Silesia from which the Kesslitzes sprang. Before the Catholic Habsburg Archduke Ferdinand (later Emperor Ferdinand I) became king

Silesia, mid eighteenth century

of Bohemia in 1526, the Reformers had converted almost all of Silesia. The Piasten princes themselves had gone over to Calvinism, and Protestant nobles lived throughout Silesia by the end of the sixteenth century.[3]

During the early stages of the Thirty Years' War, Silesia, along with other Habsburg domains, experienced a vigorous recatholicization. Wallenstein received the duchy of Sagan and the town of Glogau as rewards for his services to the imperial cause, and the force of his presence in these central places of Lower Silesia returned their urban populations to the old belief. Recatholicization engendered a deep resentment among Silesia's population, however, which lingered on throughout the early modern period. It was especially pronounced in Lower Silesia, so much so that some in 1740 "could interpret the Prussian conquest . . . as a confessional liberation."[4]

The Peace of Westphalia (1648) allowed Silesia to maintain its territorial integrity and recognized the Augsburg Confession de jure for the principalities of Brieg, Liegnitz, Münsterberg, Oels, and the city of Breslau. Everywhere else recatholicization proceeded apace, although the agreement permitted Lutherans to set up so-called "peace churches." The resulting tilt toward Catholicism brought with it important consequences for the European nobility. Catholic officers, either from Silesia itself or from elsewhere in the Habsburg/Austrian lands, seized the chance to acquire Silesian estates, making Silesia their new home.[5] One lineage that profited from the opportunity was the von Kesslitz family.

Religious tensions between Catholics and Protestants colored the closing decades of the seventeenth century. The conflict simmered but never boiled over, although a vigorous struggle persisted over the placement and the number of churches allowed Protestants. The new emperor, Joseph I, solved much of the problem in 1707 by signing a religious settlement with Karl XII of Sweden (a guarantor of the Peace of Westphalia). The Altranstädter Convention (1 September 1707) returned numerous churches to the Protestants, admitted three consistories (Catholic, Lutheran, and Calvinist), and in general ended the most grievous religious discrimination against non-Catholics.[6]

Thus, the period between 1707 and 1740, before the beginning of the conflict that history knows as the War of the Austrian Succession, has often been characterized as "halcyon," especially by Catholic historians. Life was hardly perfect, of course, but internal conflicts within Silesia had died down to such an extent that "a condition of political, economic, and social stability had been achieved."[7] The Silesian nobility as a whole benefited from this tranquility. Whereas the confessional period and religious conflict had persisted longer in Silesia than in many other parts of the Germanies (or Europe as a whole), so, too, did older structures—the dominance of the nobility, entrenched estate hierarchies, and traditional administration. Larger "processes typical of the epoch," such as the introduction of educational and agrarian reforms or the progress of the Enlightenment, arrived in Silesia later than in western Europe.[8] Particularly for Silesia's nobility, the period between the Altranstädter Convention and the appearance of Frederick the Great's troops in Silesia in 1740 was an era of calm and well-being.

The economic history of Silesia in the years of Habsburg overlordship was mixed. The nobility profited from many aspects of Habsburg rule. They retained control over their vassals, although many fled to Poland. In Upper Silesia, the hand of the nobility rested more heavily on peasants than in Lower Silesia.[9] From the time that Silesia became part of the

Habsburg domains in 1526, rulers labored to develop its economic capacity. Habsburg initiatives ran the gamut of measures typical of early mercantilism: they built roads, dug canals, reformed taxes structures, tried to bridle the power of the guilds, sought to encourage exports while reducing imports, and endeavored not only to increase the population of Silesia but also to improve living conditions. Success crowned some of these efforts, especially in Lower Silesia, where, by the middle of the sixteenth century, Breslau had become a major center of international commerce. Integral to attempts to improve Silesia economically were innovations that directly profited the nobility. Nobles who read the signs of the times and heeded them enriched themselves by enclosing fields, consolidating properties, introducing three-field crop rotation, and planting cash crops, such as hemp and flax. They also stimulated rural industries, focusing on the production of linen and the brewing of beer. These agricultural capitalists successfully pushed many small producers out of the market. The resulting concentration of money and power nurtured a "notable noble culture" that found its principal physical expression in the many sixteenth- and seventeenth-century castles that dotted the Silesian countryside.

By the closing decades of the seventeenth century, linen production for the market and trade for export accounted for healthy, even robust, economic growth throughout Silesia. The cities of Landeshut, Greiffenberg, Schmiedeberg, and Hirschberg anchored a trade that extended as far as the Netherlands and Hamburg. The nobility in Silesia profited most from this business, for their political and legal position enabled them to control production and marketing. Enterprising estate owners fostered capitalist ventures of virtually every sort on their properties: taverns, breweries, mills (for flour, lumber, oil, and polishing), smithies, tile works, and so on. Estates themselves were generally held as "closed, connected areas" that included one or more villages. This situation facilitated running estates as businesses and made the introduction of manufacturing easier. Although most estates were modest in size when compared to the huge latifundia of East Prussia and rarely exceeded 2,000 acres, they were nonetheless quite thickly populated with peasants and gardeners. The nobility, and not urban merchants, ran a thriving protoindustry in the countryside, encouraging their peasants to weave and often providing them with equipment. Thus, despite problems and the inevitable ups-and-downs (especially the textile crisis of the 1720s), the links to a world economy guaranteed that the material power of the Silesian nobility remained considerable, even if the Silesian economy as a whole still suffered under antiquated tax and customs systems and experienced serious agricultural dislocation.[10]

Uncertain succession in the Habsburg family loomed as the darkest cloud on the early eighteenth-century political horizon for all Europe, but most ominously for Silesia. Karl VI, the Holy Roman emperor, king of Bohemia, and head of the Habsburg lineage, had no male offspring, only three daughters, of whom Maria-Theresa was the eldest. To assure her succession to the Habsburg lands, he formulated the Pragmatic Sanction in 1713 (as a woman she could not become emperor, which was elective in any case). By the early 1720s, the estates and princes of the empire had unanimously agreed to the Sanction and thus to Maria-Theresa's right to rule. The estates and princes of Silesia did so ceremonially in Breslau on 25 October 1720. This document, signed thirteen years before Kesslitz's birth, would have a determinant effect on him, both as a young man and in his later years as a soldier in the armies of Frederick the Great.

Almost certainly the most important event in the life of the young Kesslitz was the invasion of Prussian troops on 16 December 1740. Quick victories at Glogau, Brieg, and Breslau over the next eight months laid the groundwork for a peace that made Lower Silesia Prussian in 1742. Over the next twenty years, fighting in and about Silesia would recur in the form of the Second Silesian War (1744–45) and then the Seven Years' War (1756–63). Joseph was too young to do more than observe the first two conflicts, but he experienced the Prussianization of the province under Frederick's rule thereafter and participated as a junior officer in the last of these wars.

The integration of Lower Silesia into the Prussian fold deeply altered certain aspects of life in Frederick's new province: government, religion, education, and economics. The first and last of these particularly affected the position of the Silesian nobility. Silesia was to become "more Prussian," and that quickly. Frederick the Great intended to reorganize or rather to Prussianize Silesia on the model of the older parts of his monarchy. Still, the process, if thoroughgoing and, at times, roughshod, always went forward in a manner that "preserved certain Silesian peculiarities," and especially that of its mixed confessionality. Thus, some characteristics of pre-1740 Silesia remained virtually untouched, although other things changed. The Prussians overhauled the financial system, restructured military recruiting, and reconfigured the legal system. Protestants gained ground vis-à-vis Catholics, and Jews came to enjoy new civic freedoms.[11]

Overall, however, the rights and privileges of the Silesian nobility remained inviolate. In particular, the process of reforming the agricultural constitution and practices to the advantage of the peasants (the program generally known as *Bauernschutz*) achieved little headway against the continued prerogatives of the nobility. Because Prussia did little to upset its social, economic, and political hegemony, the Silesian nobility rather quickly came round to Prussian rule. The Prussians broadened the nobility's major avenues to power, preserving, for example, its near-monopoly of the position of district administrators (*Landräte*). Until almost 1800, the agrarian constitution of Silesia retained the form that typified most German territories east of the Elbe and Saale and that allowed the nobility to dominate rural life, both in terms of the property they owned or controlled and in the ways they controlled it.[12]

Of the approximately 8,000 Silesian nobles in 1796, 1,300 no longer resided in Silesia, and many of these expatriates served the Habsburgs. About 2,700 held no land in Silesia and made their livings either as civil servants or military officers, although some possessed estates elsewhere. Nonetheless, some 4,000 people of noble blood (931 noblemen and their dependents) retained their Lower Silesian properties in 1785–86. Their lifestyles before the Seven Years' War can be summed up as unpretentious, although apparently toward the end of the century, a certain trend toward greater cultural refinement and sophistication set in. With the integration of Silesia into the Prussian state, a number of noble newcomers also did well in Silesia. Count Johann Baptist von Ballestrem (the family originally came from northern Italy) was one such outsider who marched into Silesia with the troops of Frederick the Great. He married a Silesian noblewoman of the von Stechow family and settled on an estate there. The Ballestrems prospered as manufacturers: they opened mines, constructed sugar refineries, and established the first large-scale modern zinc foundry in the German territories.[13]

Despite efforts of the Prussian government to stimulate the economy in Silesia and the undeniable successes of individual entrepreneurs like the Ballestrems, the general results were, at best, modest. Attempts to increase the population, to spread settlements in underpopulated areas, and to found new cities were unsuccessful. Breslau was a major commercial center, but Lower Silesia remained overwhelmingly rural. In fact the urban population over the course of the eighteenth century actually declined, from 22 percent in 1756 to 19 percent in 1777 to 17 percent in 1807. From midcentury on, the production of linen and other textiles moved increasingly into the countryside. Mercantilistic attempts to stimulate industry tended to hinder commerce and eventually had serious negative effects on what had long been the primary industry in Silesia: textile manufacturing, especially linen. Over the period 1740 to 1806, the manufacture of linen for export suffered from the serious fluctuations of prices and demand in the export market. After the Seven Years' War, trade with the Habsburg Empire was completely destroyed. Hamburg remained an important buyer and transporter of linen cloth for Silesia, however, and, with the demise of the Habsburg connection, the city assumed an even

greater significance in the trade. This shift would have fateful consequences for Joseph von Kesslitz in the 1770s.[14]

The Silesian Nobility

In the middle of the nineteenth century, the poet Joseph von Eichendorff,
who had been born in Upper Silesia in 1788, composed a short, biting
satire on the Silesian nobility at midcentury. "The nobility of Silesia,"
he wrote, fell into three very different categories. "The most numerous,
soundest, and by far and away the most amusing" were the large estate
owners, who existed "in an almost insular isolation . . . that can scarcely be
believed [to have existed] anymore." The "happiest" among them lived in
"total satisfaction" in their "very modest houses, which were, of course,
invariably termed 'castles.' " They built these edifices not in places that
took advantage of "even the most charming views," but rather to keep
sharp watch on their outbuildings, stalls, and household members. To be a
"good husbandman" was the greatest ambition of the men; a "good house-
wife" for the women. They lacked all "sensitivity to the beauty of nature,
for they were themselves natural products." They possessed little more
education than the peasants they dominated.

The second category of nobles saw themselves as completely superior to
the first. (In fact, each group regarded the others with contempt.) These
nobles inhabited real castles and kept as far away as possible from the nasty
smells and the boorish sights of the farmyard. They sought to be "progressive" in culture, but the sole outward manifestation of that endeavor was
their chase after "fashion."

The third group, Eichendorff sarcastically termed "the most brilliant."
These were the "extremists." Among them one found "completely thoughtless wastrels" and "shallow libertines." Instead of a real education, their
children learned to dance, fence, ride, and prattle a little French, instructed
by "ignorant foreigners" or "those lacking all conscience."

Eichendorff's profile was, of course, neither real nor uniquely Silesian. It
paralleled similar portraits drawn by the writers in weeklies such as *Der
Patriot* (Hamburg) and reflected the forms propagators of enlightenment
frequently used. These tropes and models were convenient mental conventions. Certainly, too, the reformers, and the broader public they addressed,
at least half-believed them.[15]

Eichendorff rightly noted the varied nature of the Silesian nobility. One
scholar has observed that "in almost no other German territory was the
nobility so diversified and were the differences in property and legal rights
as great as in Silesia." The gulf separating the higher nobility from the

lower (the group to which Kesslitz and his family belonged) was wide and, under the Habsburgs, basically unbridgeable.[16] Of course, the division between "nobility of the sword" (the old nobility, whose power and privileges derived, at least theoretically, from their military service and their many quarterings of nobility) and the "nobility of the robe" (those ennobled more recently for service to the state, generally as judges, councilors, and bureaucrats) still existed, although the dichotomy proved less simple than the terms imply. Besides these divisions, nobility also split into rural (*Landadel*) and court types (*Hofadel*). Rural nobles tended to live from their estates (and some could and did live well), while court nobles traded on their positions in Vienna and Potsdam and in the monarch's service to grow rich, often extraordinarily so.

Of course, differences pertained not only between kinds of nobles but also within families. Such variances resulted from—and facilitated—the blossoming of noble life and power in Silesia before 1740. The von Liechtensteins offer one dazzling example. Among the widely ramified Liechtenstein family, one found court nobles and high officers of the Bohemian crown; military men of distinguished reputation; literati, academics, and musicians; and, of course, those who were deeply engaged in economic endeavors, in which they developed a finesse and discernment that would rival any Hamburg merchant's. This was equally true of the Reichenbach family. In 1727, at the age of twenty-two, Freiherr Leopold von Reichenbach acquired an estate of five villages, five farms, and a market town. He then embarked on a series of entrepreneurial ventures, adding more estates, engaging in market forestry, and building a paper mill. Such commercial and industrial exertions, combined with the old-fashioned method of aggrandizing estates by buying up other holdings, catapulted the Reichenbachs into the ranks of the European princely elites who lived in splendor and entertained lavishly. Such large clans also had their share of lesser lights, drunkards, ne'er-do-wells, gamblers, and even "cranks and cretins," of course, and often noblemen suffered financial difficulties that stemmed from their own flaws. Some, for instance, scorned estate work as unworthy and preferred a cavalier's life, running up debts and swishing through the world flaunting their titles and trading on their blue blood.[17]

Lesser families, too, could demonstrate economic and political flexibility, like the von Zedlitz family, which traced its ancestors back to the late fourteenth century. Of more interest here are the accomplishments of the family members after the Thirty Years' War. Caspar von Zedlitz's entire estate in the 1670s was valued at a mere 8,000 Silesian Thaler, but he proved to be a man of great enterprise and considerable ingenuity. He resettled deserted villages and bought and ran a quarry. When he died, he left a restored estate to his son, Conrad Gottlieb, who then followed faithfully in his father's economic footprints. In 1742, Conrad's son, another Conrad Gottlieb, became district administrator for the Hirschberg district. He invited a master damask weaver, Johann Friedrich Dietze from Zittau, to settle with his family on the Zedlitz estate of Tiefharmannsdorf, and one of Dietze's sons went on to make an important economic career in the nineteenth century in the firm of S. G. Weber and Company in Schmiedeberg. Another relative of the family, Carl Abraham von Zedlitz, served as Frederick the Great's education minister and was especially influential in reforming the Ritterakademie in Liegnitz, which Kesslitz later attended.[18]

Probably more like the Kesslitz family were the von Nostitzes, who held the estate of Nieder-Zedlitz for more than three hundred years (1404–1745), to which they added Ober-Zedlitz in 1569. Both holdings lay in the district of Steinau, near Breslau and not far from the Kesslitz home of Salisch. Friedrich Leonhard I von Nostitz was born in 1600 and survived the Thirty Years' War. Even before war broke out in 1618, other disasters had struck repeatedly, each succeeding one preventing a full recovery from the previous event. In 1613, plague raged. The drought of 1617 hugely inflated prices and caused widespread hunger, even starvation. In 1622, the Silesian economy suffered from a severe depreciation of currency. Then the war broke out in Bohemia, and the flames soon engulfed most of central Europe. By the time peace was signed in 1648, the Zedlitz estate was "tragically desolated"; it took decades for the family to recover.[19]

In the 1690s, the properties fell to the then four-year-old Caspar Otto von Nostitz, grandson of Friedrich Leonhard. His guardians administered the property in his name. As still quite a young man, he was named district representative for Steinau. In November 1724, he married Maria von Lestqitz from Groß-Ober-Tschirnau, and his finances began to improve. A smart marriage had set him on the road to prosperity, but it was mostly his own energy and skill as a manager that mattered. During the closing years of Habsburg rule in Lower Silesia, he had acquired enough wealth to erect one of the Renaissance-style manors that decorated the Silesian countryside, at least until World War II.[20] Unfortunately, he died suddenly in 1744 while still quite young, leaving a underage male heir—Otto Melchior von Nostitz—and several daughters. These were difficult times during and just after the First and Second Silesian Wars. And fate was not kind to the Nostitzes, as it was equally unkind to the Kesslitzes. The heir's guardians considered it "not prudent or perhaps not possible" to preserve the estate for the boy, which could only be done by depleting his sisters' dowries. They decided, therefore, to put the property on the market, and as no member of the family wished to take on the burden, the estate was knocked down to "the first best stranger" who presented himself, and the heir could do nothing about it. The estate passed into the hands of Wilhelm Bernhard Gottfried von Schmettau. But Schmettau did not hold on to the estate for long either and, like so many other Silesian estates in these years, Zedlitz was soon up for sale again. In 1751, Ludwig Anton, Reichsfreiherr von Wechmar, purchased it. Wechmar had commanded a hussar regiment for the first three years of the Seven Years' War, earned the *Pour le mérite*, and was invalided out of the service; he died in Zedlitz in 1787. His heirs were still on the estate at the end of the nineteenth century.[21] Thus we have here, if not quite a typical Silesian story, one that could be repeated many times in its outlines and even in many of its details; an encumbered estate, no heir available to take it on; and thus property that changed hands several times.

If the Silesian nobility under Habsburg rule called the tune in Silesia politically and administratively and had cemented a strong economic position for themselves as well, did the coming of the Prussians change everything? Or even anything? From the time of the annexation of Lower Silesia at least until the outbreak of the Seven Year's War, Frederick the Great and his ministers preferred to rule through the existing power arrangements, in particular "[to arrange] everything if possible with the property-owning nobility."[22] The Silesian nobility probably felt quite at home after Prussia incorporated Silesia. Not all of them, of course, made their peace (literally) with their new masters: a considerable number remained in Habsburg service, some left Silesia and, although holding estates there, chose to reside elsewhere. The high nobility forfeited much of its status simply because it had linked its own fate so tightly to that of the Habsburgs. Once Silesia became Prussian, many of these nobles either had to sell their estates or settle for a loss of political clout. Either way, the once-large difference between higher and lower nobility in Silesia began to disappear, and the Prussian state did little or nothing to brake the process. As early as 1741, Frederick began selecting district administrators in Silesia from the "well-situated noble knights." Frederick clearly viewed the rural nobility as the best source of officers for his army (and not only in Silesia, of course). He did much at the very beginning of his reign in Silesia to woo the nobility, in particular prohibiting the bourgeoisie from buying or otherwise acquiring noble estates. Likewise, he resisted ennobling men from the middle classes, commenting tersely on one such suggestion: "One becomes a noble by using his sword, not otherwise." Nonetheless, he sometimes—albeit very infrequently—ennobled middle-class officers who had proved their worth on the field of battle.[23]

Frederick the Great supported the nobility because of its key role in his army, which demanded its preservation as a socioeconomic class. The Prussian officer corps became increasingly noble under Frederick, to a degree far greater than in most German lands. Nobles virtually monopolized the officer corps, contributing over 90 percent of its members. Only two branches of the military—the artillery and the hussars—had *any* non-noble officers. Frederick considered only nobles suitable officer material. He admitted that one might occasionally encounter talent without birth, "but it is rare." The most important resource nobles possessed was their swords. Concepts of honor, too, forged a nobleman into a soldier, for "once having lost his honor, he would find no refuge in his father's home." Honor was unique to a nobleman. A commoner who had "done something base" would not "blush" to take up his father's occupation, and no one (including the man himself) would consider him "dishonored."[24] How different it was for noblemen, and how useful such concepts of honor were in staffing an army. Frederick drew all the officers from the hereditary nobility and from the rural nobles who resided on their estates, from families like the Kesslitzes, the Kreckwitzes (Joseph's maternal uncle was a Kreckwitz), and the Nostritzes.[25]

Allowing nobles a monopoly of the officer corps was one way to preserve the aristocracy. Preventing the alienation of their lands to bourgeois purchasers and land speculators was another. *Rittergüter*—manorial estates—were thus kept intact for future generations of the noble families that owned them. Here, two problems had to be solved. The first was to halt the splintering of estates; that is, the partition of immovable property among all children. To curtail such practices, Frederick recommended to his nobility that they pass their undivided estates as a whole to their eldest sons. Far more determinant were financial measures Frederick introduced after the Seven Years' War, when speculation in estates, particularly in Silesia, grew enormously and when indebtedness (again especially pronounced in Silesia) threatened to drive the rural nobility as a whole into bankruptcy and to cause the loss of the very estates that endowed them with income and social position. The bargain struck earlier in the century was cemented more firmly during the course of Frederick's long reign: the more the nobility relied on the state for its financial stability, the more the nobility had to accede to the state in other ways, and the more of its sons would become officers.[26]

In addition, in Prussian Silesia, the lower nobility, and especially those who had served in the army, enjoyed considerable advantages in the selection of district administrators. Frederick specified that such appointments should go only to "competent, right-thinking, and well-loved" inhabitants. Theoretically, one did not have to be a nobleman. Yet almost all were. In

Silesia, unlike some other parts of the Prussian state, no examination was required for assuming office, although a certain, if not very great, level of wealth was thought necessary to forestall corruption. After the Seven Years' War, Frederick used the position of district administrator to reward his invalided officers (at least those who had attained higher rank). In the 1770s, only ex-officers had a chance to become administrators of a district. Still, it was usually a dead-end job. The pay was relatively low (no more than 300 Reichsthaler annually), and there were few opportunities for advancement to higher positions. Most of these men continued to live on their estates and, because of the meager pay, continued to farm or combined one administrative position with others. Significantly, Kesslitz was not placed in one of these positions, for he never achieved the necessary higher rank. Thus, one of the avenues of advancement, or at least security, open to other ex-officers seemed closed to him. Moreover, by 1765, he had lost his estate, and his financial situation was anything but secure.[27]

During years of peace between the Second and Third (Seven Years') Silesian Wars, many Silesian nobles seized opportunities to expand their holdings, often snapping up properties deserted by those who remained true to the Habsburg cause. Several other factors contributed to rather good prices for the properties and often quite considerable incomes for their owners.[28] That favorable situation, however, flipped over during the Seven Years' War, and the financial woes that began during the war persisted, or even worsened, in its immediate aftermath.

The chronic indebtedness of Silesian noble properties in the years immediately after the Seven Years' War undercut the financial and social position of the Silesian nobility. While some suffered less and some not at all, of course, the general impression is one of decay in stark contrast to the relative well-being of the Silesian nobility in the first half of the century. Older, partisan (pro-Habsburg) historiography painted a picture of almost total ruination in Silesia that affected all classes, the nobility included, immediately after the peace in 1763. One scholar drew particularly grim conclusions: "Forced deliveries [of goods] and plundering drove almost all noble estate owners to the very edge of the precipice."[29] Yet the economic crisis of the Silesian nobility, while real enough, was a story of differences, as, for that matter, was the overall story of the economic situation of the nobility in the last decades of the ancien régime: some adapted, prospered, and grew rich; others failed; and not a few sank into self-inflicted destitution.

Apparently, the Silesian nobility (or rather significant parts of it) actually benefited from inflation during the war. Johann Heinrich von Carmer, the chief Prussian official in the Breslau region, reported to the king in September 1767 that "the reduction in liquid funds caused by the war has hardly affected the rural nobility at all, or at least far less than the other groups and occupations in the area." Many nobles wiped the slate clean using inflated currency and enlarged their holdings. Property values rose, and ownership rapidly turned over.[30] Thus, many nobles bounced back quickly from the war and, more important, from the changed economic circumstances of the postwar era, when demand for agricultural products (in particular those that fed the army or provided timber or fuel) declined precipitously. Many, as Carmer put it, "who had experienced no pronounced tragedy during the war and [had been able] to preserve their credit, found enough money to carry them through." They were in fact by far the majority of the rural nobility. Four years after the end of the war, most noble fortunes were nearly restored, and their possessors required no further assistance from either the monarch or the state. But there were others to whom fate had been less kind, and whose survival depended on "a charitable gift" from their ruler. Those families whom the misadventures of war had struck especially hard and whose credit had been weakened by real disaster were unable to profit from the return of peace. Many could no longer pay the interest on their debts. Chance and circumstances had left many insolvent. Others were less innocent. Their debts derived from "embarking on foolish or too grandiose projects" or from simple indolence and neglect.

To remedy these problems, Carmer recommended a "gift," but only to "those who had suffered true tragedies during the conflict," and who, after the peace, were no longer in a position to reestablish their credit or return their estates to a firm financial footing because money was tight. Even those men who were not yet "insolvendo" could qualify. As a result, the royal treasury distributed monetary assistance to some eighty-three Lower Silesian noble families in 1768. Carmer noted that "most of the Silesian nobility applied." Not all could be helped. It was decided to assist only those who actually possessed estates in Lower Silesia and lived on them, whose estates were mortgaged (or whose owners were indebted) for at least half their values, and who had either served in the army themselves or whose sons had. This covered the vast majority of recipients. All help came too late for Joseph and his brother, who had already lost their estate, Salisch, in 1765, but their uncle received 4,000 Reichsthaler. One of Joseph's cousins, Hanns Carl, had served as cornet in the war, and the Kreckwitzes (Joseph's mother's family) thus qualified. The Salisch estate at the time was valued at about 30,000 Reichsthaler and was indebted to the tune of 16,000 Reichsthaler.[31]

Infusions of cash could only partly bridge the yawning financial gap in Silesia. It not until the establishment in 1770 of a Silesian credit organization (*Schlesische Landschaft*) for noble property that mortgage insurance —calculated to deliver approximately 3,200 Silesian estates from financial disaster—came into existence.[32] This initiative reduced the total indebtedness of noble estates in Silesia from twenty-two million to eight million Reichsthaler by 1825; even in the first years of its existence, it probably saved around 400 noble families in Silesia from ruin. At the same time, however, it also promoted speculation in noble property in Silesia and led to a rapid turnover in ownership. No reader of either the *Berlinische Nachrichten von Staats- und Gelehrten Sachen* (Berlin Political and Learned News) or the *Schlesische Provincial-Berichte* (Silesian Provincial Report) could miss the accelerated trade in estates. In two Silesian districts, almost all estates changed hands at least once between 1764 and 1770.[33] This also held true for the various Kesslitz holdings. Speculation enriched many others, and the period after 1770 opened a new era of good times for the Silesian nobility. They, too, now jobbed in land. Because property taxes remained more or less fixed, their indebtedness as a group declined, and their prosperity increased, often multiple times. Thus one can say that when Frederick died in 1786, he left the nobility of all his territories in a better economic, social, and political position than when he ascended the throne, The Silesian nobility had probably benefited the most.[34] That the Kesslitzes did not was bad luck, bad timing, or perhaps something else entirely: mismanagement.

An Illustrious Family

The Kesslitz family, an "Illustres Geschlecht" bearing the title of barons (*Freiherren*), is found in Silesia (now part of Poland), as early as the fourteenth century. A "Hans von Kesslitz auf Lettnitz und Schweinitz" flourished in the Glogau area around the end of the Thirty Years' War. His son Johann von Kesslitz was our Joseph's great-grandfather. Johann (I) had two sons, Johann (II) (1629–1709), who settled on the estates of Lettnitz and Schweinitz, and then Joseph's grandfather, Maximilian I (d. 1716), who held the estates of Salisch, Merzdorf, and the Bergvorwerke. In 1685, Maximilian I purchased the estate of Golgowitz from Johann Bernhard, Reichsgraf von Herberstein. Joseph's grandfather put the family on the map of social and political elites in the areas around Glogau and Grünberg in the early eighteenth century. As deputy head of the provincial government in Glogau, Maximilian became an important political figure in the albeit small world of Lower Silesian administrative life.

Joseph von Kesslitz's parents, Maria Francisca von Kesslitz (née von Kreckwitz) and Maximilian II von Kesslitz (1696–1763), Herr auf Salisch, Merzdorf, und die Bergvorwerke. Courtesy Andreas Kutschelis, private collection, Northeim.

Almost certainly as a result of Maximilian's service to the Habsburg regime, the family was raised into the "Böhmischer Freiherrnstand" on 13 June 1704.[35]

Maximilian I and his wife produced three sons (all of whom reached adulthood, married, and procreated) and two daughters. Joseph's older uncle, Johann Karl, became provincial head in the more important principality of Sagan. The second uncle, Christoph Friedrich (1685–1760), was "Herr auf Golgowitz," and his son, Franz, born in 1730 (d. 1766), served as a captain in the Habsburg forces during the Seven Years' War. Thus, Joseph and his slightly older cousin, Franz, fought on opposing sides in that conflict. The second son of Joseph's grandfather, Christoph Friedrich (1685–1760), inherited Golgowitz, while the youngest, Maximilian II (1696–1763) (Joseph's father) took over the estates of Salisch (where Joseph was born), Merzdorf, and the Bergvorwerke. He married Maria Franziska von Kreckwitz, and they had four children: Joseph in 1733, his sister Augustine in 1737, then Maria Antonia, and the youngest, Maximilian III, in 1741 (d. 1815). No lesser a personage than Frederick the Great nominated Augustine (Sister Maria Benedicta) to a place in the Poor Clares' cloister in Glogau in 1754; she became abbess in 1780 and died in that office a year later.[36]

Thus, since the Thirty Years' War the Kesslitz family had acquired many of the common characteristics of Silesian noble families. The family made its fortune during the consolidation of Habsburg rule when several members served in the military and the provincial administration. There existed far greater political animals in Silesia than the Kesslitzes, of course. Still, when multiplied by the dozens, lineages like the Kesslitzes administered Silesia for both the Habsburgs and the Hohenzollerns, and some even filled relatively important posts. Almost all exercised magisterial and judicial powers in the villages that belonged to them.[37]

In other ways, too, the Kesslitzes offer a model of Silesian nobility. The family was Catholic, and Joseph's father married into another Silesian noble family—of somewhat greater prominence than his own—who were deeply Catholic, the von Kreckwitzes. Joseph's own Catholicism seems to have been lukewarm, although his mother was more than devout, at least according to him. She was so dedicated to the Church that she squandered more of her family's wealth on it than the financially strapped Kesslitzes could afford in the 1750s and 1760s. Joseph's parents certainly brought him up Catholic: a "K" for "Katholisch" indicated his confessional allegiance in the matriculation register of the Ritterakademie in Liegnitz.[38]

As we have seen, Silesia in the eighteenth century moved from a Cath-

Rittergut Salisch. Courtesy Andreas Kutschelis, private collection, Northeim.

olic ruler to a Protestant one, from Habsburg to Hollenzollern rule. Moreover, since the Reformation, the Protestant presence in Silesia had been a considerable if often also a contested one. Frederick the Great's incorporation of Lower Silesia (by 1742) considerably strengthened the Protestant position, although he continued the policy of the eighteenth-century Habsburgs in being—comparatively speaking—even-handed in his treatment of Catholics and Protestants. In fact, he quickly and thoroughly won over the Silesian nobility. Thus, hot-blooded youths like Joseph von Kesslitz (even those of Catholic background) might well have preferred serving with the dashing young king than with the imperial troops. In January 1757, for example, shortly after the outbreak of the Seven Years' War, seven orphaned sons of Silesian noble families who were entrusted to an *Orphanotrophium* for their education and who were all ultimately intended for clerical careers, pleaded with the canon who ran the institute to be allowed to transfer to the Berlin cadet school in order to be able to become officers in Frederick's army.[39] Yet others, such as Joseph's cousin, Franz, remained true to the Habsburgs. This split of loyalties typified many Silesian noble families, and one could not predict with absolute reliability the political decisions each family or each individual family member would make based solely on religion. Joseph's sister, after all, ended up as abbess in a Catholic foundation, and there were several nuns as well as a captain in the imperial army among his cousins. Moreover, an individual could move from one service to another, and from one religious regime to another. Carl Emanuel von Warnery auf Langendorf served in the Austrian army during the First Silesian war but then transferred into Prussian service in 1742. He subsequently commanded a Prussian hussar regiment and won the *Pour le mérite* for bravery against Austrian forces. In 1758, however, in the middle of the Seven Years' War, he changed his uniform once again, becoming a major general of Polish cavalry and finally ending up as adjutant to the (Saxon) king of Poland. Atypically for Silesian noble families of that era, however, the Kesslitzes, with the sole exception of Joseph, preserved their links to the Hapsburgs and to Catholicism. Later, the family split into distinct Prussian and Austrian lines.[40]

The financial difficulties that plagued many noble families during the late eighteenth century troubled the Kesslitzes too. Over time, the various estates of the family were split among the sons. One need look no further than Joseph's father's generation. The eldest brother held Schweinitz; the second brother, Golgowitz; and Joseph's father, Salisch, Merzdorf, and the Bergvorwerke. While it is very difficult to judge the worth of these estates, none of them seem to have been especially valuable. Wars and the political and economic dislocation that they caused exacerbated financial difficulties for many families, including the Kesslitzes. The tax records for 1765 offer some indication of property values.[41] Schweinitz, owned by Joseph's uncle, Johann Karl, was a modest property, assessed at 20,570 Reichsthaler, and the number of tenants was eighty-six. Joseph's aunt, the widowed Baroness (*Freiin*) von Kesslitz (the wife of Kesslitz's other uncle, Christoph Friedrich, who had died in 1760) held Golgowitz. This was a far less valuable property, whose assessed worth was a mere 7,231 Reichsthaler; there were only ten tenants.[42]

What Kesslitz's father owned until his death were the estates of Salisch, Merzdorf, and the Bergvorwerke, all in the district of Glogau. Salisch's worth was somewhat less than that of Schweinitz; it was valued at 14,266 Reichsthaler (and had thirty-nine tenants). Merzdorf was even smaller than the widow's estate, being assessed at only 4,398 Reichsthaler (although some forty-five tenants lived there). The total value of what Kesslitz's father controlled was 18,664 Reichsthaler. Such figures are tremendously deceptive, however, because they fail to account for other critical factors, such as indebtedness and the market. When the estate sold in 1765, Joseph's portion amounted to 7,000 Reichsthaler.[43] From this sum alone we cannot estimate its worth. One assumes that the four children shared equally—in which case the sale price must have been something like 28,000 Reichsthaler. Yet one can plausibly suppose that the proceeds from the sale covered the outstanding debts, so the property might have sold for considerably more, or perhaps Joseph's uncle assumed the debts. These are mere conjectures, although there is no reason to doubt Joseph's statement in 1776 that he and his brother (Maximilian III) had sold the estate because they could no longer carry the debt. The reasons for that indebtedness remain unknown, and it is hard to say, therefore, if the Kesslitzes counted among the landlords Carmer designated "unlucky" or those he dismissed as "improvident." In any case, neither brother had the wherewithal (or perhaps the inclination?) to rescue the estate, although evidence suggests that Joseph's father was neither a lazy nor an unenterprising landlord. (And Joseph himself refers to his father's preference for a quiet life in the country where he could devote himself to his economic pursuits.) In 1762, while Joseph was still in the army, his father approached the district government of Glogau for permission to break his contract with a tenant on his estate of Merzdorf. The man, one Christoph Nitsche, was apparently unproductive and, as a result, virtually bankrupt. He owed the district fees of 400 marks. He owned no plow oxen (although according to the terms of his contract, he should have had four), and he planted very little grain. Moreover, "he sends his only child out to beg and lives from this." Neither Kesslitz nor anyone else could imagine how Nitsche could pull himself out of debt. Kesslitz therefore advanced the following solution; if the district allowed him to evict Nitsche, he would try to induce someone from just over the nearby Polish border to take up the vacant position. He preferred a "somewhat well-off fellow, with a wife and children."[44]

The Kesslitz family, then, probably differed little from dozens of other hard-pressed estate owners in the late 1760s. Little distinguished them financially, socially, and culturally from the Nostitzes, Kreckwitzes, von Pohlenzes, von Persdorfs, von Prittwitz und Gaffrons, and all the others. After the Seven Years' War, not only Joseph von Kesslitz found his survival as a nobleman threatened, and not only he and his brother were obliged to alienate their estates. His capital reserves had worn thin, and his chances of finding employment in a peacetime army were rapidly vanishing. The outlook for him, as for many others, was bleak.

Joseph von Kesslitz

Joseph von Kesslitz (1733–1813) was born while Silesia still belonged to the Habsburgs, held as a fief of the Bohemian crown. That background certainly shaped his early life, as it did that of his parents. The alterations that convulsed Silesia after 1742, when the territory became part of Prussia, profoundly influenced his life.[45]

Joseph's childhood remains a closed book. The eight-page autobiography he composed in 1775 began nineteen years before. It tells us virtually nothing about his early education. Presumably, this took place on his father's estate, in the "castle" his grandfather had built in 1690 and his father had restored in 1754 after a disastrous fire the previous year. Young Joseph first enters the historical record, therefore, on 31 January 1750. The archives of the Liegnitzer Ritterakademie preserve the following, signed by Frederick II: "After being informed, that at our Ritterakademie in Liegnitz, the *Fundatist* position previously held by [Herr] von Galen has fallen vacant, so . . . we command you [the Academy's director] to make the necessary arrangements to inscribe . . . Freiherr [Joseph] von Kesslitz among the *Fundatisten* of the Royal Academy and to allow him to enjoy all the advantages and funds associated with that position."[46] That Kesslitz was admitted as a kind of scholarship boy indicates that his family was already experiencing financial difficulties and certainly did not count as one of the wealthier Silesian noble clans. His younger brother, Maximilian, followed him to Liegnitz—also as a *Fundatist*—in 1760.

The Silesian nobility, like their brethren throughout western and central Europe, built their positions and their power on a combination of qualities. Military service and bloodlines still bedrocked their standing and their consciousness, but they increasingly recognized the value of education for the maintenance of their position, especially vis-à-vis increasingly prosperous and assertive merchants and professionals. Education at universities and at special schools for the nobility alone had become a hallmark of the social group since the sixteenth century. Inspired originally by Renaissance ideals of the courtier, the academy movement quickly became a Europe-wide phenomenon. In the seventeenth century, these academies combined "a society, a university, and an elevated [form of] riding school," all rolled into one. To some extent, their establishment represented an attempt on the part of nobility and monarchs alike to perpetuate aristocratic distinction in a world where the older warrior values had forfeited much of their worth. On the other hand, education received there, while remaining partly noble and even feudal in character (the emphasis placed on horsemanship, for instance), was also academic and therefore an admission that a nobleman had to be able to do more than fence adequately and stay upright on his mount.[47]

How successful the academies were in elevating the educational standards of nobles and officers remains debatable. Special schooling first

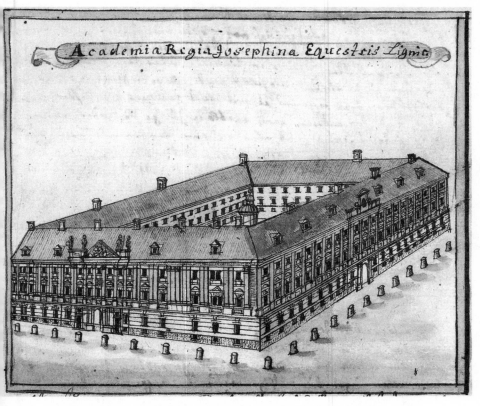

*The Ritterakademie, Liegnitz. Courtesy Archiwum
Panstwowe we Wrocławiu, Wrocław.*

came into existence for artillery officers, but few noblemen (and usually only the most penurious) chose the artillery. The most important function of the academies was apparently to preserve the threatened social position of the European nobility, rather than to educate young men to be officers. And by no means all graduates pursued a military career. During the Austrian period, of some 416 students at Liegnitz, only 20 chose the army as their vocation. Not surprisingly, that changed once Silesia became part of Prussia: more than half of the students entered military service, and during the Seven Years' War many left to join Frederick's army. Some academy graduates (including Joseph von Kesslitz) attended universities afterwards.[48]

Thus the academies offered an education that roughly paralleled a university one and in particular benefited the sons of noble families of restricted means. How much education the young men received varied considerably from school to school. How much education a young noble was *supposed* to receive (or it was thought desirable for him to receive) also raised debate. The ignorance of young army officers, especially Prussians, was proverbial in the late eighteenth and early nineteenth century. Many high military leaders felt that experience was by far the best teacher and regarded these cadets as toy soldiers. In this regard, Frederick the Great is as inscrutable as in other respects. Clearly, he preferred nobles as officers but was not blind to the need to educate them better. He reacted hostilely to the well-known "contempt for education" his generals expressed and dismissed their blind reliance on learning-by-doing with a stinging bon mot: "If experience alone was sufficient to make great generals, then Prince Eugene's mules would have been stupendous ones."[49]

In Silesia, the academy of choice for the nobility was the Ritterakademie in Liegnitz, which Joseph von Kesslitz entered at age seventeen. He remained for the normal course of three years.[50] The Ritterakademie, or to use its full name, the Josephenine Ritterakademie zu Liegnitz, had opened in November 1708. In the wake of the religious settlement of the Altranstädter Convention in September of that year, Joseph I set up the academy on the principle of parity. The Ritterakademie admitted Protestants and Catholics in about equal numbers and was to be administered equally by Protestant and Catholics. The institution had no pastor and neither theology nor religion found a place in the curriculum. Rather, the founding statutes constrained each student to "act in a quiet, honorable, and God-fearing manner . . . and attend church regularly," specifying the nearby St. Johannes Church for Catholics and St. Peter and Paul for Protestants. Each confession prayed separately within the academy. At the time of its establishment, and throughout the Habsburg period, the Liegnitz Ritterakademie got by with only a small teaching staff. Typically for such academies, the curriculum included instruction in law, mechanics, civil and military architecture, history, philosophy, religion, Italian and French, natural history, and geography. In addition, the students acquired the attributes of nobility: dancing, riding (at least two hours a day), and fencing. From the opening of the academy until late summer 1741, 415 young nobles attended; about 20–30 were admitted each year.[51]

Students were divided into two groups: the *Pensionisten* and the *Fundatisten*. The latter were "twelve poor and needy nobles . . . of whom five are to be Catholic and seven Lutheran." Preference was given first to natives of the district of Liegnitz, then Brieg and Wohlau, and finally Silesia as a whole. *Fundatisten* paid an entrance fee of 30 Reichsthaler. They then received from the funds free instruction, housing, and meals for three years. No *numerus clausus* applied to the *Pensionisten*, who paid 40 Reichsthaler upon entry and 200 Reichsthaler annually. After Prussia incorporated Silesia, the number of paying students decreased sharply, and between 1741 and 1774, only 95 matriculated, as opposed to 145 royal and 23 *Kospothsche Fundatisten* (a private endowment supported the latter). Moreover, as demand for entry to the academy continued to decline, it was necessary to offer Catholic *Fundatisten* positions to Protestants and to admit foreigners, that is, those born neither in Liegnitz nor, for that matter, in Silesia. Sons of Prussian officers and bureaucrats from elsewhere thus often gained admittance.[52]

According to the founding statutes, the director of the academy was to be a Silesian nobleman, and the post was to alternate between a Protestant and a Catholic. However, after the first director—a Protestant when appointed—converted to Catholicism, all the subsequent directors until the annexation of Silesia by the Prussians were Catholic. Thereafter, the academy developed a more Protestant character and was always headed by a Protestant. When the Catholic nobleman Joseph von Kesslitz entered in 1750, he joined three other *Fundatisten*: one was Catholic, two Protestant.[53] Exactly what led to Kesslitz's selection is not known, but clearly his father must have applied for admission by explaining the family's rather precarious economic situation. Already by 1750, the Salisch branch of the Kesslitz family was financially embarrassed and the estate encumbered.[54]

In the life history Kesslitz composed while under arrest in Hamburg, he relates how he returned to Salisch in 1756 after completing his studies at "Universitaeten und academien." The university in question was Frankfurt an der Oder, which Kesslitz, an *eques Silesius*, entered in January 1754. According to his own account, he remained for two years (and probably did not take a degree). We have no idea what he studied or with whom. Overall, however, nobles vastly preferred the legal faculty. Generally speaking, the higher nobility—those who anticipated careers in the upper reaches of the bureaucracy—attended universities. But it was also the newer nobility, those "somewhat insecure in their birth status," who were "more likely than others to back it [their position] up with the status of education."[55]

In 1756, after leaving Frankfurt an der Oder, Joseph returned to his father's home in Salisch. Apparently, life on the relatively small and not especially prosperous estate held little appeal for the then twenty-three-year-old nobleman. "The reclusiveness and quiet of rural life," instead of dampening his ardor for military life, stimulated it. The dullness and isolation of Salisch were not the only problems. His father's plans to arrange an "advantageous match" for his son distressed Joseph even more (in fact, he never married). The outbreak of the Seven Years' War soon after his return to Salisch inflamed his desire for action: "My only wish, even then, was to offer to my king, my most gracious master, my loyal service." His father stood squarely, obstinately, in the way, preferring "a peaceful life in the country and his economic pursuits" and thus thwarted the ambitions of a "fiery youth." For three years (until 1759), Joseph had to accommodate himself to his father's wishes, and not until his father actually sought to marry him off did he rebel. He wrote to Major General Moritz Franz Kasimir von Wobersnow and asked for help, eventually receiving the answer that he could join the Garde du Corps. (Perhaps his decision to join the *Prussian* army represented another sort of rebellion against his family, as he was the sole member to do so in these years.) This offer came too late, however: Joseph had already engaged himself in the cuirassier regiment under the command of the brother of Frederick's famous minister in Silesia, Ernst Wilhelm von Schlabrendorff. He enrolled as a "standard noble" (*Etandert Juncker*) in Major von Lehwald[t]'s company, and, "because I was unwilling to take any pay [as a soldier]," was regarded as a volunteer. In this capacity, he saw action in several campaigns. At the same time, he applied himself "diligently" to learning the military arts, "not only in a mechanical manner, which comes from constant routine," but also "according to theoretical principles." Here Kesslitz projects the image of an ardent young nobleman, full of fire and dedication, committed to becoming a good officer and serving his king.

Even if we accept that Kesslitz (at least in this account written in late 1775) deliberately emphasized both his dedication to Prussia and his soldierly bent in order to assist his case in Hamburg, the overall picture rings true. Obviously, it is shaped by conventions and filled with platitudes, even banalities, but just as obviously, such emotions inspired many men like Kesslitz. The enthusiasm they felt for Frederick was also quite real. Growing up in Silesia after the Prussian successes of the first two Silesian Wars—five glorious victories without a single defeat—must have left many young noblemen starry-eyed with admiration for the Prussian Alexander. Writing after the war, even the sober British diplomat Nathaniel Wraxall acclaimed Frederick's accomplishments: "Never was a Prince more calculated to elevate the family of Brandenburgh, at the expence of that of Austria. Silesia, the first conquest of his arms, has been retained against the utmost exertions of Maria Theresa, by eleven campaigns, by torrents of human blood, and by the greatest efforts of military skill."[56] How much more compelling must Frederick's image and achievements have been for young men of noble birth, especially someone like Kesslitz, whose homeland was the casus belli and who felt isolated from the action, as well as stifled by the humdrum bucolic existence his father preferred.

The twenty-five-year-old Kesslitz joined a regiment under the command of Friedrich Wilhelm von Roeder as a cornet on 26 July 1759 (there-

fore pretty much in the middle of a war that had been going on since 1756).
He served with the 5th Squadron stationed in Breslau. During the course
of the war, he was promoted to lieutenant on 10 December 1761. He requested his discharge on 29 June 1763, some four months after the signing
of the treaty ending the war.[57] His was a cuirassier regiment, part of the
army under General Gustav Albrecht von Schlabrendorff. Cuirassiers were
heavy cavalrymen who wore a massive breastplate (the cuirass, weighing
more than twenty-five pounds), as well as an iron helmet to prevent head
wounds. The regiment had covered itself with glory early in the century.
Then, during Frederick's wars, the regiment distinguished itself again in
some of his most important actions: Collin, Hohenfriedberg, Prague,
Breslau, Lissa, Chotusitz, Kai, and Kunersdorff. Kesslitz's first real battle
was a famous one: at Kai (22/23 July 1759). His second major action, the
legendary Kunersdorf (12 August 1759), almost finished Frederick.[58]

The Seven Years' War from the point of view of those who fought it—
and perhaps from everyone's perspective—was a confused and confusing
affair: "one hardly knew which enemy one should fight first, for there were
Austrians, Russians, Frenchmen, Swedes, Saxons, Württembergers, Ba-
varians, and [also] a large imperial army," all arrayed against Prussia.[59] The
year 1758 had been, relatively speaking, a good one for Frederick and his
forces, after two notably bad ones. In the course of that year, Frederick, in
brilliant, lightning strikes, had won back much of the territory he had
earlier lost to the Russians, the Swedes, and the Habsburgs. However, 1759
was less successful altogether. If the thrilling victories of 1758 had inspired
martial enthusiasm in Kesslitz, his first year of campaigning must have
been far more sobering for him—as for the Prussians in general.

During his first engagement, at Kai, Kesslitz distinguished himself: "As
the fighting began, I hoisted the standard to my shoulder . . . and drew my
sword. My major fell beside me and I found myself alone with the flag,
right in the middle of the enemy infantry. My horse, although badly
wounded, managed to carry me about 300 feet from the action, where I
used [the flat of] my sword to drive the scattered riders together in order
to shield the royal standard." This action drew the attention of his commanding general and led to his promotion to cornet. His superiors cer-
tified all of this, as well as his later exemplary conduct on several occasions.[60] Thus there is no doubt that Kesslitz was a good, diligent, and brave
officer in the field.

Yet, perhaps diplomatically, Kesslitz does not mention that Kai was a
foul-up, probably due to the mistakes of Major General Karl Heinrich von
Wedel, the very man who had raised him to the rank of cornet. The
butcher's bill was high: Wedel lost over 8,000 men dead or wounded. Von

Wobersnow, one of Kesslitz's early military patrons, was killed, and thirteen cannon, four flags, and several standards fell into the hands of the Russians. Kesslitz protected his company's colors and was apparently one of those few who managed to prevent the defeat from turning into rout.[61]

If the cudgeling at Kai was serious, the defeat at Kunersdorf a little more than three weeks later (12 August), was catastrophic. Frederick was beaten, and badly. The total of dead, wounded, and captured mounted to almost about 26,000 men; a shattering defeat for the Prussians, a splendid victory for the Russians, and Frederick's darkest hour. The king despaired of recovering from such a resounding defeat. "Our losses are very great," Frederick wrote to his brother in a mood of despair. "Out of an army of 48,000 men, I have at this moment no more than 3,000." Defeat turned to havoc, and Frederick no longer controlled his forces. "It is a terrible event; I won't survive it. . . . I have no idea what to do and, to be totally honest, I think all is lost. I shall not survive the fall of my Fatherland. Farewell!"[62]

The defeat almost destroyed the indomitable Frederick, while his army felt not merely the shame of the loss but the full horrors of war. Whether Kesslitz, too, experienced despair and desolation, we do not know, but a young fellow Silesian, also a nobleman and from a family of similarly modest resources, Christian Wilhelm von Prittwitz und Gaffron, did, and his memoirs reflect these trying times.[63] The battle raged fiercely as the Prussians and their allies moved against the well-entrenched Russians. Despite early advances, Russian reinforcements arrived, and the tide rolled against the Prussians. Prittwitz himself received a foot wound that ended his active military career and made him an invalid. What first looked like a victory for the Prussians all too quickly turned into a defeat. While Prittwitz was lying wounded with others, the "horrible news" filtered back to them that the battle was lost and the army dispersed. Strategic retreat turned into headlong flight. Prittwitz testified to the tragic conditions. "One ran here, the other there, and many threw away their weapons in order to lighten their load." The king, whose horse had been shot out from under him, sent messengers to plead with the fleeing troops to stand their ground and return to their ranks, but nothing helped.[64] Then on 4 September, Dresden fell to the Habsburg forces, although Prince Heinrich—under whom Kesslitz was now serving—managed to hold onto the rest of Saxony. Frederick then joined Heinrich in Saxony, where both armies spent the cold winter in the field. It must have been grim.[65]

Early in 1760, Prussia and England sent out peace feelers, but their opponents (France, Austria, and Russia) felt the situation had shifted so dramatically in their favor that they believed they could defeat Frederick if they only fought on. And so the war continued. Frederick no longer could rely on his seasoned troops, many of whom were now dead or captured. Still, at least from the view of a Prussian partisan, "although his soldiers were now rather young . . . they had courage and good leaders." Summer 1760 was a miserable time for Silesia. The bombardment of Breslau reduced its suburbs to rubble and ashes. Habsburg troops plundered Landeshut and overran Glatz. Frederick's position in 1761, despite his almost uncanny ability to escape disaster, worsened with each passing day. No one believed he would survive another year of campaigning. Yet if Frederick was a brilliant general, he was also a lucky one. On 5 January 1762, his old enemy, Elisabeth, the tsarina of Russia, died. Her nephew, Peter III, a fervent admirer of Frederick and all things Prussian, succeeded her. He not only ended hostilities with Frederick but also provided him a modest contingent of troops and returned all Prussian prisoners in Russian captivity. When a palace coup engineered by his wife, Catherine (later "the Great"), and her favorites deposed Peter, little changed. Admittedly, she no longer helped Frederick with troops, but neither did she reenter the fray on the Habsburg side. That summer, Frederick returned to Saxony, where he and his brother achieved notable military successes. Here, Joseph von Kesslitz once again distinguished himself. After England and France concluded a peace in November 1762, it was simply a matter of time until the Treaty of Hubertusburg on 15 February 1763 ended fighting in central Europe. Frederick kept Silesia.[66]

All that was in the future, of course, and during the years after Kunersdorf, Kesslitz was busy. He fought at the battle of Tropau, where "I found myself on the other side of the [enemy's] trench among the Austrian troops and [then] was able to rescue myself and my small band." In 1761, he rose to lieutenant. In the final full year of the war (1762), he fought under the command of Frederick's militarily talented brother, Prince Heinrich. At the battle of Freiburg (29 October 1762), his conduct drew notice. His quick-witted flanking action allowed three squadrons to escape being overrun and resulted in the capture of two enemy battalions, three sets of colors, and two cannon. So resolute was his action that his superior, Major General von Mayer, presented him to the prince "after embracing me on the *champ de bataille*." Prince Heinrich "expressed his complete satisfaction with me in a letter dated Freiburg, 13 November." He included a gift to Kesslitz of 300 Reichsthaler, "because my best horse had been completely shot up" in the battle.[67]

Freiburg formed the last real engagement for the Prussians and the termination of hostilities in 1763 tossed cold water on Kesslitz's further military ambitions. Moreover, events at home mandated his attention. In June 1763, his father died and left behind "an estate completely ruined by debts and war," as well as a younger brother (about twenty-three) and two sisters. Joseph's presence was essential "in order to preserve my small inheritance." The dire financial situation of his estate was exacerbated, in his words, by the "extravagances" of his mother, who gave everything to "monks and the [Catholic] Church." Although his commander offered to furlough him for as long as he needed to set straight his affairs at home, he refused, for "in my opinion the most honorable service of the king allows for no separation between private life and the total dedication required of every officer." Besides, peace had been signed. Thus, he preferred to take his discharge, feeling that he could not attend to his familial responsibilities without neglecting his duties as an officer. Now twenty-eight years old, Joseph von Kesslitz turned his back on a military career with obvious reluctance. Whether Kesslitz was ever compensated for his services in the military or not is unclear (remember he joined as a "volunteer"). His military pay, however, would never have been enough to allow him to save his estate or even live as a nobleman, for not until one reached the rank of captain did one have any hope of drawing an appropriate (*standesgemäß*) salary. Whereas many officers who reached higher rank in Frederick's armies—that of colonel—and then retired to their estates could continue to serve Prussia as civil officials, such as district administrators, that path was closed to Kesslitz.[68]

Salisch, in any case, was soon lost to him and his immediate family as well. Like many other estates in Silesia, Salisch emerged from these years heavily burdened by debt. The property had suffered grievously during the war, although probably more from taxes and lack of income than any physical devastation. Neither Joseph nor his younger brother was able to maintain the estate, and thus they sold the property to their maternal uncle, Johann Karl Ferdinand Leopold von Kreckwitz, for a sum that netted about 7,000 Reichsthaler for Joseph.[69] Kesslitz's income now became exceedingly precarious. Separated from his lands and no longer in the army, he had to live off what he had received from the sale, and 7,000 Reichsthaler would hardly last forever.

Joseph decided to settle in the nearby town of Glogau, where his relatives had once held land and offices. At first, he saw this as a temporary solution: "and [I] always hoped that perhaps new wars might occur, [in which case] I would not be the last to offer His Majesty my services [again]." Despite living "frugally," as he described it, he was soon dipping into his capital, because the interest he drew "was not sufficient to cover my expenses [while living] in the style to which I was raised." While his material circumstances had never allowed for much indulgence, a noble lifestyle required some accouterments: proper dress, a horse, some minor luxuries and ornaments like a watch, rings, stockings, riding boots, and perhaps a manservant. Kesslitz quickly realized that he could not manage for long on the tiny sum he commanded, and so "I had to think of something to save me from complete destitution." Faced with financial insolvency, Kesslitz took a step that might first seem strange for a nobleman; he went to work, or rather he began a small trade in gems to maintain himself. He had developed "a rather good knowledge of [precious] stones, antique coins and cameos, and jewels." Exactly how, we do not know, but we can speculate. Kesslitz's willingness to take such a step suggests either a growing desperation or an ability to adapt to changing times and circumstances. The trade in gems and cameos could be immensely profitable. Mayer Amschel Rothschild laid the basis of his family's fortune in it in the 1770s: "there is no question that without the capital Mayer Amschel was able to accumulate by buying and selling 'curiosities,' he would never have had the resources to move into banking."[70] Kesslitz, of course, was no Rothschild, but the demand for curiosities had burgeoned in the eighteenth century, making room for many suppliers, large and small alike.

Collecting precious and half-precious stones, coins, and cameos had become a hobby for serious connoisseurs, as well as for not-so-serious amateurs and not-so-knowledgeable dilettantes. Already in the sixteenth century, north of the Alps, numerous princes had compiled vast quantities of jewels, stones, prints, musical instruments, stuffed animals and other *naturalia,* and paintings, all of which they then displayed in their "cabinets of wonder." The most extensive was that of the Emperor Rudolf II in Prague, but throughout central Europe, the rulers of smaller territories, such as Saxony, Württemberg, and Braunschweig, also acquired impressive collections. High clerics and nobles used antique gems as jewelry or signet rings. Almost certainly more important for Kesslitz's trade were the many smaller collectors and the tradition of collecting that had sprung up among the bourgeoisie, as well as among nobles of less exalted pedigrees and less substantial means. The events of the late seventeenth and early eighteenth centuries—the rise of the new science and the growing wealth of the bourgeoisie—allowed such activities to spread ever more widely. Individuals situated far lower in the social rankings than monarchs, princes, and great nobles built collections that often reflected special interests—in coins and cameos, for example—and their more modest financial situation. Goethe, who cannot, of course, be viewed as in any sense ordinary, assembled his own selection of stones, coins, and antique cameos. Like many other enthusiasts, he often made expeditions to Italy. He warned others not to waste money by buying from large dealers, because their prices matched the size of their trade. Smaller, ambulant traders could give better prices, but they were often ignoramuses and cheats. Forgeries abounded. Where Kess-litz fitted into the extensive trade in antiquities is unknown, but a sizable market existed for the wares he offered to the burghers and nobles of central Europe.[71]

For four years then, until 1773, he lived from a enterprise that kept him on the move. Traveling throughout central Europe, but particularly in Saxony, Bohemia, and Prussia, he collected "whatever came my way." (On one of these trips, to Breslau, he met Visconti.) Despite his restricted circumstances, however, he quickly assured Berlin that he had always lived in a noble fashion and never earned money in a contemptible manner. Thus, although he, in a sense, labored for his bread, he preserved his nobility unsullied (at least in his own mind and probably in the eyes of his contemporaries as well). Sustaining a noble lifestyle was, of course, impor-tant for his own self-esteem. In the context of when he wrote this memoir (while under arrest in Hamburg), it was vital to convince the Prussian court that he had never done anything to sully his lineage or reduce his status, or, for that matter, Prussia's. It was important for him to prove that his nobility remained intact and that his still-untainted honor deserved full protection. Thus, despite years of need, or at least greatly straitened circumstances, he had neither taken any work incompatible with honor nor consorted with common folk or hired himself out as a mercenary. Nothing he had done in the years since the war damaged his position as an *eques Silesius*. How he achieved this is not completely clear, but as any reader of Casanova's memoirs knows, nobles—even impecunious ones—found it relatively easy to keep up appearances. Invitations to dinners, to country homes, and to town houses could tide one over for days, weeks, or even months. Such sojourns could also give a man like Kesslitz (or Cas-anova) a chance to offer their wares or talents without entangling them-selves in vile commerce.

An Eques Silesius *in Hamburg*

In 1773, Kesslitz's fortunes shifted again. Since the sale of his estate, he had struck up a friendship with Friedrich, baron von Schlabrendorff, the son of his "one-time commander and great benefactor." From him, Kesslitz received an offer that would eventually bring him to Hamburg. Schlabren-dorff at the time held the rank of cavalry lieutenant. Ordered to Hamburg to facilitate Prussian recruitment, he suggested that Kesslitz accompany him to the city, "where I [Kesslitz] might find something advantageous." Our two Silesian knights thus arrived in Hamburg on 29 November 1773 and took up lodgings in the Riga Inn on the Großer Neumarkt.[72] If the move to Hamburg turned out in the long run to be a disaster, at first it seemed a godsend—a stroke of good luck for a man in a tight place. Yet how much of this can be written off to mere serendipity, and how much did historical circumstances channel Kesslitz (as well as Romellini, Sanpelayo, and Visconti) to Hamburg? Schlabrendorff's presence in the city was hardly accidental. He went to Hamburg as one of a long series of Prussian recruiters. We have seen how frequent and troublesome such recruitment was, and Schlabrendorff's own stay ended in an ignominious, headlong flight from the authorities after a duel. The recruitment activities of many northern and northwestern European powers centered in Hamburg, so it was hardly strange that Berlin dispatched Schlabrendorff there. One current that swept people along into Hamburg, in this case, Prussians, nobles, and army officers, was thus the same one that washed recruits back to Prussia. While recruiters worked in other places, territorial states like Denmark or the other north German states were less bountiful hunting grounds for them. Their own recruiters combed the field, and Prussians would have been unwelcome and unlikely to find volunteers. The Prussians, moreover, could, as we have seen, put a price on their benevolent support of Hamburg, a backing crucially necessary at midcentury, but never superfluous. Simply put, in return for protecting Hamburg from the aspirations of other, mightier neighbors, Prussia wished Hamburg to allow its recruiters free hand. Other countries, in particular Spain and France, employed similar diplomatic blackmail to achieve similar goals.

His friend's invitation only partially determined Kesslitz's presence in Hamburg. In moving to the Elbian metropolis, he joined literally hundreds of other nobles who found Hamburg a pleasant and exciting place to live. The city was the news center of all northern Europe, and its bookstores displayed all the current publications. Its coffeehouses were the best known in Germany. Graceful villas and ornamental gardens adorned the approaches to the city, and the inns offered varying degrees of comfort at several price levels. Servants abounded and cost little. Some nobles must have also hoped to acquire suitable brides from among the unmarried daughters of wealthy merchants. For all these reasons, Hamburg attracted the flotsam and jetsam of Europe's nobility like a magnet attracted filings. Of course, it was also home to other foreigners of rank. Few places in northern Europe could offer a more congenial or agreeable atmosphere, combining urbanity, comfort, elegance, excitement, and entertainment. Not incidentally, it was also an excellent place for imposters to pose, cardsharps to pounce on prey, and a whole range of others to slip into an anonymity that furthered their own interests. Inevitably, the rich, the famous, and the gullible mingled with the destitute, the humble, and the cunning, sometimes by choice, sometimes almost unconsciously.

Hamburg was an exhilarating place to live, not only because it formed the nerve center of northwestern Europe, but also because it offered more opportunities for enjoyment than almost anywhere else in the region. Not only were the city's theaters, opera, and coffeehouses unrivaled in northern Europe, other amusements were cast on a greater scale or staged more lavishly. Kesslitz, for instance, went coaching with Sanpelayo and Romellini. The many villages that then surrounded Hamburg (and now make up its suburbs)—Hamm, Billwerder, Eimsbüttel, Eppendorf, Poppenbüttel, Wellingsbüttel, and Wandsbek—were favored places for such excursions. Or one could venture farther afield, to Bergedorf, Neuengamme, or Ahrensburg. One traveled in gigs and carriages, or on horseback in summer; on sleighs in winter. If one had wealthy friends, as Sanpelayo and Kesslitz did, an invitation to lunch or dinner in a garden villa was a delightful way to spend an afternoon or evening. In addition, opera, theater, French comedies, and church concerts were there to be enjoyed. The city itself, its markets and street life, was another unending show: carnivalists exhibited exotic animals, and supple young men and women danced on narrow cords strung between two beams. Fireworks illuminated the evening and celebrated royal visits. Less savory, but wildly popular, were bearbaiting and cock- and dogfights, which attracted groups to St. Pauli, near today's Reeperbahn.[73] Hamburg spilled out a cornucopia of diversions, catering to tastes of all kinds (including the venereal ones), furnishing distractions to the wealthy and the not-so-wealthy alike.

Nobles in Hamburg created a social life enlivened by dinners, teas, parties, masked balls, and more casual get-togethers, which centered on the diplomatic corps and Countess von Bentinck's salon. To these festivities, they invited their diplomatic opposite numbers and prominent foreigners, as well as distinguished locals and others who might offer in glitter what they lacked in substance. Kesslitz quickly moved into these circles or flitted along their edges. Soon after his arrival in Hamburg, he met Sanpelayo at the house of the French minister, Baron de la Houze. Immediately, the two hit it off. Kesslitz discovered in Sanpelayo a soul much like his own, and they "shared a way of thinking about many things." These affinities, along with "the good recommendations I had brought with me," led Sanpelayo into a closer acquaintance with Kesslitz. Finally, there developed between the two men, both relatively new to Hamburg, "a band of friendship." Sanpelayo offered more to Kesslitz than congenial company, however. He also volunteered to help him out of his financial embarrassment. According to Kesslitz, Sanpelayo's "noble feelings of generosity, which suffused his entire character" led the Spanish consul to inquire (delicately at first, one presumes) into Kesslitz's all-too-apparent poor financial situation. Sanpelayo suggested that Kesslitz "take part in his [Sanpelayo's] commercial accomplishments." Kesslitz confidently placed what was left of his estate, only some 2,000 marks on account and about 1,200 Reichsthaler in cash ("almost everything I had left"), in Sanpelayo's hands. A casual encounter at the house of the French resident minister had turned into a piece of amazing good luck for Kesslitz. By all reports, Sanpelayo lived up to his reputation as a canny businessman who had made fortune in Bilbao before transferring to Hamburg. His luck and skill did not desert him when he moved north. In his hands, Kesslitz's meager riches rapidly multiplied. Sanpelayo invested the money Kesslitz had given him in "such an advantageous manner . . . in his Silesian linen trade, that up to the point of my misfortune on 18 October, my small capital had increased, even though I had also lived on it for more than two years."

Kesslitz was hooked. His success with Sanpelayo drove him to consider launching his own business venture. Assisted by Sanpelayo, he drew up a plan to open a direct trade in linen cloth between Spain and Silesia. In the 1775 statement that describes this project, Kesslitz may have been "playing to the audience" of the Berlin court, but his expressions and aspirations corresponded very closely to those others had broached to animate trade and commerce within a mercantilist system.[74] This was precisely what Kesslitz and Sanpelayo planned, or at least this is how Kesslitz presented the scheme to Berlin. He proposed entering into an agreement with Sanpelayo to develop trade with Spain, which "was sure to be successful," he argued, when directed by a man like Sanpelayo, who possessed "the financial know-how and the requisite contacts in Spain." They crafted a somewhat grandiose but hardly impractical scheme: to set up "their own trading office" in Landeshut (Silesia). From there, they would ship linen to Cádiz, thus circumventing Hamburg's exporters and avoiding its transshipping fees. This would be easy, for in the 1770s, Spain remained the major customer for linen from Landeshut (which was generally reexported to the virtually insatiable markets in its American colonies): that trade passed almost exclusively through Hamburg first. Hamburg had long been "Silesia's most important door to foreign markets," especially for its textiles.[75] An earlier project to encourage the export of Silesian cloth, which involved a Hamburg merchant, Friedrich Christoph Wurmb, had been suggested in 1750. Despite enjoying Prussian support, it came to nothing.[76] If at first one might regard the scheme floated by Sanpelayo and Kesslitz as far-fetched or even absurd, one should remember that projects and projectors proliferated in these years. Many were busts, but even men of quite humble origins—like Heinrich Carl von Schimmelmann, who began his life as a simple boatman—could by dint of hard work and clever wheeling-dealing acquire great wealth and even come to exercise enormous political clout, as Schimmelmann did as a Danish cabinet minister.[77]

Sanpelayo immediately pounced on Kesslitz's idea. The two men began to plan an expedition to Silesia for the winter of 1775–76, "in order to investigate more closely [the feasibility of] this project." The trip was never made, because of the "accident" on 18 October. Here Kesslitz intimated that the Hamburg magistrates had seized the opportunity to throw a spanner in the works. They had always jealously resented Sanpelayo's flourishing business, Kesslitz contended, and they were now exploiting his own misfortune "to cause [Sanpelayo] huge expenses [and] even, if possible, to destroy him utterly."[78]

This was a clever move on Kesslitz's part (or was it perhaps ghostwritten for him by his lawyer, Detenhof?). This version of events transformed Kesslitz's problems with the Hamburg magistracy from a criminal investigation into an attack on Prussia's own economic interests. His condemnation would effectively eliminate a pesky competitor. Linen export was the backbone of Silesia's economy, and the wars had considerably reduced its scope. The 1750s and 1760s were especially lean years for Silesian weavers and merchants. In the early 1750s, for example, the price of Silesian cloth sank appreciably in its most important markets: Hamburg, London, Amsterdam, and Spain. One solution broached in these years would have established direct trade with Spain (in order to obtain higher prices for the cloth and greater profits for the Silesian merchants) along the lines Kesslitz and Sanpelayo later proposed in the mid 1770s. Emancipation from the transit trade and commission business seemed too risky a solution for some, who pointed out that insurance costs would rise, and that payment would only be forthcoming a year after delivery. Many thus believed it safer and perhaps more profitable to continue employing the Dutch and the Hamburgers as middlemen. The real advantage of Silesian linen was its low price; its quality lagged far behind that of French textiles.[79]

The desire for a direct trade in linen with Spain became more attractive again once Silesia was Prussian. Earlier worries about costs seemed to have receded, and the general feeling was now that forging a commercial link with Spain would enormously benefit Prussia's newest province. Frederick the Great himself firmly advocated such a policy and tried several times to implement it, but with notable lack of success. In 1750, as Prussia labored to negotiate a favorable commercial agreement with Spain, the linen trade became a major issue. Frederick wrote to his representative in Madrid urging him to do his utmost to facilitate the movement and sale of *des toiles de Silèsie,* to no avail. A later attempt in 1754 collapsed as well. Clearly, however, a project like the one Kesslitz and Sanpelayo thought up would quickly attract Berlin's attention. In the 1760s, trade with Spain occupied the many officials in Berlin and merchants and officials in Silesia who were concerned with the linen trade. One of the legacies of the war was that the Austrians pressed several commercial offensives against Prussia, seeking to win back by diplomacy some of what they had lost in battle. Rumors reached Berlin that the Austrians were trying to persuade the Spanish to forbid the import of Silesian linen and to replace it with Bohemian products. In the depressed economic circumstances of postwar Silesia, any economic inroad could only be extremely troubling. Once again, the Prussian king supported endeavors to protect trade with Spain. Likewise disconcerting was the way in which the Austrians tried to compete with Silesian products in Hamburg, Holland, and Spain. In the end, however, very little came of either the Austrian or Prussian attempts.[80]

Kesslitz's appeal to the court in Berlin, however, managed to hit all the right notes. If in some ways, his memoir seems a bit crude, or even naive, and if his repeated assertions of his sense of duty and his zeal in Prussian service seem too crass, nonetheless the phrases had power. Kesslitz reminded the Prussian court that Hamburg had acted in a high-handed, even arrogant, manner, and that it was hardly the first time that the upstart city had thumbed its nose at Prussia. More cleverly, Kesslitz gave Prussia yet another pretext for taking his part: the interests of the Silesian linen trade. Even if official Berlin was not thoroughly convinced of his innocence, Detenhof and Kesslitz must have known that the terms they had chosen would not be without effect. One can easily believe that at least some important people in Berlin saw the case as a good place to wring political and economic concessions out of Hamburg.

Fragments of a Life

Everything about Kesslitz comes in bits and pieces. The testimony in the case, although voluminous, conveys only fragments of a life and slivers of a personality. These kaleidoscopic images have brighter shards and denser spots, and it is inevitably the more lustrous ones that catch the eye. This is not only true of Kesslitz, of course: time has similarly pulverized the personae of Romellini, Visconti, and Sanpelayo. Sometimes the fragments seem incongruously juxtaposed, but they formed patterns contemporaries thought they recognized and understood: hot-headed noble, shady imposter, lustful Spaniard, flighty libertine.

About Kesslitz's time in Hamburg, we know little, and almost all of it comes from testimony collected in the murder case. Kesslitz socialized with officers and nobility in Hamburg and frequented the houses of diplomats such as the French resident, Baron de la Houze, and the Prussian minister, Hecht. With Sanpelayo, and perhaps with Romellini on occasion, he went out riding or in a carriage. Accompanied by Sanpelayo, or on his invitation, he had contact with the mercantile elite of Hamburg, visiting the garden villa of the broker Woltersdorff outside the gates on at least one occasion. He whiled away many hours in Dreyer's coffeehouse, where he played cards and billiards. In Hamburg, Kesslitz had hired a valet, one Johann Pfeiffer, whose testimony gives us an inadequate sense of the man whose boots he polished and clothes he brushed. Pfeiffer knew little about Kesslitz, because he did not live with him, but came in to "do" for him each day, helping him with his morning toilet and then running whatever errands Kesslitz assigned him, visiting shopkeepers or delivering messages. He had accompanied Kesslitz once to Woltersdorff's garden. "The rest of the time," he did nothing for Kesslitz, who rarely required his services, because "he spent most of the time during the day [and evening] at Dreyer's."[81]

If we know little about Kesslitz's daily routine, his personality is almost as mysterious, or rather it, too, is only glimpsed momentarily. What Kesslitz was like as a man of forty-some years can only be pieced together from hints in the documentation. He described himself as having been a hot-blooded youth who had found rural life unbearably dull. He had bolted from the family's estate when faced with a marriage for which he expressed the deepest revulsion. Throughout his military career, he had served gallantly, and even—it seems—with great bravery, although some might call it impetuosity. He certainly did not shy away from action, but flung himself into the thick of it whenever the opportunity presented itself.[82] We cannot judge whether the more mature man of forty was as fiery or as brash as the youth of twenty. His younger friend Schlabrendorff considered him an "honest and upright cavalier" who never sought out trouble but preferred to make things right. Here, as in his life as gem merchant, we find a smooth operator who seems to have had a knack for striking up acquaintances, making friends, and winning confidence. Indeed, he often sorted out quarrels between other men. One might imagine an older, more settled Kesslitz here intervening with his younger friends (Schlabrendorff was thirty-one) to prevent the very kind of affair—a duel—that involved Schlabrendorff in December 1775. Moreover, while Schlabrendorff probably worded his statement to impart a favorable picture of Kesslitz, he also added that Kesslitz did "have a somewhat hasty temper that could be easily aroused." Schlabrendorff felt that he was capable of killing "to save his own or a friend's life."[83]

Kesslitz left no diary, and we have no correspondence of his. Nonetheless, we can rough out a plausible sketch of his daily life. Enough is known about Hamburg and life in the city for us to envisage him relaxing around a rubber of whist in Dreyer's coffeehouse, strolling on the Jungfernstieg promenade, or enjoying the air of a garden villa, and to give us a picture of the social locale. Simply put, we can paste Kesslitz onto several well-known backgrounds. If this method works well enough to create a pattern of daily life that is credible in its outlines (if necessarily fuzzier in its details), it serves less well in understanding him as a person. We can use what is known about life in Hamburg to draw lines between the points where we actually see Kesslitz; scraps of a personality, however, are less easily assembled into a convincing whole. Kesslitz's contemporaries certainly considered personality important as a direct indicator of motivations. They did not, of course, speak in modern terms of personality as an integrated pattern of collective character, behavioral, temperamental, emotional, and mental traits. Rather, they discussed what Sillem called *Beschaffenheiten*, that is, "qualities" or "nature." A person's nature alloyed temperament to social milieu. In Sillem's account, for example, Visconti appears as a rogue and a bandit; the first was a inherent trait, the second a social description. Likewise, Kesslitz was "noble" and "soldierly." While they recognized that circumstances often produced occasions for violence, they also understood a person's qualities as fundamentally determinant. Such evaluations were those of observers who were not impartial. Moreover, no one had much to say about the man that went beyond platitude: "noble," "a bit hasty in temper," "honest and upright." Still, if we set these observations against the position of the commentator, asking, for example, why was it useful for someone to portray Kesslitz as noble in character and not only lineage, then these descriptions offer insights into the man himself, although they say almost as much about how observers used narratives to construct their own Kesslitz (and Visconti, Romellini, and Sanpelayo, as well, of course).

Syndic Sillem in his "Historical Narrative" judged Kesslitz to be an honorable man of unblemished record. Sillem presumed that he based his own estimation on a careful sifting of relevant evidence. He believed himself to be an objective observer who had weighed the facts. His underlying desire to prevent a blowup with Prussia and to avoid turning an incident into a diplomatic embarrassment may well have molded his beliefs, however. Thus the narrative of events Sillem fabricated *required* Kesslitz to exhibit nobility of soul. For Sillem, Kesslitz was only perhaps guilty of a too zealous self-defense, as well as some rather poor judgment in choosing his friends.[84] His is, all in all, a positive assessment of Kesslitz, even if it lacks detail and texture. Others offered similar appraisals. His commanders during the Seven Years' War (including Prince Heinrich) testified to the sterling quality of Kesslitz's war record. His friend Schlabrendorff also crafted a very favorable description; Kesslitz was a peacemaker by nature. Yet he could not deny that Kesslitz's temper was at times "a bit hasty," especially if provoked in a just cause. The innkeeper Dreyer knew him only as a frequent customer with whom he had no trouble. He, too, believed him to be "an honest and upright cavalier," news of whose "unhappy circumstance" (his arrest) had been received with "regret" throughout the city.[85] Of course, Dreyer had little reason or incentive to portray his clientele as shady customers. Speaking ill of a well-liked noblemen with a number of friends in the city was not the best way to attract business. Almost everyone questioned had good grounds for stressing Kesslitz's inherent nobility of character. These estimations were neither lies nor fabrications (or at least there is no reason to brand them as such out of hand) but rather reflections of a particular view of the world, and of their and Kesslitz's place in it. In addition, and also in Kesslitz's favor, the several men at the coffeehouse that evening stressed that Kesslitz had only very unwillingly participated in the encounter with Visconti. Schlabrendorff reported that when Kesslitz went off with Sanpelayo, he had followed him and offered his assistance (suspecting that a duel might be on). Kesslitz demurred, however, replying "Oh, no, I am not involved in anything like that, it is only something awkward."[86]

Thus, the investigation turned up almost nothing negative about Kesslitz except some indication of a slightly greater tendency to anger than desirable, but that was hardly unusual or damning. The characterizations are disappointing; they seem so clichéd and bland. Does no other material give us a better look at the flesh-and-blood man who stood behind the hackneyed terms "upright" and "noble"? Such evidence usually crops up in the historical record only when trouble brewed. Historians have assiduously tapped the richness of criminal records and civil court cases to understand a whole range of early modern topics, including social relationships. In Kesslitz's case, his misfortune tells us somewhat more about the man than we would have known otherwise. His two brief memoirs are unusually productive and immediate sources. A few other documents also crack his shell: the papers in his possession when the authorities detained him are especially intriguing. In one letter case lay a notarized document that set down the details of an incident that had occurred some time previously. (It was not unusual for a person to use notaries to create the early modern equivalent of a paper trail.) Here, Kesslitz explained the circumstances under which he had sheltered a runaway "Moor," possibly a slave, in his lodgings.[87]

For more evidence, we can analyze how Kesslitz behaved during his arrest. He consistently acted with gentility and civility. Immediately after his apprehension (he surrendered voluntarily, of course), he contented himself with protesting that he had only struck Visconti down in self-defense; he asked to be released on his own recognizances or into Hecht's custody. He had, after all, not tried to flee, which surely attested to his innocence, he argued, especially when one realized how frequently officers involved in duels took to their heels and escaped to other jurisdictions (as Schlabrendorff would do some months later).[88] He rarely complained about his captivity. Over the months, he requested the attendance of his own physician, more varied company, greater opportunity to enjoy fresh air and exercise, and a change of room; he got the first three. The legal case was more irksome. When first confined, he submitted himself meekly to the Senat's authority and explicitly to its "well-known fairness and mercy." Yet when later informed that the fiscal procedure had been decided upon, he was by no means so *sobmiß* (submissive). Still, even after receiving that unwelcome news, he never objected to how his guards treated him; "[They] care for me as if I were a general." He also insisted that everything his friends had attempted on his behalf in Berlin had been done without his knowledge or approval. That was, of course, not true, for he had already written his memoir for the Prussian king on Detenhof's instructions and had therein accused the Senat in no uncertain terms of taking the opportunity to ruin Sanpelayo in order to advance Hamburg's commerce.[89] By December, his anxiety had grown and his patience had diminished. As the fiscal procedure moved inexorably forward, he came to dread the outcome. Professor Nölting, with whom Kesslitz had repeatedly conversed during his captivity, reported that Kesslitz had sunk into "depression and disquietude." Kesslitz shuddered at his prospects. Even if in the end the courts totally exonerated him, the criminal investigation alone would make him ineligible for further military or civil office in Prussia under a royal decree of 1755.[90]

All this evidence, too, seems only to enhance the portrait of a man of honor, if also one understandably dismayed by a process that appeared to him unjust and that, moreover, threatened to place him in an untenable future position. He bore his captivity stoically: he complained only rarely and was unfailingly polite to the Senat and to the members of the guard who watched over him. He volunteered information and submitted to the magistracy's "justice and mercy" with little worry. Of course, the sentence and the swearing of the *Urfehde* that accompanied it upset him, but that distress was not difficult to comprehend and did nothing to detract from an understanding of him as inherently "noble."

But was there another Kesslitz? Was there something in the relationship —that strange four-sided affair among Kesslitz, Romellini, Visconti, and Sanpelayo—that revealed a rather different, considerably less honest fellow and less noble character? One curious piece of evidence lay buried in the papers the magistracy confiscated from Kesslitz's lodgings. It was a letter in French, written anonymously and lacking date, address, place, and any other identifying marks. There is no way of knowing how it came to be in Kesslitz's possession. Addressed to "Votre Excellenz," it informed "His Excellency" about the scandalous conduct of his son with "a female adventurer and prostitute" of common birth, a "bold and practiced coquette, impertinent enough to try to usurp a name illustrious in their country." The comment added by the magistracy suggested "that it probably referred to Romellini." But who then was the addressee? Kesslitz's father had died in 1763. Had Kesslitz perhaps known Romellini before then? It seems unlikely. Is this a letter to Sanpelayo's father that somehow Kesslitz had gotten his hands on? Or was Romellini having an affair with someone else altogether? And if so, why did Kesslitz have the letter and how had he obtained it? Do we perhaps perceive a whiff of blackmail here? None of these questions has an answer. The presence of the letter in Kesslitz's effects could be completely innocent, but it raised prickles of suspicion among the magistracy that all might not quite be as it at first seemed. Was the connection between these four longer than anyone suspected and of a different kind?[91]

In his own testimony, Kesslitz let slip information that hinted at a less favorable interpretation of his relationships with Sanpelayo, Romellini, and perhaps also Visconti before the night of 18/19 October.[92] Soon after Kesslitz had become acquainted with Sanpelayo, he met Romellini, but wanted little to do with her. About this same time, Sanpelayo and Romellini had "a little spat," and they separated for a time. Romellini quickly took up with a Count Matusky, perhaps seeing in him her next supporter. Matusky was, in Kesslitz's opinion, a man "of good family but bad intentions." The count told Romellini that he was currently out of pocket but expecting a substantial money draft "any day now." Could she help him in the meantime? She gave him some of her possessions so that he could pawn them and then redeem them once his money came through. It never did. The whole swindle quite annoyed Sanpelayo, for what Matusky had pawned, Sanpelayo had originally purchased for Romellini. Matusky had, of course, disappeared in the interim. Could he have been the one referred to in the anonymous letter as having been sucked into a *mésalliance* with a calculating adventuress? Then how did Kesslitz obtain the letter? Soon after this incident, Sanpelayo and Romellini reconciled. Kesslitz again urged his friend to give her up. Kesslitz's exertions went beyond persuasion. He penned an anonymous letter to Romellini, threatening to denounce her to the authorities as a whore. His sole motive, he insisted, was to scare her into packing up and leaving the city secretly, thus liberating his friend from her clutches. The result was hardly the one he intended or said he had intended. Instead, it led to a confrontation with Romellini and perhaps laid the basis for the charges she later raised against him: that he had agreed to assume the blame for the death of Visconti (when in fact Sanpelayo was responsible) in return for payment. Moreover, she later accused Sanpelayo of having induced a "strong Prussian officer" (Kesslitz?) to insult her publicly and threaten her with physical harm. Romellini, as we shall see, had reasons of her own for launching these charges. Yet whatever the truth of the matter, Kesslitz's conduct, by his own account, was less than admirable and hardly chivalrous.

Thus, not enough evidence exists for us to assemble a portrait of Kesslitz that fleshes out the man's personality and character. In the end, we cannot know whether he was an honest broker, gullible pawn, or unscrupulous and venal co-conspirator, but it was those very possibilities—all of them—that made his role in the affair so baffling, so intriguing, and so controversial to his contemporaries, and to us as well.

Post Scriptum

What happened to Kesslitz after he left Hamburg in the summer of 1776 remains a mystery. It is probable that he returned to Silesia and perhaps to the life of an itinerant gem trader that he had led between 1765 and 1773. But that is pure speculation. Apparently he never married and there is no record of any children. He died in Liegnitz on 3 August 1813, eighty years old. The causes of death were listed as weakness and age.[93] A dramatic life had ended unremarkably.

CHAPTER FIVE

A Woman of Pleasure

Had Daniel Defoe lived in the 1770s, perhaps we would today read *Anna Maria Romellini: Woman of Pleasure* as a nonfictional counterpart of *Moll Flanders*. No Defoe nor even a Pitaval, however, wrote her life story and spread her fame (or rather her notoriety) across Europe and through the generations. Yet her career was no less exciting or scandalous than Moll's, although we do not know if it had as happy (and implausible) a resolution. Romellini, like Defoe's eventually repentant harlot, experienced the heights and depths of fortune, careening from triumph to defeat and back again in a succession of often improbable events that in truth seemed stranger than fiction. Like many other women of ill repute, Romellini moved at the edges of high society, tumbling with surprising swiftness from the arms of royalty into the embrace of a down-and-out gambler. And she traveled—from Venice to Poland to Paris to Bordeaux to London and Hamburg and then off again to Altona, the Hague, and Rotterdam, where we finally lose her trace. Anna Maria's life crossed with those of the great and mighty and with base adventurers and vile scoundrels, partly because their lives so frequently overlapped in eighteenth-century society.[1]

Most of what we know about Romellini comes from the investigation of the Kesslitz affair. Had it not been for that fateful night of 18/19 October, only fleeting mentions in private correspondence, scandal sheets, and notary records would remain to register her passing. The Kesslitz case caused her great distress but also gave her a chance to tell all. If she narrated her story involuntarily, she nonetheless spun out a captivating tale that mirrored (if incompletely and imperfectly) the eighteenth-century world. Her statements to the magistrates over the course of October and November 1775 tell us much about her previous life. Although her narrative was neither an autobiography nor a memoir, but rather an account elicited by a criminal investigation, it rivals the inventions of the most accomplished novelist. As a romance of everyday life, Romellini's story is hard to beat.

A Life Unfolds

The most complete information that exists on Anna Maria Romellini comes from her statements given in late October and early November 1775. These were recorded in the third person, albeit as immediate transcriptions of her words.[2] Prompted by the magistrates who, like Sillem, linked motives and actions to personal backgrounds, she began by describing her family, birth, and early life. Her father was the chevalier Saby, and her mother came from the family Romellini; she had always used the latter name. She had never known her mother and had no idea whether she was still alive. She also could not say if her parents had been "properly wed." Her father had always called her Romellini, "because he was an officer and . . . thus did not want her to go by his name." She believed herself to have been born in Venice. The exact date of her birth (like her age) is unclear. In her 1775 testimony, she gave her age as twenty-four (or "not yet twenty-four"); accordingly, she would have been born in either 1751 or 1752. Of course, she might well have been somewhat older. It was advantageous for her to present herself as younger, first as a selling point but also to impress on her questioners her youthful innocence and lack of experience. "Ordinary people" had raised her until she was six. Then her father had reappeared, removed her from foster care, and "carried me off on his tours." She was still so young that she had no idea where they went. In fact, she did not even know until some years later, when he told her, that Saby had fathered her. For a while, she and he journeyed throughout the Italian peninsula and occasionally crossed into the duchy of Savoy; she offered no clues as to what he did there. When she was about nine, her father shipped her back to Venice, where she boarded with a widow, whom she only knew by a Christian name, Catarina, because "in Venice it is usual for people to go solely by their first names." Catarina had instructed her in religion and taught her how to cook, sew, and do household tasks. Whether she also studied singing and dancing, she does not say. She lived there for another two years, until she was eleven, when Catarina sent her to Parma to reside with a friend in a furnished room.

At age eleven, Anna Maria began to earn her keep "by performing at the court opera [in Parma]." Joining a troupe of dancers did not necessarily require either great talent or rigorous training. One of the many actresses of Casanova's acquaintance remarked how a girl could perform in the

Unknown lady. Courtesy Museum für Hamburgische Geschichte, Hamburg.

opera chorus or the corps de ballet "without ever having learned to sing or dance."[3] A fresh face and attractive limbs, especially fine legs and well-turned ankles, were far more important. Romellini vaguely remembered that she had received a salary of about 100 ducats a year directly from Guillaume du Tillot (the statement renders his name as "Thillau") then director of the opera.[4] As the repertoires of operas and ballets changed every two or three months, and as companies migrated regularly from one city to another, she, too, alternated between Parma and Mantua. During the two or so years she spent in the two places, she never so much as glimpsed her father, who was then, he told her, a major in the infantry of Friedrich August, elector of Saxony and king of Poland (August III). Although she could not recall the name of his regiment, she remembered that he had worn "a red uniform with blue facings and a medal" around his neck. He acted principally as a courier for the royal couple. She knew that her father was French by birth, but nothing more about his family or origins. Where Saby was in 1775, she had no idea, because she had not had heard a word from him in over three years. The earlier letters (from the mid 1760s) in her possession had been sent to her in Warsaw from Augsburg, Frankfurt, and Vienna.[5] She was not absolutely certain that Saby was her father, although he had cared for her and told her so.

In Mantua, she had danced "with a private troupe under the direction of Magnanigo." Magnanigo had arranged lodgings for her with a Bolognese woman in Mantua and paid for her keep. She was then (in 1763–64) about twelve years old. From Mantua, she went back to Venice in order to locate "a respectable [honnête] engagement." At this point, her father had returned. For the entire time of his absence, dancing had supported her. She portrayed their reunion in Venice as an accident: "Her father encountered her by chance in church . . . and was delighted to have found his child again so fortuitously." He had accompanied the duke of Courland and a person she called "Prince" Poniatowski (the brother of the king of Poland) to Venice.[6] The two princes and her father boarded at the same inn, and there she got to know both of them and, in particular, Poniatowski. The Polish prince "first debauched" her, and it was on his orders that her father took her back to Warsaw with him. According to her account, she must have been no older than thirteen. Later, her father returned with her to Venice (again on Poniatowski's commission), where she gave birth to a child; this was the young girl of about nine who was with her in Hamburg in the early 1770s. Her daughter had been born in 1767, when Romellini was about fourteen or fifteen years old. They baptized the girl Carolina Antonina Johanna du Chene. The name Du Chene, or Duchène, was "completely invented" and referred to no one in particular. Poniatowski had given Romellini no money but rather jewels (especially diamonds) and other presents worth over 20,000 ducats.

After the birth of his daughter, Poniatowski apparently lost interest in Romellini and ceased supporting her. She quickly took up with another Polish nobleman, Count Poniński Nepomus (Jan Nepomucen Poniński),[7] with whom she already had, however, concluded "an agreement." Later, as Countess Poniński, she traveled with him to Dresden, Leipzig, Frankfurt an der Oder, and Danzig. As with many nobleman, no matter what their status, Poniński's purse was often empty, and he rarely got out of debt. When creditors had him detained in Linz, she sold all her diamonds to buy him free. Poniatowski had known about her liaison with Poniński even before she bore his daughter, but "thought nothing of it." Perhaps he regarded Poniński as a godsend, a convenient deus ex machina who obligingly took over a now-unwanted mistress. Soon thereafter, in 1768, in Warsaw, Poniński fathered her second daughter. By 1775, Romellini could no longer recall what they had christened the child, but she did remember that the name was written on a card "that must be in [my] correspondence somewhere." (It was, for Romellini had recorded the birth of a girl, subsequently baptized Paulina Anna Maria Teresa Giovanna, on 10 or 16 June 1768.)[8] Poniński placed the child with an orphanage in Warsaw *aux enfants Jesus,* where, as far as Romellini knew, she still lived.

In December 1769, Dresden's magistrates imprisoned her lover Poniński (for dueling with the powerful magnate Prince Jablonowski) and her father (for debt). In order to free them, she struck a bargain with Karl Johann Gustav von der Osten, called Sacken, who was the Saxon plenipotentiary to St. Petersburg from 1763 to 1768 and then a cabinet minister in Saxony. During these years, he orchestrated the convoluted maneuvering between France, Poland, Saxony, and Russia. His coded dispatches reported in great detail, for instance, on the scheming of the Poniatowski and Czartoryskis families and on the affairs of the dukes of Courland, which, he warned, should be treated with "the greatest discretion."[9] In return for Sacken's intervention on behalf of her father and lover, Romellini agreed to carry "addressed letters" from Dresden to the maréchal de Richelieu in France. Her father was involved "in the secret correspondence about the confederation and Count Poniński was its head."[10]

The "confederation" of which she spoke was probably the famous Confederation of Bar. A significant portion of the Polish nobility remained unreconciled to the 1764 election of Stanisław August as king, viewing him (to some extent correctly) as a Russian puppet. Catherine the Great kept a very close eye on Poland and interfered repeatedly—and vigorously—in its internal affairs. The Polish nobility detested her minister to Poland, Count Nikolai Vasilievich Repnin, for his high-handed, imperious manner. James Harris, the British representative to the court of Poland, found Repnin despotic and overbearing and judged him more powerful than the king himself.[11] Matters came to a head in 1768 when Catherine and Frederick the Great championed (cynically one assumes) the religious rights of dissidents, that is, non-Catholics, in Poland. Pressure from the Prussians and particularly from the Russians forced the Polish Diet (the Sejm) to grant toleration to non-Catholics and to place them under the protectorship of the tsarina. In response, the Polish gentry gathered in the small town of Bar (in Podolia, near what was then the Turkish border) and organized an alliance to defend their rights, Polish Catholics, and the traditional Polish constitution. Violently anti-Russian sentiments characterized the Confederation. On 20 August 1770, the Confederation declared Stanisław August deposed. In November 1771, hot-headed members of the Confederation kidnapped the king (holding him very briefly, about forty-eight hours) and rumors of assassination plots filled the air; all of which discredited the Confederation even with some of its sympathizers. For a while, however, the Confederation's activities amounted to virtual civil war in the eastern part of Poland and war with Russia in the western Ukraine. The Confederation was not effectively squelched until 1772, when Poland was first partitioned. The larger international situation greatly facilitated the Confederation's (albeit limited) successes and its ability to survive despite its mighty enemies. Turkey supported the Confederation and in 1768 declared war on Russia (the "Polish" Turkish War). The French, too, fished in these troubled waters. France had long been interested in Poland, but its course of action was muddled by the competing initiatives of official and secret diplomacies. The organization called "Le Secret du Roi," or the King's Secret, had been established in the 1740s to secure the Polish throne for a French prince. The head of the King's Secret, Charles François, comte de Broglie, regarded the Confederation of Bar as a "shambles" and advised Louis XV to support Stanisław August. (De Broglie's opinion of Stanisław August had shifted drastically since arranging for his dismissal as Polish representative to St. Petersburg in 1758, or at least he felt it in France's best interests to support the king at this juncture.) French *official* policy under Foreign Minister Choiseul "took a diametrically opposed course" and fervently supported the Confederates, conspiring with the Saxons against Frederick and Catherine to set the Polish crown on the head of a Saxon princeling. Romellini's lover, Poniński, immersed himself in Confederation affairs, and the letters his mistress carried between Warsaw, Dresden, and France helped the rebels communicate with Stanisław's enemies.[12]

So Anna Maria became a spy or at least a secret courier. "And . . . she traveled around" in this capacity, wearing men's clothes and conveying letters "pertaining to the secret correspondence, sometimes [going] to Warsaw, sometimes to Dresden." When she visited Richelieu, however, she dressed as a woman and, in return for the dispatches, he "gave her all sorts of valuable gifts." Once while on secret mission, Russian troops stopped her and took her (in male garb) to the Russian general Stepan Stepanovich Apraxin (the conqueror of Kraków in 1768). Despite her disguise, he quickly discerned her true sex "and, as she offered him much amusement, he repaid her with many presents, in all worth more than 6,000 ducats." "Presents" given in return for "amusement and distraction" is code for sexual favors. One reasonably assumes that Romellini slept with both the Russian general and the French marshal. If Sacken and Poniński were feeding Richelieu tasty bits of secret information, they also may have served up a tender *amuse bouche* of another sort entirely.[13]

Everything she earned as courier and spy, she turned over to her father and Poniński. Her efforts soon freed her father, but Poniński languished for some nine months, until almost 1770. In the interim, her father returned to France, although she did not know what he intended doing there. Poniński eventually went to Belich (Bielsko) "to seek service with the Polacks," that is, with the Confederation.

Her father gone, and with Poniński in jail and then in Poland, Romellini had to look out for herself. Sometime in 1769, she decided to "try her luck" in France. Once in Paris, she came to know the Venetian ambassador there, "Matzenigo," actually, Alvise Mocenigo. Through him she subsequently met a "certain cavalier attached to the Venetian embassy." This was probably Antoine Niccoló Manuzzi, the son of Giovanni Battista Manuzzi, whose activities as a spy for the Venetian Inquisition had led to Casanova's imprisonment in the notorious Leads in Venice. Casanova described the younger Manuzzi (whom he met in Spain in 1767) as "a handsome, rather well-built youth who makes a very good impression." Mocenigo, at least according to Casanova, came to be "much talked about in Paris because of his unfortunate inclination for pederasty." A grandee of Spain gossiped maliciously to Casanova that "everyone knew that Manuzzi played the part of wife to His Excellency the Ambassador."[14] Romellini began an affair with Manuzzi and bore him a son in 1770 in Dresden, whom they named for his relatives, the duke of Courland and his sister. Again, she was unsure about the infant's exact name, and he soon died of smallpox. He was buried in the Catholic chapel in Dresden. (Once again her papers revealed what she had forgotten: Charles August Christian Maria, born on 4 August 1771, died on the 30th of that month.)[15] Manuzzi had given her nothing, because "he himself had naught." Rather, she earned "much money" in Paris singing, dancing, and entertaining "the princes and other great men" in the city. She denied having any sexual relationships there (with the exception of Manuzzi), because she "could not stomach the French."

When she returned to Dresden in 1770 to bear Manuzzi's child, he followed her to pursue his business at court. As soon as she finished her lying-in, she left Dresden and went to Bordeaux. Apparently, she was still working for the Confederation, or at least for someone connected to it. She brought letters from Richelieu to the commandant in Bordeaux, Monsieur Duamill. Manuzzi departed from Dresden about the same time and returned to Paris. In Bordeaux, Romellini engaged in "no other love affairs." She stayed there for three months and then embarked with a merchant ship captain named Barcker (presumably Barker) who was on his way to Hamburg. Eventually, Visconti followed her.

She had known Visconti since her childhood, having first encountered him during her early career on stage. He pursued her wherever she went and repeatedly, fervently "declared his love for her and swore that he would marry no one else." She knew nothing about his family. The name itself revealed little, because in Italy there were "many families that call themselves Visconti, among them very grand people as well as very common ones." She possessed no inkling to which of these he belonged, merely that he always called himself Comte Visconti. He confided to her that his uncle was the papal nuncio in Warsaw and would be the next pope. The nuncio from 1760 to 1767 was indeed named Antonio Eugenio Visconti and, moreover, became a leading candidate for the Holy See when Clement XIV died in 1774. (Despite the support of the Polish king and of Maria Theresa and Joseph II, Visconti lost out to Gian Angelo Braschi, who became Pius VI, after 265 days of wrangling at the electoral conclave.)[16] Comte Visconti, however, held "neither posts of honor nor [had] any other business," but was always mired in debt and survived solely "from his schemes." For example, he could no longer allow himself to be seen in Vienna because of unpaid bills and his (bad) reputation there.

After the birth of her first child (Poniatowski's daughter), Visconti offered to marry Romellini and legitimize the girl. Because "she could not stand him," however, she rejected his suit. Yet Visconti continued to plague her, employing "spies" to ferret out her whereabouts and then turning up almost everywhere she went to "pester her with declarations of love." Occasionally, he gave her trifling sums of money, something like twenty or thirty ducats. Far more often she paid him to go away. He frightened her, for he was a man "athirst for revenge" (although on whom and why we do not know) and existed only "to work his vengeance" on others, as he repeatedly confided to her.

No more princes, real, rich, impoverished, fraudulent, or otherwise materialized to save her while she was in Dresden. Rather, a humbler man altogether, named Thonus, whom she described as "a Polack of low birth," became her companion. Thonus had originally been a valet, but he had made his own luck in Dresden by prostituting his daughter to Count Marcolini "for a piece of gold." The count had rewarded him by "making him a baron" (!), she said. Romellini became acquainted with Thonus soon after the birth of Manuzzi's son and found him "an entertaining man, who engaged in all sorts of amusing and diverting enterprises." She testified to having had "lots of fun" in his company. The letter he had written to her from Strasbourg found in her papers during the investigation should not, she insisted, be taken too seriously, because its language reflected his normal jocular, teasing manner. "As a joke," he addressed her as "son fidèle épouse." She denied being married to him, that she had any sort of understanding with him, or that she had sexual relations with him. Thonus's wife and children resided in Berlin, where he seems to have been known under the name of Torns or Tonus; two of his sons served as cadets with the Steinkeller Regiment. Herr Brentano, the Saxon minister to Hamburg, could vouch for her story, she offered.

On the voyage from Bordeaux, while tossing up the Channel to Hamburg, she became Captain Barcker's paramour. It was a rather steep fall in status from being the mistress of princes-even rather threadbare ones—to that of a fairly ordinary if seemingly prosperous coastal skipper. She said she left Bordeaux with Barcker because Visconti had found her in France and "because she disliked Bordeaux anyway." Once in Hamburg, Barcker used his connections with the many Englishmen there to lodge her with an innkeeper named Brown (sometimes Teutonized in the documentation as "Braun") while he arranged for cargo to be taken to Malaga. She admitted that on the trip she had become his mistress, not out of inclination or even passion but out of concern for her safety. To prevent Visconti from discovering her location, she called herself Madame Barcker. She remained only a few days with Brown, because Barcker considered the place "not reputable enough" and quickly moved her to lodgings owned by a man named Holtermann. Barcker had never stayed overnight with her at Brown's, "because [Brown's] wife would not allow it." Barcker introduced her to Holtermann as his spouse in order to avoid similar inconveniences. She stayed there about eight weeks until Barcker contracted and loaded his cargo. Once Barcker sailed off to the Mediterranean, Brown appeared at Holtermann's and insisted that she return with him, for she owed him considerable money for room and board. More important, Barcker had written to Brown asking him to remove her from Holtermann's establishment "due to an ungrounded jealousy, because he feared that she would be seduced" while living there unsupervised. Whom Barcker suspected, Romellini did not specify.

During her second sojourn at Brown's, Visconti reappeared. Perhaps this was what Barcker had feared all along. Romellini related how Visconti had noticed her "by chance" while she lounged on the window seat. Such happenstances, such as the lucky meeting with her father in a Venetian church years before were, one assumes, often staged. They play a large role in Romellini's account and are frequently used by her to move the plot forward, a function they also perform in many eighteenth-century romances, novels, and true crime stories. Lovers, friends, siblings, and parents and children are forever being separated and reunited by chance or, just as frequently, passing one another by unnoticed. Reacquainted by accident, Visconti subsequently visited her a couple times in the company of Brown's wife and "conducted himself entirely properly, and they chatted away in an amiable manner about all sorts of trivial matters." Nonetheless, Visconti also revealed to her how desperate his circumstances were and how few his resources. To be quit of him, she gave him a gold medal on a chain. A few days later, however, he came back and insisted that she go away with him, "employing all manner of threats . . . to retain her as his mistress. He packed all her things at Brown's and wanted to carry them away [with him] absolutely without her knowledge." She described him as "engorged with anger" and he carried pistols and a sword. As Visconti was trying to force her to leave, Brown stopped him. Enraged, Visconti drew his sword and cut Brown over the hand with it and fought with him and two sailors who happened to be present. He finally succeeded in hustling Romellini off and into a carriage he had waiting and then transported her (against her will, she claimed) to the house of a language teacher, La Farque, on the Mühlenbrücke. They stayed there together for only a single day, then Visconti moved her to lodgings owned by the Buhrbanck sisters (where their house stood in Hamburg is unclear). He forced her to live with him for a while as his mistress, "threatening to run her through or shoot her dead" if she endeavored to flee. She neither protested nor informed the authorities, for she did not want to cause any trouble and she also felt impotent as an "unknown woman lacking protectors."

For several days she tarried at the Buhrbancks' lodgings under the name Madame Barcker. In the interim, Barcker had returned, and when he finally located her, he hastened there to see her. When Barcker appeared at Buhrbancks' house, he and Visconti argued, each one "asserting that she was *his* wife." Finally, Barcker conceded the point and left her in Visconti's possession. Soon, however, Barcker and Visconti struck on a modus vivendi that divided Romellini between them. Visconti, always in need of money, seemed perfectly amenable to this arrangement and acted, perhaps not for the first time, as Romellini's pimp. Once Visconti realized that Barcker was willing to pay him for Romellini's favors, "the [two] became good friends." Barcker was soon supping with Visconti and Romellini, remaining over night, and sleeping with her on occasion. On "Barcker's nights," Visconti stayed out "gambling and carousing." "As long as Barcker made free with his funds," according to Romellini, Visconti happily acquiesced in this profitable ménage à trois. When Barcker refused to lend Visconti more money, however, Visconti closed off access to Romellini.

Soon thereafter, Barcker fell deathly ill, and for two months, he kept to his bed. Cut off from this source of income, Visconti quickly ran up bills. To elude his creditors, he quit Hamburg in fall 1773; Romellini remained at the Buhrbancks' house. On the evening of his departure, Visconti revealed only that "he no longer found [Hamburg] diverting" and intended to go to Celle for his amusement. Not unexpectedly, Visconti left a mountain of debt behind him, and all those to whom he owed money soon came knocking on Romellini's door. While in Hamburg, he had bespoken a whole range of pretty things: jeweled watches, gold braid, silver spurs, and lacquerwork. Visconti informed his creditors that he had been called out of the city unexpectedly and that his wife would settle up with them. Nothing could have been further from the truth. Besides the artisans who wanted to be paid, an officer unknown to her, but whose uniform seemed Prussian, turned up and demanded the return of the hunting knife Visconti had borrowed. He bullied her and threatened to swear out a complaint with the authorities. She only managed to pay off these debts after a notary named Erdmann brokered a deal. He had subsequently acted several times on her behalf.

About then she became acquainted with Sanpelayo, because "she had decided on a whim to go to Spain" to seek her fortune there, and she had approached Sanpelayo for the necessary passport. That initial meeting must have gone extremely well, because soon thereafter Sanpelayo "magnanimously" offered her money to cover Visconti's obligations and her own. At the time, however, she had concluded no "engagement" and had "no sexual relationship" with him. She had hoped that she was now rid of Visconti, but, predictably, she was not. He soon returned from Celle, completely broke. "Impudently," he took a separate room at the Buhrbancks' house and often slept with her. All the while her connection to Sanpelayo remained merely that of "good friends." Inevitably, considering these living arrangements, Visconti and Sanpelayo became acquainted. Romellini occasionally called on Barcker, who had requested to see her while he was ill. Once he recovered, his sexual visits to Romellini resumed. She intensely disliked the situation, because she feared that Barcker had contracted a venereal disease, and she therefore wanted nothing to do with him (or was it perhaps because three competing lovers proved a bit difficult to manage?). Eventually, she (or Visconti?) persuaded him to stay away. At the time, she engaged in no other love affairs and survived by pawning or selling the clothes and other belongings she had brought with her from France. Neither Sanpelayo nor Visconti had at the time impregnated her.

Visconti's second sojourn in Hamburg lasted a mere three weeks. While packing his bags, he told Romellini that he had to return to Russia. She now maintained that she had entered neither into a legal marriage nor a *mariage de conscience* with him. What then about the papers the notary Erdmann had prepared and that she and Visconti had witnessed to the effect that "she was his legitimate wife and had been properly espoused to him by a priest?" Romellini denied it. She had only signed because she "lacked the courage to oppose him." She knew him as a "brutal man," who had repeatedly threatened to kill her. He had boxed her ears several times, pulled her around the floor by her hair so violently that he tore loose several handfuls, and even stabbed her in the leg with his sword. She was afraid to deny him whatever he demanded.

When she complained to Visconti that she had been left to pay his debts, he blamed his servant for uncommissioned purchases and items borrowed without his knowledge or permission. While in Hamburg, Visconti maintained himself by "wheedling" money from friends and chance acquaintances. He now left Hamburg for the second time, "to seek [his] pardon" in Russia or so he said. He had been furloughed from the tsarina's army (still preserving the fiction that he had actually served as an officer). His leave ran for a year, but he had stayed away two. When he arrived in Hamburg, he presented himself as a Russian major. His claims quickly aroused the suspicions of the Russian minister there, Fyodor Ivanovich von Groß (Romellini referred to a "Herr von Groth"),[17] and, when he checked with St. Petersburg, the latter discovered that "no such major [currently] serves in the Russian military." Once he was exposed as a pretender, Visconti's already precarious hold on respectability slipped entirely. His friends at the coffeehouses stopped lending him money and would no longer associate with him. The clock had run out on this particular imposture, and it was time to move on.

Although Romellini usually portrayed Visconti as a pest and a menace, the two of them nonetheless cooperated on many occasions, perhaps thrown together more by the desperateness of their circumstances than by elective affinities. In January 1775, Visconti represented her in a case she was pursuing against the baron von Schwicheldt ("Schwiegelt"), who may well have been Heinrich Ernst von Schwicheldt, son of the Hanoverian cabinet minister August Wilhelm von Schwicheldt.[18] She had first come to know the younger Schwicheldt years before in her Dresden days. More recently, their paths had crossed again in Hamburg, where she had entrusted some diamonds to him to sell on her behalf. He had accepted the commission, then vanished. Visconti went to Hanover to find Schwicheldt and eventually struck a bargain with him—how we do not know—for about 110–120 louis d'or. Little honor reigned among thieves. Schwicheldt's noble rank did not put him above such swindles, especially since Romellini could hardly sue him for fraud.

When queried about Visconti's affairs in Breslau and about his dealings "with a certain Matusky," Romellini pleaded innocence. She could only repeat what Kesslitz had confided to her about the Breslau incident: "that Visconti had cheated some young gentlemen at cards" and that, as a result, he had been forced to restore the money he had conned from them. Kesslitz also related the story of how Visconti had used a fake bar of gold to swindle three merchants in Breslau and taken to his heels before the deceit was uncovered.

According to Romellini, Visconti had "known very well" at the time that she lived on intimate terms with Sanpelayo, although she insisted that she was not yet sleeping with the consul. She admitted that she had still occasionally had sex with Visconti. She had not sealed her love contract with Sanpelayo until after Visconti abandoned her yet again, and Visconti had had no knowledge of this later understanding. When he left, he had (disingenuously?) entrusted Romellini to Sanpelayo, saying that he expected him as a *cavalier fervent* to keep an eye on her, protect her, and amuse her. Visconti also promised to send money and actually did so at least once. Far more frequently, Romellini posted cash to him. As he was leaving, he warned her that he would not soon return, for he expected that he would be confined to prison in Russia for overstaying his leave and would never be allowed to travel again. When the promised funds failed to arrive, she had little choice but to make her transaction of sex for support with Sanpelayo, who agreed to maintain her as "his proper mistress." This arrangement amounted to neither a regular marriage nor a *mariage de conscience*. Sanpelayo rented a furnished house for her on the ritzy Neuer Wall. (At the time, the Neuer Wall was the longest, toniest, and probably the straightest street in Hamburg. Large houses built of stone and brick adorned its length, and Hamburg's most notable home, the Görtz "palace," stood there. This fine edifice also served Binder von Kriegelstein as his official residence.)[19] All the furniture, silver, and other trappings, such as the curtains and even the knickknacks, belonged to him. The sole condition he imposed was that she have sexual relations with no one else; a bargain she had "kept faithfully." Thus she settled down as the kept woman of the Spanish consul and so remained for about two years. She bore Sanpelayo two children. One arrived too prematurely to survive; the other, a daughter, died the very night of her birth.

During this time, Visconti wrote to her (and also a couple of times to Sanpelayo) from several places in Italy, Venice and Bergamo among others. In these letters, he rather tenderly enquired about her well-being and informed her that the Venetians had arrested him for the murder of a dancer. Still, he assured her, this was "only a minor inconvenience" (!), because he had "not really killed" the woman. He expected to regain his freedom soon. Romellini replied with a letter filled with sympathy for his plight, but that included no money. In October 1775, another message arrived, this time from Augsburg: Visconti had obtained his release and was traveling from Augsburg to France by way of Braunschweig. First, however, he intended to return to Italy to sue the judges there for injury and libel. They had published his name in the newspapers in connection with the case of the dancer. Despite his unsavory reputation and his dubious exploits, Visconti may well have felt his honor impugned. He never revealed that he planned to come to Hamburg to see her, and his appearance on 18 October was therefore "a total surprise."

What Others Saw

Romellini dished up a right spicy tale. One suspects that the magistrates greedily gulped down large chunks of it, especially those in which she bared her soul, describing a dissolute lifestyle, several lovers, and shady financial dealings. Still, was she merely Visconti's victim? Or had she, Sanpelayo, and Kesslitz perhaps cooked up her story to conceal a premeditated murder? One thing was certain, her version did not immediately satisfy the magistrates, who went to work assembling testimony to corroborate or disprove her account. The magistrates interrogated many who had known Romellini in the few years she had been in Hamburg. The testimony gathered on her far exceeded what they learned about Visconti or, for that matter, Kesslitz. The judges followed the twisted plot lines of her life from when she first came to Hamburg in early 1773 until the death of Visconti in October 1775, but they also tugged at the skeins leading into her past. And although she told the magistrates much, others added the finishing touches.

It is quite remarkable how many people had met Romellini before either they or she arrived in Hamburg. Each witness provided useful pieces of information that helped the magistrates—and help us—recreate her life. Those interrogated for what they knew included her daughter, Antonina de Romellini (then just nine years old); her servant, Maria Anna Engauen; her landlords (Thomas Brown, "citizen and innkeeper" in the Beydenhoff near the Vorsetzen, Friedrich Christoph Holtermann, and the two sisters Maria Coecilia and Magdalena Elisabeth Buhrbanck); the notary Heinrich Christian Georg Erdmann; and numerous other acquaintances, some of whom she knew well and some hardly at all. Among these last were Catharina Guido, wife of an Italian tutor; Philipp Jacob Marechall, keeper of a French school; Joseph Caledon, instructor in Spanish; Abraham Roose, a next-door neighbor on the Neuer Wall; the broker Johann Gottfried Bruchbach, resident in the inn Stadt Dammthor; the

Italian bankers Brentano Buvarro and Jacob Greppi, with whom Visconti had an account; the seventy-two-year-old Jewish surgeon Jacob Gonsalez Montesanto; three servants hired by the day (two coachmen and a valet); Catharina Ilsabe Köhlern, a woman who sold milk; Joseph Pini, an Italian trader; and, finally, Joseph da Fonseca, a Portuguese-Jewish merchant.[20] The circle of acquaintances Romellini, Visconti, and Sanpelayo frequented while in Hamburg is well mirrored in this lengthy list.

Romellini's friends and more casual contacts overlapped with each other and with several entirely different social groups. The magistrates identified and interrogated her landlords and her servants (in particular, her maid-of-all-work, Engauen) to ferret out the hidden details of her life. Mostly they sought information on the relations among the four principals in the case: Romellini, Sanpelayo, Visconti, and Kesslitz. The foreignness of this little colony immediately strikes the eye. Barcker, for instance, placed Romellini with another Englishman, Brown. Romellini socialized with teachers of Italian, French, and Spanish, but also with Italian bankers, Jewish surgeons, and Italian and Jewish merchants. Perhaps more striking, however, is how many people had known Romellini often long before either they or she entered the city. The French schoolmaster Marechall, for instance, had encountered her in Warsaw a decade earlier, and the Jewish surgeon and tooth drawer Montesanto had met her briefly in Paris in 1770.

The magistrates were especially eager to learn what had originally drawn Romellini to Hamburg and what had occupied her during her first weeks and months in the city. According to Thomas Brown, whose lodgings near the Vorsetzen catered to many English mariners and merchants, Romellini had arrived in Hamburg in April 1773 with the English sea captain Barcker, having sailed with him from Bordeaux a month previously. (Until she took up with Sanpelayo, who moved her to a much better quarter of the city, Romellini had lived near the water, either in St. Michael's parish along the Elbe or close by, near the inner harbor, in the parish of St. Nicolai.)[21] Although Barcker had never expressly acknowledged Romellini as his wife, he allowed people to think she was. Yet he also confided to Brown (perhaps facetiously?) that he intended to introduce one of his female passengers to Baron von Schimmelmann, one of the richest men in northern Europe and also a major politico in his capacity as the Danish minister to the Lower Saxon Circle. He was thus a counterpart and colleague of Hecht, Binder von Kriegelstein, de la Houze, and Sanpelayo. Schimmelmann, a parvenu and a social climber par excellence, had sprung from extremely humble beginnings. He went bankrupt twice before cleaning up as a profiteer during the Seven Years' War and as the manager of the Prussian porcelain manufactories. He lived lavishly in

Hamburg and built a veritable palace for himself and his numerous family outside the city in Ahrensburg. Did Schimmelmann differ so very much from Visconti or from the thousands of other adventurers who tried to scheme their way to wealth and power? Perhaps only in his successes.[22]

Barcker probably only joked about his desire to match Romellini and Schimmelmann, although he certainly tried to keep Brown in the dark about his real relationship with the attractive young stranger. Brown could not say whether Romellini was or was not Barcker's mistress, for Barcker and Romellini occupied separate chambers. She stayed with Brown for six to eight weeks. Before sailing to Stettin to take on additional cargo, and thence to Malaga, Barcker sought new lodgings for Romellini with the grain dealer Holtermann, who lived auf der Kayen. Despite moving Romellini from Brown's establishment, Barcker instructed Brown and his wife "to keep a sharp eye on the lady and to report back to him on her conduct." Brown's wife visited her often, especially while she recovered from a late miscarriage (Barcker's child, one assumes). At Holtermann's, Romellini associated with a Genoese merchant named Pini and "several other Italians and young men." These liaisons displeased Barcker, and he instructed the Browns to find her another place to live, preferably with them. The Browns placed her in a small house behind their own eating establishment, so that they could, as Barcker wished, watch her closely.

Visconti now appeared in Hamburg for the first time. He ate a few times at Brown's inn, having heard that "Madame Romellini," as she was then calling herself, resided there. Because Visconti appeared clad in a green coat with red cuffs and small half-boots "such as hussars wear," Brown assumed that he was an officer. Officers in foreign service were a common sight in Hamburg, and it may not have been easy for laymen to keep them and their uniforms straight. Visconti inquired of Brown if there was not a young Italian woman living there; if so, might it be possible to speak to her? Brown did not know if "an Italian woman" was his lodger, but rather that Captain Barcker had brought a lady with him from Bordeaux and entrusted her to his supervision. Visconti pressed: he greatly desired conversation with the woman; he had something important to convey to her; he had a letter addressed to her. Visconti's insistence raised misgivings in Brown. He told Visconti that Romellini was his responsibility and he could not let her see or speak to "just anyone." However, if Visconti's need to communicate with her was really so intense, Brown would summon her from her room, which he did. Visconti and Romellini thus met again (perhaps for the first time in several years?) under the watchful eye of Barcker's bulldog. They began their conversation in French, but soon shifted to Italian (from which Brown brightly concluded "she must be an

Italian woman"). Visconti handed her an envelope, which she took upstairs. A few days later, Visconti returned, this time mounting the stairs to Romellini's rooms and entering without Brown's knowledge or permission. When she asked Brown to bring up a meal for two, he became alarmed. He went into her parlor and, finding Visconti there, rebuked him: "What did he think he was doing? Why was he upstairs with the lady like this? If he wanted a meal . . . he should come downstairs and be served with the other guests. He would send no food up to him and would not abide such conduct." Brown took Visconti by the elbow and led him outside into the courtyard. Visconti apologized profusely for his importunity and withdrew quietly.

Visconti's next meeting with Brown, a few days later, proceeded far less genially. To his dismay, Brown learned that Visconti was once again alone with Romellini, and that, moreover, he had spent the night there. Now "very angry," Brown charged up the stairs and found Romellini lying in bed with Visconti standing next to her. Brown laid his hand on Visconti's shoulder and reminded him that he had been warned never to enter Romellini's rooms unchaperoned. Brown insisted that "he did not keep a whorehouse." Visconti immediately reached for his sword and had pulled it about halfway out of the scabbard when Brown seized him by the arm and dragged him out of the house. Had Visconti resisted further, "I would have tossed him out the window," Brown boasted. The next day, Romellini ordered a carriage, left with her maidservant, and went to live with Visconti. Inasmuch as she still owed Brown money, and he feared that Barcker would not pay, given that she had run off with another man, he refused to send her possessions after her. Once he was paid in full, "which took some time," he released her effects and then quickly forgot about the incident and about Romellini as well.

During her time at Holtermanns (May–July 1773), and before she went back to Brown's (where she stayed until the end of October 1773), Romellini suffered several bouts of illness, including the miscarriage Brown described. He knew about it because his wife had taken the fetus away "in spirits." Who fathered this untimely child, he could not say. Holtermann admitted that he had attended little to Romellini's comings and goings, for, as far as he know, she was "an honest woman." While she lived at his house, he had observed nothing either "dishonorable or discreditable" about her. He could offer scant information as to her lifestyle, except that several Italians, including the merchant Pini, had visited her frequently. He had also once seen her out riding in Wellingsbüttel (a village outside of Hamburg). She was "dressed brilliantly . . . and surrounded by men." Pini, a thirty-two-year-old Italian and a citizen of Hamburg, had known Romellini since she lived with Barcker. He had met her in the chapel of the imperial resident and visited her a number of times in her lodgings auf der Kayen, conversing with her and some of his friends as they stood on the stoop or leaned against the wall, while she bent out the window. He denied making covert visits to her and did not think that, at the time, she was conducting an affair with anyone. Still, he also believed that she was a "loose woman." Rumors had reached him that she had been the mistress of first Barcker, then Visconti, and finally the Spanish consul. His familiarity with Visconti was slight. He had spoken to him a couple of times in the coffeehouses. Since his absence from Hamburg, news had circulated that he had been imprisoned in Italy "for a certain crime" and had only recently regained his freedom. Pini knew nothing more.

Several people painted virtually an identical picture of Romellini's life in the months before she took up with Sanpelayo. Visconti frequented coffeehouses, played cards, and sponged. Romellini attracted many male friends. She went out riding with some of them, supped with a few, and chatted pleasantly with others; she preferred those with whom she could rattle away in Italian. Joseph da Fonseca, a Portuguese-Jewish merchant, had known Romellini casually for about eighteen months, meeting her when Visconti was still in the city and while they dwelled together at Buhrbancks' house. He, too, had first encountered Visconti over a game of cards and had once lent him a few ducats. Because many spoke of Romellini as "a clever and vivacious person," he had occasionally called on her and spent a while in idle conversation. Most of the time, Visconti was also present. Romellini had referred to Visconti as *il suo marito*. He knew little about her life thereafter, except for the general rumor that she "was habitually seen with the Spanish consul . . . and went out on horseback with him, or [attended] the Comèdie or other parties and entertainments."

The Buhrbanck sisters, with whom she lived from the end of October 1773 until February 1774 (and then later between mid March and July 1774), told a similar story. They had rented a room to Romellini for twenty-five shillings. She had presented herself as a merchant's wife and told them that her baggage and husband had been delayed. During the first three or four weeks, she had resided alone with only a single servant. Visconti stayed elsewhere. Usually, however, he drove up in a rented carriage each morning, whiled away the entire day with her, dined with her, and then left again about 10 P.M. After the first month, however, he moved in permanently. While lodging with the sisters, Romellini did not throw money about. Admittedly, she hired a footman and dressed him in a livery of yellow and silver, although she neglected to pay the tailor's bill for his finery. The footman left with Visconti, however, just eight days after his arrival. Romellini then removed herself to less expensive lodgings with Frau Malo on hinter den Bleichen. The Buhrbancks ventured the opinion that Romellini might have first met Sanpelayo at Malo's place, because he had previously lodged there. The magistrates never questioned Frau Malo, because she had gone home to France.

Soon after Romellini moved to Malo's house, she sought to return to her previous quarters with the Buhrbancks. They happily agreed, and she moved in again on 15 March. After an absence of many weeks, Captain Barcker reappeared. During her first stay with the Buhrbancks, Barcker had called on her there. Even though she was then cohabiting with Visconti, Barcker often remained overnight. Although Visconti had once had an understanding with Barcker (and later developed a similar compact with Sanpelayo), that was not the case *this* time, probably because Barcker would no longer pay Visconti for Romellini's "use": "indeed," according to the sisters, "Barcker and Visconti . . . could not stand each other and squabbled over whose 'wife' she really was and who should maintain her." After one particularly nasty flare-up, Barcker stormed out in a rage, and he never came back.

Over the next several months, with Visconti gone, Sanpelayo visited her almost every day but never stayed the night. On 28 March, Visconti moved in with her again. This upset her relationship with Sanpelayo hardly at all, at least as far as the two women could tell: "Herr Sanpelayo came as before and went riding and coaching with her and the count together." This pleasant triangle continued less than a month, for Visconti set off again on 19 April. If Sanpelayo paid him to disappear we do not know, but it seems probable. Romellini remained at the Buhrbancks' house until 19 July, and then she, too, left; they believed she had gone to Altona after having quarreled with Sanpelayo. This was when she took up (albeit briefly) with Matusky.

The landlords' testimony allows us to shadow Romellini as she moved around the city for the two years before October 1775. Their observations provide good snapshots of her three lovers: Barcker, Visconti, and Sanpelayo. Significantly, Kesslitz is mentioned just once and then only briefly. The many others whom the magistrates subpoenaed and queried added other blocks of information on Romellini and connected the dots between her and her intimates. These witnesses revealed much about her life before 1773, that is, while she was living in Dresden, Warsaw, and Paris. That very knowledge suggests how historical currents swept people together, apart, and then—often years later—together again. While such meetings might appear random events or chance encounters (as they undoubtedly sometimes were), they were often not mere coincidences but represented the avenues people traveled through northern Europe and, simultaneously, the paths open to them as they wove their way through the layers of eighteenth-century society. None too surprisingly, many made station in entrepôts and capitals like Hamburg, Bordeaux, Dresden, and Warsaw. They switched cities as they switched identities, dearly hoping for better employment, ceaselessly seeking fortunes, or anxiously avoiding the law.

Philipp Jacob Marechall, who ran a French school, was one of these many unquiet souls. Marechall knew Romellini in Hamburg but had also been acquainted with her from 1766 until 1769 when she was living in Warsaw under the name of Madame Duchène. There she "allowed herself to be used as a mistress by several prominent men." Marechall had departed Warsaw in 1769 and did not see Romellini again until sometime in 1774, when he met her unexpectedly in the chapel of the French resident. She called herself first Madame Barcker, then Madame Visconti. Soon after the encounter in the chapel, she asked him to admit her daughter to his school. Marechall and his wife called on Romellini once in a while, and she was also an occasional guest in their home. After her daughter had been at his school for a few months, they sometimes dined with her. No "society of men" congregated at these gatherings, and the only other male they met there was the broker Bruchbach, who periodically accompanied Romellini when she picked her daughter up at school. Marechall could say little else about her or how she lived, except that he was aware (as it seems the whole city was) that she had taken up with the Spanish consul and "as is said, had become his mistress." This hardly shocked him, because he had always known her as a "*galante* woman, who entertained many distinguished lovers and for a long time made a profession of it." She had always, he summed up, been "a great adventuress." He knew her father as well and his testimony helped piece together in the magistrates' minds a comfortable picture (for them, anyway) of a family of strivers, con artists, ne'er-do-wells, and miscreants. Her father styled himself "Chevalier Saby," but was, according to Marechall, really only a wigmaker's apprentice from Paris who had been uncommonly lucky: he had "carried the happy news" of a royal birth from Paris to Dresden (why this message was entrusted to a "wigmaker's apprentice," Marechall does not say), where the king of Poland and elector of Saxony, August III (the child's grandfather) had rewarded him with the order of St. Ludwig and the title of *chevalier*.

This much-awaited child, Louis, duc de Bourgogne, was the grandson of Louis XV and the eldest brother of Louis XVI. His death in 1761, followed by his father's death in 1765, made Louis XVI the heir-apparent. His mother was Maria-Josepha of Saxony. The duc de Richelieu had negotiated the marriage. Romellini and her father formed small, single links in

*Maria-Josepha, mother of three kings of France. Courtesy Staatliche
Kunstsammlungen, Dresden, Porzellansammlung im Zwinger.*

the chains that bound Dresden to Warsaw and Paris, and thus they hooked
up with formidable eighteenth-century personages. Saby was, for whatever reason, happily in the right place at the right time. Marechall dismissed the idea that Romellini descended from "either a distinguished
noble or a countly family," because she had divulged to him that she was
illegitimate. He understood that she had adopted the name Duchène either from her first husband or a lover in Poland. Another casual acquaintance, the broker Johann Gottfried Bruchbach, repeated what she had told
him when he visited her once while she was Sanpelayo's mistress: "that she
herself was a Venetian, her father [stood] in the service of Saxony and

[later] was a valet to Prince Poniatowski." (To make the switch from being an intimate of the Saxon kings of Poland to serving the new royal family in Poland, the Poniatowskis, certainly required some political agility on Saby's part or maybe just reflected his chameleon character, or his insignificance.) Bruchbach also had known Visconti for about two years. They had occasionally dined together in the city's inns and often spent evenings at Dreyer's coffeehouse. Bruchbach himself was a drifter, a broker living on commissions who had rented rooms in Hamburg during the previous four years.

Romellini made Warsaw her home from 1766 to 1769. In 1770, she was in Paris, where the Jewish surgeon Jacob Gonsalez Montesanto met her at the home of a friend, an Italian fellow dentist named Palermo, to whom she had come to have a tooth extracted, arriving "in a carriage like a lady, and [she called herself] the Baroness de Romellini." Soon afterwards, Montesanto left Paris and, after journeying first to England and then Holland, moved to Hamburg, where he discovered her again "among the Englishmen" who frequented Brown's establishment. Mrs. Brown told him that an Italian woman was residing with them. Would he come to tea, because she would welcome the opportunity to speak Italian with him? When he arrived, he failed to recognize her. She was thrilled to have someone who spoke her own language, and they conversed for a while quite happily, each equally unaware of their previous contact. Then, however, having taken a closer look at him as she moved her chair forward to pour tea, she placed him. Did he not perhaps remember "a certain lady de Romellini" whom he had seen at Palermo's in Paris? She revealed herself to be that woman. After this reacquaintance, he occasionally visited her as she moved from Brown's to Holtermann's and to Buhrbanck's, visits that "considering his age [he was seventy-two], no one could take amiss." He had no other relationship with her. He was neither her foster father nor "anything like it." The only other contact he had had with her was about a year previously, when she had written asking him to recommend a "good opportunity" for her in Amsterdam, because she might not be able to remain in Hamburg much longer.

The extensive testimony of the notary Heinrich Christian Georg Erdmann filled in other missing parts of her story. He had acted on her behalf on numerous occasions and in several capacities. Functioning as an intermediary in their tangled financial matters was perhaps the service he performed most frequently for Romellini and Visconti. He had, for example, brokered agreements with their creditors and had also drawn up the papers for the *mariage de conscience* the two had entered into. Around Easter 1774, Erdmann persuaded Visconti's creditors to accept 25–30 percent of what he actually owed. This agreement "delighted the count." While Erdmann was explaining the arrangements to the two, the oldest daughter of one of the Buhrbanck sisters entered the room and told them that while Romellini was out that morning, the swordsmith Gevers had come with two other persons and had vehemently demanded payment from Visconti for a hunting knife—a "stag killer"—that Gevers had forged for him. Visconti had denied all knowledge of the commission and categorically, indignantly refused to pay. Gevers had fallen into a rage, swearing to return and thrash "that so-called count." Frau Buhrbanck sent someone to inform the magistrate in an attempt to preserve the peace. None of this satisfied Gevers, who informed the neighbors that he would return that very afternoon and "no matter what it cost him" beat Visconti "to a pulp." Terrified by the threat, Romellini begged Erdmann's assistance. Visconti, however, "booted and spurred, and reclining aloofly on the chaise longue," told Erdmann that if the smith and his friends dared attack him, it would be easy to dispatch them with "un coup de Pistolett," although he hoped it would not come to that. Erdmann went to the praetor and procured from him the eighteenth-century equivalent of a restraining order.

Erdmann's services to Romellini and Visconti extended beyond managing their debts and staving off their creditors. Soon after the incident with Gevers, they summoned him again. Romellini wanted him to execute a power of attorney for Visconti so that he could go to Hanover to demand from Baron von Schwicheldt the 100 Reichsthaler owed her from the supposed sale of her diamonds. Erdmann prepared the document and had it notarized. At the same time, Visconti and Romellini revealed to him that "although they were legally husband and wife," they had no marriage certificate, which was inconvenient, especially for her. She worried that in her spouse's absence, she would suffer humiliating "accusations and indignities" that would undermine her position in society and subject her to unpleasantness, although she was "a born baroness de Romellini." Thus, *she* not Visconti (and here Erdmann's testimony differed from hers) had requested Erdmann to prepare a "statement or certification . . . in which the supposed count would swear on his word of honor and his conscience" that she was his lawfully wedded wife.

Both Visconti and Romellini employed legal forms to bolster their positions, assert their fictive names, and combat their enemies. In these endeavors, notaries and solicitors like Erdmann were essential. The case in Hanover produced—through compromise or blackmail—a tidy sum, which disappeared directly into Visconti's pockets. Romellini further requested Erdmann's assistance in trying to obtain compensation from "a certain count Matusky," who had, she maintained, taken some of her jewels and other possessions to pawn for her (the Schwicheldt situation all over again). Erdmann advised her not to press a civil suit against Count Matusky, because he was not subject to local jurisdiction. Soon after this, and perhaps referring to threats from Sanpelayo, she asked Erdmann "to find some protection for her." What she had in mind is unclear. Erdmann replied that she could rely on the Hamburg authorities to defend her. "That was no help," she insisted, breaking into tears, for the Spanish consul was "unbelievably jealous" and had, moreover, induced a "Prussian officer" (Kesslitz?) to accost her on the street and call her a "dissolute slut" to her face. He had harangued her with the most "astonishing obscenities." The consul himself threatened to denounce her to the authorities as a common whore and have her punished. Erdmann countered that, if innocent, she had nothing to fear. "Ach, you don't understand the Spanish," she replied. "If he doesn't kill me, he will publicly [accuse me of] prostitution."

In the opening months of 1775, she asked Erdmann to assist her in retrieving clothing she had pawned with a "Jew-woman." In April, she again solicited his services. Although she had recently borne a child to Sanpelayo, the relationship was rapidly falling apart. She was unable, she insisted, "to put up with him" any longer. He had the pox, and yet he still demanded that she lie with him. His jealousy had transformed him into "a real tyrant." Her life was hell: "She dare not so much as greet anyone [on the street], for [if she did] he swore to beat her with his cane and had even raised it to her. He accused her of illicit relations [with other men]. He gave her no money for housekeeping. That same strong Prussian officer [the one who had abused her verbally] . . . had even begged her pardon for insulting her on the consul's instigation. He [Sanpelayo] threatened to murder her."

She now forged plans to flee from Sanpelayo once and for all, even though the consul said that he would kill her if she tried, "or at the least have acid thrown on the axles of the coach so that she would break her neck" or have her arrested for theft. To prevent him from accusing her of stealing his possessions, she asked Erdmann to draw up an inventory that separated her property from his. Erdmann alone could do this, she maintained, because if Sanpelayo found any other man in the house, "he would drive him out with a stick." She then asked Erdmann to obtain a "magisterial attestation" stating that she had left no debts behind her in Hamburg. While Erdmann was writing out the inventory, she confided to him that the consul had taunted her, saying that her husband, "that so-called count," had been hanged in Venice. How, she beseeched him, could she be held responsible for this? She admitted that the Venetian authorities had arrested Visconti, but then his family ("the illustrious Viscontis") had interceded and had the sentence commuted to life imprisonment in a castle in Madrid. The only other commission she had entrusted to Erdmann was to write to the Edelsheim cloister to inquire how much it would cost to educate a young girl "in all female skills, but particularly in voice and music," for her daughter was, she insisted, learning nothing in Hamburg. Again she told Erdmann that although she still fully intended to leave Sanpelayo, she had to postpone the break until she could get away "with her honor intact."

One who should have known more about Romellini's intimate life was Maria Anna Engauen, the forty-year-old woman from Ritzebüttel who cooked for her. Sanpelayo had engaged Engauen for the house on the Neuer Wall. Despite her position in the household, she seems either to have been curiously uninformed or was reluctant to reveal what she knew about her employers (or perhaps her silence had been bought; see Chapter 6). Before taking the job, she had neither met nor heard of any of them. Romellini had introduced herself as a countess, but Engauen had no idea whether this was true or not. Moreover, she, "as a person of low estate," could not "concern herself with counts and the like." Before Engauen's arrival, the establishment had been set up on a rather more elaborate footing: in addition to a cook, there was a lady's maid. During her time with Romellini, however, Engauen had worked by herself. At first Sanpelayo came only once in a while, but then his visits became far more regular; he often stayed overnight as well. If Romellini was his "proper mistress," Engauen could not—or would not—say, but Romellini had "no special or extensive contact with any other gentlemen." Kesslitz had, however, called on Sanpelayo there and frequently eaten Sunday dinners together with the consul and Romellini. Other than Kesslitz and Sanpelayo, the only other man who entered the house was a person named "Brodtback" (Bruchbach), an acquaintance of the consul's who resided in the nearby Dammthorstraße. In short, as far as Engauen knew, only the fact that "she had so lived with Herr Sanpelayo" blotted Romellini's reputation.

Witnesses to Romellini's and Sanpelayo's cohabitation provided the raw material others used to construct a narrative of their lives and, ultimately, to judge them. We already know what the agents of foreign powers in Hamburg and at courts across Europe thought of Romellini: she was a *putain*—a whore—and a giddy female. The Hamburg magistracy shared those sentiments. In his "Historical Narrative," Sillem characterized the qualities of everyone enmeshed in the affair. Sillem reviewed the story Romellini had told about her parents—Saby and her unknown mother—and her supposedly noble descent. "Both of them, the sire as well as the dam, if the story is in any way factual, appear to be adventurers, or she is illegitimate." She had been the mistress of at least six men in Warsaw between 1766 and 1769, he reckoned. That she had sunk into prostitution he hardly doubted, although he had to admit that the documentation contained not "the least evidence of it." That is, nothing indicated that she had involved herself promiscuously with other men or was a common whore, although she did not conceal that the had lived with Sanpelayo "sometimes . . . in happiness, sometimes in discord." She spoke, he noted, "very freely" about her many erotic adventures "with some great men." Her actions were "thoughtless," her temperament "rash," and her habits "extravagant." In a letter she had written to Visconti from Hamburg, she spoke with great vehemence of an enemy (one Frei), who she felt had betrayed her. She wished to see him thoroughly trounced: "I am insane with malice and only await the day when I can revenge myself on him."[23] Still, Sillem doubted whether she could actually formulate or carry out such plans: "For she seems incapable of . . . anything that requires meticulous planning and well-thought-out execution."

The letter referred to here reveals much about Romellini and about her long-term relationship with Visconti, a relationship that had more warmth to it than her testimony otherwise indicated.[24] In the latter, she suggested that she had often tried to break with him, but unsuccessfully: he pursued her everywhere. The letter reveals rather different feelings for the man, although it is fully possible that she was drawn to him, feared him, and wished to be quit of him all at once. "Visconti *carissimo*," she began. She thanked him for the packet she had recently received from him and for the portrait he had included, "although it was almost completely ruined" when it arrived, because he had wrapped it carelessly. Still, she promised to have it repaired and assured him that "[it] pleased her . . . because it was so unexpected." The likeness was good, although he appeared "quite old" in it and the artist "lacked skill." Yet, nonetheless, the trinket made her fonder of him "than if you had given me the best present" possible. When she showed the image to her daughter, the little girl broke into tears and cried out for Visconti, her "Venetian papa." Romellini then ticked off a long catalog of woes: the child was not doing well in Hamburg, the air seemed bad for her, she had passed "an unbelievable number of worms," and Romellini feared that she would never reach maturity. The girl appended a postscript in her own, shaky handwriting, signing herself "your most obedient and loving daughter, Antonina Romellini." The document as a whole hardly portrays a woman who dreaded her correspondent or desperately wished to be rid of him. She solicited his advice, she asked favors of him (could he please send her the cards she desired?), she hoped "that his affairs prospered," and she prayed that God would "preserve him from further troubles." Finally, she closed: "I have now nothing else to say except to embrace you with love, and to call you from my heart, your true friend, Nina."

If terms of love and endearment characterized her thoughts for Visconti, the rest of the letter throbbed with other emotions entirely, producing the sentences that Sillem used in judging her rash, quick-tempered, and even violent. She was experiencing difficulties with "that scoundrel" von Frei. (I have not been able to identify him.) "I cannot tell you," she wrote "everything he said when I spoke of you." Frei had insulted her, called her "the most shameless" of women, fabricated and spread a "thousand infamous lies" about her: that she had had to flee Warsaw in the dark of night "with bag and baggage" and that she had shacked up with Visconti in a bordello. Frei insisted that the child, Antonia, was Visconti's, but "he cannot prove it." Even though all this was false, "my friend [Sanpelayo] is not a man who will listen to reason." Her tormentor was, fortunately, in Amsterdam at the time but awaited the money that "my friend" had promised him (to leave Hamburg and stop pestering Romellini?). "If I could get away from here," she continued, she would go to Amsterdam and there "take the greatest pleasure in beating him up and when he recovered from those first blows, I'd start all over again!" Not only the insults stung; Frei could do her real damage. Even a woman of Romellini's questionable past trembled at the thought of slander. Her value as a mistress to someone of Sanpelayo's stature depended, curiously enough, on her preserving a degree of respectability. Obviously, the façade signified. A "fancy woman" or a "*galante* lady" was a desirable mistress as long as public rumor did not brand her a common whore or associate her with gross venery. Romellini had attained considerable status in the world of courtesans as the mistress of the brother of the king of Poland and of other high nobles in Warsaw; these affiliations were real assets for her. However, her liaisons with Visconti, Barcker, and what may have been a series of less prestigious or even common lovers, such as Thonus, had diminished that capital. Thus, when Frei accused her of being a prostitute—having been in a brothel—that salacious bit of gossip, if spread in the wrong places, could have endangered her position with Sanpelayo, even if he had not been (as it seems he was) a jealous man.

The Many Lives of Anna Maria Romellini

Romellini existed in and on the edge of many worlds: the glitzy world of aristocratic privilege; the shadowy world of secret diplomacy; and the racy world of libertine Europe. She moved easily in all three milieus because they merged as thoroughly in real life as they did in eighteenth-century literature and imaginations.

Several people labeled Romellini "a *galante* lady" and "a great adventuress." The French word *galant(e)* only imperfectly approximates what we today understand as "gallant" and, in fact, in many ways denoted its opposite. In the eighteenth century, the term *galant(e)* overlapped with "libertine" and "amoral." It was found among those adjectives that described a certain kind of high life and a refined (perhaps overrefined) society that valued pleasure as a positive good and worried little about the rules of God or man. *Galant(e)* society was elegant and showy on the surface, fashionable, gay, polished, and courtierlike. Yet *galant(e)* equally pertained to sexual love and indicated a more questionable dedication to amorous or even lecherous pursuits. German usage rendered *galant(e)* as "good or well-balanced" or "in accordance with a good and discriminating way of life," but it also meant "being in love" physically. Throughout the eighteenth century only a hair-thin line divided *galant(e)* from libertine conduct. In its broader context, libertine society included and catered to those unrestrained by moral law. While libertines tended to be men, by the late eighteenth century, the word also applied to women and thus Romellini's character as "*ein galantes Frauenzimmer*"—a *galante* woman—situated her in a respectable if slightly "fast" high society, as well as in the dissolute world of libertinage.[25]

The word "libertine" possesses fewer ambiguities. Today we understand it much as the eighteenth century did, in terms of slack morals and lack of restraint, especially in the realm of sexuality. Libertinism has a complex pedigree, however, having first appeared in theological thought in the sixteenth century, when Calvin used it to denounce the Anabaptists; later, it referred to atheists. In the next century, libertinism comprised a school of thought roughly equivalent to free thinking and accepted by those opposed to dogma in all fields of study. These *libertins érudits* practiced skepticism. By the opening decades of the eighteenth century, the usual sense of "libertine" had shifted to mean both a dissolute lifestyle connected with sexuality and eroticism and an aristocratic way of life. Both were closely associated with the French monarchy beginning in the Regency of Philip d'Orleans and continuing well into the reign of Louis XV.[26]

Not all courts condoned or tolerated libertine styles or values. Maria-Theresa's court was pious and prudish. In his memoirs, Stanisław August found all the women there "virtuous" and not very warm to strangers; he suffered considerably from "boredom."[27] Frederick the Great, despite his deep appreciation for French culture and for art, music, and literature, kept a very masculine court. Few women had access to the inner circle at Potsdam, although Frederick had led a considerably freer life in his younger days as crown prince in Rheinsburg. Other courts, especially in Dresden, Warsaw, and Paris, were far more lively, or dissolute, depending on one's perspective.

Whereas the term and concept of "libertine" came, ultimately, from theology, *galant(e)* had closer links to belles lettres, and particularly to a form widely read in the early eighteenth century. Much *galant(e)* writing of the time approximated what we might today call escapist or light reading. The *galant(e)* literature that developed in late seventeenth-century France related the stories of the court and, especially, its scandals. Although few of these works count as first-class fiction (Madame de la Fayette's *La Princesse de Clèves* is one conspicuous exception), they were wildly popular. In early eighteenth-century Germany, the prolific scribbler Christian Friedrich Hunold, writing under the pen name Menantes, published many. His most celebrated novel, *Die liebenswürdige Adalie* (The Charming Adalie) first appeared in 1702 and subsequently went through numerous editions. *Adalie* is the romantic tale of a Frenchwoman who falls in love with a German prince, and he with her; she eventually becomes his wife (it was based on the true-life story of Duke Georg Wilhelm of Celle and Elénore d'Olbreuse). In such novels, romance and sex, chance encounters and contrived situations entwined to drive forward the (often otherwise weak) plots. Just as important, Hunold's novels, like those of many contemporaries, built on, then embellished, real histories. His biting roman à clef *Satryrischer Roman (Satirical Novel)*, which appeared in 1706, spread transparently fictionalized scandals about Hamburg personalities. The resulting uproar (and his unpaid debts) caused him to flee the city in some haste.[28]

Galante novels often drew their material directly from the scandal sheets, or from the half-real, half-fictitious memoirs of a series of scandalmongering courtiers. One of the most famous (and least reliable) of these was a German named Karl Ludwig von Pöllnitz. Pöllnitz's stories of the legendary sexual exploits of August the Strong, elector of Saxony and king of Poland, who, according to Pöllnitz sired as many as 300 illegitimate children, leave something to be desired as history, but they were a great read and shaped the picture many Europeans had of court life, especially Polish court life.[29] True stories of private affairs that focused on love and sexual intrigue counted among the most avidly consumed literary forms throughout the eighteenth century.[30] Even if the thirst for the *galante* novel abated by midcentury, the stories continued to circulate, and the audience for tales of amorous conspiracies and sexual thrills never waned.

The duc de Richelieu, after Jean-Marc Nattier.
Courtesy Wallace Collection, London.

Romellini's life crossed with three of the gayest, most *galante,* and most sensation-ridden courts of eighteenth-century Europe: Warsaw, Dresden, and Paris. Romellini knew two of the century's great libertines: Prince Poniatowski, the brother of the king of Poland, and *le maréchal libertin,* Louis François Armand de Vignerot du Plessis, duc de Richelieu.[31] Poniatowski surely bedded Romellini as she claimed. She certainly met that famous roué the duc de Richelieu. Contemporaries regarded Richelieu, the grand-nephew of the great cardinal, as "the professor of pleasure," "the prince of vice," and "*le Lovelace français*," in short, as the very embodiment of an eighteenth-century *galant*-libertine. His long life (1696–1788) spanned almost the entire century, reaching from the last years of the reign of Louis XIV into the twilight of the French monarchy. He was in his youth a charmer; as an adult, a don Juan; and, in his senescence, a debauched Sadean. He may well have inspired Pierre Choderlos de Laclos's vivid portrayal in *Les Liaisons dangereuses* of that most famous of dissolute beaux, Valmont. Richelieu was no mere hedonist ne'er-do-well; he was not merely a "prince of pleasure" but also an "excellent diplomat, a lucky general, a sensible provincial administrator, and friend of the arts and letters, and a patron of actors and dancers." As a soldier, he distinguished himself in the Wars of the Austrian Succession (he was named marshal of France in 1748) and in the Seven Years' War. Frederick the Great appreciated him in both roles, writing to him in 1757 in a vain attempt to make peace: "I am persuaded . . . that the Nephew of the great Cardinal . . . is made for signing treaties no less than gaining battles." Richelieu had served as ambassador to Vienna as quite a young man, from 1725 to 1728. He negotiated the marriage of the old dauphin to Maria-Josepha of Saxony, the mother of three future kings of France: Louis XVI, Louis XVIII, and Charles X. He was as relentless in the pursuit of pleasure as in the pursuit of power. "In short, he was an example of the perfect 'grand seigneur' of the eighteenth century with all that the term covered, both good and not-so-good."[32]

Equally fascinating was the kindredness of libertines such as Richelieu to the entire world of diplomacy that ranged from the ceremonial meetings of kings and ministers to the darker, danker corners of European affairs that spies and con men inhabited. A dense thicket of secret, semisecret, or amateur diplomacy paralleled or disrupted official actions. Talented schemers like Frederick the Great preferred to negotiate sub rosa, working, for example, in 1744 to renew the Franco-Prussian alliance without informing the official representatives.[33]

The best-known, most extensive, and longest-lived—if also perhaps the least well-conceived—of these unofficial ventures was the King's Secret constructed by Louis-François, prince de Conti (1717–76), and Louis XV in the 1740s. Few efforts in diplomacy were as covert, as muddled, or as ineffectual as the King's Secret, but it is hardly the sole example of diplomacy that proceeded outside of official channels or behind official backs. Its raison d'être was to place a Frenchman on the Polish throne. The recurring issue of the Polish succession more than once gave rise to international tensions. France's link to Poland had been established early; Henri III (then the duc d'Anjou) was king of Poland briefly in 1573–74; Louis XV's father-in-law, Stanisław Leszcyński, had also held the crown for a short time in the early eighteenth century. The King's Secret became active in 1745 "to promote the candidacy of the prince de Conti to the elective crown of Poland," and from the early 1740s until 1774 (when Louis XVI disbanded it), it ran a network of up to twenty-five spies in eastern Europe. Conti's grandfather (François-Louis de Bourbon) had also been elected king of Poland (1697), although he never mounted the throne, which August the Strong, elector of Saxony, had seized by force. In the 1760s, when some in France conspired to topple Stanisław August and replace him with a Saxon duke, Romellini's "Ninski" (Poniński) schemed to stir the pot. Romellini carried letters that linked the Polish rebels to Saxony and France. In two ways, then, Romellini moved in this diplomatic milieu. If she never exercised real influence, she nonetheless helped spin the webs that bound France to Poland, Poland to Saxony, and spies, libertines, and adventurers to crowned heads and government officials everywhere.[34]

Romellini's life, her years in Dresden and Warsaw, and especially her connections with various princes (shabby and not quite so), played out, therefore, against a backdrop of eastern European politics of great complexity and fluidity. One need only think of the tumult in Polish affairs—as the Saxons lost the throne and Russia's candidate, Stanisław August, gained it, only to see his realm relentlessly cut away in the three partitions that wiped Poland off the map of Europe for over 100 years—to grasp the immense transformations afoot. Poland was an integral cog in the political machinations of far more puissant countries: Prussia, Russia, and France. The years after 1756 were a period of decline and then rebuilding for another German power, Saxony, and that state, which had once rivaled Brandenburg-Prussia, no longer competed at the level of a major power. Changes were under way farther east and north as well. The Russian Empire was slowly assimilating the duchy of Courland (one of Saby's cronies, it will be recalled, was the duke of Courland, who may well also have been Romellini's lover), whose story in these years is as melodramatic, tragic, and intricate as Poland's. Competing dukes and their families were all buffeted about by the forces greater powers exerted. Courland and Poland both had Saxon pretenders, and the lines of power and connivance ran from Mitau and Warsaw to Dresden, St. Petersburg, Berlin, and Paris. This net caught up Romellini and her father. Thus, the wider European diplomatic framework determined the contours of Romellini's life, but she was hardly alone in feeling its pull. Europe swarmed with mobile, unattached, and sometimes desperate people who nonetheless moved in close proximity to the great and the powerful. They became foot soldiers in the diplomatic wars that toppled princes and shoved them from one side of the continent to the other.

Poland in the years Romellini lived there experienced a last fevered burst of brilliance just before it descended into the virtual civil war that led to the First Partition (1772). It was a key piece in the jigsaw puzzle that made up the *concert européen* created at the beginning of the century. Poland (or rather, the Commonwealth of Poland-Lithuania) was a gentry republic (*Rzeczpospolita*) in which the Diet played a crucial role, not least in selecting a ruler.[35] This system of elective kingship offered exquisite opportunities for internal chaos. Repeatedly, perhaps inevitably, Poland attracted the hardly benign interest of its increasingly powerful neighbors. The War of the Polish Succession broke out in 1733 after the death of Poland's king, the Saxon elector, August the Strong. He and his son, August III, held a position that was "in one country [Saxony] . . . hereditary and absolute, and in the other [Poland] elective and constitutional." Joint rulership meant that Poland's vulnerability stretched in two directions: internally, to endemic Polish bickering and externally, to European conflicts beginning in the Germanies. The War of the Polish Succession (1733– 35) pitted the Saxon candidate and his supporters against the popular Polish nobleman Stanisław Leszcyński, who had once been elected in 1704 but had never actually ruled. Leszcyński lost again and spent the rest of his life in Lorraine as its duke; his daughter married Louis XV. The reign of the new (Saxon) king, August III, proceeded for the most part more calmly, although near its end, factional conflict within Poland escalated. "Patriotic" reformers (a group that included the Czartoryskis, the extended family of Stanisław August) sought to establish a stronger administration and a more centralized form of government. Conservative republicans preferred the status quo and defended Polish liberties. When August died, just as the Seven Years' War was ending, one of the cadet members of the Poniatowski family, Stanisław August—"polished, pliant, [and] cosmopolitan," the one-time passionate lover of Catherine the Great while she was still a grand duchess—became king (and his brothers, princes). Russia, Prussia, and England successfully achieved his election.

Catherine's partiality for Stanisław August rested on shrewd political calculation. She deduced rapidly and accurately that Stanisław at the time of his election was neither particularly well liked in Poland nor strong enough to oppose her. Once crowned, he would be far more dependent on Russia than either a foreign candidate (a Saxon prince, for instance) or a

Pole who enjoyed a greater following among the nobility.[36] Stanisław August walked forward with eyes wide shut into this morass. A fervent reformer and an intelligent man, the new king set to work trying to change Poland, but the interests of larger powers, especially Russia, and his many enemies at home thwarted his plans. Stanisław August was not the most forceful of rulers, although he was also not, as Frederick the Great slightingly called him, merely a *roi de théâtre* or, as de Broglie viewed him, good only for seducing women. While Frederick could hardly resist the jab, historical and contemporary judgments range from regarding Stanisław as an outright traitor and a Russian hireling to believing him to be a talented and hard-working statesman, if flawed and none too clever, who accepted the political necessity of Russian influence and tried to work with it. Few deny his good education, his real appreciation of culture, his literary and linguistic talents, and his great personal charm. And although it is wise to avoid casting Poland in the role of inevitable victim and of overstating its political impotence, the task of maintaining Polish independence was enormous; and Stanisław August was no political miracle worker.

After 1763, several states had designs on Poland. The Prussians, Russians, and Austrians viewed Poland as a tasty morsel to be gobbled up. France's interest predominantly focused on using Poland to frustrate the aspirations of those countries that eyed Polish territory most rapaciously. Moreover, for France, Polish affairs after the Seven Years' War became deeply entangled with ways to revenge itself on England by reducing Prussia's influence on its eastern frontier. For others, such as Saxony, but also for France, the repeatedly empty Polish throne beckoned cadet princes. By 1795, three partitions had effectively wiped Poland off the face of Europe. Stanisław August had, Casanova remarked, outlived his country.[37]

The competition for the throne of Poland in the period following the Seven Years' War played out in exceedingly complex variations, however, and thus begot an equally complex diplomacy. When August III died in 1763, for instance, his oldest son became elector of Saxony, but not king of Poland. The Prussians and Russians opposed his nomination, and Louis XV dithered, unable to chose between two Saxon candidates: Karl Christian Joseph (August III's third son and erstwhile duke of Courland; this was almost certainly not, however, the duke of Courland Romellini knew in Italy) or his younger brother, Xavier. After months of wavering, Louis finally decided in favor of Xavier, but that support meant little in the face of the overwhelming Russian preference for Stanisław August and the more important presence of Russian troops at the Diet that elected Catherine's favorite.[38]

If this were not labyrinthine enough, the Polish-Saxon question and that of Courland were stacked like dominoes. The same Karl of Saxony who became one of the candidates for the Polish throne in 1763–64 had been duke of Courland since 1758. The previous duke, Ernst Johann Biron, had been deposed in 1740. For almost two decades (1740–58), Courland existed as a dukeless Russian satellite. The Saxon-Polish-Russian connections ran deeper, however. In 1733, when August II of Poland and his designated successor, August III, needed the help of Russia to frustrate the ambitions of Stanisław Leszcyński, they turned to Biron, then the influential favorite of Tsarina Anna. The two Augusts promised Biron that if he weighed in on their side in the 1733 election, they would recognize him as duke of Courland, and thus he became duke in 1736. In 1740, he was deposed and exiled to Siberia for twenty years (although he made a stunning comeback in 1763). One of the other contenders for duke at the time was Moritz of Saxony, an older brother of Karl.[39] It was Karl Ernst, baron von Treyden, Biron's son, who befriended Saby and Prince Poniatowski and who went with them to Venice, where they all met Romellini. Thus the

---

Kings of Poland, 1506–1795

Sigismund I	1506–1548
Sigismund II	1548–1572
Henry of Valois	1573–1574
[Henry III, king of France,	1574–1589]
Stephen Bathory	1575–1586
Sigismund III	1587–1632
Wladisław IV	1632–1648
John II Casimir	1648–1668
Michael Wisniowecki	1669–1673
John III (Sobieski)	1674–1696
Stanisław I Leszcyński	1704–1709, 1733–1735
[Duke of Lorraine,	1735–1766]
August II (Saxony)	1697–1733
[Friedrich August I, elector of Saxony,	1694–1733]
August III	1733–1763
[Friedrich August II, elector of Saxony,	1733–1763]
Stanisław August (Poniatowski)	1764–1795

Note: Brackets indicate other titles—for example, King August II of Poland was simultaneously Friedrich Augustus I, elector of Saxony.

---

life and the loves of Anna Maria Romellini replicated *en petit* the Saxony-Courland-Poland diplomatic nexus.

In the late 1760s, Romellini was in Warsaw, the crossroads of this eastern European diplomacy. It was a time of turmoil, with civil war and foreign intervention the order of the day. The opponents of Stanisław August belonged to one of several confederations, that of Bar being the most important.[40] Romellini's lover Poniński, although something of a will-o'-the wisp in his political affiliations, became deeply involved, and it was on his behalf that Romellini acted as courier. Despite political upheaval, Warsaw remained one of the most elegant, expensive, and refined cities of Europe. Casanova, who was there in late 1765, found it "brilliant."[41] "Warsaw," it was said, "danced to an endless succession of aristocratic balls, where all that mattered was the size of one's partner's latifundia." The arts flourished under August III and Stanisław August. But beauty masked corruption. During the reign of the last king of Poland, self-serving nobles like Adam Poniński (described, admittedly by an enemy, as "a man whose self-interest was matched only by his delusions of grandeur" and one of "those creatures who are born and mature only in the sewers of revolution") schemed to benefit themselves. This Poniński (possibly a distant relative of Romellini's "Ninski"?) served as Catherine's henchman in engineering the partition of 1772–73. As Stanisław August became increasingly unable to do much to stop the downward spiral of events, his private life filled up with "innumerable mistresses." He rarely passed up a pretty face or a gracefully turned ankle. He married only late (1783) and then morganatically. His amours were legendary. His affections ranged from the wives of residents and ambassadors, "la marquise Lucchesini," and "la baronne Schitter" to a Miss Harriet (a young protégée of the English ambassador) and a whole series of others whose names are known to us from a secret register in which he recorded the presents or pensions he gave them. Some lived temporarily in the castle, some were set up in houses in Warsaw, and almost all received some tangible token of their sovereign's affection in the form of clothing or jewels. Stanisław's brothers broke almost as many lances on the field of love as he, and between them, they sired a number of illegitimate children. There is, therefore, every reason to accept Romellini's claim to have been the mistress of "the brother of the king of Poland."[42]

By all accounts, in the years Romellini lived there, Warsaw offered a dazzling array of delights for anyone who possessed some pertinent combination of authority, money, beauty, and good birth. It was not necessary to possess them all. Was it any surprise that this bright candle lured many moths to its flame? Warsaw in the 1760s and 1770s was home to many adventurers, among them Casanova and the Italian charlatan Cagliostro, who flocked to the Polish capital seeking fame, fortune, or just a good time living high off the largesse of friends, admirers, and dupes. Casanova turned up in 1765, when Romellini must have just been getting her start as a *fille de joie*. Saby and his mysterious wife were two more nomads drawn inexorably to Warsaw. Warsaw and Dresden formed the staging ground for some of the greatest imposters of the day, including Stiépan Zannovitch, or Annibale, the famous (or infamous) false prince of Albania.[43]

Because of the personal connections between Saxony and Poland during the first half of the century, the court moved freely between the two places, which had much in common. Under the Wettin electors of Saxony, Dresden had become one of the most magnificent cities in Europe, a center of art, music, literature, and architecture, all revolving around the electoral court. It was "the pleasure center of Germany," and its spectacles differed little from those of Paris. Herder referred to it as a "German Florence," by which he indicated not only the efflorescence of culture but also the pronounced Italian influence. Dresden showed "a thoroughly un-German stamp. . . . [It was a place where] the daughters of the elector wrote Italian and French poetry," making it a congenial home for other Italians as well.[44]

Things changed, however, at midcentury. In August 1756, the Prussians attacked neutral Saxony at the outset of the Seven Years' War. Within days they had occupied Dresden, but they lost it to the Austrians seventy-two hours later. As they marched out, the Prussians torched two suburbs, and two years later, they bombarded the old city center. According to an eyewitness, "Dresden is no longer completely intact . . . its best and most beautiful [buildings] lie in ashes. . . . The richest inhabitants are impoverished and what the [bombardment] left to them, thieves did not." The population shrank from about 63,000 before the war to about 40,000 at its conclusion. After the Seven Years' War and until the end of the Napoleonic period, Dresden possessed only a shadow of its former elegance, and the war damage was only slowly repaired. Though the death of August III snapped the human link, the political ties binding Saxony to Poland and vice versa did not instantly dissolve. The intense diplomatic maneuvering that typified French-Polish relationships centered in Dresden, at least until the death of Louis XV in 1774.[45]

In capitals like Warsaw and Dresden, diplomacy intersected with sex, and power on the throne with power in the boudoir. Being a ruler and keeping mistresses is hardly solely a Polish, Saxon, or exclusively eighteenth-century phenomenon, but in the eighteenth century, the sense that

View of Dresden from the right bank of the Elbe.
Courtesy Staatliche Kunstsammlungen, Dresden.

power and sexuality, great diplomatic affairs and bedroom politicking, were inextricably interlocked, was a dominant political mentality and shaped a whole political discourse. The closing decades of the ancien régime bred a welter of agents and missions that blurred the political and the sexual to an extent that one could hardly tell them apart. One need think only of the powerful mistresses of Louis XV, the influential Madame de Pompadour, for example, who could make and break ministers, to comprehend the disgust with which many in the eighteenth century regarded the "monstrous regiment of women." Even if their real power was less than perceived or feared, perceptions counted.[46] (And perhaps sexuality rather than femaleness was critical. Although there were more mistresses than male favorites, the latter also evoked great jealously, hatred, and inflated apprehensions of their influence, and they almost always wielded far more real power than any woman.)[47] The fertile worlds of libertinage, diplomacy (secret and overt), and *galanterie* cultivated strange flowers like Monsieur d'Eon, a member of the King's Secret and a cross-dressing man, as well as many less exotic blooms such as Anna Maria Romellini. Cross-dressing women or women who occasionally dressed as men were commoner and less troubling than one might think. Indeed, when visiting her lovers, including Stanisław August, Catherine the Great often donned breeches. The story of d'Eon became so well known as to be eponymous. A local Silesian paper reported in 1786 on one Susanna Urban, a woman who clothed herself as a man, as the appearance of the "Chevalier d'Eon" in Silesia.[48]

Poor girls of low or suspect birth often traveled the road from singer and dancer to bedmate of nobility, sometimes with *succès fou*. Few achievements startled contemporaries as much as the real-life, rags-to-riches surge of Eléonore Desmier d'Olbreuse (1638–1725) who eventually became the duchess of Lüneburg-Celle by marrying the duke, albeit after passing through the stage of official mistress. Her origins were not entirely base, however; she was the daughter of a minor provincial nobleman from Poitou. Mincke Encke (1753–1820), known as "Madame Rietz," first met her royal lover, the future Friedrich Wilhelm II of Prussia, when he visited the Polish Count Matuschka in Potsdam. The then twelve-year-old Wilhelmine Encke lived with her sister, an opera extra and the count's mistress. Her parents, both musicians, were certainly complicit in the arrangement. Wilhelmine soon became the heir's companion and finally went on to enjoy the title of countess von Lichtenau. The assertive Madame du Barry, the mistress of Louis XV, was born Jeanne Bécu in poor circumstances, first earning her living as a hairdresser and salesgirl, then moving into a bordello catering to the aristocracy. Jean du Barry, a client of the powerful minister Choiseul, choreographed her rise. He married her off to his obliging brother, thus acquiring for her the necessary noble imprimatur to allow her presentation at court. There the two brothers managed, by bribing the comtesse de Béarn, to bring her literally under the eyes of Louis XV. The rest is history.[49]

Even Friedrich Wilhelm's dour old uncle, Frederick the Great, had in his younger years been beguiled by a charming dancer, known as "La Barbarina." Barbara Campanini had appeared on stage in Venice, Paris, and London when Frederick, by a combination of coercion and bribery, brought her to Berlin to dance at the Opera, where she received a huge salary. She soon became "the talk of Berlin and the accredited mistress of the sovereign." A famous picture of her, painted by Antoine Pesne, hung in his office (and a comedy published almost a century after her death made her its heroine). Besides Frederick, she had many admirers: Count Rothenburg, Count Algarotti, and other foreign noblemen—French, Italian, Russian, and Polish. One of her paladins was Carl Ludwig von Coccejii, son of Frederick's famous chancellor Samuel von Coccejii. His attentions landed him in Spandau prison. In 1751, after his release he secretly married Barbarina. The marriage had no happy ending, however. It endured only a decade before the two separated; they divorced in 1789. Barbarina in the meantime had become Countess Campanini and purchased three Silesian estates; she died a wealthy, respected woman in 1799.[50]

Romellini, like Barbarina and many others who began their rise from the footlights, combined two types: courtesan and actress. The courtesan was a product of the late Renaissance. At the end of the fifteenth century, "authorities in Dijon, Venice, Florence, and elsewhere railed against the appearance of a better sort of prostitute"—the courtesan—a more refined, more talented, and more presentable prostitute than an ordinary whore.[51] In the eighteenth century, as the secularization of morals gained speed, the figure of the "virtuous courtesan" (a variant of the honest whore of British literature) began to appear in novels.

As a courtesan, Romellini hardly attained the stature of Ninon de Lenclos (1620–1705), the educated and witty friend and inspiration to men of literary genius, nor did she qualify as one of the principled courtesans French literature imagined or, for that matter, as one of the "saved" courtesans modernized from biblical tradition.[52] If she was no muse, Romellini was also not a women of the "stews." Rather, she resembled the youthful actresses (or dancers and singers) whose ties to the theater pulled them into a demimonde of illicit sexuality. Erotic magnetism, but also nubile vulnerability, characterized them all. Their successes on stage and with the public virtually demanded their prostitution. Casanova admitted that if one of them "tried to live virtuously, she would die of starvation." Toward the end of the eighteenth century, as the once-strong prejudice against actresses as people without honor (and thus inadmissible in respectable society) began to break down, they became even more useful as objects of erotic desire for princes, officers, and wealthy bourgeoisie (or their sons). Kathryn Norbert, in examining Parisian police records from the 1750s, found that "[t]he typical Parisian courtesan was an adolescent opera dancer," a description that fits the young Romellini, as it fits Mincke Encke's sister and thousands of others, to a t. Like dancers in Paris, Romellini, too, found that her lovers and keepers rarely offered her money, but were far more willing to provide lodgings, clothes, furniture, and expensive trinkets, such as jewels.[53]

Barbarina's progress from dancer on stage to wealthy countess marked a noteworthy accomplishment, but other women made similar or ever greater jumps in the eighteenth century. Obviously, one could go on almost indefinitely relating the stories of dancers who made good, actresses who left behind their greasepaint and scandalous reputation for a respectable life, and women of bourgeois or lower origin who ended up the mistresses of kings, wielding the scepter from behind the throne. The eighteenth century had no monopoly on such phenomena, although it may have democratized the type. For whatever reason—the increasing wealth of the bourgeoisie and their wish to attain nobility, which was slowly obliterating many of the older differences between blue blood and commoner; greater social mobility overall; more expansive roles for women (women came into their own as actress and dancers on the respectable stage in the eighteenth century); more populous and thus more anonymous cities; a new emphasis on pleasure and the pursuit of pleasure as positive goods—the opportunities open to female adventurers and "*galante* ladies" multiplied.[54]

Clearly, no young girl of Romellini's background in the 1750s when she first began her career on stage thought purposefully of using that position as a springboard to wealth and power or plotted out a careful progression of steps leading from dancer to mistress to courtesan or higher. Nonetheless, the paths existed and many women followed where they led. Some scaled the heights and stayed there; others, like Romellini, slipped from bed to bed, passing from nestling with near-royalty through the caresses of a series of noble lovers before coming to rest on the humbler chests of men like Sanpelayo and Visconti. Elaborate planning and foresight surely existed but perhaps more among the parents, relatives, and brokers of the most successful courtesans and social climbers, at least in the initial stages of their careers. Saby was one of these sexual impresarios. These avenues grew ever broader and more beckoning, and many women (and men as well) were launched on similar trajectories. Women, moreover, now formed an integral part of the world of pleasure and not only in the obviously physical sense of sex. Beautifully attired and coifed, they ornamented the stylish world. Endowed with wit and talent, they became the salon women who nurtured the Republic of Letters. They were just as obvious and just as necessary elsewhere: strolling on city promenades, lounging in pleasure gardens, applauding fireworks, listening to concerts, filling boxes at plays, operas, and comedies, adorning carriages while taking the air in parks, and serving at country picnics. Sociability (even for women) rapidly migrated from homes to the streets after midcentury. In the beau monde, all played roles, but each role had multiple shapes and meanings. Some actors and actresses became divas, others—like Romellini—remained understudies and extras.

Romellini and her sisters were seductive adornments. Da Fonseca noted in his statement that Romellini had become well known in the city in the company of Sanpelayo at plays, parties, and other entertainments. The French teacher who remembered her from Warsaw in the later 1760s, when she called herself Madame Duchène, reported to the Hamburg magistracy that she "had always lived well" as the mistress "of various distin-guished men." She, or someone like her, was to all her fanciers as indis-pensable to their gallantry as their finely tempered swords, flashy clothes, dressed hair, fiery horses, luxurious coaches, and expensive perfumes. In the fast society of Stanisław August's Warsaw, a man of fashion seemed naked without a mistress or at least the appearance of having one.

A Courtesan in Hamburg

If the *galante* world of the court and of aristocratic society in Warsaw and Paris basked happily in, and even flaunted, an aura of libertinism, gaiety, and culture (be it ever so shallow), how then did the good citizens of Hamburg regard the lifestyles of the many not-so-rich and possibly in-famous who flocked to their city? As we have already seen in discussing their attitudes toward the nobility as a whole, feelings about the fast-living dandies of Warsaw and Dresden are not simple to analyze. One might expect disdain and even contempt; and those sentiments existed. Still, it is facile and wrong to imagine that all Hamburg burghers were stodgy sorts, easily offended by, and scornful of, the fleshy pleasures and carnal sins such fluffy packages as Romellini or distasteful adventurers as Visconti embodied. Disapproving rhetoric sounded everywhere but should not be taken for representing more than it did. Merchants could share with no-blemen considerable distaste for Sanpelayo's "scandalous behavior," al-though a goodly part of their revulsion arose from his self-destructive besottedness. The story is complex, as are the sensibilities, and to tell it properly we must be willing to accept that not everything can be wrapped up neatly, for contradictions of thought, word, and action were structured by what Kant called the "crooked timber of humanity."[55]

Sillem told van der Lepe that Romellini was nothing more than a "bold libertine" who had "passed through several hands." Moreover, he argued that customs differed in Germany (and in Hamburg) from Spain, because the laws of Germany were "more severe in regard to libertinage than those of other countries."[56] Here again the dissonance of appearance and reality confronts us. Hamburg was a worldly city, and its citizens and magistrates were fully conversant with the customs and practices, including the sexual customs and practices, of most European states. While no doubt exists that they all accepted, at least rhetorically, that morals needed to be purer in republics like Hamburg than in monarchies, little under the sun shocked them. Anyone sitting in the Senat had grown used to dealing with a range of distasteful, even horrible, crimes: dismemberment murders, sexual per-versions, bestiality, homosexuality, rape, and incest. Members of the Senat, moreover, rotated through a series of offices that made them conversant with a large catalog of human foibles and miseries. They were themselves, of course, not all paragons of republican and civic virtue. Far from all of them lived regular and respectable lives, and not all condemned the imperfections of others out of hand. Many had spent several years outside Hamburg, in merchant branches in Spain, France, Poland, and Russia, or at universities hardly famed for their puritanical restraint. Yet the rhetoric of "purer morals" remained politically and diplomatically expedient, especially in dealing with monarchies.

Hamburg was, moreover, a Lutheran stronghold. Its clergy continued to defend orthodoxy throughout the eighteenth century, although once-small cracks in the bulwark of strict Lutheranism gaped by the 1770s. Still, if the strictures of religion and traditional morality were loosening, two movements combined to reinforce the call for hardier forms of civic virtue and morality in Hamburg (and in other republics like Hamburg) than elsewhere. One thread was the Enlightenment; the other was the disapproval (enlightened and traditional alike) of foreignness, luxury, and courtly values. Both proselytized for a return to republican virtues to preserve (or restore) older habits of modesty, sobriety, and hard work. One way to do this was to condemn the scandalous lives of the nobility as inherently anti- or counterrepublican. "Republican" frequently functioned only as a code word for traditional morality, yet its use was not merely rhetorical. While many attacks on "new values" (which always meant "poorer values") were platitudinous and repetitive, they and the rhetoric that expressed them nonetheless played a role in the strategies magistrates and a wider public used to understand and denounce Romellini and the *galante* world she, Visconti, and Sanpelayo inhabited. "Purer values" like "republican virtues" could be flung down as trump cards in diplomatic clashes with other states. And, while the demimonde repelled many, it fascinated others. Some gawked and some deplored what they saw, while others participated in that world and relished it. Clearly, men like Pini, da Fonseca, Marechall, Erdmann, and the rest of Romellini's intimate little circle hardly wished to sacrifice their respectability. Yet they saw little harm, and perhaps a good deal of allure, in brief and essentially meaningless encounters with it. It was all a bit risqué, but not too much so. They did not want to sink down to Romellini's or Visconti's level, but they enjoyed what they could of it, fleetingly or vicariously, while always keeping enough of a distance to be warmed by the glow but not singed by the flame.

Nonetheless, traditional morality and the ideals of the Enlightenment combined to censure the morally loose lives of a Romellini, a Visconti, a

Sanpelayo, and even a Kesslitz, if for different reasons. The German Prot-estant Enlightenment never shed its religious coloration, and the morality it preached, while more forgiving of lapses engendered by poverty or the human frailties all people shared, often looked very much like what the godly approved.[57] The enlightened press of the early and middle decades of the century deployed a rhetoric hostile to court life, but that also casti-gated a bent toward luxury that undercut good republican values. These reformers insisted on recovering older virtues, creating a less frivolous and more didactic literature, and educating women as mothers and compan-ions to their husbands. Romellini's *galante* life, Sanpelayo's concupiscence, and Visconti's falseness all ran counter to *both* enlightened and traditional beliefs.

While we must not forget that the early Enlightenment was probably more moral and Christian than its later manifestations, a glance at Ham-burg's most famous moral weekly, *Der Patriot*, written by a group of self-identified enlightened thinkers from a variety of walks of life, helps us understand these attitudes. All were, of course, men; many came from mercantile backgrounds, many were trained in law or in theology, some were academics, and some served at the highest ranks of Hamburg's gov-ernment as senators. *Der Patriot*, published from 1724 to 1726, attracted a broad readership. Some 5,000 copies were printed and sold. A later group, the Patriotic Society of 1765, built ideologically and generationally on the earlier exemplar, but shifted its purpose toward gradual social betterment through institutional improvements. Thus one can speak of a tradition of republican patriotism spanning the century in Hamburg. Patriotism rep-resented engaged civic duty, a "civil-republican . . . identity and a sense of social responsibility."[58] A caveat should be inserted here. Republicanism in Hamburg was never a well articulated or thoroughly thought-out political program; it had next-to-nothing to do with the republicanism of, for example, the French Revolution. Still, republicanism was the identity Hamburgers adopted. It meant something vaguely like "those good old time-tested values" that characterized Hamburg's political culture as it had developed since the Reformation. Thus, as *Der Patriot* described the su-perficiality and hypocrisy of court life, it praised the civic virtues that pertained—or should pertain—in a republic like Hamburg. What, then, was the role of women to be in such a republic?

The enlightened version of female education, as it developed in the second half of the century, argued, unoriginally, that women were des-tined "for the household life of motherhood, wifehood, love, nurturance, and frugality."[59] Earlier, *Der Patriot*, as well as other moral weeklies, such as Johann Christoph Gottsched's *Der Biedermann* (The Upright Man), attacked the "courtly *galant*," frenchified ideal of female education. The physical allure of a woman bestowed only "the worthy shell on a far more beautiful disposition." Her virtues included innocence, naturalness, a good temperament, pleasant demeanor, and chastity. She should possess the character of "a rational friend."[60] Over the course of several issues, *Der Patriot* developed a picture of the model woman who embodied these female virtues perfectly. Her education required careful planning. Here one found the obligatory religious instruction (but not of a narrow or bigoted type) yet also a significant dose of practical knowledge, including all the attributes of being a good housekeeper, as well as an intelligent conversationalist and a well-read person. These ideals differed not all that much from the merits of the old-fashioned matron (*Hausmutter*) as the economic and familial counterpart of the prudent husbandman, or of its version in the mercantile republics, the merchant-trader. Such publications described the well-educated republican woman as modest in her appetites. Her preceptors taught her to avoid everything that smacked of opulence and voluptuousness. Her existence, however, was as substantial— or as ephemeral—as that of the "honest burgher," himself as much myth as reality.

A later article, censuring the dissolute life of students in "scenes from a comedy," addresses the perils of female lust. The protagonist is Prodigo (a student and a fop) who, although of bourgeois origins, apes the nobility: he wears a wig, drinks, duels, plays games of chance, chases women, and squanders money. In one episode, the "galantes Frauenzimmer," Amanda (the daughter of his landlady), enters his room and informs him that a jeweler is downstairs trying to sell her some pearls. She coyly "asks his advice." She would like the pearls, but they are expensive. He suggests that he might "contribute something," a sum of fifty Reichsthaler. She hurries away to pay the gem dealer, but before she leaves, Prodigo says:

> *Prodigo:* Just a little word [before you go]. May I request the pleasure of your company this afternoon?
> *Amanda:* As soon as Mama takes her afternoon nap, I shall be entirely at your disposal. Until then!

A seduction has taken place, with both the profligate youth and the shallow young woman happy to pay up. Is it hard to see Romellini doing likewise?[61]

What turned silly girls into licentious women was lack of a proper education—or perhaps an improper one?—as well as yielding to passion. One of the sharpest satires that appeared in *Der Patriot* embodied female prurience in a woman named Geilemine (which might perhaps be translated as "Hot-Pants"). The picture is that of a flighty woman, whose lasciviousness has combined with superficial, or even hypocritical, piety to produce a monster. It portrays a woman who has deliberately sold her body and her beauty. This "harlot's progress" could serve, if not in all its aspects, as scenes from the life of Romellini. "Geilemine had inherited in her youth more beauty than estate. As she grew up, she had her admirers. The presents they lavished on her fed her love of the male sex. She chose the richest and most generous of them and let him pay much for the pleasure of an illicit union [with her]. Later she sold herself more cheaply, and finally she sank so low through her licentious behavior that she offered herself to all comers in the most disreputable houses."[62]

When it came to women's sexuality, most scholars have argued that the eighteenth century believed that both men and women had "a strong, natural, God-given sexual drive" and that, in fact, sexual activity was a medical necessity to preserve health. It could no more be denied without penalty than the need to eat, sleep, or excrete. A woman achieved sexual gratification, however, only by "subordinating herself completely to her husband's sexual wishes."[63] Thus, a Romellini was not so much a sexual predator as a victim of her own inability to regulate her appetites. That lack of control derived principally from her poor upbringing, but it was also her biological destiny as a child of rogues. If enlightened belief and rhetoric could—on occasion—excuse the woman as a victim, the language of the men who judged Romellini shows little sympathy for her fallibility. A much harsher picture emerges, one closer to an older vision of a "sinful woman," as well as a frivolous, almost feeble-minded one who fell prey to her desires.

Obviously, such models were just that, models, and the various moral weeklies and their successors formulated prescriptions not descriptions. They must not be read as evidence of the existence of real persons. Moreover, while the moralists of the second half of the century might continue to wring their hands over "declining morals" and "burgeoning luxury," the compromise in favor of luxury, human pleasure, and happiness in this world had long been made. In 1702, Christian Wolff wrote that society's purpose lay in encouraging the common good and promoting the welfare —that is, the felicity—of the population, its groups, and its individual members. "After Wolff, most cameralists simply assumed that (especially material) happiness was the main purpose of the state/society."[64] Still, the very real triumph of a pleasure ethic neither dissolved morality entirely nor stopped the mouths of enlightened critics; they continued to attack extravagant lifestyles and loose living. Discussions about luxury compared the fashionable women of the mid to late eighteenth century unfavorably to their more traditionally inclined republican "mothers"; it mattered little to the rhetoric whether one or the other actually ever breathed. Critics castigated a love of fancy clothes as foreign and dangerous to the maintenance of true prosperity and corrosive of republican freedom. Battles over proper dress, the issue of servants, and even the curling of hair all reflected the ability of such debates to agitate the public mind. Of course, a good deal of this was platitudinous, but it could still be used, and used effectively, to register disapproval.[65] It was, moreover, a rhetoric hardly unique to Hamburg. Other cities, for example, Amsterdam, nourished similar debates tying love of luxury and the cultivation of foreign tastes to economic decline. And the same criticisms, if perhaps not as sharply, could be found in monarchies and territorial states. None of that, of course, prevented Hamburg's magistrates from using the rhetorical tool of a "better morality necessary for republics" at home and abroad. Thus, the condemnation of Romellini fits as neatly into larger political and diplomatic strategies as it did into a moral discourse.

Afterwards

Like so many of history's bit players, Romellini exits the historical stage quickly, although not without some final lines. By the time Kesslitz left Hamburg in July 1776, Romellini had already gone. In May, the magistrates had disposed of her as follows: "because of her dissolute lifestyle, whereby she at the very least gave the first impetus to the fight with the so-called Visconti, [and that resulted in] his death . . . [she] is to be banished from the city and its territories, with the warning that, if she ever returns, she will be immediately arrested. She is also told that she must take her daughter with her." They simultaneously informed Sanpelayo of this decision "so that he would have the opportunity" to make private arrangements with Romellini. Clearly, the Senat expected him to provide for her and her daughter in some way.[66]

After the decision of 24 May, Romellini tarried a while in the city, asking for a week's grace (until 1 June), because "she was afflicted with fever." The Senat granted her request, but by the middle of June she had departed. Very soon afterwards, she began a campaign of letter writing, bombarding the Senat with petitions, posted first from Altona, then from the Hague, and finally from Rotterdam.[67] Toward the end of July, while still in Altona, she beseeched Sillem to force Sanpelayo "to settle up with her." She dispatched the same plea to Binder von Kriegelstein and, trying a different channel, to the countess von Bentinck. Binder von Kriegelstein communicated a copy of her letter to his superior in Vienna, Foreign Minister Rudolf Joseph, count von Colloredo,[68] noting, "Of course, I won't respond." The reaction of the Senat was virtually identical: "to let it lie unanswered." Still in Altona, she renewed her supplications twice in August. On the 14th, she explained that her penniless state confined her to Altona. Her repeated requests to Sanpelayo for assistance had produced absolutely nothing, not even an expression of sympathy. Bad enough was that he ignored her rightful claims; worse was that he had caused anonymous intimidating letters to be sent to her. She asked the Senat to appoint a commission to wrap up the affair, without, however, requiring her to go to court, which she could not afford. Her pleas fell on deaf ears.[69]

Romellini's letters had dynamite in them. She boldly took the offensive, refusing to be quiet about how Sanpelayo and others had taken advantage of her. She suggested that the story of Visconti's death differed from the one she had originally told, and that Sanpelayo's involvement had been of a far more criminal nature. She began by pointing out that she had really wanted to get away from Sanpelayo for over a year before the events of mid October and would have done so "if I had been allowed to exercise my free will." Sanpelayo had done everything possible to prevent her. Her youth—she was "still not yet twenty-four"—and the frailty of her sex had sapped her will and made her susceptible to his blandishments and threats. He had employed underhanded methods to attach her more tightly to him. He had even used her daughter against her. "It was not unknown to him that some time before making his acquaintance I had borne a daughter to a very high gentleman": Poniatowski. She loved that child "most dearly." By agreeing to provide for the girl's future, Sanpelayo manipulated her maternal feelings, binding her ever more firmly to him. When they first met, the child was "well cared for in Venice," but Sanpelayo insisted that she be brought to Hamburg. He told Romellini that "it did not matter to him in the least whose child it was, as long as I was its mother." Thus, Sanpelayo arranged for the girl to come to Hamburg, and, according to Romellini, "we would probably still be together now, if the tragedy with the unhappy Visconti had not occurred."[70]

She had avoided unnecessary expenses while living with Sanpelayo, although "many want to say that I was very extravagant." Everything he had done for her, she argued (probably honestly), "he did freely." Occasionally, he gave her fifty or more ducats, but that was quickly consumed when he brought friends with him to dinner "the very next day . . . and entertained them lavishly." Thus the money vanished again almost instantly. Even the sums she had received from Hanover twice in the last year, about 778 Reichsthaler, he had frittered away on his amusements, and "I saw nothing more of them." The consul placated her, saying "Nina! My property and your property are one and the same!"

While she was under house arrest, he had reassured her that he would never abandon her "but would share his goods and blood with her equally," a promise he had repeated whenever he visited. In fact, he betrayed her. He had not only removed from her lodgings all her household items "but also, and especially, silver worth about 300 Reichsthaler that he had given me as a present when I was lying-in [with his child]." He swore to restore everything to her later, explaining that unless he took these things into his custody, the magistracy would seize them to offset the costs of her maintenance. He had spirited her daughter away to a cloister in Hildesheim. (It is not clear that the child actually went; if she did, she returned and left Hamburg later with her mother.) Moreover, Sanpelayo had assured her orally, in writing, and "in the presence of several people of high rank [in the city]," that once she was freed, he would give her 1,000 Reichsthaler to set her up again. Not only Sanpelayo had extended such guarantees. Both Kesslitz and Detenhof had offered exactly the same thing. Upon his release from the Eimbeck'sches Haus, Kesslitz had confided "that he actually had the money in his hands," but because it was in silver, he needed to exchange it for gold ducats. He named the very hour when this was to take place and gave her "his word of honor" in writing. All of these papers were "now in my safekeeping," but she did not produce them or copies of them. In the next chapter, we shall learn what happened to these damning documents.

In the end, she got absolutely nothing from any of them. At the very least, she insisted, law obliged the consul either to return her silver or to reimburse her its value. He should be required to restore her daughter to her and then provide for the child's education, her dowry, and her trousseau. When Romellini left Hamburg, she had "not a penny of cash" to her name and had been forced to borrow fifteen ducats from the procurator Tode. Delays and false assurances had strung her along for weeks, and eventually she auctioned off her wardrobe to make ends meet. She lacked the financial wherewithal to initiate a civil suit against Sanpelayo, which would run on "too long and [be] too costly," and besides, "I wanted to be kind to the man with whom I had [once] enjoyed the greatest intimacy." She hoped to spare him the indignity of a civil suit in a case that could only greatly discomfit him.

Sanpelayo was then preparing to leave Hamburg forever, however, and as she had still received absolutely nothing of what was due her, she found it necessary to act before he eluded her and slipped out of reach of the magistrates entirely. Thus she appealed for assistance to Binder von Kriegelstein as "[his] unhappy co-religionist" and a wretched person who "after having been led astray by the evils of the world into youthful errors, now wants only to make it all good again." If she were allowed to return to Hamburg, she would throw herself at his feet, but since she could not enter the city, she must needs take up her pen and beseech him in writing to rescue two people (herself and her daughter) from "utter ruin."

Her protestations left the Senat and Binder von Kriegelstein unmoved, but Romellini's continued agitation on her behalf and the broad hints she dropped that there was more to the story than she had revealed did have an effect. Binder von Kriegelstein, although disinclined to believe the tale in its entirety, nevertheless allowed that *perhaps* there was more to the matter than at first met the eye. Her charges had reanimated the "suspicions of the [larger] public" that the Senat had shown "much partiality" to the consul, and that much money "had been spread around" to achieve a desired—not necessarily a just—outcome. People whispered that Sanpelayo was the true murderer, and that Kesslitz had acted "infamously enough" in accepting the blame for money. Such delicious rumors did not remain safely captive behind Hamburg's thick walls but flew off to Berlin and Spain to set the diplomatic pot boiling again. The fury blew over quickly, however, and Binder von Kriegelstein reported by the end of July that now "everything has quieted down again."[71] That lull was momentary, for Romellini had not yet abandoned her quest for justice.

How long Romellini remained in Altona, when she went to the Hague, and when she left there are not clear. In November, she wrote from Rotterdam. Her letters from Rotterdam no longer conveyed veiled threats or murmured vague innuendoes; she now openly charged Sillem, Detenhof, Sanpelayo, and Kesslitz with collusion. She attacked Sillem head on, accusing him of concealing the truth and of bribing her to lie. An account of the true course of events followed. Baron de la Houze had visited her "in mufti" while she was under house arrest. Sillem had accompanied him, and he told her that de la Houze was "hunting for a way to turn the process to the good of the murderers." De la Houze offered Sillem a "gift" of 150 ducats, which de la Houze had brought with him wrapped in paper and which he personally handed to the syndic in her presence: "and immediately in the next days the case took on an entirely different aspect." She begged the Senat's compassion for a woman who had been so shamefully deceived and barbarously used. What had she done to serve her hard fate? "Saved the lives of two murderers by her testimony" and "prevented a consul's destruction." She had been "very badly paid," and everyone had turned against her in an attempt to destroy her completely. "What if I had said," she continued, "that Kesslitz had struck the first blow and that Sanpelayo had then immediately split his [Visconti's] skull with his cane." "Then," she added, "perhaps everything would have looked very irregular" to the authorities. Instead, she had lost all because she had trusted in the false assurances of an assassin and a corrupt official. Now she regarded her troubles as God's punishment "for preserving that murderer from his just earthly deserts."[72]

Romellini leveled serious charges, of bribery and the subversion of justice. But no one—at least not officially—believed her. The Senat quickly asked another syndic, Paridom Anckelmann, to draft a letter to the magistrates in Rotterdam, which he did. Anckelmann's dispatch briefly summarized the facts of the case, emphasizing Romellini's character as a woman who "from her youth associated with various men in a shameful manner." He heaped blame on her: her "debauched lifestyle" was the *primum mobile* of Visconti's death. After being banished, she sought revenge on the city by smearing the good name of an honorable magistrate. Anckelmann's letter, however, never left Hamburg. The Senat decided to pass over the matter in silence rather than risk more trouble. Her letter "deserved not a moment's attention," for "the honor of a respected and reputable man cannot be marred by the babble of a hussy." There ended Romellini's affairs as far as Hamburg was concerned, and she then disappears from the historical record.[73]

What then, finally, are we to make of Anna Maria Romellini: gold digger or victim? Shrewd manipulator or hapless dupe? The historian is powerless to answer such questions definitively and perhaps should not even pose them. If the moralist or the psychologist might venture opinions about her intentions, the historian must be satisfied with less certain conclusions. They are, however, just as complex and far more valuable as part of the historical record. One can, of course, cast Romellini as a type, as has to some extent been done here: courtesan, adventuress, libertine, *galante* creature, actress, and dancer. Typecasting, however, inevitably smooths away the ambiguities and intricacies not only of her character and her life but also of the world she inhabited. She cannot, therefore, merely be pressed into convenient molds, as valuable as that exercise is for portraying the richness of the eighteenth-century milieu where sex, law, and diplomacy entwined. Her story was unique. Moreover, she was not merely batted and buffeted about by historical currents that she could neither understand nor direct. Obviously, she could not control the circumstances of her birth and her sex. Still, she made choices and acted as much as she was acted upon, and that is where the real Romellini enters, and also leaves, the historical record. Traveling with her on that exciting yet often sad journey has brought us closer to understanding her and the several worlds she inhabited.

CHAPTER SIX

A Real Polish Prince, a Fake Italian Count, and an Authentic Spanish Hidalgo

Romellini's life with men began early. She was little more than pubescent when Prince Poniatowski impregnated her. Few of her lovers, however, provided for her well; many ran up debts; some gave with the right hand and took again with the left; and others proved violent and abusive. While her paramours were not always blue bloods (Barcker and Thonus were certainly not), most were. Thus, the story of Romellini's men overlaps with the history of the European nobility, but also with a crepuscular world of would-be nobles, imposters, and adventurers.

In the eighteenth century, heterogeneity characterized Europe's nobility. Within its ranks one found rich nobles; poor nobles; entrepreneur nobles; peasant nobles; well-educated men and women and coarse boors; new nobles and those whose family trees stretched back into antiquity. Scions of some families staffed state administrations, while others could only be categorized as feckless. Known by a baffling multiplicity of titles, the size of the groups varied enormously and, as a crude measure, the countries with the most nobles (proportionately)—Spain, the Italian states, and Poland—tended to have the most poverty-stricken and indolent ones. Yet striking anomalies broke up general patterns. In some countries, like Spain, with its grandees at the top and the vast, assorted hidalgo class at the bottom, the concept of "nobility" had especially vague and imprecise meanings. In Poland, no legal rules differentiated the high from the low nobility; all equally belonged to the *szlachta*. Among the Poles, political power, social standing, wealth, and cultural predominance rested, however, with the magnate families: the Czartoryskis, Poniatowskis, Ponińskis, Potockis, and Radziwiłłs. In Lombardy, patricians in cities like Milan and in Venice had long mixed socially and politically with noble families like the Viscontis, and they habitually intermarried. Romellini's

234

lovers, therefore, represented a cross-section of this variegated nobility, but also its faux penumbra in Poland, Courland, Lombardy, Venice, and Spain. One is tempted to estimate that at least one doppelgänger dogged the steps of each real nobleman.[1]

A Real Polish Prince

Romellini started her career almost at the pinnacle of the aristocratic pyramid. Her testimony revealed that she was "first debauched" by Prince Poniatowski, the brother of the man who had been king of Poland since 1764, Stanisław August. Considering the approximate date of her defloration, probably in 1765 (the child was born in 1766), three of the Poniatowski brothers (besides the king) were of a sexually active age: Kazimierz, Michał, and Andrzej. Many of the male members of the Poniatowski family, but particularly the king and his older brother Kazimierz, were well known for their amative even profligate ways.

"Les amours du roi" were legend. Stanisław August's fate—and that of his country—was largely determined by his famous love affair with the grand duchess of Holstein-Gottorp, the future Empress Catherine the Great, in the years 1755–58. The handsome young courtier had perhaps not really conquered the heart of the young duchess, but he had certainly shared her bed. When the old Saxon king of Poland, August III, fell ill, Poniatowski's extended family (the famous Familia of the Poniatowskis and the Czartoryskis) planned to place one of their own on the throne after his death. Powerful elements, including other ambitious magnates and the Saxon party, opposed the election of any reformist Czartoryski candidate. ("Reform" in the context of midcentury Poland meant any wish to modernize the administration, curb magnate power, achieve religious toleration for so-called dissidents [i.e., non-Catholics], and do away with the *liberum veto* that made every noble malcontent a potential political spoiler. The Reform party often turned to Russia for support.) As the moment of crisis approached, the Czartoryski party planned a coup d'état and enlisted the aid of Catherine, expecting her to chose one of their family. The still youthful Stanisław, often dismissed by his own family as profligate and superficial, despite his obvious gifts, was not their first choice. Russian troops ensured his election, however, and, in 1764, the thirty-two-year-old Stanisław become the last king of Poland. Once king, Stanisław continued his amorous ways, and the list of his mistresses soon ran to pages.[2]

But which brother "first debauched" Romellini when she was little more than a child? Prince Michał, born in 1736, was younger than the king.

A rather dour, even sardonic man, he became bishop of Plock in 1773 and archbishop of Gniezno in 1774. Like his enthroned sibling, he embraced the Enlightenment and dedicated himself to the promotion of education and general reform in his diocese. His office as archbishop and primate of Poland does not automatically clear him from suspicion in Romellini's case, yet it does seem unlikely that this "extremely passionless" man (noted for his "sécheresse extrême du coeur") would have been Romellini's lover, or that no contemporaries would have remarked on the lecherous conquests of a high churchman. His slightly older brother Andrzej distinguished himself in Austrian service during the Seven Years' War and rose to the rank of general. In 1765, however, when Romellini met Prince Poniatowski in Venice, Andrzej was in Warsaw; he left Poland for Vienna in December 1766 and never returned.[3] If neither Michal nor Andrzej can be completely exonerated, the most likely candidate remains the king's eldest brother, Kazimierz, who was notorious for his many affairs. A sexual encounter with a (barely) nubile Romellini would have been entirely in character for him.

A famous biography of King Stanisław August characterizes Kazimierz as "debauché, sinon dévoyé" (debauched, if not depraved), saying that as a young man he cared for little more than extorting money from his father and amusing himself with dancers, actresses, and lovers of both sexes. More balanced accounts agree that his conduct as a young man caused concern. "His talents and abilities were undeniable, but his cynicism, his violent temperament, and his profligacy worried" his parents. He was handsome and his personality was outgoing, at least until his political career stalled in the 1770s. Before Stanisław's election, he was "the leading skirmisher of the Familia in the Seym [Diet] and one of its best negotiators out of it." After the death of the last Saxon king of Poland, Kazimierz strongly supported Stanisław's bid for the throne, and during the early years of Stanisław's reign, he urged his brother to resist, as much as possible, the assertiveness of the Familia and the influence of the Russians. Thwarted in his ambitions to become hetman, he resigned his offices after the first partition and withdrew entirely from politics, retaining only a titular role as royal chamberlain. As he grew older, according to an unfriendly account, he became "hideous, pusillanimous, and indolent." His retreat at Solec on the banks of the Vistula was celebrated for its hothouses of tropical fruit, his art collection, a miniature court theater, mock Gothic ruins, and his menagerie of monkeys. Above the door of his residence hung the device: "To friendship and amusements." If in these years his life was not quite one of "scandalous futility," he nonetheless "occupied [himself] with giving louche parties . . . and most of all with his new mistress, the actress Agnieszka Truskolaska." (He outlived his royal brother by two years, dying in Warsaw in 1800.)[4] Was this Romellini's first lover? Was this the man for whom her father pimped?

Romellini's father, Antoine (de) Saby, introduced the prince (whichever one it was) to her on a trip to Venice in 1765. Saby or Sabiski, as he called himself in Poland, had accompanied the Poniatowski prince and Karl Ernst, Baron Treyden, duke of Courland (the second and favored son of Biron, the ruling duke of Courland), to Venice. He was French and probably born in Montauban in about 1716. A practiced adventurer and professional gambler, Saby's path crossed Casanova's several times. Like many of his fellows, indeed, like Casanova himself, he spent his life on the road, moving restlessly from one city to another, perhaps out of necessity. In 1749, he was in Warsaw; in 1753–58, in Paris; in 1758–59, in Amsterdam (where Casanova first met him); in 1766, in Dresden, Frankfurt, Augsburg, and Vienna; in 1775, in Venice; and after 1778, in Paris and elsewhere in France. In 1743, he married the daughter of a French royal courtier, only to abandon her when he went to Warsaw. He earned his title of "chevalier" and the Order of St. Ludwig from the Saxon elector (August III, also king of Poland) for the magnificent deed of carrying to Dresden the news of the birth in 1751 of Louis-Joseph-Xavier, duc de Bourgogne, son of the dauphin (and the heir to the French throne).[5]

Casanova repeatedly ran across the man he called "the perfidious major" in the late 1750s and 1760s. In fall 1759, when Casanova encountered Saby in Amsterdam, he was associating with "a collection of scoundrels" at an inn called the City of Lyon, where "count Piccolomini" held court. This count was himself counterfeit. His real name was Ruggieri Rocco, and he lived as a professional gambler and fencing master. "Countess" Piccolomini accompanied him, and they associated on intimate terms with a colorful crew: a Bohemian baron, Johann Carl von Wiedau (a real nobleman, but also an adventurer); a "gaunt bravo" going by the name of the chevalier de la Perrine; and a French officer, adventurer, and professional card player "who had broken the prince-bishop's bank at Pressburg." Typically, the company incorporated the genuine and the bogus, but all were, as Casanova recognized, rascals and hustlers. At that time, Saby wore the uniform of a major in the service of the king of Poland. Saby's "pretended wife . . . a rather pretty Saxon woman who was paying court to the Countess Piccolomini, speaking very broken Italian," accompanied him.[6] Could this have been Romellini? If so, she would have been terribly young for a "pretended wife," just seven or eight in 1759 (if she was, as she claimed, only twenty-four in 1775). It is hard to believe too that Romellini spoke Italian badly, because she was born and raised in Italy,

King August III of Poland. Courtesy Staatliche Kunstsammlungen, Dresden.

although, of course, Casanova might have meant she spoke an ungrammatical rather than a halting Italian. Still, nothing compels us to identify this "pretty Saxon" with Romellini. Saby could easily have taken up with another woman while in Dresden or Warsaw and while serving the Saxon elector–Polish king. Before the end of 1759, Casanova met Saby again. The "perfidious major" warned him to be careful of a Venetian officer who felt that Casanova had dishonored him. Saby told Casanova that the man had spread the tale that "since he had vainly asked me to give him satisfaction he had the right to murder me. He said he was desperate, that he wanted to leave [town], and that he had no money." Saby suggested that Casanova offer the man fifty florins to be rid of him, which Casanova did. Might this have been Visconti? Could he and Saby have been in cahoots?[7]

When Casanova arrived in Warsaw toward the end of October 1765, he once again ran across Saby, finding him encircled by a crew of "grecs" (*grec* was eighteenth-century slang for a cardsharp). At that time, Saby "had set up shop with a Saxon woman," who may have been the same pretty Saxon from Amsterdam (although Casanova does not say so, and his memory of previous acquaintances, even fleeting ones, was generally excellent) or, now quite plausibly, Romellini. We know from the testimony in the Kesslitz case that at least one man placed her in Warsaw in 1766–69. In Warsaw, Saby and his woman associated with Italians from the theater and opera, including Carlo Tomatis, director of the opera buffa; a Milanese dancer named Caterina Catai, "who, by her charms far more than her talent, was the delight of the city and the Court"; and a Veronese woman named Giropoldi, who was living with an officer from Lorraine who "kept the bank at faro." Catai later married Tomatis and, while his wife, became mistress to Stanisław August. One of Stanisław August's biographers, described Carlo as a pimp for the king whose "villa at Królikarnia was little more than a high-class brothel." Another face in the crowd was Baron Saint-Hélène of Savoy, whose principal talent, according to the Italian wag, lay in running up debts and then persuading his creditors to wait for payment. And so on.[8]

Saby, Prince Poniatowski, and the duke of Courland had earlier journeyed to Venice together. (Casanova records that a "prince" of Courland departed for Venice sometime in spring 1766, soon after Easter, 30 March. He may have been there earlier, or Romellini misremembered her dates.)[9] Karl Ernst of Courland was a good friend to Casanova, and he appears frequently in the memoirs. While Romellini never explicitly admits that

---

Reigning Dukes of Courland, 1641–1795

Jakob Kettler	1641–1682
Friedrich Kasimir Kettler	1682–1698
Friedrich Wilhelm Kettler	1698–1711
Ferdinand Kettler	1711–1737
Ernst Johann Biron	1737–1740
[Ducal council	1740–1758]
Karl of Saxony	1758–1763
Ernst Johann Biron	1763–1769
Peter Biron	1769–1795

she became the mistress of this "prince" (duke) of Courland (and she seemed proud to recount her other affairs with royalty or near-royalty), it is hardly improbable. Karl Ernst was the younger, favored son of the reigning duke, Ernst Johann Biron (or Bühren). The story of Courland (itself technically a Polish fief) in the mid to the late eighteenth century was, as we have seen, a complicated one and intersected with and echoed that of Poland. Its reigning duke, Ernst Johann, was simply another adventurer who had made good. Indeed, he was one of the most talented of the many eighteenth-century political upstarts, and much of his political success rested on his masculine charms and his ability to cozen women in powerful positions. Tsarina Anna (who was the widow of a previous duke of Courland, Friedrich Wilhelm Kettler) fawned on the young Biron. Admittedly, he descended from a family of Westphalian counts, but he aimed, and rose, much higher. As his reward for backing them in the struggle for the Polish crown, the Saxon Wettins helped make Ernst Johann duke of Courland in 1737. When Anna died in 1740, however, Russian support for him collapsed. He was deposed and exiled to Siberia, where he and his family (including the young Karl Ernst) remained for twenty years. A dukeless period followed, during which Russia basically ran Courland. Between 1758 and 1763, a new duke, Karl Christian of Saxony, the third son of August III (and the man to whom Casanova referred in his memoirs as "the *other* duke of Courland"), ruled in Mitau. But Biron's luck with women did not desert him, and in 1763, another virago, Catherine the Great, restored him to his duchy, which he and his son Peter (r. 1769–95) controlled until Russia finally absorbed Courland in 1795. Karl Ernst held the rank of major general in the Russian army from 1762 on, although he performed few duties for it. The contentious and entangled history of Courland made it rather easy for all sorts of people to pretend to the title, often with some right.[10]

Casanova met this "real" duke of Courland, Karl Ernst, at his father's court in 1764 at Mitau and fraternized with him in Riga, finding him a most congenial comrade. Then thirty-six, Karl Ernst had "a pleasant though not handsome face" and was "polite without stiffness, speaking French well."[11] They struck up an intimate friendship, and Casanova promised to provide him with, among other things, a formula for invisible ink. Despite his position and his family's unhappy stay in Siberia, or perhaps because of them, Karl Ernst pursued "an undisciplined, profligate life, [and] associated with all sorts of adventurers," much to his father's dissatisfaction. Twenty years in Siberia had substantially cooled the old duke's ardent nature, and his patience with his sons' failings quickly wore thin. Not surprisingly, Karl Ernst and his father quarreled, and the flow of money from his family trickled to a stop. The young duke soon sought funds where he could, sometimes in unsavory places. Hounded out of Courland by his creditors, he traveled to southern and western Europe, going to Poland, Germany, Italy, Holland, England, and France. In 1766, he was associating with Casanova's circle in Warsaw. In Holland, his boon companion was none other than Romellini's father, Major Saby. The Florentine Segreteria di Stato detained him for bad debts. Once released, he crossed into France, accompanied by a numerous retinue, including his then-mistress, an Italian woman, who may have been Caterina Pulcinelli of Rome. One wonders if Saby might have been one of this entourage. In Paris in 1768, Karl Ernst turned to the favorite device of all eighteenth-century schemers for raising money: falsifying bills of exchange and forging signatures. Some reports speak of him as a leader of a band of cutpurses. His plotting landed him in the Bastille, from which only his father's money finally rescued him. His obligations at the time amounted to almost 50,000 livres. His name was ruined, and he died in Prussian territory in 1801.[12]

Besides noble scoundrels, pretenders galore abounded, and some, like the many who claimed to be the "true" tsar, the husband of Catherine, Peter III (who had disappeared under mysterious circumstances during the coup d'état that brought his wife to power), caused great trouble. The tangled lineages of the Courland-Saxon-Polish thrones nourished much humbuggery. Besides the two Karls who were authentic, if not reigning, dukes of Courland, there was also one Charles Ivanov who tried to borrow money from Casanova in Grenoble, pretending to be "Charles, second son of Ivan, Duke of Kurland." (Although Casanova was not deceived, he was not unsympathetic: "since it was not for me to be the avowed enemy of adventurers, who are all imposters in one degree or another.")[13] Some upstarts, like Biron, personified a particular type: "the genius-adventurer of great stature . . . who is so frequent in, and so characteristic of, the history of seventeenth- and eighteenth-century Europe."[14] Others swished their way through the capitals of Europe trading on their supposed titles, good looks, or brash demeanor. Not all were believable or believed, and not all were capable of stepping into powerful positions and holding on, but even those of small stature had their entertainment value. All of these connections replicated at a higher level the world Romellini, her father, and her lovers inhabited.

Romellini and her kind not only reflected this larger environment; they created it. Throughout the eighteenth century, but especially after its midpoint, the pillars that had once so firmly anchored the aristocratic world began to crumble. While they certainly did not tumble (retaining much of their substance even after the French Revolution), they never again stood quite so solidly as they once had. The whole world seemed bewilderingly fluid. As noble hierarchies dissolved, merged with other groups, or were turned on their heads, pseudo-nobles or would-be nobles could work their way in and up to hobnob with their social betters or—with increasing frequency—lord it over them. Politically, nobility no longer enjoyed a virtual stranglehold on power (if it ever had). Talented newcomers (among them the erstwhile physician Johann Friedrich Struensee in Denmark), flimflam men, and even Jews (such as, earlier in the century, Josef Süss Oppenheimer in Württemberg), became factors to be reckon with. They rose and they fell, and although individuals disappeared, the type persisted. If flux characterized the political, diplomatic, and social worlds of the nobility, the economic sphere, with its cycles of booms and busts, was considerably more permeable and slippery. The Brions, Casanovas, Sabys, Viscontis, and Romellinis both benefited from this universe in motion and contributed to its spin.

Only innuendo supports speculation about a relationship between Romellini and Karl Ernst, but she fully informs us about her other princely affairs. Her second lover, and the father of her next child, the prince or count "Poniński Nepomus," was the Pole Jan Nepomucen Poniński. Born in 1735 (died 1782?), he would have been about twice her age when he met Romellini in 1765 or 1766.[15] Poniński proved an even less reliable protector than Poniatowski. Debts and duels trailed him wherever he went. The Dresden magistrates would not allow him to leave the city in 1768 because of bad bills of exchange, and that not for the first time. Financial irresponsibility, doubtful morals, and a quick temper hardly disqualified him, however, from becoming deeply involved in politics or from playing a substantial role in the European diplomatic world. According to Romellini, Poniński and her father were up to their necks in "the secret correspondence concerning the Confederation, of which correspondence count Poniński was the chief."[16] To this man, she bore a daughter.

Poniński displayed all the contradictions and dissonances that exemplified many politically involved nobleman of the mid to late eighteenth century. To dismiss him as a rake and bumbler denies the complexities of eighteenth-century society, politics, and diplomacy alike. Few, however, embodied the amalgam as neatly as Poniński, and perhaps few moved as nimbly from one side to another in the shifting alliances of Polish internal politics. In his youth, he had prepared for a military career at a *collegium nobilium*, where he soon demonstrated the literary skills he later used to attract patrons. During the Seven Years' War, he was aide-de-camp to a commander of Saxon forces, General (*hetman*) Jan Klemens Branicki (who as a man of sixty had married Stanisław August's eighteen-year-old sister). Like Kesslitz after the war, Poniński found his modest estate in severe financial difficulties. His friendship with the royal treasurer, Teodor Wessel, constituted in these lean years "toute sa resource." In 1763, when the future of Poland hung in the balance, he ghostwrote for Wessel a paper proposing the establishment of a purely republican government. In the wrangling over the Polish throne in 1763–64, Poniński took the side of the elderly (seventy-four) but popular hetman Branicki (Branicki's son, Ksawery, was a friend of the king's and fought a famous duel with Casanova). In these troubled times, a confederation arose to back Branicki's candidacy and forestall Stanisław August's election. In early July 1764, Poniński traveled to Dresden to secure financial aid for the project. The election of Stanisław August dashed Poniński's hopes of exerting influence in the new Polish government, however, and he slid into political isolation and economic disaster. Reduced to pleading with Branicki, he suffered a sharp rebuff, because the hetman wished to avoid "relationships with people [i.e., Poniński] whose indiscretions may humiliate us." Over the course of the next two years, political impotence and financial instability did little to increase his affection for the new king. In 1767, he was involved in the Confederation of Radom, a ragtag assemblage of Polish malcontents, which Repnin (Russia's much-hated minister to Poland) had conjured up to counter the king's reform plans and block the influence of the Familia.[17]

Poniński's opposition to Stanisław August threw him in with this Russian endeavor. In 1767 and 1768, Poniński accepted payments from Repnin. The latter never fully trusted him, however, and gradually Poniński moved —or was pushed—out of the Russian orbit. In spring of 1768, Poniński came into contact with members of another, and far more famous, confederation, that of Bar, although it is not certain that he actually joined it. The Confederation of Bar had been formed to request (or, if necessary, to coerce) Catherine the Great to restore the Polish constitution in its old form. It protested Russian interference in internal Polish matters and particularly targeted the new rights for non-Catholics forced on the Diet by Catherine and Frederick the Great. In 1767, the conflict over the rights of non-Catholics in Poland came to a head, or rather formed the pretext for increased Russian control and Russian intervention to prevent any reform that might strengthen the Polish state. The extraordinary diet held in October 1767 was, according to the British minister, James Harris, "immediately under the direction of Russia . . . eight thousand Russian troops surrounded the town, and a thousand encamped in the Russian Ambassador's [Repnin's] garden, who, for the time being, was in every respect absolute monarch."[18]

By early 1768, the rebellion launched by the confederates of Bar had burgeoned into a formidable insurrection, "occasioned," Harris opined, "by a taedium of oppression and dread of slavery, mixed with their natural turbulent spirit" on the part of the seditious Polish gentry.[19] Between the outbreak of the rebellion and its end (1772), some 100,000 people had taken part in about 500 skirmishes as the revolt flared first in one place and then another. In November, Poniński journeyed to Saxony, where the Confederation's list of demands was drawn up: abolition of reforms initiated since 1764; invalidation of the election of Stanisław August; and the renewed candidacy of the Saxon elector, Friedrich August. To what extent Poniński acted in pursuit of higher political goals and to what extent for himself is open to interpretation. In December 1769, he was arrested in Dresden on three counts (and not merely for the duel Romellini mentions): misappropriation of Confederation funds (which he seemed to have squandered on wine and women); attempted blackmail of the Saxon electress; and cheating his main creditor, Prince Josef Alexander Jablonowski (with whom he dueled). Once released (in part through Romellini's good offices?), he went to Bielsko, where his old patrons Wessel and Branicki supported him. By 1771, and although now pretty much a political has-been, he still apparently ran errands to France on Wessel's commission, and he was occasionally there from mid 1771 through 1775. By the early 1780s, after becoming deeply involved in the Masonic movement (possibly seeking thereby an alternative avenue to political power), he returned to Warsaw, where he fought a pistol duel. Once there, he attempted to convince Stanisław August that he repented his past opposition to the king. Stanisław August remained skeptical and became uneasy when Poniński departed for St. Petersburg in 1782, for the king considered him "more evil, two-faced, and treacherous than he previously thought." As it turns out, Stanisław August had little to worry about; despite his scheming, Poniński's stay in Russia produced nothing substantial. While Catherine's favorite Gregori Potemkin found Poniński's "malicious prattle" amusing for a time, he soon tired of him. Poniński had left St. Petersburg by midsummer 1782, and he then vanishes; he probably died in the same year. Poniński hardly lacked talents, but his indiscretions and his shape-shifting earned distrust and suspicion even from those who once been his advocates and associates. One of his (many) enemies admitted that he possessed "a noble posture, regular features . . . a pleasant voice, and broad knowledge" and knew how to prettify his speeches with "fine words" like virtue and patriotism. Yet he was also base, devious, mean-spirited, and all that went with his "boundless, passionate ambition." It was a devil's brew, but one that fermented well in the Polish cauldron of the 1760s and 1770s.[20]

A Fake Italian Count

"Comte" Visconti first appears in this story as a corpse. The examining physicians described him, it will be remembered, as a man of about forty, whose "well-formed and healthy body" was badly disfigured by some twenty-three fresh wounds, of which at least two were "absolutely fatal."[21] On that morning, little else was clear about the man. Over the ensuring weeks, however, the Senat and city of Hamburg would come to know him and his life history well. Yet of all the principals in the tragic events of 18/19 October 1775, he remained the only one who could not—who could no longer—speak for himself. Who was this robust forty-year-old man? Where did he come from? And what had he sought in Romellini's lodgings the previous night? Why was he now dead?

By now these questions have been addressed and partially answered. Sillem, in his "Historical Narrative," summed up Visconti's existence succinctly and unflatteringly: he was "nothing more than a barber's son," a gambler, adventurer, bandit, wanderer, and imposter by profession and a "quarrelsome, sneaky, and desperate fellow" by temperament. He was manifestly what good citizens were not: disguised, showy, migratory. This explanation as Sillem crafted it, or rather the identity he gave Visconti, drew on a series of familiar types. Visconti's identity was not merely that which respectable society imposed on him after his death, however, it was also the one that Kesslitz, Sanpelayo, Romellini, and Detenhof, as well as Visconti himself, consciously shaped.

Each witness, each participant, and each statement from those who had known Visconti told much the same story, at least on the face of it: Visconti was an adventurer, a crook, a thief, and a parasite. He had been born in Italy in the mid 1730s, making him a close contemporary of Kesslitz. We know little about his life before he came into contact with the young singer and dancer Romellini. His connections with her from when she was twelve or thirteen were sporadic but repeated; he faded in and out of her life. She knew little more than that he called himself Visconti, and she had always understood him to be a soldier and a nobleman. "Of his [actual] family, birthplace and occupation," she professed to have no clue. "There are," she added, "so many families of the name Visconti [in Italy] . . . [and] some are very distinguished." She knew only that "he had always presented himself . . . as Count Visconti."[22]

Of his religion there was no doubt: Visconti was, like Romellini, Kesslitz, and Sanpelayo, a Catholic, and thus it fell to Catholics to bury him. Sanpelayo quickly stepped in to do so, perhaps persuaded by the praetor.

Four days after the fight, on Monday, 23 October, while Kesslitz sat in the Eimbeck'sches Haus, gravediggers quickly and quietly interred Visconti in the Catholic cemetery in Altona.[23] That hardly closed the Visconti file. Even though his physical remains were safely underground, his specter haunted all involved: was he perhaps a member of the powerful and extensive Milanese family of Viscontis? Three days later, the Senat asked Binder von Kriegelstein to take "the next convenient moment" to find out. Could Vienna say if this man was indeed a member of that clan? Binder von Kriegelstein was ahead of the Senat: he had queried his superiors on the previous Saturday about whether Visconti was "an imperial subject." By the 15th of November, it still remained uncertain whether he was or was not part of the Visconti family. Two days later, however, the Senat breathed a sigh of relief to learn from Binder von Kriegelstein that no Visconti of note had been involved. From Vienna, came the news that "the Visconti recently killed in Hamburg in no way belongs to the respected noble family of that name from Milan. Rather, he was a barber's son and an accomplished adventurer. Two years ago, he left here [Milan] for Vienna wearing the uniform of a Russian [officer]. . . . That he called himself . . . Visconti was as you observed . . . nothing very remarkable in Italy, because clients of the great families [there] often take their names with impunity." Binder von Kriegelstein placed a notice to this effect (and in almost identical words) in the *Hamburgischer Correspondent* "to preserve the honor of the noble Visconti family."[24]

It should surprise no one that "Comte" Visconti could carry off the imposture for so long and be so thoroughly believed. In the eighteenth century, the Visconti family was huge. Rich and puissant Viscontis were as numerous as impecunious and undistinguished ones. Its origins lay in feudal antiquity, and Viscontis held extremely important positions. Almost all Lombard noble families were well represented in the hierarchy of the Catholic Church, and the Viscontis were no exception. Joseph, "Comte" Visconti, claimed the very real papal nuncio in Warsaw, Antonio Eugenio Visconti, as his uncle. Besides the nuncio, the Viscontis boasted twenty-nine other male clerics and thirty nuns. Another Visconti was archbishop of Milan and a general of the Jesuit Order. Although it is very doubtful that our "comte" belonged to any part of this family in a regular sense, it is possible (and maybe even probable?) that he was an illegitimate son. Moreover, precisely because the family had threaded itself throughout Italian (and European) political, religious, and cultural structures, his story had some credibility. The large number of Italian states in the eighteenth century also meant that the number of Italian ambassadors, consuls, and other members of diplomatic missions—such as the "cavalier" connected to the Venetian mission in Paris, Manuzzi, with whom Romellini had an affair—mounted exponentially.

The investigation failed to pin down Visconti's identity precisely, but it did reveal more of his background and gradually filled in some of the blanks. None of the evidence came from Visconti directly. He was, after all, dead. Thus, he, far more than either Romellini or Kesslitz, remains a cardboard cutout figure and little more than an eighteenth-century type.

In order to understand Visconti, and in order to explain why he had ended up dead, the Senat and its members reconstructed what they considered a plausible version of his life, scratching away at the record to follow him from his early years until October 1775. Above all, they wanted to know how, and how often, his path had crossed those of Romellini, Kesslitz, and Sanpelayo. Encounters that seemed entirely accidental were considerably less so. Not that anyone had necessarily planned them; rather, historical currents tended to deposit people in the same places. Imposters often came together in Breslau, just as they did in Warsaw and Dresden.

In the early days of the case, as the Senat began gathering testimony, it became clear that many people in Hamburg had known Visconti. The merchant Johann Christoph Reiss spun a captivating tale relating Visconti's escapades in Breslau just a few years earlier. On his commercial travels, Reiss had lodged in Breslau with a Visconti. At that time, Visconti had, according to Reiss, "conducted himself in an orderly manner" and, moreover, had "moved in the best company and in elite society." Still, word soon circulated that he was "really nothing more than an upstart and a gambler." One of the fascinating things about the eighteenth century is the ease with which fakes and frauds, or adventurers and gamblers, penetrated respectable society. One strongly suspects that while imposters and their impostures duped some people, most had a pretty shrewd idea of what men like Visconti were. They produced a frisson of excitement, however, by providing flirtatious contact with a seedier, faster world. They probably fooled few. For instance, many in Breslau knew Visconti's title to be false.[25]

Yet if some people were not taken in by Visconti's affectations, others were more gullible. While he was first in Breslau, Reiss never saw or heard anything "adverse about [Visconti] or detrimental," except that he pretended to be what he was not. When Reiss returned to Breslau, after some months' absence, however, he discovered a "very unfavorable history" of Visconti's actions in the meantime, in which Visconti appeared as a "great scoundrel" and a "deceiver." Visconti had neatly scammed a Greek merchant from Thessaloníki named Kyrani.[26]

This was how it went. One evening in the inn where both Reiss and Visconti lodged, two well-dressed Italian merchants had openly approached Visconti and "asked him, as one of their countrymen, if he were not able to accommodate them with a sum of money"; Reiss understood it to be about 800 ducats. They were awaiting a letter of exchange and needed a short-term loan to tide them over. They offered a thick gold bar as security. It was a thoroughly credible situation. By the last quarter of the eighteenth century, bills of exchange, often drawn on persons or companies far removed in space and time from the bearer, quickened commercial transactions, and almost everyone engaged in business relied on them. The increased use of paper instruments in business—bills of exchange, letters of credit, and stocks—inevitably accompanied and facilitated economic growth but also further distanced business partners and deals from one another, as well as rendering them more anonymous. Anonymity and distance abetted frauds but simultaneously caused situations like this one to seem thoroughly credible.[27] Larceny in bills of exchange occurred frequently. Bills functioned not just as the tools of small-time con men like Visconti; their use, or rather misuse, had landed a quite real duke of Courland in the Bastille and inconvenienced hundreds of nobleman strapped for cash. The conjunction of imposters, nobles, and pretended nobles with forged or bad bills of exchange was so familiar to the eighteenth-century public that it hardly required explanation.

Visconti merely shook his head, regretting that he could not help them out. He planned to leave Breslau soon and thus "needed all his cash." He promised, however, to inquire if one of his acquaintances among the merchants might be able to assist them. The whole scene was, of course, staged; the two "Italian merchants" were Visconti's accomplices. Of course, their pigeon, the Greek merchant, was conveniently in the room, where he overheard the entire conversation. He, according to Reiss, "like all Greek merchants, who, just like Jews, never want to miss the chance to turn a profit easily," volunteered his assistance. Because he could not cover the entire sum himself, Kyrani wanted to consult some of his friends. He and another businessman then lent the Italian "merchants" 200 ducats on the security of the gold bar. Kyrani was not a total idiot, for he insisted that a local goldsmith first weigh the bar and assess its worth before he agreed to hand over the cash. This was done, and, in Kyrani's presence, the merchants placed the gold bar in a leather bag, pulled the drawstring tight, sealed it with their signet rings, and entrusted it to another trader in Breslau to hold as surety.

Soon thereafter, Kyrani learned that Visconti intended to leave Breslau and went to bid farewell to "his good friend." To his amazement, he found out that Visconti had left town the day before. Although Kyrani thought this a bit odd and somewhat precipitous, "he suspected no evil." Then, however, he discovered that not only had Visconti gone, but the other two Italians had likewise disappeared, and "his heart dropped." Fearing that the three had pulled a fast one on him, he hurried to the merchant who held the bar as collateral, insisted on breaking the seal, and took the bar to the goldsmith who had originally verified its weight and worth. To his great consternation, the goldsmith informed him that the bar in his hands was not the one he had assessed before, but rather a bar made of some metal "that looked like gold" and weighed the same. Immediately, Kyrani realized that "he had been skinned out of [his] 200 ducats."

Rumor had it that the three crooks had crossed the border into Saxony, and Kyrani pursued them from post station to post station, finally catching up to them in either Bautzen or Görlitz; Reiss believed it was Görlitz.[28] Kyrani had them brought before the magistrates there. After an investigation, the magistrates condemned Visconti's two partners to be whipped publicly and then banished from Saxony. Reiss was not, however, sure whether Visconti, too, had been caught or suffered the same penalties, or even if Kyrani had retrieved his money, "for the Greek merchant Kyrani . . . really disliked talking about the whole affair." He was understandably chagrined, for he regarded himself as "a very prudent and clever merchant" and felt mortified that he had been "so easily deceived and that such rogues had plucked him clean." The story spread throughout Breslau and ruined Visconti's reputation there. Good society in Breslau could accept a harmless pretender, whose posturing might cause them to laugh behind his back; a thief was another matter altogether.[29]

Curiously (or perhaps not), several people implicated in the events of 18/19 October had also been in Breslau several years earlier. One of them was Kesslitz. In his testimony, he revealed that he had encountered Visconti three years earlier in Breslau. He had met Visconti on the parade ground. The latter had worn a Russian uniform and introduced himself as a captain in the Russian navy. He had a servant with him "and had [this servant] address him as 'count.'" In Breslau, however, Kesslitz had had little contact with Visconti, only meeting him occasionally in public places, where he passed the time of day with him, "as one does with a stranger [conversing] about nothing in particular."[30]

Impostures, such as those Visconti practiced in Breslau and elsewhere, mixed the believable, the fantastic, and the transparent. Faking the identity of an officer, even one from a distant place like Russia, had its perils, especially in a garrison town like Breslau, where officers abounded, and where military men continually bumped into old acquaintances. Kesslitz, for instance, quickly embarrassed Visconti, perhaps intentionally. Kesslitz had been perplexed that, as a Russian officer, Visconti had not "paid his compliments" to the local Prussian commandant, as usual military and polite practice dictated. Innocently or disingenuously, Kesslitz advised him to do so, offering to accompany him. Visconti replied that it was not necessary, leaving Kesslitz baffled.

Servants, such as the one Visconti employed, were ideally placed to reveal all. From common gossip, Kesslitz had learned that one manservant had had a falling out with Visconti. Visconti had beaten him, and the servant threatened to "expose all his master's secrets." Visconti's landlord had requested Visconti to leave his premises and go elsewhere, but Kesslitz did not know why. Had he not paid his rent? Visconti moved out and into seedy accommodations, where he kept company with "storekeepers' clerks and the like." He entertained them, playing hazard and other games of chance with them, and apparently cheating them all along. When one of his dupes discovered that Visconti was gulling him, he forced Visconti to restore his money. This story, too, according to Kesslitz, quickly made the rounds in Breslau. From that time on, Kesslitz assiduously avoided Visconti's company. Whenever he met him, he only said "this and that to him," treating him entirely as a stranger. When the Prussian commandant became aware of Visconti's tricks, however, he warned him to leave Breslau; one assumes that his young officers were Visconti's prey. Visconti went, but not far. Rather, he settled in the area known as auf dem Sand, a suburb of Breslau. This was where he and the two other Italians orchestrated the scene with Kyrani.

Kesslitz's version of the gold bar scam follows the outlines of Reiss's story. In Kesslitz's telling, Kyrani lent the money, 300–500 ducats, for a term of two to three months. Kesslitz reported that Visconti had actually been arrested in Görlitz and as a result been compelled to make full restitution. Kesslitz also suggested that the authorities in Görlitz would be able to verify the story. He was careful to add, however, that his knowledge of the whole affair came simply from rumors, lest it be thought that he commonly associated with traveling merchants like Kyrani or lowlifes like Visconti.

Soon after the encounter with Visconti in Breslau, Kesslitz accompanied Baron von Schlabrendorff to Hamburg on his recruiting mission. The two officers then met up again, "quite accidentally," with Visconti at a coffeehouse. Visconti was "in a miserable condition," Kesslitz said, and he had made no effort to renew the acquaintance—he did not wish to have anything to do with Visconti, because "[he] could never respect such a person." At the time, he knew nothing about Visconti's affair with Romellini and, in fact, had only recently met Romellini through Sanpelayo and Baron de la Houze. Romellini had became aware of Visconti's deceits in Breslau from Kesslitz, or at least so she said. Under interrogation, Schlabrendorff related an almost identical story about Visconti's swindles in Breslau.[31]

After crossing in Breslau, the paths of Visconti and Kesslitz soon diverged again. Kesslitz moved to Hamburg, while Visconti continued to roam through eastern Europe, the Empire, and the Italian states. As the Senat pressed its investigation into the prehistory of the murder, if such it was, it peeled back the layers of Visconti's life like an onion, uncovering a series of tawdry affairs, as well as links between the four principals and several places: Warsaw, Dresden, Breslau, Bergamo, and Venice. For instance, in about 1772 (that is, very soon after he had fled Breslau and probably indeed on that trip into Saxony), Visconti had been in Dresden, again posing as a Russian officer. This time he engaged in fictitious, and illegal, recruiting, which, when exposed, got him tossed out of the city. The French schoolmaster Philipp Jacob Marechall, who had also known Romellini in Warsaw, provided details of this incident.[32] Besides these testimonies and rumors, other sources revealed the rather sordid details of Visconti's life before 1775. Romellini had, of course, told what she knew about him in Venice and Parma from her youth.

More damning still were his adventures in several Italian cities. Here, again, Romellini was the primary source of information, yet much had also been revealed in the letters Visconti wrote to her while she was Sanpelayo's mistress. Although when he left Hamburg in 1773 or 1774, he had said he was going to Russia, he in fact went south. His letters first related the story of the "murder" of a dancer or singer in Venice. Visconti admitted that he had been arrested for this crime, but told Romellini not to worry, because "the matter is insignificant." He expected a rapid release, for he had not "really" slain the woman. A dispatch from the *Gazette de France* reported, however, that the "soi-disant Comte Visconti de Milan, who had passed himself off as a officer in the service of the tsarina . . . having refused to leave the [Venetian] Republic, was arrested and imprisoned."[33] Early in October 1775, he wrote to Romellini from Augsburg, revealing that he had recovered his liberty, but betrayed no intention of coming to Hamburg; thus, on the night of 18 October, he appeared, according to Romellini, "completely unexpectedly."[34]

Not until that evening, as she sipped tea with Visconti (before Kesslitz and Sanpelayo arrived), did she get a full account of his Italian misfortunes from Visconti himself. In Venice, he had met an opera buffa singer, with whom he entered into a "love agreement." Not surprisingly, Visconti was scarcely her only suitor; she attracted many men. A rich Venetian merchant, whose name Visconti did not recall, maintained her as his mistress. Visconti, driven in part by jealousy but also by greed, proposed that she invite the merchant to join in a game of cards, in which he intended to cheat him "with her connivance." She "remained true to her clerk," however, warning him to be on his guard, and thus checking Visconti's scheme. To spite her, he denounced the singer to the authorities in Venice, accusing her of stealing a diamond tiara and other objects that he had actually given her as presents. The Venetian Republic placed her under house arrest but allowed her to fulfill her contract at the opera. The police escorted her back and forth to the theater each evening. Eventually, the authorities released her (for lack of evidence?) and she went to Brescia. Her detention did not assuage Visconti's wrath. He pursued her and, when he caught up to her, beat her with his riding whip and threw ink on her. Having wreaked his vengeance on this "unfaithful woman," he returned to Venice but had to leave again quickly because the merchant and several of her other admirers threatened him when they learned what he had done in Brescia. He escaped to Bergamo, but reports from Venice had preceded him there, and the magistrates apprehended him for his attack on the singer. Here his Russian uniform saved him from ignominious arrest; he was confined "honorably." The Bergamese authorities permitted him to return to Venice so that he could present his case to the Venetian magistrates. In Venice, however, when it was discovered that he was not a Russian officer at all, "the city executioner broke his sword over his knee" in St. Mark's Square and Venice expelled him. He resumed his wanderings, going to Augsburg, Braunschweig, and then back to Hamburg. Romellini's story corresponded to what the Hamburg Senat heard from its Bergamese counterpart later in November. Count Barthy wrote to the Senat expressing the Bergamese magistrates' "great astonishment" when they received word of Visconti's fate in Hamburg, for "we know him." The Bergamese had arrested him at the request of the Venetian authorities, and he was subsequently banished for good from Venetian territory on pain of more severe punishment if he dared show his face again. Supposedly, he had gone to Poland from Bergamo; in any case, they had no further news of him.[35]

The dancer-courtesan who had so fatefully attracted Visconti's attention suffered the violence many prostitutes did in the Italian states in the eighteenth century. Of course, their lives were probably no more dangerous in Venice than elsewhere, although blood-drenched tales about them and their lovers titillated Europe. Moreover, Venice seemed the home of a wide variety of women for sale, ranging from stand-up prostitutes to famous courtesans who held court in stately houses on the Grand Canal. Of course, rumor only approximates reality, but such widely dispersed stories predisposed people to believe in the stock and stereotypical characters of knife-wielding, hot-blooded Italian noblemen and cutthroat *banditos* (and the two types tended to merge in fact and fiction) ready to clash over honor at the drop of a hat and capable of attacking anyone, male or female, who insulted them or seemed to. Their "bellicose nature" inclined them to "unbelievable acts of violence."[36]

While in Hamburg, Visconti's behavior departed not at all from its previous brutal and dissipated course. Much of what we know about him comes from Romellini, and it was, of course, advantageous for her to portray him as a fierce and dangerous person, but others corroborated her words. According to her statement, Visconti had pursued her relentlessly from one place in Europe to another; from Venice to Warsaw to Dresden to Paris to Bordeaux to Hamburg. In all the time she knew him, he had never held a position or had funds; rather, he had "lived from his intrigues." He had run up debts in Vienna and had been arrested or detained in cities virtually across the continent for bad bills, cheap swindles, and physical violence. Soon after Romellini reached Hamburg in 1772, Visconti found her (or followed her) there. In her testimony, she represented his attentions as unwanted and burdensome; she trembled in fear of his brutality and impetuosity. While she was the mistress of Barcker, and then Sanpelayo, Visconti never strayed far from the scene, leeching on her and her men, kicking up a fuss when someone got in his way, threatening to beat or even shoot those who argued with him, stacking up obligations, posing as an officer, forcing or trying to force his way into better society, and throwing money around lavishly when he had it. Twice he had had to flee the city when his creditors or victims bore down on him.

Not only Romellini had witnessed such behavior; others also testified to it and to Visconti's character. Thomas Brown, one of Romellini's landlords, had quarreled with Visconti for visiting Romellini in her boudoir without his permission. They almost came to blows when Visconti reached for his sword. Catharina Guido added that he had also clashed with Barcker himself, calling him "a son of a bitch" and putting on airs, trying to lord it over a mere ship's captain. He had threatened to dispatch the swordsmith to whom he owed money with a pistol shot if he dared pester him again.[37] If we can never know the truth about his relationship with Romellini or fully unravel who was using whom or whether lingering affection besides greed and mutual benefit bound the two together, it seems indisputable that on more than one occasion, he had assaulted her physically: he struck her; warned her that he would "cut open her belly" if she betrayed or defied him; ripped her clothes; dragged her around by the hair; and, on the night of his death, stabbed her in the hand with a scissors. Her protestations that she lived in dread of him could certainly be true, even if she addressed him in letters as "my dearest" and even when she—apparently of her own free will—continued to see him and sleep with him. Yet, by October 1775, she was no longer willing to share her life with him even episodically. Surely calculation determined her refusal to leave Sanpelayo on the night of October 18th, for Sanpelayo was a far better provider than Visconti would ever be. But the terror Visconti evoked in her also made her loath to go. Just as clear, however, was her continued regard, even fondness, for him. Moreover, her picture of Sanpelayo's temper and temperament hardly flattered the consul. He, too, was a jealous, vindictive, petty man.

Almost wherever he appeared, Visconti styled himself a count and tried, evidently with some success, to assume the ways of the nobility. He acquired a taste for luxury; he kept a manservant whenever he could possibly afford to, although he did not always pay them and often treated them poorly. The servant he beat in Dresden threatened to reveal the truth about Visconti's impostures. He craved fine clothes, jewels, and other trinkets, such as the sword he had ordered and for which he refused to pay when the bill came due. He cadged money from anyone foolish enough to lend it to him. Romellini pacified him with small sums, never very much, but enough—she hoped!—to stop him from coming back for more. More casual acquaintances, the men he met in coffeehouses, for example, often loaned him a few coins. Romellini's lovers in Hamburg (and probably elsewhere) seemed perfectly amenable to paying for the privilege of enjoying her; both Barcker and Sanpelayo had provided him with money and lodgings in exchange for his willingness to look the other way.

Wherever he went, Visconti dressed in an officer's uniform. Donning a uniform made his impersonation of a count more believable and additionally forced authorities to treat him with more circumspection than they might otherwise have done. His assumed title and his affected status, until disproved, kept him clear of ignominious situations as well as foul common prisons and corporal punishments. At least for a time, he would be treated well. If released on parole of honor, he could always skip town. Officers of foreign powers received a certain degree of consideration and could not simply be snapped up and dumped in the most convenient lockup. Thus the uniform he wore had many benefits besides endowing him with a phony status. It had prevented the Bergamese from placing him under common arrest, for example. He typically kitted himself out as a Russian officer, although why is a mystery—perhaps because of the remoteness of Russia? Mid eighteenth-century Europe pullulated with officers and even ex-officers, many of whom had uniforms and swords. Thomas Brown described him as clad in a green coat with red lapels, yellow leather breeches, and "half-boots, like hussars wear"; "one concluded therefore that he was an officer." Others described basically the same appearance. Even officers like Schlabrendoff and Kesslitz said he wore some sort of Russian uniform, and surely they must have known.[38] Passing for an officer was laughably simple; Casanova did it many times, and he was hardly the only one who appreciated the psychological and legal benefits military apparel conferred. Even in a *bürgerliche* society like Hamburg's, clothes made the man, and the city authorities prudently respected the uniforms of all the European powers.

On the final evening of his life, Visconti remained true to form. He was impetuous in his visit to Romellini, brutal in his treatment of her and her maid, furious when thwarted, and violent when challenged, but his behavior was equally maudlin and farcical. Such conduct made it easy for others to take these events and use them to shape convincing portraits of a cruel and desperate yet also rash and foolish man.

One of the most important analyses of Visconti's character came from the "Historical Narrative" that Sillem laid before the Senat in December 1775.[39] This marked the point of sharpest discord between foreign courts (especially Prussia) and Hamburg over the Kesslitz affair. Sillem tapped toward a solution that would spare Kesslitz as much humiliation as possible, while still taking into account that he had probably used excessive force in self-defense. For this purpose, Visconti's character and his deeds had to be presented in a particular light. Thus, Sillem stressed what he referred to as the "vast difference" between the two men. Kesslitz was "a man of honor . . . whose statements deserve a modicum of belief, keeping in mind, however, that he is hardly disinterested." Visconti was a "quarrelsome, sneaky, and desperate fellow," who had perhaps even been branded as a criminal. This proved untrue. The city's jailer and executioner, Georg Hennings, had examined the body in October and detected a mark (rather like a V), but he did not think it was a brand of the kind usual in Germany.[40]

Visconti was a desperate, brutal, and even cruel man. He had, Sillem reported, threatened on several occasions to harm people, to disembowel Romellini, and to shoot creditors. His speech was equally inflamed and unrestrained: those who opposed him were "scoundrels," "liars," "bastards," "sons of bitches," and "pricks." His desperation rendered him indifferent to his own self-preservation. He was virtually suicidal (had he then committed a form of suicide by "running upon" Kesslitz's blade?) and had told Romellini that his final purpose in life was to wreak vengeance on (unspecified) others. In him, cowardice and ignobility paired with brutality and hopelessness. Kesslitz judged him so craven that he lacked even the courage to draw his sword to defend himself. He was exactly the sort of person to plan and carry out a dastardly attack or fling his life away in a stupid and needless brawl.[41]

Yet, despite his base and skulking nature, Visconti proved a formidable foe, for he was an Italian street fighter armed with a large knife, which he wielded all too effectively. Italians were "known," Sillem insisted, for their skill with knives. Even the best swordsmen often failed to parry their strokes, and they almost always succeeded in killing or maiming their opponents.[42]

Knife-fighting cultures existed in many places in early modern Europe, flourishing "along the border of the 'respectable' and the 'disreputable' segment of the urban lower classes," as Pieter Spierenburg notes of early modern Amsterdam. This was exactly the kind of milieu from which Visconti sprang. Here, knife fighting approximated what might be called lower-class dueling. Bandits in many countries preferred knives as deadly yet easily concealed weapons. Not until near the end of the eighteenth century, when small firearms became more common and more reliable, did the pistolet begin to replace the knife. But Visconti carried pocket pistols as well.[43]

While the bad reputation of Italian knife fighters was a matter of common lore, Sillem had also been provided with this ammunition against Visconti by Detenhof. Thus, collaboration between the two of them generated a compelling picture of Visconti. Detenhof's description of Visconti highlighted his aggressiveness, vulgarity, and self-destructiveness. In particular, Detenhof stressed his reputation as an Italian brawler. Visconti represented an almost superhuman adversary, whom Kesslitz, even armed with a good, strong sword, barely fended off. In his written defense, Detenhof wove together reasoned arguments and almost idiomatic prejudices against Italians as exotic, disruptive foreigners; their honor codes differed as well. "It may seem to some," Detenhof began, "that an attack with a knife or stiletto is not very dreadful." This was a common misconception. Several incidents involving a single knife fighter against a group of men with swords demonstrated the opposite, with the man wielding the knife killing or seriously wounding his opponents before they finally cut him down. An Italian knife fighter of this caliber presented a perfectly serious threat to two men, one armed with nothing more than a cane and the other, although having a sword in his hand, already wounded. Yet not only their ability with knives made such "bandits" (the word Detenhof consistently used to refer to Visconti and his ilk) so formidable; they also relied on drugs to enhance their stamina and to dull their pain. In such a state, light wounds did not bother them at all and even when severely hurt they battled on. If such bandits thought they would be involved in a fight, they swallowed in advance "a powdered mixture of opium" to fire them up and impart courage. The bailiff had dug out of Visconti's pocket some finely ground powder wrapped in paper. Could one not expect, Detenhof queried rhetorically, that a vagabond and hotspur like Visconti would possess an opiate or something like it?[44]

Virtual unanimity existed on Visconti. He was a bandit, vagabond, cardsharp, imposter, and thief. He was violent, perhaps even suicidal, vengeful, and desperate to the point of irrationality. In addition, however, he was a strong, well-built man in the prime of life (in his early forties), trained in knife fighting and used to a rough-and-tumble world. The characteristics of his personality, his personal history, and the way he as an individual represented a series of contemporary types, reflected and personified traits distinctive to his times and his place in them. Obviously, brutal and unpredictable men inhabit every historical period. The late eighteenth century, however, also nurtured a unique brand of adventurer. Sillem, Detenhof, Romellini, Sanpelayo, Kesslitz, and others pieced together a "Visconti" from parts of a real and an imagined world of bandits, adventurers, and imposters. In his case, it was imbued with an emblematic Italianness. He was a type that not only belonged to the milieu of outcasts and outsiders, however. His successes depended on a seamy penumbra of bandits, adventurers, and imposters snugly overlapping with the glitzy, yet quite respectable, world of nobles, officers, and courts. Shifting social hierarchies, greater social and geographical mobility, and the written and read world of the adventure yarn, the novel, the true-crime story, and the romance, contributed vital parts to his creation. We have already seen how the fast world that encompassed drifters like Romellini and Visconti, profligate nobles like Poniński, and Beau Brummel pacesetters contrasted with a *bürgerliche* universe peopled by merchants, moralists, and magistrates.

Imposter, adventurer, and bandit; all three types played an important role in the eighteenth-century world of the city, the court, and the imagination.[45] Casanova immediately leaps to mind, and the connection is absolutely pertinent. Casanova, by birth a Venetian and the son of an actor, was variously a cleric in minor orders, writer, soldier, spy, diplomat, and librarian, as well as being an adventurer, imposter, and libertine. One knows Casanova so well because of his memoirs, but a series of other libertine adventurers also became famous or notorious for their impostures, financial double-dealings, deceptions, and often for their exploits in the twilight world of secret diplomacy and espionage. Casanova himself mentions at least fifty of them in his memoirs.[46]

And this is the mere tip of the iceberg. In 1710, for example, the Irish rake Patrick Hurley played the Dutch for fools: "acting the part of a Nobleman, he travell'd with his Retinue into Holland, where passing for an Irish Person of Quality at the Hague, by his cunning Insinuations of Generosity, and outward Splendor among the Dutch, he obtain'd so much Favour among them, as to borrow Ten Thousand Pounds of the Bank of Amsterdam, which he carried clear off the Ground, without ever coming to Account for their unusual Civility to Strangers." John Law partook of this world and, although generally known for his financial schemes during the Regency in France, he was a shadowy figure in his early years as well. The chevalier d'Eon dressed as a woman pretending to dress as a man and yet was a principal agent in the King's Secret. The master charlatan Giuseppe Balsamo (1743–95) was born of poor parents in Palermo, but by 1781, he moved in Warsaw's high society, even persuading Kazimierz Poniatowski to try out his elixir of youth. Styling himself Alessandro, count di Cagliostro, he for a while cut a very successful path through fashionable Paris as a magician, adventurer, and magnetic healer (like a proto-Mesmer). After his involvement in the Diamond Necklace affair that ruined the reputation of Marie Antoinette, however, he was imprisoned in the Bastille, where he died.[47]

The successes of Casanova, Law, Hurley, d'Eon, the "false prince of Albania," and Cagliostro in deceiving their contemporaries testify to how well they represented the eighteenth century and how they actually shaped that world. Law was a visionary and in many ways "the father of paper money." Cagliostro linked occultism and the broader world of the Enlightenment, and some scholars have actually cast him as a "prophet of revolution." D'Eon may have been odd, but he facilitated a secret diplomacy that schemed to topple kings.[48]

Adventurers, imposters, thieves, and even murderers seem to have been very much cut from the same cloth. Such individuals crossed the boundaries demarcating the real and the hypothetical with complete ease. In them, real-life morphed into fiction and back again almost seamlessly. One of the most famous murder cases of the late seventeenth century became a stock true-crime story of the eighteenth century, reprinted, retold, and embellished many times. It involved the marquise de Brinvilliers, who, despite being married, took up with the ne'er-do-well sieur Godin, known as Sainte-Croix. Sainte-Croix, the illegitimate son of a man of distinguished family, served in Marquis Brinvilliers's regiment. He was, according to Pitaval, "one of those souls born with the seeds of the greatest crimes [within them] but who, with a genius for deceit, had the skill to conceal their bad characters beneath an imposing exterior." The marquise's father had Sainte-Croix sent to the Bastille, where he became acquainted with an Italian, who taught him the secret arts of poisoning. Once released, he and his mistress proceeded to murder her father and her two brothers; her sister barely escaped their plot. Like Visconti, Sainte-Croix was gallows-bait, a seducer of women, and a violent man with an attractive exterior. It was not incidental to the success of the story that an *Italian* had instructed him in the nefarious skill of poisoning.[49]

For each grandiose character who occupied the center of the eighteenth-century stage, a whole chorus of bit players peopled its edges. Distinguishing duodecimo imposters and adventurers from the lumpenproletariat of bandits, cutpurses, and ordinary crooks was not easy, however, and Visconti's own career shows how often these categories overlapped. Nonetheless, while the great imposters and adventurers possessed considerable theatrical talent, their smaller counterparts were far less adroit and, in fact, played only buffoons. The illusions they created were tinsel and quickly collapsed when they stumbled over their lines and missed their cues. Where the great ones seemed to enjoy the risk, expanding their deceptions ever outward, those of smaller talents and means feared discovery and skipped town when the going got hot.

Let us also not mistake fiction for reality. The origins and early lives of men like Visconti and women like Romellini approximate the novels of the eighteenth century in their tropes, but the frequent happy conclusions— the successful reunion, for example, of lost sons with their wealthy and honorable parents; the marriage of the poor but honest maiden to a propertied or noble spouse; the making good of, for instance, a Tom Jones or a Moll Flanders—rarely came to pass in real life. Rather, many ended, like Visconti, dead in a pool of blood, while the Kesslitzes and Romellinis of that world soon faded back into the historical woodwork.

An Authentic Hidalgo

No one would seem less like Visconti than Antoine de Sanpelayo, the official representative of the Spanish crown in Hamburg, an established and wealthy *homme d'affaires* and son of a prominent hidalgo and mercantile family from Bilbao. Whereas Visconti moved on the fringes of respectable and fashionable society and scavenged its leavings, Sanpelayo inhabited its core and fed on its fruits. He socialized with notable merchants and with nobles in Hamburg. He enjoyed an intimate friendship with the French resident, Baron de la Houze, moreover, and often supped with him. Even had Romellini never lived, the paths of Visconti and Sanpelayo might nonetheless have crossed, however, for the fashionable rubbed elbows with a much broader public in coffeehouses, on the promenades, at the opera, theater, and in public gardens and squares.

The story of Sanpelayo begins in Spain, or rather in Bilbao, where he first made his mark as a merchant. Spain's trade with Hamburg had been considerable since the sixteenth century, and the colonial traffic through Spain remained extensive. While we do not know what prompted Sanpelayo to resettle in Hamburg, he was hardly the only Spanish merchant who lived or worked there and certainly not the only merchant whose business with Hamburg was substantial.

In the rich Iberian trade, Hamburg functioned as an intermediary. Central ports in the transshipping trade were first Cádiz and Málaga, then Seville, Barcelona, Sanlúcar, Alicante, Gibraltar, and—Sanpelayo's home base—Bilbao.[50] Bilbao facilitated commercial traffic between northern Spain and the Hanse cities, particularly in four major Spanish products: iron, wood, Castilian wool, and colonial goods. Far greater in volume, variety, and worth, however, were the wares sent from Hamburg to Bilbao. Of these products, linen assumed pride of place. Although the trade with Spain in the middle years of the eighteenth century stagnated somewhat, it bloomed again after the Seven Years' War and flourished at least until the end of the century. By the 1780s, about two-thirds of all Silesian linen went to Spain, and most of this passed through Hamburg. Total ship traffic between Hamburg and Bilbao was impressive even when compared to that of other major European ports. In 1769, for instance, 31 ships sailed between London and Bilbao and in 1774, 24; between Amsterdam and Bilbao in 1769 and 1774, 25. Traffic between Bilbao and the ports of Bordeaux and Bristol only slightly exceeded that with Hamburg: in 1769, 17, 11, and 10 ships respectively; in 1774, 13, 14, and 13.[51]

We can thus safely assume that Sanpelayo came to Hamburg for business purposes. Hamburg's vast economic hinterlands and burgeoning markets nourished a commercial vitality that begot grand fortunes but also lured the less lucky or less financially adroit onto the rocks of bankruptcy and ruin. Thus, Hamburg attracted aggressive businessmen who thrived, or thought they could thrive, in a heated economic environment. Sanpelayo, by all reports, appears to have been one such entrepreneur. Kesslitz believed that the venture they planned—to open direct trade between Silesia and Bilbao—could hardly fail when directed by a man like Sanpelayo, "who possesses the abilities and the many [necessary] connections in Spain."[52] While one might reasonably doubt Kesslitz's ability to judge commercial qualifications, Sanpelayo's position as consul, his duties of facilitating commerce between the two states, and his excellent contacts in Spain and Bilbao, as well as with the Spanish crown itself, testify to his acuity as a man of affairs. Precisely what that business entailed is not completely clear, although, considering the massive trade in linen cloth from Hamburg to Spain (and especially to Bilbao), as well as the plans he and Kesslitz concocted, it is reasonable to conclude that Sanpelayo was involved in it. Such trade required him to maintain close contact with Hamburg merchants, as well as with his many clients in Bilbao.

If not Spain's most important port in the eighteenth century (Barcelona probably held that honor), Bilbao nonetheless was an ideal site from which to foster commerce with northern Europe and across the Atlantic to New Spain. Bilbao was then, as it is now, the capital of the province of Vizcaya (Biscay). A Basque city, first settled by seafaring folk, Bilbao boasts a long tradition of fierce communal independence, as well as a well-developed commercial identity. As early as 1511, the city, like the great early modern commercial center Burgos, obtained the right to have its own commercial tribunal promulgate laws. Trade with New Spain made eighteenth-century Bilbao extremely rich and prosperous. This was Sanpelayo's home, or at least where he first won his spurs as a merchant.

Bilbao was unlike most of Spain. In some ways, it resembled Hamburg more than, for example, Madrid, in having a well-developed commercial elite, of which the Sanpelayos formed a part. In the eighteenth century, Spain experienced a modest revival in trade, to which the Basque commercial nobility substantially contributed and from which they profited. Moreover, in Bilbao (as in Valencia, for instance), "merchants fortunate enough to obtain places on the rolls of a *consulado* (chamber of commerce) had acquired for all practical purposes an honorific social position of a quasi-noble character."[53] The family of Sampelayo or Sanpelayo had attained nobility by the late fifteenth century. Even if our Sanpelayo did not belong to this clan, he was almost certainly a hidalgo. By early modern times, the term *hidalgo* comprised the lower nobility or gentry who had no other particular title than Don, "Sir." In Vizcaya, virtually every native male was awarded hidalgo status. Many lived in little more than poverty, but many others, like the Sanpelayos, were prominent and moneyed.[54]

Hamburg differed notably from Bilbao. It was an independent republic, whereas Bilbao was part of a monarchy, and it had no nobles per se or any significant surrounding territory, whereas Basque hidalgos were quite important in both Bilbao proper and its rural agricultural hinterland. Nonetheless, the commercial milieu in Hamburg probably felt quite familiar to Sanpelayo. Citizens in economic pacemaker cities, and especially the prosperous merchants among them, probably had more in common with one another than with their rural countrymen or courtly administrators. Thus the merchants of Bordeaux, Lisbon, Bilbao, Livorno, and elsewhere probably felt far more at ease in one another's society than with many of those who resided either at court or in the countryside, despite the religious differences separating the Catholic Spanish, French, and Italians from the Lutheran Hamburgers. The commercial aristocracy—overseas traders and bankers—of the eighteenth century had accustomed itself to living and working in several economic centers, and a kind of mercantile cosmopolitanism thus distinguished them all. If they fervently supported their own cities and civic traditions, their amphibiousness made them comfortable elsewhere, too. Many Hamburg merchants ("at home and overseas," as one of their best historians refers to them) had often worked in company branches in Spain, France, England, and Russia and had grown accustomed to the customs of their counterparts, often speaking several languages well. As we have seen, durable ties linked Hamburg to Spain and vice versa. In his tripartite identity as consul, merchant, and nobleman, Sanpelayo gained entrée to some of the best circles in the city. He was a merchant among merchants, a noble among nobles, and, of course, a diplomat among diplomats. He filled, as Hamburg merchants themselves often filled, a diplomatic niche of some importance both to his own country and to Hamburg as well.

In May 1758, the Spanish consul to Hamburg, Giacomo Poniso, died. He had represented Spain in Hamburg since 1741. At first, the Senat and the city's Chamber of Commerce had equally expressed great unhappiness about Poniso's appointment. Both bodies had hoped to avoid accepting a Spanish consul, for they believed that trade with Spain could be more advantageously conducted in the absence of one. Moreover, once the precedent of a consul had been established, it would be hard to break. After Poniso's death, however, ten years elapsed before a new consul arrived in Hamburg. Not until 1768 was the position filled, this time with the relatively young (he was about thirty) Bilbao merchant Antoine (Ventura) de Sanpelayo. It is unclear how long Sanpelayo had been in Hamburg before being named consul.[55] Official word reached the Senat in late November 1768, when its agent in Madrid, van de Lepe, reported that a colonel of the elite Walloon Garde had notified him that the king of Spain intended to appoint a consul to Hamburg "to facilitate Spanish recruitment [there] under the direction of Baron d'Herma." This was highly unwelcome news to the Senat. First, all the objections it had originally raised to the appointment of Poniso remained valid: the members of the Senat and the Chamber of Commerce still agreed that trade with Spain would proceed more profitably (at least for Hamburg) if there were no Spanish consul. Second, Hamburg was already at odds over recruitment (with Vienna, Prussia, and Denmark) and confronted with the problem of piracy in the Mediterranean. Ideally, Hamburg's leaders would have liked to do away with Spanish recruitment entirely, but they feared that a refusal to allow Spanish recruiters in the city would evoke royal displeasure and reduce or even curtail commerce with Spain. The imperial government had nevertheless forbidden such recruitment, and Hamburg had long been trying to hammer out a compromise. About a week after receiving this notification, the Senat replied that the appointment of a consul general on these grounds (to facilitate recruitment), was unnecessary, because the Senat was already working to persuade Vienna to make an exception for Spanish needs. Too late. Two days later, Sanpelayo rather suddenly materialized outside the Senat's chambers, credentials in hand. The Senat reflected on its vain attempts to deny the appointment of Poniso and reluctantly agreed "to accept Herr Sanpelayo as consul here." When so informed, Sanpelayo expressed his gratitude and replied "that he was only here in order to protect [the existing] good relations between his court and this city and, if possible, to expand them."[56] The Spanish had stolen a march on the Senat, and it could only put the best face on the situation.

A rocky beginning, perhaps, but worse followed. The position of consul (or consul general) did not in the eyes of the Senat equal that of a resident minister, such as those of France, Prussia, and the Empire. The Senat also preferred to establish special understandings with each of the foreign representatives in the city, if possible keeping each in the dark about the rights and privileges the others enjoyed. Moreover, the Senat insisted (not always successfully) that privileges must be mutually held. In other words, the Spanish consul in Hamburg should enjoy only the rights and privileges accorded to Hanseatic consuls and representatives in Spanish cities. Debates over these sorts of freedoms clouded the relationship between the Senat and Sanpelayo, although he was not the only foreign representative who experienced such annoyances.

The court in Madrid explicitly appointed Sanpelayo to expedite Spanish recruitment; in fact, during his consulship, it ended. In spring 1770, the last Spanish recruiter returned to Spain. Sanpelayo in Hamburg and van der Lepe in Madrid worked hard, and eventually successfully, to convince the Spanish government that Hamburg could no longer allow Spanish recruitment without driving the city into an unacceptable conflict with the Empire.[57] Recruitment constituted an internal problem as much as a matter of foreign relations, however. Recruiters quarreled among themselves and with the locals and clashed repeatedly with the soldiers of the city's garrison and its night-watchmen. Duels between recruiting officers occurred frequently and often ended in death (as in the case of the Prussian recruiting sergeant Carl Rolff, who killed his Danish counterpart in December 1775), thus breeding sticky diplomatic situations for the municipality as it tried to keep order and assert its sovereignty and yet avoid treading on the tender toes of mightier neighbors like Prussia and Denmark. A fracas that broke out between several Spanish recruiters and their Prussian counterparts twice in January 1770 was only too typical and stirred up an all too typical diplomatic hornet's nest. In the wake of the fray, Johann Julius von Hecht, the king of Prussia's representative in Hamburg, passed on to the Senat a request from his master "that Spanish recruitment . . . be completely terminated." Hecht, as always a good friend of the city, had pointed out to his superiors that as much as Hamburg might want to halt Spanish recruitment, it was virtually impossible for the city to do so "without destroying their commerce entirely." The Prussian court satisfied itself with the demand the Senat forbid Spanish recruiters "from taking Prussian subjects under any pretext." The Spanish director of recruitment, d'Herma, quickly agreed to do so, provided "Prussian officers were also told to refrain from recruiting Spanish noncommissioned officers."[58]

The principle of reciprocity upon which d'Herma played was equally favored by the Senat. Hamburg's governors would allow Sanpelayo only the same rights that Hamburg or Hanseatic consuls enjoyed in Spanish cities. Sanpelayo tested this principle many times during his ten years as Spain's representative. Some of Sanpelayo's dealings with the Senat and the city matched or differed only slightly from the relations other consuls or residents had. Admittedly, he represented his government and its subjects considerably less actively than did Hecht (who bristled at real or supposed slights to Prussian prerogatives) or the imperial resident, Binder von Kriegelstein. The French and Danish representatives appear more frequently in the Senat protocols. The relatively small number of Spaniards who lived in Hamburg, compared to Prussians, Danes, or even Frenchmen, in part explains Sanpelayo's lower profile. Moreover, Sanpelayo, by virtue of his somewhat ambiguous position as consul, had less to do and less clout with the Senat in any case. Hecht and, later, Binder von Kriegelstein and de la Houze were much busier diplomats, but they were not also running their own businesses, as Sanpelayo was. As we have seen, when Sanpelayo invoked his consular immunity in 1775, the Senat only reluctantly acknowledged it, and then only to avoid offending Spain. Van der Lepe had several times warned the Senat that it must deal cautiously with

Sanpelayo, because he enjoyed "important protection" in Madrid. None other than the marquis de Grimaldi, Spain's powerful foreign minister, championed his cause.[59]

One issue in particular bruised relations between Sanpelayo and the Senat: Sanpelayo's position as consul and its peculiarly indeterminate status. Many people in Hamburg, including the magistrates and at least some members of the diplomatic corps regarded him more as a private person than as an official of his government. Binder von Kriegelstein, in writing to Vienna about the events of October 1775, referred to Sanpelayo as a consul "only in name" (*Titular-consul*) and actually "nothing more than a businessman." The Senat had always meticulously avoided endowing him with the rights and privileges residents like Hecht and Binder von Kriegelstein enjoyed. Yet no policy statement spelled this out. Individual decisions taken over the course of his consulship, however, clearly show that the city quite deliberately left him uninformed about the rights other diplomats enjoyed, used every opportunity to impress his lesser position upon him, and pushed for return of any favor it granted him.[60]

If Sanpelayo and the Spanish government viewed Hamburg's attitude toward him as less than satisfactory, others saw it in a far different light, especially when they considered the deference the city paid him throughout the Kesslitz investigation. While Kesslitz was incarcerated, Sanpelayo remained free. The city "never detained [him] or even regarded [him] as an accomplice." Moreover, he conducted his activities as usual, appeared in public without restrictions, supped with his friend and protector de la Houze, attended the theater, and—most infuriating of all—visited Romellini while she was under arrest. All of this, but especially the last, offended many in the city, not least Binder von Kriegelstein and the other members of the diplomatic corps. Binder von Kriegelstein understood the reasons behind the special treatment accorded the consul: personal, economic, and diplomatic motives had induced the Senat to handle him with kid gloves. De la Houze was Sanpelayo's friend; Sanpelayo, one recalls, dined with the French diplomat on the night of 18 October. De la Houze and the French court had quickly gone to work, Binder von Kriegelstein wrote to his superiors in February 1776, to ensure that Sanpelayo would neither directly nor indirectly be involved in any sort of criminal investigation or procedure; specifically, he would "under no pretext whatsoever" be summoned to appear in court. Binder von Kriegelstein's perception of favoritism may have been wrong, for the Hamburg Senat was actually exceedingly annoyed by the fervor with which de la Houze took Sanpelayo's part, about which it had complained to Paris and Madrid.[61]

Two incidents perfectly illustrate how diplomatic maneuvering crossed with, and crossed up, the Senat's attempts to preserve the rights Hamburgers enjoyed in Spain and to gain new concessions for them by using Sanpelayo's own demands as a wedge.

In his first year of residence in Hamburg, Sanpelayo had battled with the Senat over the payment of excise taxes on wine and beer. Ministers plenipotentiary and residents imported wine and beer duty-free for their own use (and that of their suites). To what extent this right also pertained to consuls—and, in particular, to the Spanish consul—was another matter altogether. In June 1769, Sanpelayo had requested from the director of the wine excise "free passage of some wine, a part of which was only in transit . . . to the Spanish ambassador in Copenhagen, another part of which, however, was on his own account." Virtually simultaneously, he solicited a similar exception for ten tuns of Altona beer. The wine headed for Copenhagen posed no problem: it passed through Hamburg duty-free. The wine and beer "for Herr Sanpelayo's own reckoning," however, raised a completely different point. Was he importing the beverages for sale? If so, the duty clearly applied. More important here, however, loomed the issue of whether the wine and beer were for his own consumption. To permit him that freedom would elevate him to the level of the other foreign representatives in the city, and that the Senat dearly wished to avoid. A quick conference with the merchant Steetz, who had once served as Hamburg's consul in Cádiz, produced the response that this right "in no way pertained." While Steetz had lived in Cádiz, he had enjoyed no such privilege. Still deep in the delicate negotiations involving recruitment, and still, of course, dependent to some extent on Sanpelayo's good offices in that respect, the Senat decided on accommodation, however. Steetz volunteered to speak to Sanpelayo "as a friend," while the Senat agreed to allow Sanpelayo a one-time exemption from duties. The Senat nonetheless stipulated that "it could not permit Herr Sanpelayo such freedom from fees in the future." On the surface, the decision rested on the completely transparent dictum of reciprocity: Sanpelayo should receive no exemption from import duties on wine, because Hamburg consuls in Spain paid them. The Senat stood by this decision, and, when Sanpelayo again claimed duty-free imports in February 1770, it refused. The Senat knew that its denial might cause trouble with Madrid, so it wrote to van der Lepe to forestall the harm done if Sanpelayo appealed to his king. In this note, the Senat indignantly rejected Sanpelayo's demand as "improper."[62]

The Senat had painted itself into a corner, however, and its legal advisor, Syndic Faber, warned it against filing an official protest in Madrid. First, the consul "enjoyed much standing" with the Spanish foreign minister, Grimaldi. Second, Sanpelayo and the French consul, Lesseps, were in frequent contact, and he would quickly learn that Lesseps paid no duties, and would, therefore, "pretend to the same." Thus, Faber proposed that because all Hamburg and Hanseatic consuls in Spain paid import duties, Sanpelayo must do so as well. If Sanpelayo could succeed in changing those circumstances, he, too, would benefit. This time the consul protested vigorously. He penned a "disrespectful note" to the director of the wine excise. His quick temper was becoming noticeable. He sent the offensive memorandum in August, and not until November did he apologize: "[the lines] had been [written] in the first heat of the moment and in response to what one of his servants had told him; he [now] wishes that he had never sent them." Nonetheless, his instructions from Madrid ordered him "to make sure that he obtained the same rights as other consuls [had]." Thus, he hoped that he would be placed on the same footing as the French and British representatives. The Senat told van der Lepe to request similar rights for the Hamburg consul in Madrid. At the same time, the Senat moved to decide future cases as they arose. In other words, without freeing Sanpelayo from paying duties, the Senat temporized, allowing him a grace period until Madrid responded. That solution dissolved as soon as the Senat received Grimaldi's uncompromising decision: "that no such reciprocity can be shown to Herr van der Lepe because no [other] consul in Spain possesses such exemptions." At the same time, Grimaldi demanded that Sanpelayo receive "whatever consuls from the other most favored nations" enjoyed. If Grimaldi was unwilling to compromise, the Senat remained equally adamant: "if our consuls in Spain enjoy no similar privileges," then duty-free passage of goods would no longer be permitted to Sanpelayo. And that was that.[63]

These relatively minor matters were, of course, only small steps in a much more elaborate diplomatic dance over sovereignty and prestige. Obviously, not only Spain and its consuls were involved, and such probings were the quotidian stuff of diplomacy. Alone, each incident could hardly crab relationships between the two powers. Yet even small disagreements such as those over wine and beer duties could accumulate and incite bigger battles or provide the ammunition to wage them. Several other episodes in the late 1760s and early 1770s, ranging from annoying to more serious, also unsettled Sanpelayo's relationships with the governors of Hamburg and occasionally made him the talk of the town. And once the Visconti affair became public, earlier missteps and peccadilloes rendered his position more precarious. Earlier unpleasant episodes bolstered the Senat's case against him (even in Madrid), reduced sympathy for him in the city, and caused the consul considerable discomfort.

Sanpelayo's troubles in Hamburg had begun just six months after his credentialing, when he complained to the Senat vigorously about an injury done him by the night-watchmen. One had "actually struck him with his lance," wounding him so severely that he was bedridden for several days. He did not exaggerate. A member of the Senat confirmed that Sanpelayo "had really received a dangerous blow to the head." What exactly had happened was not determined, and Sanpelayo seems to have been satisfied that the responsible parties had been arrested and questioned. He later agreed to forgive them, and the city released them with a sharp warning to proceed more prudently in the future.[64]

Sanpelayo's problems went beyond run-ins with the night-watchmen and bickering over duties. Twice he had requested special legal consideration from the Senat. In 1771, he asked the Senat to expedite a civil case against Jacob Schultz for unspecified reasons; the Senat quietly pushed the matter in Sanpelayo's favor. Then in 1775, mere months before the death of Visconti, he wanted to have one of his employees arrested for his "dissolute lifestyle" (!) and packed off to his relatives in Spain; the Senat arranged it. Sanpelayo himself was the occasional object of legal requests to the Senat. In 1774, for instance, a commercial court in Berlin asked the Senat to help it collect 6 Reichsthaler and 21 groschen in fees from Sanpelayo. In 1771, he again came to the attention of the Senat as the defendant in a paternity suit.[65]

None of these troubles was, taken by itself, especially worrisome or even unusual. Other prominent members of Hamburg foreign or diplomatic groups had also, for instance, knocked heads with the night-watchmen or suffered at the hands of outraged inhabitants.[66] Anti-Catholic sentiment in Hamburg persisted, especially among the lower classes, and helped fuel resentment of foreigners. An illegitimate child, a minor set-to with municipal officials, a spat with a local, and an unpaid debt hardly stacked up to the stuff of great scandal. Still, these incidents lay not far in Sanpelayo's past and all too close to the surface. His occasional harsh words to the Senat, his arrogance in demanding freedom from import duties, and his slightly scandalous personal life were all common knowledge among the political and social elites, in diplomatic circles, and in the broader, if vaguer, arena of rumor and idle talk. In light of the events of 18/19 October 1775, actions that could have been easily forgotten as minor missteps or excused as human blemishes more amusing than dangerous, and a temper that was perhaps a bit hasty but typically, perhaps even attractively, "Iberian," became unheeded warning signs. Moreover, such things could be marshaled against him. After 1775, Sanpelayo was no longer like other diplomats, all of whom had experienced their own problems with locals and with city government. Those who already disliked him, or found him unsympathetic, could now justify their feelings as the reaction of the honest and respectable to the corrupt and disreputable.

In late 1775 and 1776, as the drama of the Visconti death unfolded, and as the roles Kesslitz and Sanpelayo had played in it elicited comment in the fora of government and law, in the streets, coffeehouses, and sitting rooms, and in the correspondence that passed between Hamburg and capitals like Berlin, Vienna, Madrid, and Paris, Sanpelayo emerged in several guises. In Madrid and Paris, he was an innocent bystander who, despite having lifted no hand to strike Visconti, had nonetheless suffered public humiliation, great expense, and even blackmail. Another Sanpelayo emerged in the dispatches Binder von Kriegelstein sent to Vienna. This Sanpelayo had purchased a mistress "for a piece of gold" from a cheap adventurer who was little more than a pimp and subsequently killed him and bought Kesslitz's silence. He had connived with de la Houze to bribe Syndic Sillem. He was a bad-tempered man, a jealous lover, a libertine, and even a crook.

Extracting Sanpelayo's personality from such historical sources is an arduous task, because all too often the information we have on him comes from those who were his enemies or whose agendas remain obscure or dubious. Binder von Kriegelstein disliked Sanpelayo intensely, as he also disliked de la Houze, one of Sanpelayo's strongest protectors and advocates. Broader political considerations affected the situation, too. Although Austria and France had recently been allied in the Seven Years' War, the relationship between Spain and France warmed in the 1760s and 1770s, producing a new convention over consular representation and trade, while that between France and Austria cooled (despite the dynastic tie). The trade agreement France and Hamburg signed in 1769 underscored the importance of France and its colonies, like Spain and its colonies, to Hamburg's commerce.[67] Such factors strongly affected how various people viewed Sanpelayo.

A short temper and a tendency to act precipitously characterized the man. Although Sanpelayo's dealing with the Senat were not extensive in the late 1760s and early 1770s, they show that he was rather quick to anger and already renowned in the city for his temperamental outbursts. Kesslitz, although a good friend of Sanpelayo's and perhaps also financially dependent on him, had by his own testimony on the night of Visconti's death at least twice warned Sanpelayo not to "do anything rash," suggesting that he had reason to believe that Sanpelayo was easily provoked. Kesslitz had made sure that Sanpelayo only carried a walking stick with him to Romellini's lodgings. A man with a short fuse, perhaps? Romellini drew an even less flattering portrait of the consul, although it should be remembered that this negative testimony came *after* her expulsion from Hamburg. Her understanding with Sanpelayo was, at least on the surface, a completely straightforward one: she would be his mistress; he would pay her expenses; and she would agree not to take any other lovers. Although Sanpelayo rented housing for her, he also borrowed money from her, took back gifts he had given her, and expected her to entertain his friends extravagantly without compensation (at least that was her version). Apparently, she and Sanpelayo did not live in tranquility; they had fought and made up several times. Even before the night of Visconti's death, she told the notary Erdmann that Sanpelayo was "unbelievably jealous" and frequently threatened her when he thought she was flirting with other men. Moreover, he had induced a friend of his, "a strong Prussian officer" (Kesslitz?), to insult her in public saying "the most obscene things" to her face. Sanpelayo swore that he would denounce her to the magistrates as a dissolute woman and would have her punished if she ever deceived him. Although she had had two children with Sanpelayo, his temper had poisoned their relationship. A few months before Visconti reappeared, she had told the same notary that "she could not hold out with the consul much longer." His possessiveness had made him "a real tyrant" and her life a misery: he insulted her, threatened her with physical injury, forced her to sleep with him although he was diseased with the pox, and told her that if she tried to leave, he would kill her.[68]

While neither the Senat nor Countess von Bentinck nor Binder von Kriegelstein acted on Romellini's accusations, or perhaps even believed them fully, Binder von Kriegelstein thought enough of them to forward them to his superiors in Vienna. He regarded Sanpelayo in the same light as the Senat apparently did by June 1776 when it requested his recall as a man "who has led a very lascivious and debauched life [here]." Binder von Kriegelstein and others were only too well aware of the "many beastly habits" Sanpelayo had acquired during his time in Hamburg. Sanpelayo and Kesslitz had bad reputations, he noted. Their conduct "appalled our [Catholic] churches here . . . [and] they spent entire nights gambling in the coffeehouses and more or less made a profession of it." After the city released Kesslitz in mid May, Sanpelayo continued to offend public sensibilities by visiting "that wanton" at a rented house in Altona. Worse still, he went to see her in the company of "his 'worthy' companion," that is, Kesslitz, and one could only anticipate, Binder von Kriegelstein sighed, that sooner or later some new disturbance would arise out of these connections. The Senat and diplomatic circles had a right to be annoyed.[69]

Moreover, Binder von Kriegelstein (and others) came to believe (or at least believe it probable) that Sanpelayo had been considerably more involved in the murder than first suspected, and that the Senat (or certain members of that body) had shown Sanpelayo extraordinary preference, for diplomatic, economic, and political reasons, and winked at the real facts of the crime. For instance, Binder von Kriegelstein noted that a few years previously, the Spanish crown had explicitly and publicly acknowledged that "consuls enjoyed no legal immunity," but rather were subject to the laws of their posting. Despite that, "Sanpelayo continues to enjoy [here] the most perfect freedom of movement. He is regarded [almost] as a real citizen because of his considerable business. To give the appearance of his being under house arrest, a watch stands before his door. Many [magistrates] are easily corrupted, and Sanpelayo knew how to spend large sums to rid himself of all these [inconveniences]. He will soon use the same means to liberate Baron Kesslitz [from his debts to the city]."[70]

A month later, Binder von Kriegelstein conveyed his suspicions to Vienna in even stronger terms. A cover-up was under way, and it involved the Senat. Inexplicably, "these [magistrates] did not even have the nominal Spanish consul arrested, although he is really nothing more than a businessman. [They] used the excuse . . . that he must be considered a public person. Yet he was clearly regarded as a flight risk for a substantial caution was demanded of [him]." If Sanpelayo was a public person, Binder von Kriegelstein reasoned, then he enjoyed immunity, and the Senat had no right to demand a deposit to secure his compliance. If not, then the magistrates should have placed him under strict house arrest at the very least. What had happened, however, contributed to the "revulsion of the public." Mere days after the murder (and Binder von Kriegelstein was by no means bashful about calling it that), Sanpelayo had dared show his face at the Exchange, conducted his normal business, and even attended the theater. All of this seemed to demonstrate "a pronounced favoritism" but also a far more sinister "massive and well-thought-out bribery" campaign. This was hardly mincing words.[71]

What was being covered up, by whom, and to what end? Suspicions of malfeasance had arisen early. By mid November, barely a month after the killing, rumors of bias and corruption animated diplomatic circles and circulated widely among the public. They never died out entirely. The final disposition of the case seemed to substantiate those misgivings and impart to them more sinister and cynical meanings. In May, after the courts reached the decision that Kesslitz would be released after paying expenses, Binder von Kriegelstein once again pointed a recriminative finger at Sanpelayo. Clearly, Kesslitz had not covered the costs, for his penury was proverbial; Sanpelayo had probably done so to seal Kesslitz's lips. According to Binder von Kriegelstein, the two friends had come to an under-standing, agreeing to conceal the fact that Sanpelayo, not Kesslitz, had slain Visconti. Rumor reported that on the night of the murder, Kesslitz had been able to spend some three or four hours alone, speaking to his lawyer, Detenhof. "The [real] story is that he [Kesslitz] had no part in the affair other than striking the first, by no means fatal blow, on the head [of Visconti]. Sanpelayo and his whore then [together] inflicted the other twenty-two wounds." Kesslitz had agreed to stick to this story in return for a lump sum payment of 10,000 Reichsthaler. Sanpelayo, Detenhof, and Kesslitz had all banked on the intervention of the Prussian government to protect Kesslitz, as an erstwhile Prussian officer, from prosecution and punishment. "If, however," Binder von Kriegelstein concluded, the local magistrates had "done their job properly, this [deceit] would never have worked."[72] So, who, supposedly, had been bought? Garlieb Sillem.

Binder von Kriegelstein ticked off a series of improprieties that had distinguished the investigation from its inception and that continued to pervert the legal procedure; all ran counter to the statutes and customs of Hamburg law. For instance, Sillem, the most junior, the "fourth," syndic, the one normally responsible for criminal investigations, had supposedly been "promoted" to the position of third, the one most directly responsi-ble for foreign affairs. Sillem then accepted a hefty bribe to bend the case to Sanpelayo's benefit and subsequently falsified reports written to Berlin and Madrid. "If one had been able to examine the originals" Sillem sent, Binder von Kriegelstein argued, one would see that the contents "differed entirely from the drafts read in, and approved by, the Senat." They had been changed, he suggested, in Sillem's office and with the connivance of Sillem and his clerk.

The imperial resident correctly understood that Hamburg's constitu-tion and administrative practice made the fourth syndic responsible for criminal prosecutions. Sillem had been appointed syndic in 1768, and from then until 1775, he was the most junior. In December 1775, following the death of the venerable Johann Klefeker, Paridom Anckelmann (until then a secretary to the Senat) became syndic. Thus, in the very middle of the Kesslitz affair, Sillem in normal fashion moved up in seniority. Under these circumstances, it was not unusual for him to continue to have a hand in criminal affairs for which he had earlier been responsible. As third syndic, Sillem quite properly conducted Hamburg's foreign affairs and his correspondence with van der Lepe in Madrid and Wever in Berlin about the case, for example, was standard operating procedure.

Be all this as it may, a significant number of people in Hamburg, including many among the elite and the foreign community, perceived irregularities in the case from its onset and were apt to interpret these "disorders" as proof of a conspiracy to cover up the involvement of Sanpelayo. The collegial bodies in Hamburg had always mistrusted the Senat's dealings with foreign powers, believing that the Senat was altogether too chummy with other governments and, by catering to their wishes, jeopardized municipal freedoms. Such a whitewashing might have resulted from a desire to protect Sanpelayo as consul, to accommodate more important people like de la Houze, to avoid annoying crowned heads, or—the most ominous of the interpretations—because Sillem had been bribed and his colleagues had been unwilling to expose his dishonesty publicly. No trace of any of this appears, of course, in the Senat protocols. (Still, one suspicious piece of evidence had surfaced earlier in the investigation. While under house arrest, Romellini continued to be attended by her cook, Engauen, although another woman—Catharine Rouget—was hired as an additional servant. Apparently, Engauen and Romellini had an argument that Rouget overheard, in which Engauen threatened to reveal that she had lied for Romellini and the consul. Although the praetor questioned both Rouget and Engauen about the incident, nothing further was done.)[73] Official dishonesty, if and when it existed, almost never became part of the senatorial record. Over the course of the eighteenth century in Hamburg, virtually no instances of political corruption came to light, a circumstance that indicates either the relative probity of the governors and governing process in Hamburg or a completely effective closing of senatorial ranks. Numerous political commentators, however, have been less reticent and have argued that the Senat often swept corruption under the carpet.[74]

In short, his enemies charged that Sillem had turned the investigation in the direction he desired by using scare techniques on the Senat and by adroitly manipulating what he wrote to Madrid, Paris, and Berlin and craftily editing what the Senat learned from him. None of this could be proven, but everyone knew that Kesslitz enjoyed a suspiciously comfortable house arrest. He was allowed congenial companionship, unhindered speech with anyone he chose, and complete freedom of movement around the Eimbeck'sche Haus. The Senat tolerated grossly offensive behavior from Sanpelayo, again something that was inexplicable unless someone had been bought. Sanpelayo, who was at very least to be regarded as "the source of the entire ruckus," pranced off to see his "whore" whenever he pleased. He had even impregnated Romellini while she was under arrest. Detenhof himself had let it slip to Binder von Kriegelstein that "the prosecutor had done more good for the accused than he ever could have [achieved]." "Evidently," Binder von Kriegelstein concluded, "something rather fishy is going on behind the scenes." The way in which justice had been done (or not) in this case had "mortified many senators and caused general disgruntlement among the [broader] public," as well as among the nonsenatorial parts of city government.[75]

In June, after the case had been more or less wrapped up and Romellini banned from the city, Binder von Kriegelstein learned from some of his confidants that a good number of senators were absolutely convinced of Sanpelayo's guilt and few believed him totally innocent. The diplomatic situation, however, dictated caution. Only Grimaldi's "baseless threats" and fear of hamstringing Hamburg's commerce with Spain, "as happened several years ago over the signing of the Algiers agreement" (with the Barbary pirates), could have caused the magistracy to be so ill-advised as to treat Sanpelayo so solicitously, damaging its own authority and "counter to the proper course of justice." Public reaction had been appalled that Sanpelayo, in distinction to Kesslitz, had remained at liberty. People were repelled by Sanpelayo's "extreme licentiousness" and aghast at the effrontery and poor taste the Spanish consul showed in continuing to flaunt a sexual relationship with his "whore." Again from his sources in the Senat, Binder von Kriegelstein knew that the Senat fervently wanted Sanpelayo recalled.

As we know, Romellini stayed in Altona only a few months and then went to the Hague and to Rotterdam, where we finally lose track of her. Sanpelayo, on the other hand, never left Hamburg. From Altona, Romellini launched an offensive of her own. She carried out a campaign on several fronts: pleas to Sanpelayo were certainly her first step, although we have no written record of them. When those failed, she broke with him, and put her case before others: among them, the Senat, Countess von Bentinck, and Binder von Kriegelstein. We have seen what she wanted; money to "set herself up again," the restitution of her jewels and silver, a dowry for her daughter, and so on. Far more intriguing here is the entirely different story that Romellini bruited about. She pointed her finger directly at Sillem. Her letters to Countess von Bentinck and Binder von Kriegelstein, in the words of the latter, "confirmed the suspicions of the public": Sanpelayo was the murderer, and Kesslitz had been "base enough to take the blame on himself for money."[76]

Although Binder von Kriegelstein consistently referred to Romellini as the "notorious Romellini," whose communications to him and to the countess merited no response, nonetheless he accepted as true, or partially true, many of the charges she raised. He acknowledged that a cabal of powerful men had conspired against her. She insisted that if the king of

Spain and Grimaldi knew the truth about "the horrible deeds of this monster [Sanpelayo]," they would have quickly withdrawn all support for him. Moreover, they would also have been impelled to think twice in the future "about using frivolous threats to impede the workings of a sacred justice." Binder von Kriegelstein was fully convinced that the Senat would have punished Sanpelayo (if not as the actual perpetrator, then at the very least as a culpable accomplice), if for no other reason than to assuage the wrath of the public, had it not been terrified of losing Spanish trade.[77]

Binder von Kriegelstein reported to Vienna that conclusive evidence of the plot to murder Visconti existed, and was, or at least had been, in Romellini's hands. In her account to him and to Countess von Bentinck, Romellini maintained that she possessed "original letters [from Sanpelayo] that spoke of the decision made to free her from her persecutor [Visconti]." She had intended to entrust these to "a talented solicitor" who would prepare a *species facti* to be published and thereby reveal to the world the "true sequence of events." Binder von Kriegelstein felt that this could probably not be done in Altona, for "due to a wonderful set of circumstances, those two evildoers [Sanpelayo and Kesslitz] still find great support [there]" from foreign powers.[78]

Publishing a *species facti* summarizing the facts of a case was a favored method of appealing to the court of public opinion in the eighteenth century. The exact titles often differed: one might offer a "Missive to the Public" or a "Complete Documentary Record" and express indignation or wrath ("the innocent victim of . . . ." appeared in many titles). Each, however, adopted a quasi-legal structure and tone. While such publications often saw the light of day in political cases (involving accusations of corruption, for example) and frequently conveyed a partisan position, as during the virtual civil war that reigned in Hamburg in the late seventeenth and early eighteenth centuries, they were also the tools of private persons involved in criminal or civil proceedings. Those who felt their rights trampled upon, their honor impugned, or their motives misconstrued grabbed a pen or, as Romellini proposed to do, hired a collaborator to tell their side of the story. Scandals produced the most striking examples. For instance, in the Guyard incest case of 1760s, both Charlotte's father and her husband felt deeply aggrieved and mishandled by Hamburg's justice system. Both put their suits before the public (earning, in each case, senatorial ire). The audience they addressed was not, however, merely a vague general public. Nor did they seek only self-justification. They also appealed to larger political entities, seeking redress of grievances and palpable support. Denis Martin, Charlotte's father, clearly intended to attract the attention of Prussia, which he did.[79] Romellini's purpose was much the same. *Species facti* assumed many forms, but one of the most effective was the kind Romellini envisioned: a compilation of damning letters that aired the "true state of affairs."[80]

Binder von Kriegelstein confided an even more incredible—and villainous—story to Colloredo seven months later. He drew this information from the Russian minister in the Hague, (at the time, Prince Dimitri Golitsyn, who had also served in France as the Russian minister plenipotentiary from 1763 to 1768, directly after the Seven Years War),[81] where Romellini now resided. Romellini had been forced to leave Altona quickly and silently "after first receiving all sorts of promises and then suffering all sorts of alarming threats." She went to Holland, hoping to have published there "the true circumstances and exact events" proving Sanpelayo's "guilt in this bloody affair" from his own words in the letters. Her plans became known in Hamburg through "confidential channels," however, and these then alerted Sanpelayo and his cronies. The latter, "both with good intentions and evil ones," marshaled "all human means" to persuade Romellini to abandon her course, but rather than deterring her, their efforts reinforced her determination to bring her side of the story to public notice. With this purpose in mind, she had journeyed to Amsterdam to discuss the situation with her lawyer. Unfortunately, on leaving the Hague, she had imprudently entrusted Sanpelayo's letters to the priest at the Spanish embassy, and when she asked for them back, she received the "startling answer, that the Spanish ambassador [there] . . . , the vicomte de la Herreira, had demanded that the priest surrender the entire correspondence to him." Herreira then returned it to Sanpelayo.

Obviously, once the originals were back in Sanpelayo's control, an "authentic *species facti*" would, Binder von Kriegelstein asserted, be "forever denied to the public." Such an accurate recounting of the circumstances was, in his opinion, highly desirable. Not only would truth be served but, perhaps more important, such publication would forestall accusations against others whose actions were neither felonious nor false. This dirty trick had caused a sensation in the Hague, Binder von Kriegelstein reported; according to rumor, Romellini had now decided to take herself and her case to Madrid. Sanpelayo was undaunted. The entire course of events barely inconvenienced him. Binder von Kriegelstein felt that his recall in January 1777 was a mere feint, for Sanpelayo remained in Hamburg, and "[it] is said that he intends to enter the so-called Aliens' Contract . . . which will license him to continue all his business here" under the most propitious circumstances. (The Hamburg Aliens' Contract allowed certain favored groups, English Merchant Adventurers, Dutch Calvinists, Portuguese Jews, and Mennonites, among others, to settle in Hamburg and conduct business there without obtaining citizenship.) In the meantime, Sanpelayo's cousin had arrived and been accepted as the new Spanish consul. One expected that he would continue to support and protect Sanpelayo, which proved true.[82]

At this point, Sanpelayo's story was almost, if not quite, finished. For several months after his dismissal as consul, he was involved in the suit his former landlady, the widow Amberg, had brought against him for unpaid rent on the Neuer Wall. Numerous other outstanding bills also hung over his head. Despite the vigorous intervention of Grimaldi and the new consul, Urqullu, the Senat refused to intervene in the case. After Sanpelayo died, on 28 November 1778, aged forty, Urqullu pressed the Senat to release some of Sanpelayo's property that had been seized to pay his debts, with unknown results.[83]

Once Sanpelayo was buried, the uproar over the affair subsided. Sanpelayo's reputation, of course, never recovered. Still, it cannot be proved that support for him in Hamburg relied on his ability to bribe important men. Baron de la Houze was his friend but was also, as representative of the French court (and, by proxy, also of the Spanish court), obliged to take his part, particularly in defending the diplomatic rights of consuls. He did at times, as the protocols amply demonstrate, become rather heated in dealings with the Senat, but so, too, on occasion did Hecht in his defense of Kesslitz. De la Houze's interest may have been mercenary, but it may also have been unbiased. Likewise, although the details of Romellini's version fit the story excellently, we must distrust her account as well. Of course, it *may* have been true, in part or even entirely. Sanpelayo's flouting of good manners and his lack of good sense—in refusing to give up his sexual affair with Romellini during the investigation and while Kesslitz languished under arrest, for example— offended and alienated many people in Hamburg. But was corruption involved? Did Sillem take money to assist Sanpelayo's case? Again, we cannot know for sure. The correspondence between van der Lepe and Sillem as preserved in the Hamburg archives offers no evidence to support the allegations of Romellini and Binder von Kriegelstein, but there could always have been a *second* set of letters to van der Lepe or even information conveyed to him more privately. What of Kesslitz? Was he base enough to accept money to hush up the real truth? He clearly needed money desperately, but he can hardly be convicted of complicity on need alone. Thus as we close the story of Romellini, Kesslitz, Visconti, and Sanpelayo, many questions remain unresolved and, for that matter, historically moot. Yet the quest for answers has been a fruitful one, opening up, as it has, the lives of people who would have otherwise gone silently and unremarked from the historical stage, but whose existences were yoked to great and famous personages and central events of the age of Frederick the Great.

Retrospective

I never thought to write diplomatic history. All that changed in 1996, however, when a bulky packet landed on my desk in the Hamburg Archive. The label read: "Documents concerning the killing of the so-called Count Visconti by the erstwhile Prussian Lieutenant Herr Baron von Kesslitz, and what thereby came out in regard to the Italian courtesan Romellincini [*sic*] and the Royal Spanish consul, Herr San Pelaÿo, 1775–77."[1] The files stood almost a foot high. Intrigued, I opened the cover and began to read. As I pushed deeper into the stack of papers, I realized that this case would allow me to bring together diplomatic, legal, social, and cultural history in unusual and unusually productive ways.

Liaisons dangereuses is, therefore, a deliberate double entendre. It refers, of course, to the sexual liaisons that had catastrophic outcomes for Romellini, Sanpelayo, Visconti, and Kesslitz, as well as to the sexual liaisons that shaped the imaginary world of novels and the half-fictional, half-authentic genre of crime stories. But other *liaisons dangereuses* became just as relevant: the ones that contoured, and were contoured by, the diplomatic currents washing across eighteenth-century Europe. Here internal politics and foreign affairs meshed. Tussles between Hamburg, Prussia, and Spain over issues of sovereignty inflamed conflicts between the Senat and the *bürgerliche* organs of urban government. Equally compelling were the legal, commercial, and economic concerns raised. In the course of the Kesslitz affair, Prussia, Spain, and France threatened Hamburg with dire economic consequences if the city abused their subjects. These were not empty warnings, even if, in the end, no breaks occurred, and Hamburg's relations with the courts of Europe returned to a state of supple equilibrium. Thus, the Kesslitz affair demonstrates how causes célèbres never remained "mere incidents" but instead were the very hub of European diplomacy. At the same time, the imbrication of individual lives with affairs of state—for instance, Romellini and Poland or Kesslitz and Prussia —shows how deeply personal politics and diplomacy remained through- out the eighteenth century.

Liaisons dangereuses is also social and cultural history. Social historians constantly face the problem of deciding to what extent individuals' actions are determined by their membership in certain groups or categories (class, gender, ethnicity, race) and by the huge impersonal forces of history, such as secular changes in economics or somewhat faster shifts in social struc- tures. In following our characters, we have traced how each one dealt with broader social and economic circumstances and the constraints and con- tingencies that confronted them. We have seen, for instance, how a Prus- sian and Silesian background shaped Kesslitz as an officer and a nobleman. Yet while the eventualities of European war and economic decline buffeted him about, he did not merely toss in the wind. Romellini's birth and gender restricted her choices in life, but she maneuvered within them, sometimes adroitly and sometimes clumsily. The fluid social world of the eighteenth century facilitated Visconti's many impostures, making them not only believable but also fully plausible. Finally, the exigencies of a growing world economic system helped a Spanish consul fit into the *bür- gerliche* world of a north German commercial entrepôt. Many questions were answered by capitalizing on the methods and the documentation social historians have used for decades (in particular, the extensive testi- monies given in criminal cases), but diplomatic sources, too, provided crucial material for reconstructing lives.

Liaisons dangereuses has also been inspired by recent currents in cultural history that explore identity formation, self-fashioning, and narrativity. I have shown how each of the principal characters used the narratives they constructed not only to attain certain objectives but also to make sense of their lives. If there were always only a "limited number of possibilities from which individuals can create a possible self,"[2] the permutations nonetheless added up. Additionally, I have argued that the very act of narrating a life story, an incident, or a sequence of events, constitutes it for the narrator and not for the audience alone. Evidence akin to "egodocu- ments"—Romellini's extended testimony or Kesslitz's short narrative of his life—illustrates how eighteenth-century people positioned themselves within the larger social and cultural universes they inhabited. "Fashion- ing," of course, counterpointed "self-fashioning." Sillem constructed indi- viduals and types in his "Historical Narrative"; diplomats like Hecht, Binder von Kriegelstein, and de la Houze did the same in their dispatches; Detenhof's defense of Kesslitz produced a third account; and public rumor circulating on the streets and in the coffeehouses, still another. All of these versions were, in one sense "true." Finally, eighteenth-century literary forms, the fantasies they fed, and the imagined worlds they devised, present to the historian an unconventional, yet rewarding, way of situating Romellini, Kesslitz, Sanpelayo, and Visconti historically. Elements of tragedy, comedy, farce, and melodrama entwined, as they did in the fiction of Pierre Choderlos de Laclos, Christian Friedrich Hunold, Daniel Defoe, and Restif de la Bretonne (the "Voltaire of the chambermaids"), as well as in Gayot de Pitaval's *Causes célèbres et intéressantes.*

Each of these prisms focuses the Kesslitz affair differently. But not even a multidimensional approach can solve every riddle. Although archival materials, printed sources, memoirs, letters, and genealogies have allowed me to reassemble four lives, much remains unknown and probably unknowable. Rummaging in search of serendipitous finds can be immensely profitable, but it has its limits. One reaches the point of diminishing returns eventually, if not rapidly. Obviously, this book may well not be the last word on Kesslitz and Romellini. Even the two men who died during the course of the "action," Visconti and Sanpelayo, have left gaping holes in their biographies. There is undoubtedly more to know about their lives before and after *le spectacle* played out. Still, history is always incomplete, and this story is no more so than many others. If one accepts—as I do— that history is "an unending dialogue between the present and the past," then I have neither started nor ended that conversation but only added an additional voice to it.[3]

The reader may well hunger for more. Obviously, some things we can never know. The motives of all involved dangle tantalizingly near but still beyond the historian's grasp. Everyone who reads—or investigates—a "crime story" such as this one inevitably forms judgments about what "really happened." Just as involuntary are the emotions of sympathy or antipathy each character evokes as we encounter him or her in different situations. My own feelings swung wildly as I first researched and then wrote this book. I ended up believing and disbelieving, liking and disliking, each individual. Visconti's fierce temper and his abusive treatment of Romellini elicited distaste; his (allegedly) cruel behavior rendered him unsympathetic. Yet is this fair? Should we not assess the possibility that he suffered the social and psychological disadvantages of bastardy? Born on the wrong side of the blanket and forced to make his own way, he might have looked at his legitimate brothers and wondered why they, and not he, basked in the Visconti glow? The "want-to-be" personality is easy to caricature or censure, but it evokes poignancy as well. (Casanova observed that the force of circumstances made many men adventurers, including himself.)[4] Even if one cannot condone Visconti's brutality, his pretenses, his raw obnoxiousness, and his cowardliness, one may well appreciate the frustration he felt. Moreover, did he really differ significantly from the other eighteenth-century strivers who made good using methods little dissimilar from his? Romellini was born poor and illegitimate and hardly anyone would condemn her for exploiting the assets she possessed—her beauty and sexuality—to survive. If she was frivolous and perhaps even devious, circumstances had done much to push her in that direction. And yet not every poor illegitimate girl became a courtesan or involved herself with a mean adventurer like Visconti. Sanpelayo has only revealed his darker side, and the evidence skews him so badly that a negative impression comes easily. Little hints in the documentation, however, suggest that he was not quite the snide, dissipated, and irascible Spaniard that Romellini (and the magistrates) portrayed. He certainly possessed enough charm and savoir faire to move comfortably in genteel society. Moreover, he seems genuinely to have cared for Romellini. Even she testified that he presented her with a valuable gift of silver when their first child was born. He then stuck by her for almost two years, often when she was ill. She portrayed his solicitude for her daughter as manipulative, but was it? We have only her word that he deceived her and robbed her of the letters that proved his connivance in the murder. And, finally, Kesslitz. His story—like his character—eludes us. I have asked myself, as I have queried the documents, which Kesslitz was the "real" one: the "brave and upright cavalier," the gullible pawn, or the active collaborator in the destruction of Visconti? Contradictions filled his life. Often he appears as the stereotypically honorable Prussian officer and nobleman. Yet some actions marred his gallantry. He despised Romellini's hold over Sanpelayo and threatened her anonymously to free his friend from a fatal attraction. Then, on the night of 18/19 October, he defended her from Visconti. In other circumstances, a certain nobility of character and flexibility of mind defined his behavior. His willingness to earn his bread by dealing in gems and his plan to set up a linen trade, for instance, were not typical paths for men of his background. His sheltering of the runaway "young Moor" and his attempts to mediate quarrels between other officers render him more appealing to us as well. Which man was he, then? The one? The other? None? All? I do not know.

While we can speculate as to what moved these characters and who really killed Visconti, we can never be sure. Lack of certain knowledge can be historically productive, however, for it allows us to consider myriad alternatives. By following and unraveling these, we perceive more than if we knew what *really* happened. This is, of course, not to accept that all possible explanations are equally valid, but rather to affirm that history can only approximate past events, and that intelligent extrapolation is the surest measure of the historian's craft. If I have facilitated that quest, I am satisfied.

Abbreviations

ABEPI	*Archivo biográfico de España, Portugal e Iberoamérica,* ed. Victor Herrero Mediavilla and L. Rosa Aguayo Nayle (New York: Saur, 1990–94)
ABF	*Archives biographiques françaises,* ed. Susan Bradley (London: Bowker-Saur, 1988–90); 2nd ser. (Munich: Saur, 1993)
ABI	*Archivio biografico italiano,* ed. Tommaso Nappo and Silvio Furlani (Munich: Saur, 1987–90)
ACN	*Adreß-Comptoir Nachrichten* (Hamburg: n.p., 1767–1826)
ADCP	Archives diplomatiques du Ministère des Affaires étrangères, correspondance politique (sous-série: Hambourg) (Paris)
ALR 1794	Carl Gottlieb Svarez, *Das Allgemeine Landrecht: Die Texte,* ed. Peter Krause (Stuttgart-Bad Cannstaat: Frommann-Holzboog, 1996)
APW	Archiwum Panstwowe we Wrocławiu
AP-Zg	Archivum Panstwowe w Zielonej Gorze
BaBA	*Baltisches Biographisches Archiv,* ed. Paul Laegbein and Axel Frey (Munich: Saur, 1995–98)
Blank	Johann Friedrich Blank, ed., *Sammlung der von E. Hochedlen Rathe der Stadt Hamburg . . . ausgegangenen allgemeinen Mandate, bestimmten Befehle und Bescheide, auch beliebten Aufträge und verkündigten Anordnungen,* 6 vols. (Hamburg: Piscator, 1763–74)
Casanova, History	Giacomo Casanova, chevalier de Seingalt, *History of My Life,* 6 vols. (Baltimore: Johns Hopkins University Press, 1966)
DBA	*Deutsches biographisches Archiv: Eine Kumulation aus 254 der wichtigsten biographischen Nachschlagewerke für den deutschen Bereich bis zum Ausgang des neunzehnten Jahrhunderts,* ed. Bernhard Fabian and Willi Gorzny (Munich: Saur, 1982)

"Defense"   The defense presented by Detenhof to the Senat on 4 December 1775, StAHbg, Senat Cl. VII Lit. Me no. 8 vol. 6 fasc. 7 conv. 2

EHR   *Economic History Review*

"Geschichts-   "Actenmäßige Geschichts-Erzählung, wegen der Entleibung des
Erzählung"   sogenannten Visconti" presented to the Senat on 4 December 1775, StAHbg, Senat Cl. Lit. Me no. 8 vol. 6 fasc. 2

GStAPK   Geheimes Staatsarchiv, Preußischer Kulturbesitz (Berlin)

HDA   Hanns Bächtold-Stäubli, Eduard Hoffmann-Krayer, and Gerhard Lüdtke, eds., *Handwörterbuch des deutschen Aberglaubens*, 10 vols. (Berlin: Walter de Gruyter, 1927–42)

HGH   *Hamburgische Geschichts- und Heimatsblätter*

HHStAW   Haus-, Hof- und Staatsarchiv (Vienna)

HRG   Adalbert Erler and Ekkehard Kaufmann, eds., *Handwörterbuch zur deutschen Rechtsgeschichte*, 5 vols. (Berlin: Erich Schmidt, 1971–98)

Klefeker   Johann Klefeker, *Sammlung der Hamburgischen Gesetze und Verfassung in Bürger-und Kirchlichen, auch Cammer-, Handlungs- und übrigen Policey-Angelegenheiten und Geschäften samt historischen Einleitungen*, 12 vols. (Hamburg: Piscator, 1765–74)

Lexikon   Franklin Kopitzsch and Daniel Tilgner, eds., *Hamburg Lexikon* (Hamburg: Zeise, 1998)

"Libellus   [Andreas Wilhelm Uhlenhoff], "Libellus criminal Fiscalis in
criminal   Criminalibus ex Officio Inquirentis und Peinl. Anklägers,
Fiscalis"   entgegen und weiter [wieder?] Herrn Joseph, Baron von Kesslitz, Gefangenen, p.p." (n.d. [probably December 1775]), StAHbg, Senat Cl. VII Lit. Me no. 8 vol. 6 fasc. 3

OED   *Oxford English Dictionary*

PAB   *Polskie archiwum biograficzne*, ed. Dieter Hebig and Oswald Balzer (Munich: Saur, 1993–)

PSB   *Polski Słownik biograficzny* (Kraków: Sklad główny w ksieg, 1935–)

Rep.   Otto Friedrich Winter, ed., *Repertorium der diplomatischen Vertreter aller Länder*, vol. 2: *1716–1763*, ed. F. Hausmann (Zurich: Fretz & Wasmuth, 1950); vol. 3: *1764–1815* (Cologne: Böhlaus, 1965)

RHR   Reichshofrat

SäHStAD   Sächsisches Haupt-Staatsarchiv Dresden

Schriftsteller   Hans Schroeder, *Lexikon der hamburgischen Schriftsteller bis zur
Lexikon*   Gegenwart*, 8 vols. (Hamburg: Verein für Hamburgische Geschichte, 1851–83)

StADr   Stadtarchiv Dresden

StAHbg   Staatsarchiv Hamburg

SUBHbg	Staats- und Universitätsbibliothek Hamburg
VSWG	*Vierteljahrschrift für Sozial- und Wirtschaftsgeschichte*
WAP-Zg	Archiwum Panstwowe w Zielonej Gorze, Oddzial w Wilkowie
ZVGAS	*Zeitschrift des Vereins für Geschichte und Alterthum Schlesiens*
ZVHG	*Zeitschrift des Vereins für Hamburgische Geschichte*

Notes

Prologue

1. Report from 19 October 1775, StAHbg, Senat Cl. VII Lit. Me no. 8 vol. 6 fasc. 7 conv. 1.

2. Ibid. On forensic autopsies, see Theodor Georg August Roose, *Taschenbuch für gerichtliche Ärzte und Wundärzte bei gesetzmäßigen Leichenöffnungen* (Frankfurt a/M: Friedrich Wilmans, 1811). Physicians were not required to determine whether a particular wound was *in abstracto* mortal, but rather if the wound *in concreto* could have brought about the death of a certain person in certain circumstances. See Johann Baptista Friedrich, *Anleitung zur gerichtsärztlichen Untersuchung der Körperverletzungen* (Straubing: Schorner, 1841), 4, 14–40.

CHAPTER 1. *"Voilà—le spectacle!"*

1. See, e.g., reports in the *Neue Europäische Zeitung* (Hanau), 31 October 1775; *Baÿreuther Zeitung*, 2 November 1775; *Freytägige Frankfurter Reichs-Ober-Post-Amts-Zeitung*, 3 November 1775; *Nachrichten zum Nuzen und Vergnügen*, 7 November 1775.

2. *Schriftsteller Lexikon*, s.v. Sillem, Garlieb.

3. "Actenmäßige Geschichts-Erzählung, wegen der Entleibung des sogenannten Visconti," presented to the Senat on 4 December 1775, StAHbg, Senat Cl. Lit. Me no. 8 vol. 6 fasc. 2 (hereafter cited as "Geschichts-Erzählung"). See also Sillem's working notes on the case, StAHbg, Senat Cl. Lit. Me no. 8 vol. 6 fasc. 1.

4. "Das Factum ist folgendes." "Geschichts-Erzählung," § 3. The story presented here is taken from §§ 3–19 of the "Geschichts-Erzählung."

5. Described in "Geschichts-Erzählung," § 14.

6. Detenhof was born in 1730 in Stade. In 1760, he became vicar to the Cathedral Chapter (Domkapital) in Hamburg (and later syndic) and in that same year received his doctorate in law from the University of Kiel. He was apparently a rather difficult personality, who often quarreled with his contemporaries. He was "not well-loved." *Schriftsteller Lexikon*, s.v. Detenhof, Johann Hinrich; Friedrich

Johann Lorenz Meyer, *Blick auf die Domkirche in Hamburg* (Hamburg: Nestler, 1804), 94.

7. On the syndics in Hamburg, see Martin Ewald, *Der Hamburgische Senats-syndicus: Eine verwaltungsgeschichtliche Studie* (Hamburg: Appel, 1954); Klefeker, 5: 305.

8. John H. Langbein, *Prosecuting Crime in the Renaissance: England, Germany, France* (Cambridge, Mass.: Harvard University Press, 1974), 129.

9. Friedrich August Biener, *Beiträge zu der Geschichte des Inquisitionsprocess und der Geschworenengerichte* (Leipzig, 1827; reprint, Aalen: Scientia, 1965), 8–9, quoted in Langbein, *Prosecuting Crime*, 130.

10. Langbein, *Prosecuting Crime*, 130–31, 167, 179.

11. Klefeker, 5: 266–67.

12. Theodor Hasche, *Kurze Darstellung des Verfahrens im Hamburgischen Nieder-Gerichte* (Hamburg: Nestler, 1802), 7–8.

13. D[aniel] H[einrich] Jacobi, *Geschichte des Hamburger Niedergerichts* (Hamburg: Nolte, 1866), 110–11, 135. Jacobi uses the word "notorious" in describing this phenomenon. Jacobi was a knowledgeable, although hardly impartial, witness. In 1802, he worked hard to prevent further restrictions on the jurisdiction of the Niedergericht, but without success (135). Scarcely any of the records of the Niedergericht are still extant, but Jacobi had full access to them in the early nineteenth century.

14. Ibid., 47–76, quotations from 47, 135–36. Numerous incidents in the eighteenth century occasioned disputes over jurisdiction between the Senat and Niedergericht, and not solely over the application of torture. For examples, see StAHbg, Senat Cl. VII Lit. Ma no. 5 Vols. 4b4, 4f3, 4f5–6, 4f8–11, 4f13, 4f15, 4h, 4l.

15. Details of the criminal process as discussed in the following paragraphs are taken from Hasche, *Kurze Darstellung*, esp. 18–26; Klefeker, 5: 261–568; Nicolaus Schuback, "Versuch Einer Sÿstematischen Abhandlung vom Richterlichen Ampte in Hamburg . . . Beÿ Gelegenheit der vom Demselben zu übernehmenden und übernommenen Praetur" (c. 1747), SUBHbg, Handschriftensammlung, Cod. Hans. II, 139, 2, ff. 201–81.

16. On the general inquisition in Hamburg, see Klefeker, 5: 276–87; Schuback, "Versuch," ff. 202–26.

17. Klefeker, 5: 301.

18. Hasche, *Kurze Darstellung*, 19–20; Schuback, "Versuch," ff. 203–4.

19. Schuback, "Versuch," ff. 208–10.

20. Klefeker, 5: 304–5; Schuback, "Versuch," ff. 226–27.

21. Klefeker, 5: 305; "Interrogatoria, worüber Herr Baron von Kesslitz zu vernehmen ist" (n.d.), StAHbg, Senat Cl. VII Lit. Me no. 8 vol. 6 fasc. 7 conv. 2.

22. Hasche, *Kurze Darstellung*, 19.

23. Klefeker, 5: 305.

24. Ibid., 312, 320–22.

25. Jacobi, *Geschichte*, 139–45.

26. Hasche, *Kurze Darstellung*, 19–26.

27. Nicolaus A. Westphalen, *Hamburgs Verfassung und Verwaltung in ihrer allmähligen Entwicklung bis auf die neueste Zeit* (Hamburg: Perthes-Besser &

Mauke, 1841), 1: 33–55; Jürgen Bolland, *Senat und Bürgerschaft: Über das Verhältnis zwischen Bürger und Stadt-Regiment im alten Hamburg* (Hamburg: Verein für Hamburgische Geschichte, 1954).

28. Mary Lindemann, *Patriots and Paupers: Hamburg, 1712–1830* (New York: Oxford University Press, 1990), 21–22; Wilhelm Heyden, "Die Familie Anckelmann in Hamburg," *Zeitschrift für Niederdeutsche Familienkunde* 7 (1925): 273–79.

29. This section draws on the statements and testimony Kesslitz, Romellini, and Sanpelayo gave over the course of the investigation. Kesslitz's testimonies in chronological order included: Kesslitz's handwritten account from 19 October 1775 and his "Summarische Verhör und Aussage . . ." from 20 October 1775, both StAHbg, Senat Cl. VII Lit. Me no. 8 vol. 6 fasc. 7 conv. 1; interrogations of 7, 9, 11, and 13 November 1775 and "Examen des Baron von Kesslitz" from 22 December 1775 and 2 January 1776 (the latter based on "Interrogatoria, worüber Herr Baron von Kesslitz zu vernehmen ist"), StAHbg, Senat Cl. VII Lit. Me no. 8 vol. 6 fasc. 7 conv. 2. For Romellini: her statement on 19 October 1775 and then the "Fernweitige summarische Vernehmung Anna Maria Romel[l]ini wegen ihrer Lebensart und des angeb. Grafen Visconti Entleibung" (31 October and 1, 2, and 3 November 1775), StAHbg, Senat Cl. VII Lit. Me no. 8 vol. 6 fasc. 7 conv. 1. For Sanpelayo: his short "Species facti" of 19 October 1775 plus his responses to a few other questions on 20 October in ibid. and the "Summarische Vernehmung des Spanischen Consuls, Herrn Anthony de Sanpelayo" (18, 20, 21 and 24 November 1775), StAHbg, Senat Cl. VII Lit. Me no. 8 vol. 6 fasc. 7 conv. 2.

30. "Summarische Verhör und Aussage," 20 October 1775.

31. Handwritten account from 19 October 1775, StAHbg, Senat Cl. VII Lit. Me no. 8 vol. 6 fasc. 7 conv. 1.

32. "Summarische Verhör und Aussage," 20 October 1775.

33. In Sanpelayo's extended statement from 18, 20, 21 and 24 November 1775, StAHbg, Senat Cl. VII Lit. Me no. 8 vol. 6 fasc. 7 conv. 2.

34. Interrogations of 7, 9, 11, and 13 November 1775.

35. "Summarische Verhör und Aussage"; second version 7 November 1775.

36. Interrogations of 7, 9, 11, and 13 November 1775, StAHbg, Senat Cl. VII Lit. Me no. 8 vol. 6 fasc. 7 conv. 2.

37. Statement of Romellini, 19 October 1775, StAHbg, Senat Cl. VII Lit. Me no. 8 vol. 6 fasc. 7 conv. 2.

38. "Species facti" of 19 October 1775; answers to some further questions posed by the praetor on 20 October, StAHbg, Senat Cl. VII Lit. Me no. 8 vol. 6 fasc. 7 conv. 1; and extended statement from 18, 20, 21 and 24 November 1775, StAHbg, Senat Cl. VII Lit. Me no. 8 vol. 6 fasc. 7 conv. 2.

39. Ibid.

40. Natalie Zemon Davis, *Fiction in the Archives: Pardon Tales and Their Tellers in Sixteenth-Century France* (Stanford, Calif.: Stanford University Press, 1987), 4.

CHAPTER 2. *A Most Difficult Case*

1. *HRG*, s.v. "Duelle/Zweikampf," "Totschlag/Mord," and "Notwehr."

2. Klefeker, 5: 428–29.

3. Ibid., 429–30; *HRG*, s.v. "Duell."

4. Klefeker, 5: 432–33.

5. *HRG*, s.v. "Carolina."

6. Klefeker, 5: 434; Richard J. Evans, *Rituals of Retribution: Capital Punishment in Germany, 1600–1987* (Oxford: Oxford University Press, 1996), 27–64.

7. Articles 139 and 140 of the Peinliche Hals-Gerichts-Ordnung, quoted in Klefeker, 5: 434–35.

8. Klefeker, 5: 509–10; *HRG*, s.v. "Duell."

9. Giacomo Casanova, *The Duel* (1780), trans. J. G. Nichols (London: Hesperus Press, 2003), 19.

10. Karl Demeter, *Das deutsche Offizierkorps in Gesellschaft und Staat, 1659–1945*, 4th. enlarged and rev. ed. (Frankfurt a/M: Bernard & Graefe Verl. für Wehrwesen, 1965), 116, defines these two concepts of honor. See also Hans Reiner, *Die Ehre: Kritische Sichtung einer abendländlichen Lebens-und Sittlichkeitsform* (Dortmund: E. S. Mittler & Sohn, 1956), 83–85; Friedhelm Guttandin, *Das paradoxe Schicksal der Ehre: Zum Wandel der adeligen Ehre und zur Bedeutung vom Duell und Ehre für den monarchischen Zentralstaat* (Berlin: Dietrich Reimer, 1992), 234–35; A[lbrecht] von Boguslawski, *Die Ehre und das Duell* (Berlin: Schall & Grund, 1896), 4–7, 14 (quotation).

11. On dueling in Germany, see Ute Frevert, "The Taming of the Noble Ruffian: Male Violence and Dueling in Early Modern and Modern Germany," in *Men and Violence: Gender, Honor, and Rituals in Modern Europe and America*, ed. Pieter Spierenburg (Columbus: Ohio State University Press, 1998), 37–63.

12. James Kelly, *"That Damn'd Thing Called Honour": Dueling in Ireland, 1570–1860* (Cork, Ireland: Cork University Press, 1995), 10, 17–19; Hans Fehr, *Der Zweikampf* (Berlin: Karl Curtius, 1908), 14, 17, 29; Demeter, *Deutsche Offizierkorps*, 123.

13. François Billacois, *The Duel: Its Rise and Fall in Early Modern France*, trans. and ed. Trista Selous (New Haven, Conn.: Yale University Press, 1990), 6, 21–26; Frevert, "Taming of the Noble Ruffian," 38; "Ehrengericht (militarisches)" in *HRG*; Boguslawski, *Ehre und das Duell*, 29.

14. Quoted in Frevert, "Taming of the Noble Ruffian," 40.

15. Kevin McAleer, *Dueling: The Cult of Honor in Fin-de Siècle Germany* (Princeton, N.J.: Princeton University Press, 1994), 19; Heinrich Christian Senckenberg quoted in Klefeker, 5: 510–12; Guttandin, *Paradoxe Schicksal*, 230–33; François Billacois lists the edicts forbidding dueling in the Empire in *Le Duel dans la société française des XVIe–XVIIe siècles: Essai de psychosociologie historique* (Paris: Éditions de l'École des hautes études en sciences sociales, 1986), 406.

16. Quoted in Guttandin, *Paradoxe Schicksal*, 362.

17. Demeter, *Deutsche Offizierkorps*, 126–27; Boguslawski, *Ehre und das Duell*, 46.

18. McAleer, *Dueling*, 19–21; Demeter, *Deutsche Offizierkorps*, 123–29; *Sr. Königl. Majestät in Preussen, und Churfürstl. Durchl. zu Brandenburg Erklärtes und erneuertes Mandat wider die Selbst-Rache, Injurien, Friedens-Stöhrungen, und Duelle* (Berlin, 1713); Kant quoted in Frevert, "Taming of the Noble Ruffian," 44. On dishonorable deaths and burials, see Mary Lindemann, "Armen-und Eselbegräbnis in der europäischen Frühneuzeit: Eine Methode sozialer Kontrolle?" in

Studien zur Thematik des Todes im 16. Jahrhundert, ed. Richard Toellner and Paul R. Blum (Wolfenbüttel: Herzog August Bibliothek, 1983), 125–40.

19. "Mandat, daß niemand zu Duellen ausfordern, noch sich dazu ausfordern lassen soll" (29 February 1660), in Blank, 1: 170–71.

20. Billacois, *Duel,* 144–62; Frevert, "Taming of the Noble Ruffian," 40–41.

21. Whaley, *Religious Toleration,* 19.

22. Klefeker, 5: 513.

23. Kelly, *"That Damn'd Thing Called Honour,"* 14.

24. On the dishonorable occupations, see Kathy Stuart, *Defiled Trades and Social Outcasts: Honor and Ritual Pollution in Early Modern Germany* (Cambridge: Cambridge University Press, 1999); "unehrlich" in *HDA,* 8: 1398–1404; "Ehre" in *Grimms Wörterbuch.*

25. *HDA,* 2: 1016–17.

26. Lindemann, "Armen-und Eselbegräbnis."

27. "Geschichts-Erzählung," § 11.

28. Supplication and defense presented by Detenhof to the Senat on 4 December 1775, StAHbg, Senat Cl. VII Lit. Me no. 8 vol. 6 fasc. 7 conv. 2 [hereafter cited as "Defense"], §§ 22–23.

29. "Geschichts-Erzählung," §§ 21–26; "Defense"; [Andreas Wilhelm Uhlenhoff], "Libellus criminal Fiscalis in Criminalibus ex Officio Inquirentis und Peinl. Anklägers, entgegen und weiter [wieder?] Herrn Joseph, Baron von Kesslitz, Gefangenen, p.p." (n.d. [probably December 1775]), StAHbg, Senat Cl. VII Lit. Me no. 8 vol. 6 fasc. 3 (hereafter cited as "Libellus criminal Fiscalis").

30. Promemorium to French court (n.d., but probably February 1776), StAHbg, Senat Cl. VII Lit. Me no. 8 vol. 6 fasc. 6.

31. Senat, Cl. VIII no. Xa (1775), p. 312.

32. "Defense," § 124.

33. "Geschichts-Erzählung," § 21. Ute Frevert defines *rencontres* as "spontaneous clashes in which disputes were immediately settled by force and without further preparation. Rulers tended to judge such clashes mildly because they derived from 'first and sudden agitation, against which there is no resistance.' In contrast, formal duels that were planned without 'sudden agitation' were regarded as violating the 'high-courtly office' entrusted to the sovereign." Frevert, "Taming of the Noble Ruffian," 44.

34. "Defense," prefatory remarks.

35. "Geschichts-Erzählung," §§ 21–24; "Defense," §§ 2, 46.

36. *HRG,* s.v. "Notwehr"; *ALR,* II 20 § 517.

37. *HRG,* s.v. "Notwehr"; on the "duty to retreat," see Spierenburg, "Knife Fighting," 123.

38. "Defense," § 12; see also §§ 16, 28.

39. Klefeker, 5: 509, 514.

40. "Defense," §§ 21, 39–40; "Geschichts-Erzählung," § 22.

41. "Defense," § 97.

42. Ibid.

43. "Geschichts-Erzählung," §23.

44. Ibid.

45. "Defense," §§ 93–94, 101; "Geschichts-Erzählung," § 2.

46. "Defense," §§ 44–45; "Geschichts-Erzählung," § 23.

47. "Defense," § 58.

48. Ibid., §§ 105–7.

49. Sillem's report and Detenhof's brief were presented on Monday, 4 December. The Senat's decision to continue the case was made on Wednesday, 6 December 1775. StAHbg, Senat Cl. VIII no. Xa (1775), p. 315.

50. "Libellus criminalis Fiscalis."

51. Heinrich Sieveking, *Georg Heinrich Sieveking: Lebensbild eines Hamburger Kaufmanns aus dem Zeitalter der französischen Revolution* (Berlin: Karl Curtis, 1913), 416.

52. Percy Ernst Schramm, "Hamburg und die Adelsfrage (bis 1806)," *ZVHG* 55 (1969): 81–94. Schramm's article is old and, as he himself admitted, did not rest on exhaustive archival research. Still, even if one considers that his numbers are somewhat low, his general argument is nevertheless valid. Caspar Voght, *Lebensgeschichte* (Hamburg: Alfred Janssen, 1917).

53. Franklin Kopitzsch, *Grundzüge einer Sozialgeschichte der Aufklärung in Hamburg und Altona*, 2nd expanded ed. (Hamburg: Verein für Hamburgische Geschichte, 1990), 204–6; *Rep.* 3: 77, 119, 329.

54. Hans Wilhlem Eckhardt, "Hamburg zur Zeit Johann Matthesons," in *New Mattheson Studies*, ed. George J. Buelow and Hans Joachim Marx (Cambridge: Cambridge University Press, 1983), 34; Folkert Fiebig, "Johann Mattheson als Diplomat in Hamburg," in ibid., 45–73; H. Schwärzwälder, "Der 'deutsche Spion' und Bremen: Thomas Lediard, Sekretär des Britischen Gesandtern beim Niedersächsischen Kreis in Hamburg und der Gesandte Sir Cyrill Wich," *Bremisches Jahrbuch* 57 (1979): 87–123; H. C. Wolff, "Ein Engländer als Direktor der alten Hamburger Oper," *Hamburger Jahrbuch für Musikwissenschaft* 3 (1978): 75–83. On Brentano, see Peter Höfer, *Deutsch-französische Handelsbeziehungen im 18. Jahrhundert: Die Firma Breton frères in Nantes (1763–1766)* (Stuttgart: Klett-Cotta, 1982), 42.

55. Reinhold P. Kuhnert, *Urbanität auf dem Lande, Badereisen nach Pyrmont im 18. Jahrhundert* (Göttingen: Vandenhoeck & Ruprecht, 1984); Brigitte Erker, "'Brunnenfreiheit' in Pyrmont: Gesundheit und Geselligkeit im letzten Drittel des 18. Jahrhunderts," and Thomas Fuchs, "'Dieses Wasser aber ist ein natürlich / warmes und artzneyische Bad: Bürgerlichkeit und Baden am Beispiel Wiesbadens im späten 18.und frühen 19. Jahrhundert," in *Bäder und Kuren in der Aufklärung: Medizinaldiskurs and Freizeitvergnügen*, ed. Raingard Eßer and Thomas Fuchs (Berlin: Berliner Wissenschafts-Verlag, 2003), 53–97, 99–111.

56. Thomas Lediard (the Elder), *The German Spy. In familiar letters from Munster, Paderborn, Osnabrug, Minden, Bremen, Hamburg, Gluckstadt, Helgoland, Stade, Lubeck, and Rostock. Written by a Gentleman on his Travels, to his Friends in England* (London: J. Mechell, 1738), 273.

57. Fiebig, "Johann Mattheson als Diplomat," 59.

58. Lediard, *German Spy,* 89.

59. Kopitzsch, *Grundzüge*, 204–6; James Sheehan, *German History, 1770–1866* (Oxford: Clarendon Press, 1989), 135.

60. *Der Patriot,* no. 12 (23 March 1724).

61. "Mahler der Sitten," quoted in Wolfgang Martens, *Die Botschaft der Tugend: Die Aufklärung im Spiegel der deutschen Moralischen Wochenschriften* (Stuttgart: J. B. Metzler, 1971), 351.

62. Jonathan Dewald, *The European Nobility, 1400–1800* (Cambridge: Cambridge University Press, 1996), 168.

63. *Der Patriot,* no. 57 (17 February 1725). Brigitte Tolkemitt, *Der Hamburgische Correspondent: Zur öffentlichen Verbreitung der Aufklärung in Deutschland* (Tübingen: Niemeyer, 1995), 192.

64. *Der Stadt Hamburgt Gerichts-Ordnung und Statuta (1605)* (Hamburg, 1605), Art. 26; Klefeker, 5: 416–19; Hermann Conrad, *Deutsche Rechtsgeschichte* (Karlsruhe: C. F. Müller, 1966), 2: 412.

65. [François Gayot de Pitaval], *Merkwürdige Rechtsfälle als ein Beitrag zur Geschichte der Menschheit: Nach dem französischen Werk des Pitaval durch mehrere Verfasser ausgearbeitet und mit einer Vorrede begleitet herausgegeben von Schiller* (4 parts; Jena: Chris. Heinr. Cuno, 1792–95), 2: 1–60 (Morsan); 3: 3–102 (Brinvilliers); *Geheime Nachrichten aus dem Leben einiger der berühmtesten Wucherer, Unterhändler, Rabulisten, Bankerottiers, Geldschneider, und Jugendverführer unserer Zeit* (Vienna: n.p., 1798), esp. 71–77; Johann Friedrich Jünger, *Die Entführung: Ein Lustspiel in 3 Aufzügen* (Leipzig: n.p., 1792); Johann Friedrich Schütze, *Hamburgische Theater-Geschichte* (Hamburg: J. P. Treder, 1794), 633. Madame de Brinvilliers's story continues to attract attention: Anne Somerset, *The Affair of the Poisons: Murder, Infanticide and Satanism at the Court of Louis XIV* (London: Weidenfeld & Nicolson, 2003), treats the case at length.

66. Materials on the Biorenberg/Wentzhard(t) case in: SUBHbg, Handschriftensammlung, Cod. Hans. II, 171, 1; StAHbg, RHR, 17.

67. *Eilfertig entworffen Doch Rechtliche Verthädigung Des Rechtlichen Bedenckens / So vorhin occcasione der neulich geschehenen Entführung der Jungf. L.[andermann] Durch den H. Obrist-Lieut. V. W. mitgetheilet* (26 April 1699) and in his defense, *Gründliche Bedeutung Eines abgesagten Feindes der Betrigereyen / an seine durch falsche impressionen verleitte gute Freunde: Die W. und L. Entführung betreffend* (June 1699), nos. 27 and 28, StAHbg, Bibliothek, Sammelband 84; on the Pingel case, StAHbg, Senat Cl. VII Lit. Me no. 10 vol. 1 fasc. 2 (1744); decision of Niedergericht from 3 September 1745, SUBHbg, Handschriftensammlung, Cod. Hans. II, 144, 1 (91); on the Kottwitz case, see Senat Cl. VII Lit. Me no. 10 vol. 1 fasc. 5 and Senat Cl. VII Lit. Cc no. 13 vol. 5 fasc. 19; on the case involving the Baron Krohn, StAHbg, Reichskammergerichtakten, E2, pts. 1–3.

68. Demeter, *Deutsche Offizierkorps,* 71.

69. Jonathan Dewald, "Comment" at American Society for Eighteenth-Century Studies, Colorado Springs, April 2002 (personal communication to the author).

70. "[P]leasure came into its own in the eighteenth century" and, for the first time, sensual pleasures came to be viewed as "legitimate, fulfilling and to be encouraged." Roy Porter, "Introduction" to *Pleasure in the Eighteenth Century,* ed. id. and Marie Mulvey Roberts (New York: New York University Press, 1997), 1–2.

71. Testimony of Kesslitz's "Mieth-Laquei," Johann Pfeiffer, from 1 November 1775, StAHbg, Senat Cl. VII Lit. Me no. 8 vol. 6 fasc. 7 conv. 1. On patronage of the

opera, see Ernst Finder, *Hamburgisches Bürgertum in der Vergangenheit* (Hamburg: Friederichsen, de Gruyter, 1930), 383.

72. In Dewald, *European Nobility*, 152.

73. Norbert Elias, *Über den Prozess der Zivilisation: Soziogenetische und psychogenetische Untersuchungen* (Munich: Francke, 1969); Dewald, *European Nobility*, 151–55; on the Ritterakademien, see Norbert Conrads, *Ritterakademien der Frühen Neuzeit: Bildung als Standesprivileg im 16. und 17. Jahrhundert* (Göttingen: Vandenhoeck & Ruprecht, 1982).

74. Dewald, *European Nobility*, 183–84.

75. Gregory W. Pedlow, *The Survival of the Hessian Nobility, 1770–1870* (Princeton, N.J.: Princeton University Press, 1988), 142–43.

76. Otto Brunner, *Adeliges Landleben und europäischer Geist: Leben und Werk Wolf Helmhards von Hohberg, 1612–1688* (Salzburg: Otto Müller, 1949); Pedlow, *Survival*, 103–43, 154–64; Johannes Schellakowsky, "Zur Adelskultur in Brandenburg-Preußen im späteren 18. Jahrhundert—eine historische Spurensuche," in *Aspekte des 18. Jahrhunderts: Studien zur Geistes-, Bildungs- und Verwaltungsgeschichte in Franken und Brandenburg-Preußen*, ed. Peter Mainka, Johannes Schellakowsky, and Peter A. Süss (Würzburg: Freunde Mainfränkischer Kunst und Geschichte; Schweinfurt: Historische Verein, 1996), 137–65; Hermann Kellenbenz, "German Aristocratic Entrepreneurship: Economic Activities of the Holstein Nobility in the Sixteenth and Seventeenth Centuries," *Explorations in Entrepreneurial History* 6 (1953): 103–14; M. L. Bush, *Rich Noble, Poor Noble* (Manchester: Manchester University Press, 1988), 131–52; Robert Forster, *Merchants, Landlords, Magistrates: The Dupont Family in Eighteenth-Century France* (Baltimore: Johns Hopkins University Press, 1980); Dewald, *European Nobility*, 82–89, 151–55; Sheehan, *German History*, 132.

77. *Rep.* 3: 329.

78. See E. O. G. Haitsma Mulier, "De affaire Zanovich: Amsterdams-Venetiaanse betrekkingen aan het einde van de achttiende eeuw," *Amstelodamum* 72 (1980): 85–119; Casanova, *History*, 12: 119–25.

79. Kopitzsch, *Grundzüge*, 301–12, 540.

80. Pierre Jeannin, Erich Lüth, and Erich Jahn, *Gekräuselt, gepudert und mit untadeliger Anmut: Hamburg und die französische Revolution* (Hamburg: Christians, 1977), 9.

81. Voght, *Lebensgeschichte*, 18–19, 23–27, 29–30, 35–37, 42; Helen Liebel, "Laissez-faire vs. Mercantilism: The Rise of Hamburg and the Hamburg Bourgeoisie vs. Frederick the Great in the Crisis of 1763," *VSWG* 52 (1965): 207–38.

82. Voght, *Lebensgeschichte*, 44; Kopitzsch, *Grundzüge*, 394–95; Gabriele Hoffmann, *Das Haus an der Elbchaussee: Die Godeffroys—Aufstieg and Niedergang einer Dynastie* (Hamburg: Die Hanse, 1998), 25.

83. Statement of Hans Andreas Dreyer, 1 November 1775; testimony of Friedrich Baron von Schlabrendorff, 7 November 1775, both StAHbg, Senat Cl. VII Lit. Me no. 8 vol. 6 fasc. 7 conv. 1.

84. Finder, *Hamburgisches Bürgertum*, 149–55; Thomas Nugent, *Travels through Germany . . . with a particular account of the Courts of Mecklenburg, in a series of letters to a friend* (London: Printed for E. and C. Dilly, 1768), 1: 72–73.

85. Nugent, *Travels*, 1: 72.

86. Finder, *Hamburgisches Bürgertum*, 155.

87. Kopitzsch, *Grundzüge*, 417–19; Lediard, *German Spy*, 95; statement of Bruchbach, 28 October 1775, StAHbg, Senat Cl. VII Lit. Me no. 8 vol. 6 fasc. 7 conv. 1.

88. Finder, *Hamburgisches Bürgertum*, 383, 393–94.

89. Testimony of Joseph da Fonseca, 4 November 1775, StAHbg, Senat Cl. VII Lit. Me no. 8 vol. 6 fasc. 7 conv. 1.

CHAPTER 3. *A Very Diplomatic Affair*

1. Richard N. Rosecrance, "Diplomacy in the Eighteenth Century," in *Diplomacy in Modern European History*, ed. Laurence W. Martin (New York: Macmillan, 1966), 32.

2. Heinz Duchhardt, *Balance of Power und Pentarchie: Internationale Beziehungen, 1700–1785* (Paderborn: Ferdinand Schöningh, 1997), 372–73.

3. Paul W. Schroeder, *The Transformation of European Politics, 1763–1848* (Oxford: Clarendon Press, 1994), 3, 9.

4. Maurice Keens-Soper, "Abraham de Wicquefort und Diplomatic Theory" (Discussion Paper 14, Diplomatic Studies Programme, Center for the Study of Diplomacy, 1996), 7.

5. Martin Reißmann, *Die hamburgische Kaufmannschaft des 17. Jahrhunderts in sozialgeschichtlicher Sicht* (Hamburg: Hans Christians, 1975), 48. See also Hermann Kellenbenz, *Sephardim an der unteren Elbe: Ihre wirtschaftliche und politische Bedeutung vom Ende des 16. bis zum Beginn des 18. Jahrhunderts* (Wiesbaden: Franz Steiner, 1958), and id., "Unternehmerkräfte im Hamburger Portugal-und Spanienhandel 1590–1625," *Veröffentlichungen der Wirtschaftsgeschichtlichen Forschungsstelle* 10 (Hamburg, 1954).

6. Hans Pohl, *Die Beziehungen Hamburgs zu Spanien und dem spanischen Amerika in der Zeit von 1740 bis 1806* (Wiesbaden: Franz Steiner, 1963), 1–9.

7. Ibid., x–xi, 11–13; Adolph Soetbeer, "Das hamburgische Consulatswesen," *Zeitschrift des Vereins für deutsche Statistik* 1 (1847): 84–86; Werner Jochmann, "Hamburgisch-schlesische Handelsbeziehungen: Ein Beitrag zur abendländischen Wirtschaftsgeschichte," in *Geschichtliche Landeskunde und Universalgeschichte* (Hamburg: "Wihag"-Buchdruckerei, 1950), 222–25.

8. Pohl, *Beziehungen*, 15–16; Ernst Baasch, *Die Handelskammer zu Hamburg* (Hamburg: Lucas Gräfe & Sillem, 1915), 1: 427, 437.

9. Baasch, *Handelskammer*, 1: 421.

10. Johann Martin Lappenberg, "Listen der bis 1870 in Hamburg residerenden sowie der Hamburg in Ausland vertretenden Diplomaten und Konsuln," rev. Christian Mahlstedt (typescript [Hamburg, 1969], Staatsarchiv Hamburg library), 138.

11. Pohl, *Beziehungen*, 21–31.

12. Quoted in ibid., 21.

13. Quoted in ibid., 27–28.

14. Ibid., 30–31.

15. Joachim Whaley makes this point in *Religious Toleration and Social Change in Hamburg, 1529–1819* (Cambridge: Cambridge University Press, 1985).

16. *Hamburg: Geschichte der Stadt und Ihrer Bewohner*, vol. 1: *Von den Anfängen bis zur Reichsgründung*, ed. Werner Jochmann and Hans-Dieter Loose (Hamburg: Hoffmann & Campe, 1982), 269–87; more generally, John G. Gagliardo, *Reich and Nation: The Holy Roman Empire as Idea and Reality, 1763–1800* (Bloomington: Indiana University Press, 1980), 10–12.

17. Rainer Ramcke, *Die Beziehungen zwischen Hamburg und Österreich im 18. Jahrhundert: Kaiserlich-reichstädtisches Verhältnis im Zeichen von Handels-und Finanzinteressen* (Hamburg: Hans Christians, 1969), 3.

18. Liebel, "Laissez-faire vs. Mercantilism."

19. Ramcke, *Beziehungen*, 166–254.

20. My discussion of the activities of this group—the Schuback-Dorner circle—relies heavily on ibid., 244–54.

21. Gagliardo, *Reich and Nation*, 29; Kopitzsch, *Grundzüge*, 160; *HRG*, 3: 2011. Hamburg possessed two *privilegia de non appellando* (dating from 1553 and 1634, and confirmed in 1637, 1715, 1747, 1766, 1791, and 1793). These were, however, not the unlimited sort (*privilegia illimitata*) that completely prevented a subject from appealing to the imperial courts. Such unlimited *privilegia* were, in principle, only given to electors of the empire. Andreas Ebert-Wiedenfeller, *Hamburgisches Kaufmannsrecht im 17. und 18. Jahrhundert: Die Rechtsprechung des Rates und des Reichskammergerichtes* (Frankfurt a/M: Peter Lang, 1992), 16–18. For an idea of the number of cases appealed and the instances, see *Findbuch der Reichskammergerichtsakten im Staatsarchiv Hamburg*, ed. Hans-Konrad Stein-Stegemann (Hamburg, Verein für Hamburgische Geschichte, 1993).

22. My discussion of Catholics in Hamburg here is taken from Whaley, *Religious Toleration*, 45–69; quotation from ibid., 47.

23. E. R. Adair, *The Extraterritoriality of Ambassadors in the Sixteenth and Seventeenth Centuries* (London: Longmans, Green, 1929), 196–97; Alexander Miruss, *Das Europäische Gesandschaftrecht: Nebst einem Anhange von dem Gesandschaftsrechte des Deutschen Bundes, einer Bücherkunde des Gesandschaftsrechts und erläuternden Beilagen* (Leipzig: W. Engelmann, 1847), 1: 423–47.

24. Whaley, *Religious Toleration*, 69; petition to Binder von Kriegelstein included as a copy with his letter to von Colloredo (in Vienna) from 27 July 1776, HHStAW, Staatskanzlei, Berichte aus Hamburg, fasc. 10.

25. On Hamburg's relationship with Prussia in the seventeenth and eighteenth centuries, see Adolf Wohlwill, *Aus drei Jahrhunderten der Hamburgischen Geschichte (1648–1888)* (Hamburg: Lucas Gräfe & Sillem, 1897), 26–88.

26. *Hamburg*, ed. Jochmann and Loose, 1: 309. Joachim Whaley explains the eagerness of the Senat to develop a modus vivendi with Calvinists in the 1720s as deriving from "its increasing concern with the profound economic depression of the period, and in particular over the threat posed by the commercial expansion of Altona." The arguments that senators advanced in favor of limited toleration "combined traditional mercantile wisdom with new philosophical insights into the relationship between government and society." *Religious Toleration*, 129.

27. Ibid., 145–68.

28. Wohlwill, *Aus drei Jahrhunderten*, 73; Ramcke, *Beziehungen*, 244–54.

29. *Hamburg*, ed. Jochmann and Loose, 1: 355–56; W. O. Henderson, "The Berlin

Commercial Crisis of 1763," *EHR* 15 (1962–63): 89–102; Walther Vogel, "Handelskon-junkturen und Wirtschaftskrisen in ihrer Auswirkung auf den Seehandel der Hanse-städte," *HGH* 74 (1956): 50–64; Liebel, "Laissez-faire vs. Mercantilism."

30. Ramcke, *Beziehungen*, 7–12, 166; H. M. Scott, "Prussia's Royal Foreign Minister: Frederick the Great and the Administration of Prussian Diplomacy," in *Royal and Republican Sovereignty in Early Modern Europe: Essays in Memory of Ragnild Hatton*, ed. Robert Oresko, G. C. Gibbs, and H. M. Scott (Cambridge: Cambridge University Press, 1997), 519–21; Mitchell quotation, 520.

31. Wohlwill, *Aus drei Jahrhunderten*, 76–77.

32. On the Biorenberg/Wentzhard(t) case, see SUBHbg, Handschriftensamm-lung, Cod. Hans. II, 171, 1, and StAHbg, RHR, 17; the "Werbungs-Patent" issued by Prussia from 23 January 1720 is found in StAHbg, RHR, 17.

33. "Factum" presented by Hamburg to Reichshofrat, 10 November 1721, StAHbg, RHR, 17.

34. "Extractus Procolli Extrajudicalis [Hamburg]," 1 May 1720, StAHbg, RHR, 17.

35. M. S. Anderson, *The Rise of Modern Diplomacy, 1450–1919* (London: Long-man, 1993), 76–78; Erwin Matsch, *Geschichte des Auswärtigen Dienstes von Öster-reich(-Ungarn), 1720–1920* (Vienna: Böhlaus, 1980), 51–54, 107, 113.

36. On the "King's Secret," see Albert de Broglie, *The King's Secret: Being the Secret Correspondence of Louis XV, with his Diplomatic Agents, from 1752 to 1774* (London: Cassell, Petter & Galpin, 1879); Rohan Butler, "Paradiplomacy," in Arshag Ohan Sarkissian, ed., *Studies in Diplomatic History and Historiography in Honour of G. P. Gooch* (London: Longmans, 1961), 12–25. On Ripperda, see G. P. J. van Alkemade, *Jan Willem, baron van Ripperda: een diplomaat-avonturier uit de achttiende eeuw* (Apeldoorn: Semper Agendo, 1968). On Casanova, see *Geheim agent* (Amsterdam: Athenaeum-Polak & Van Gennep, 1998) and Casanova, *History*, passim.

37. Anderson, *Rise of Modern Diplomacy*, 41, 46, 69, 76–78; Ewald, *Hambur-gische Senatssyndicus*, 36–40.

38. The classification of representatives was only fully defined after 1815 (in the Vienna and Aachen Regulations of 1815 and 1817 respectively). The highest repre-sentative was the ambassador. Residents (also called ministers plenipotentiary in the late eighteenth century) formed the next level. Below them in the classificatory scheme were agents and consuls. There were no ambassadors in Hamburg, only residents/ministers-plenipotentiary and agents/consuls. Frank Hatje, *Representa-tionen der Staatsgewalt: Herrschaftstruktur und Selbstdarstellung in Hamburg, 1700–1900* (Basel: Helbing & Lichtenhahn, 1997), 147.

39. Anderson, *Rise of Modern Diplomacy*, 46.

40. Information on diplomatic missions comes from *Rep.* 2 and *Rep.* 3 and Lappenberg, "Listen."

41. *Rep.* 3: 110–12, 115, 119, 122, 124, 129 (de la Houze); 69, 77–78, 80–83, 93, 288 (Binder von Kriegelstein).

42. Ibid., 325, 329, 332 (von Hecht); 433 (Sanpelayo); Pohl, *Beziehungen*, 19, 30–31 (Sanpelayo); Georg Fink, "Diplomatische Vertretungen der Hanse seit dem 17. Jahrhundert bis zur Auflösung der Hanseatischen Gesandtschaft in Berlin," *Hans-ische Geschichtsblätter* 56 (1931): 112–55.

43. *Rep.* 3: 181 (Fabrice); 182 (Courchetet and D'Hugier); 36, 182, 233 (D'Hugier); 4, 38, 184, 234 (Wever); 38, 184, 234 (van der Lepe); Pohl, *Beziehungen,* 16 (van der Lepe).

44. List compiled from several files in GStAPK: I. HA Rep. 50 (Beziehungen zu den Reichstädten) no. 28a fasc. 271, 417, 420–21, 449; I. HA Rep. 50 no. 28 fasc. 88–89, 146.

45. Material on the Kottwitz/Mauen case is taken from StAHbg, Senat Cl. VII Lit. Cc no. 13 vol. 5 fasc. 19 and Senat Cl. VII Lit. Me no. 10 vol. 1 fasc. 5.

46. "Factum" presented by Georg Mauen, from 5 December 1771, in ibid.

47. Klefeker, 12: 449–55. Numerous ordinances were passed in the seventeenth and eighteenth centuries to regulate marriages. The most important of these was the so-called "Great Wedde Ordinance" of 30 April 1732. See Blank, 5: 1169.

48. Letter of Mauen, 26 March 1772 and presentation of Senat, 24 April 1772, StAHbg, Senat Cl. VII Lit. Cc no. 13 vol. 5 fasc. 19.

49. StAHbg, Cl. VIII no. Xa (1775), p. 348 (29 December 1775).

50. Report from Praetor Volkmann to Senat, 23 December 1775, StAHbg, Senat Cl. VII Lit. Gg Pars. 1 no. 3 vol. 5f.

51. Koschenbahr to von Hecht, 5 January 1776; Senat/Faber to Wever, 2 January 1776, both in ibid.

52. StAHbg, Senat Cl. VIII no. Xa (1776), pp. 69, 74–75 (26 and 28 February).

53. Ibid., pp. 79, 122 (1 March and 1 April).

54. Ibid., pp. 103, 196, 211, 254 (20 March, 3, 19 June, 24 August).

55. The materials on the Schlabrendorff duel, the negotiations with Berlin, and the final result are found in StAHbg, Senat Cl. VII Lit. Gg Pars. 3 no. 4 vol. 6 and in StAHbg, Senat Cl. VIII no. Xa (1776), pp. 245–48, 250, 259, 261, 264–65, 267, 279, 290, 335 (2, 9, 23, 28, 30 August, 13, 27 September, 20 November); (1777), p. 22 (27 January).

56. "Bescheid," 12 April 1776, StAHbg, Cl. VII Lit. Me no. 8 vol. 6 fasc. 7 conv. 2.

57. The diplomatic correspondence in this case is mostly found in StAHbg, Senat Cl. VIII no. Xa (Senat Protokolle) for 1775 and 1776; between von Hecht and Berlin in GStAPK, I. HA Rep. 56B no. 211k and Rep. 81 Hamburg A 133; between Binder von Kriegelstein and his superior (Colloredo) in Vienna in HHStAW, Gesandtschaftsarchiv Hamburg, Niedersächsisches Gesandschaft, Staatskanzlei und Reichskanzlei (I consulted these records on microfilm in StAHbg, Filmarchiv, Films E Sa 789–791, 812–813, 1199, 1200, 2001–2002); between Baron de la Houze and Paris in ADCP, vols. 101 (1775) and 102 (January 1776–December 1777). Because Spain's representative *was* Sanpelayo, I constructed the Spanish position from the correspondence between de la Houze and Paris, as well as from the reports of Hamburg's representative in Madrid, van der Lepe, in the Senat Protokolle, passim, and in StAHbg, Senat Cl. VII Lit. Me no. 8 vol. 6 fasc. 5.

58. StAHbg, Senat Cl. VIII no. Xa (1775), p. 266 (Wednesday, 25 October).

59. Formulas for the *Gassen/Strassen-Recht* can be found in Klefeker, 5: 559–68. See also "Erste Zugabe, eine Anmerkung über das Gassen-Recht," ibid., 569–76.

60. Hecht to Senat, StAHbg, Senat Cl. VIII no. Xa (1776) p. 11 (Wednesday, 11 January).

61. Hasche, *Kurze Darstellung,* 20–21.

62. StAHbg, Senat Cl. VII Lit. Me no. 8 vol. 2b fasc. 7; StAHbg, Senat Cl. VII Lit. Ma no. 9 vol.1i; Senat Cl. VIII no. Xa (1750), esp. p. 103 (Wednesday, 20 March); Klefeker, 5: 500–501.

63. On the Niedergericht and the defense of its rights and privileges, see Jacobi, *Geschichte,* 47–76, specifically on Kesslitz case, 60–61 (some details are misreported); and also Chapter 2. On the negotiations with the Niedergericht on this issue, StAHbg, Senat Cl. VIII no. Xa (1775), pp. 320–21 (Monday, 11 December) and p. 347 (Friday, 29 December).

64. StAhbg, Senat Cl. VIII no. Xa (1775), p. 312, 320–21 (Monday, 4 December; Monday, 11 December).

65. Copy of letter, StAHbg, Senat Cl. VII Lit. Me no. 8 vol. 6 fasc. 4.

66. StAHbg, Senat Cl. VIII no. Xa (1775), pp. 6–8 (Monday, 8 January).

67. StAHbg, Senat Cl. VII Lit. Me no. 8 vol. 6 fasc. 4. Matsen became a secretary to the Senat on 28 December 1775 and a syndic on 4 June 1784. *Schriftsteller Lexikon.*

68. GStAPK, I. HA Rep. 81 Hamburg A 133, 20 January 1776.

69. Detenhof's "Vorstellung" dated 22 December 1775, GStAPK, I. HA Rep. 46B no. 211k. Detenhof mentioned the case of the Polish subject in a letter to Berlin, 13 January 1776, in StAHbg, Senat Cl. VII Lit. Me no. 8 vol. 6 fasc. 4; see also the Special Order sent to Hecht, 20 January 1776, in GStAPK, I. HA Rep. 81 Hamburg A 133.

70. StAHbg, Senat Cl. VIII no. Xa (1776), pp. 102–3 ("des Hr. Wever Berichte nicht allemal so zuverläßig sind, wie sie billig sollte"). Wever served as Hamburg's agent in Berlin from 14 June 1771 until 29 April 1803; *Rep.* 3: 4, 38, 184, 234.

71. StAHbg, Senat Cl. VII Lit. Me no. 8 vol. 6 fasc. 4.

72. "C.C." to Hecht, in ibid.

73. Senat to Berlin, 12 January 1776, GStAPK, I. HA Rep. 46B no. 211k; "Special-Befehl," 6 February 1776, GStAPK, I. HA Rep. 81 Hamburg A 133; "C.C." to Hecht, StAHbg, Senat Cl. VII Lit. Me no. 8 vol. 6 fasc. 4.

74. StAHbg, Senat Cl. VII Lit. Me no. 8 vol. 6 fasc. 4.

75. Three "Special-Befehle" to Hecht, 10, 12 February and 16 March 1776, in GStAPK, I. HA Rep. 81 Hamburg A 133.

76. Promemorium from Detenhof, Berlin, 3 February 1776, GStAPK, I. HA Rep. 46B no. 211k.

77. Ibid.

78. StAHbg, Senat Cl. VII Lit. Me no. 8 vol. 6 fasc. 4, 29 January 1776.

79. Ibid., Sillem to Wever, 2 February 1776.

80. Ibid., Wever to Sillem, 6 February 1776.

81. Ibid., "Relation auf das eingegangene Schreiben des Königs von Preußen in der Kesslitzschen Criminal Sache."

82. StAHbg, Senat Cl. VIII no. Xa (1776), pp. 75–76 (Wednesday, 28 February).

83. The vast majority of the records of the Niedergericht are not currently able to be consulted because of extensive water damage and the resulting mold. Thus, to a large extent one must rely on the records of the Senat and reading between the lines, as well as on two valuable older works whose authors had access to the relevant documents: Jacobi, *Geschichte,* and Hasche, *Kurze Darstellung.*

84. Hatje, *Representationen,* 151.

85. StAHbg, Senat Cl. VIII no. Xa (1776), pp. 87, 89, 92–93, 102–3 (Wednesday, 6 March; Friday, 8 March, Monday 11 March, and Wednesday, 20 March). Two later cases caused similar battles to break out between the Senat and the Niedergericht: the case of Maria Wächtler, who murdered and dismembered her husband in 1786 and that of the Jewess Deborah Traub, who poisoned her sister-in-law and mother-in-law. StAHbg, Senat Cl. VIII no. Xa (28 November 1788), p. 368, and "Incomple. Acta betr. die Beschwerde des Niedergerichts wegen der Traub'schen Criminalsachen, 1791," Senat Cl. VII Lit. Ma no. 5 vol. 4f11.

86. *HRG*, s.v. "Urfehde."

87. See marginal note in French on the (German) copy of the "Urtheil des Hamburgisches Niedergerichts in der Käselitsche Sachen," 12 April 1776, in ADCP, sous-série Hambourg, vol. 102, f. 66.

88. Detenhof to Frederick, 14 April 1776; Sillem to Wever, 16 April 1776; Wever's response, 20 April 1776, StAHbg, Senat Cl. VII Lit. Me no. 8 vol. 6 fasc. 4.

89. "An der G.R. Hecht zu Hamburg," 23 April 1776; Wever to Sillem, 27 April 1776, in ibid; StAHbg, Senat Cl. VIII no. Xa (1776), p. 160 (Wednesday, 1 May).

90. Sillem to Wever, 7 and 14 May 1776; Wever to Sillem, 11 and 28 May 1776, StAHbg, Senat Cl. VII Lit. Me no. 8 vol. 6 fasc. 4; and Hecht to Berlin, 14 May 1776, GStAPK, I. HA Rep. 46B no. 211k.

91. StAHbg, Senat Cl. VIII no. Xa (1775), p. 262 (Friday, 20 October).

92. "Species facti," 19 October 1775, StAHbg, Senat Cl. VII Lit. Me no. 8 vol. 6 fasc. 7 conv. 2; StAHbg, Senat Cl. VIII no. Xa (1775), p. 262 (Friday, 20 October).

93. StAHbg, Senat Cl. VIII no. Xa (1775), p. 321 (Monday, 11 December); (1776), p. 8 (Monday, 8 January).

94. Ibid. (1776), pp. 35–43 (Monday, 31 January; Monday, 5 February). The explanation sent to van der Lepe in Madrid was dated 5 February, StAHbg, Senat Cl. VII Lit. Me no. 8 vol. 6 fasc. 5 ("Acta mit dem Königl. Spanischen Hofe p*to*. Der Kesslitzschen Criminal-Sache, A*o* 1775–76").

95. Senat/Sillem to van der Lepe, 9 February 1776, StAHbg, Senat Cl. VII Lit. Me no. 8 vol. 6 fasc. 5.

96. Ibid.

97. Promemorium to van der Lepe, 11 March 1776, ibid.

98. StAHbg, Senat Cl. VIII no. Xa (1776), p. 52 (Monday 12 February).

99. Van der Lepe to Senat/Sillem, 4 March 1776, StAHbg, Senat Cl. VII Lit. Me no. 8 vol. 6 fasc. 5.

100. StAHbg, Senat Cl. VIII no. Xa (1776), pp. 83–84 (Monday, 4 March).

101. Ibid.; Senat to van der Lepe, 1 April 1776, promemorium to van der Lepe, 11 March 1776, StAHbg, Senat Cl. VII Lit. Me no. 8 vol. 6 fasc. 5.

102. D'Hugier to Senat, 29 February 1776, StAHbg, Lit. Me no. 8 vol. 6 fasc. 6; StAHbg, Senat Cl. VIII no. Xa (1776), pp. 94, 175 (Wednesday, 13 March; Monday, 13 May).

103. StAHbg, Senat Cl. VIII no. Xa (1776), pp. 111–12, 119–20, 237, 254 (Wednesday, 27 March; Monday, 1 April; 24 July; Wednesday, 14 August); van der Lepe to Senat, 4 March 1776, StAHbg, Senat Cl. VII Lit. Me no. 8 vol. 6 fasc. 5.

104. Senat/Sillem to d'Hugier, 9 February 1776 and Senat to van der Lepe, 5 February, StAHbg, Senat Cl. VII Lit. Me no. 8 vol. 6 fasc. 6; promemorium to van

der Lepe, 11 March 1776, StAHbg, Senat Cl. VII Lit. Me no. 8 vol. 6 fasc. 5. There is here, as elsewhere, considerable overlap in what the Senat/Sillem communicated to the Spanish and French courts.

105. Promemorium to van der Lepe, 11 March 1776; Senat/Sillem to van der Lepe, 1 April 1776; and Senat/Sillem to van der Lepe, 8 November 1776, StAHbg, Senat Cl. VII Lit. Me no. 8 vol. 6 fasc. 5.

106. Sanpelayo requested his release on 30 December 1776; Urqullu arrived in January 1777 and remained in Hamburg until June 1791, and, after 1784, as consul general for the Hanse cities. Lappenberg, "Listen," 138.

107. Urqullu to Senat, 2 May 1777 and Senat to van der Lepe, 5 May 1777, StAHbg, Senat Cl. VII Lit. Me no. 8 vol. 6 fasc. 8.

108. Urqullu to Senat, 9 May 1777, ibid.

109. Senat to Urqullu, 12 May 1777, ibid.

110. Report (probably from Binder von Kriegelstein) to von Colloredo (with a copy to von Kaunitz in Madrid), 27 July 1776, in HHStAW, Staatskanzlei, Berichte aus Hamburg, fasc. 10, ff. 317–18 with an attached note from Romellini, ff. 319–22.

111. StAHbg, Senat Cl. VIII no. Xa (1775), pp. 267, 293 (Friday, 27 October and Friday, 17 November).

112. Ibid. (1776), pp. 38, 47, 48, 59, 108 (Wednesday, 31 January, Friday, 9, Wednesday, 14, and Friday 16 February, Friday, 22 March).

113. Ibid., pp. 116, 130 (Friday, 29 March and Wednesday, 10 April).

114. Ibid., p. 141 (Wednesday, 17 April).

115. 27 July 1776, HHStAW, Staatskanzlei, Berichte aus Hamburg, fasc. 10, ff. 317–18 with an attached note from Romellini, ff. 319–22. Romellini (then in Rotterdam) had written to the Senat, accusing Sillem of corruption, on 18 November 1776. The Senat concluded that it was best to ignore the letter completely. StAHbg, Senat Cl. VIII no. Xa (1776), pp. 345, 348 (Monday, 2 December and Wednesday, 4 December); Senat Cl. VII Lit. Me no. 8 vol. 6 fasc. 9.

Entr'acte

1. Davis, *Fiction in the Archives.*

2. Jo Burr Margadant, ed., *The New Biography: Performing Femininity in Nineteenth-Century France* (Berkeley: University of California Press, 2000), 9; R. Barry Rutland, "Introduction," in id., *Gender and Narrativity* (Ottawa: Centre for Textual Analysis, Discourse, and Culture, Carlton University Press, 1997), 3; Sherry B. Ortner, *Narrativity in History, Culture, and Lives* (Ann Arbor: University of Michigan, 1991), 9. See also Margaret R. Somers, *Narrativity, Culture, and Casuality: Toward a New Historical Epistemology, or, Where Is Sociology After the New Historic Turn?* (Ann Arbor: University of Michigan Press, 1990).

3. Arthur W. Frank, *The Wounded Storyteller: Body, Illness, and Ethics* (Chicago: University of Chicago Press, 1995), 23, 158. I first became aware of Frank's work while reading Alice Domurat Dreger, *Hermaphrodites and the Medical Invention of Sex* (Cambridge, Mass.: Harvard University Press, 1998), 168–70.

4. Paul John Eakin, *How Our Lives Become Stories: Making Selves* (Ithaca, N.Y.: Cornell University Press, 1999), ix.

5. Hayden White, "The Value of Narrativity in the Representation of Reality," in *On Narrative*, ed. W. J. Thomas Mitchell (Chicago: University of Chicago Press, 1981), 1–23.

6. Rudolf Dekker, "Introduction," in *Egodocuments and History: Autobiographical Writing in Its Social Context Since the Middle Ages*, ed. id. (Hilversum: Verloren, 2002), 7.

7. Ibid., 12, 15. This is the perspective of Michael Mascuch, *Origins of the Individualist Self: Autobiography and Self-Identity in England, 1591–1791* (Stanford, Calif.: Stanford University Press, 1996). See also Eakin, *How Our Lives Become Stories*, esp. chap. 3: "Storied Selves: Identity Through Self-Narration," 99–141.

8. The literature on egodocuments has grown substantially since the 1980s. Dekker, "Introduction," offers a good overview of the state of the field and of the discussions on how to analyze egodocuments.

9. For example, Restif de la Bretonne, *Le Paysan perverti, ou, les dangers de la ville, histoire récente: Mise au jour d'après les véritables lettres des personnages* (The Hague: Esprit, 1776).

10. François Gayot de Pitaval, *Causes célèbres et intéressantes avec les jugements qui les ont decidées* (Paris: Delaune, 1739–70); id., *Merkwürdige Rechtsfälle; Der neue Pitaval: Eine Sammlung der interessantesten Criminalgeschichten aller Länder aus älterer und neuerer Zeit*, ed. J. E. Hitzig, W. Alexis Häring, and Anton Vollert (Leipzig: F. A. Brockhaus, 1845–90); Charlotte Smith, *The Romance of Real Life* (London: T. Cadell, 1787); Robert Darnton, *The Forbidden Best-Sellers of Pre-Revolutionary France* (New York: Norton, 1995); Sarah Maza, *Private Lives and Public Affairs: The Causes célèbres of Prerevolutionary France* (Berkeley: University of California Press, 1993); Natalie Z. Davis, *The Return of Martin Guerre* (Cambridge, Mass.: Harvard University Press, 1983).

CHAPTER 4. *A Brave and Upright Cavalier?*

1. Julius Krebs, *Hans Ulrich, Freiherr von Schaffgotsch: Ein Lebensbild aus der Zeit des dreißigjährigen Krieges* (Breslau: Wilhelm Gottlieb Korn, 1890), 1.

2. Rudolf Endres, *Adel in der Frühen Neuzeit* (Munich: R. Oldenbourg, 1993), 38.

3. Norbert Conrads, *Schlesien* (Berlin: Siedler, 1994), 262–65.

4. Ibid., 262, 274–77.

5. Ibid., 290–91, 296.

6. Ibid., 291, 298–300.

7. Ibid., 343.

8. Ibid., 344.

9. Winfried Irgang, Werner Bein, and Helmut Neubach, *Schlesien: Geschichte, Kultur und Wirtschaft*, 2nd rev. ed. (Cologne: Wissenschaft & Politik, 1998), 112.

10. My discussion of economics in the Habsburg period relies heavily on ibid., 115–17, 128–31; Helmut Feigl, "Die Entwicklung des schlesischen Grundherrschaft unter den Habsburgern (1526 bis 1742)," in *Kontinuität und Wandel: Schlesien zwischen Österreich und Preußen*, ed. Peter Baumgart, with the assistance of Ulrich Schmilewski (Sigmaringen: Jan Thorbecke, 1990), 135–65; and Georg Frederick Knapp, *Grundherrschaft und Rittergut: Vorträge nebst biographischen Beilagen*

(Leipzig: Duncker & Humblot, 1897), 30–34, 42. On the linen trade, see Jochmann, "Hamburgisch-schlesische Handelsbeziehungen"; Alfred Zimmermann, *Blüthe und Verfall des Leinengewerbes in Schlesien: Gewerbe- und Handelspolitik dreier Jahrhunderte* (Breslau: Wilhelm Gottlieb Korn, 1885); and Otto Schumann, *Die Landeshuter Leinenindustrie in Vergangenheit und Gegenwart: Ein Beitrag zur Geschichte der schlesischen Textilindustrie* (Jena: Gustav Fischer, 1928), 5–37.

11. This discussion of developments in Silesia after 1740 is taken from the excellent accounts in Conrads, *Schlesien*, 346–464, and *Geschichte Schlesiens*, ed. Aubin et al., vol. 3: *Preußisch-Schlesien, 1740–1945 / Österreichisch-Schlesien, 1740–1918/45* (Stuttgart: Jan Thorbecke, 1999), 1–25, 104–24, 490–96. See also Andreas Kutschelis, " 'Triumph von Schlesien oder Beschreibung der Huldigung zu Breslau': Eine Flugschrift über die Huldigung der niederschlesischen Stände vor Friedrich dem Großen im Jahre 1741," *Nord-Ost Archiv: Zeitschrift für Kulturgeschichte und Landeskunde* 24 (1991): 129–48.

12. Conrads, *Schlesien*, 385–86.

13. Ibid., 356–57, 385; on the Ballestrems, see *Glogau im Wandel der Zeiten* (exhibition catalog), comp. Werner Bein, Johannes Schellakowsky, and Ulrich Schmilewski (Würzburg: Wilhelm Gottlieb Korn, 1992), 21.

14. Conrads, *Schlesien*, 384–93; Hermann Fechner, *Wirtschaftsgeschichte der preußischen Provinz Schlesien in der Zeit ihrer provinziellen Selbständigkeit 1741–1806* (Breslau: S. Schottlaender, 1907), 116–18, 488–89.

15. Eichendorff's description is quoted in Joseph von Golitschek and Robert Weber, *Schlesien-Land der Schlösser*, vol. 1: *Zeugen deutscher Kultur* (Mannheim: Kraft, 1978), 10–13.

16. Fiegl, "Entwicklung," 139–41; Colmar Grünhagen, "Der schlesische Adel vor hundert Jahren im Lichte der öffentlichen Meinung," *ZVGAS* 30 (1896): 4. More generally on the European nobility, see Dewald, *European Nobility*.

17. Fiegl, "Entwicklung," 157. For more on the Liechtenstein family, see Jakob von Falke, *Geschichte des fürstlichen Hauses Liechtenstein* (Vienna: W. Braumüller, 1868–82); Colmar Grünhagen, "Schlesien in den letzten Jahrzehnten österreichischer Herrschaft," *ZVGAS* 15 (1880): 56.

18. Carl Eduard Schück, "Die Familie derer von Zedlitz in Schlesien während dreier Jahrhunderte," *Rübezahl: der Schlesischen Provinzialblätter* 75 (1871): 59–61; Peter Mainka, *Karl Abraham von Zedlitz und Leipe (1731–1793): Ein schlesischer Adliger in Diensten Friedrichs II. und Friedrich Wilhelms II. von Preußen* (Berlin: Duncker & Humblot, 1994).

19. Carl von Wechmar, *Geschichte des Dorfes und Rittergutes Zedlitz (Kreis Steinau)* [supplement to *ZVGAS* 12] (Breslau: Verfasser, 1874), 37.

20. Knapp, *Grundherrschaft und Rittergut*, 30.

21. Wechmar, *Geschichte des Dorfes und Rittergutes Zedlitz*, 43–45.

22. Wilhelm Treue, "Schlesiens Eingliederung in das Preussische Wirtschaftssystem," in *Kontinuität und Wandel*, ed. Baumgart, 122–23.

23. Grünhagen, "Schlesische Adel," 5–6.

24. Quoted in Matthias Ludwig von Lossow, *Denkwürdigkeiten zur Charakteristik der preussischen Armee unter dem großen König Friedrich dem Zweiten* (Glogau: Carl Heymann, 1826), 167.

25. Dieter and Renate Sinn, *Der Alltag in Preußen* (Frankfurt a/M: Societäts-Verlag, 1991), 399–400, 450.

26. Otto Büsch, *Militärsystem und Sozialleben im alten Preussen 1713–1807: Die Anfänge der sozialen Militarisierung der preußisch-deutschen Gesellschaft* (Berlin: Walter de Gruyter, 1962), 47, 150–51; Demeter, *Deutsche Offizierkorps*, 2.

27. Oskar Kutzner, *Das Landratsamt in Schlesien 1740–1806: II. Teil, Die Zusammensetzung des Landratsamts* (Breslau: A. Favorke, 1911), 3–5, 17, 21, 24–25.

28. Grünhagen, "Schlesische Adel," 8.

29. Colmar Grünhagen, "Schlesien unmittelbar nach dem Hubertsburger Frieden," *ZVGAS* 25 (1891): 109–10.

30. Quoted in Otto Meinardus, "Das Gnadengeschenk Friedrichs des Großen für den schlesischen Landadel und die Ernnennung Carmers zum Justizminister (1768)," *ZVGAS* 44 (1910): 79–80.

31. Ibid., 89, 102–3.

32. The Silesian experiment was the model for similar plans established elsewhere in Prussia: in the Kur- und Neumark in 1777, in Pomerania in 1781, in West Prussia in 1787, and, finally, in East Prussia in 1778. Sinn and Sinn, *Alltag*, 400–401; Meinardus, "Gnadengeschenck," 74–109.

33. Büsch, *Militärsystem*, 47, 150–51.

34. Irgang, Bein, and Neubach, *Schlesien*, 128–29; Grünhagen, "Schlesische Adel," 8–9, 11; Sinn and Sinn, *Alltag*, 397–401.

35. Information on the Kesslitz family has been gathered from a number of historical sources. Andreas Kutschelis provided much valuable guidance. Particularly useful were the several Kesslitz family trees he constructed as well as other documents in his private collection, including a "Familien Chronik" and personal correspondence with other family members now resident in Vienna. Kutschelis's many communications with the author were equally essential for the successful reconstruction of the life of Joseph von Kesslitz and his family. See also id., "Gesucht: Personengeschichtliche Materialism zu den Glogauer Landständen in den letzten hundert Jahren der Habsburgerherrschaft über Schlesien," *Wolfenbütteler Barock-Nachrichten* 22 (1995): 119–20.

36. *Glogau im Wandel der Zeiten*, comp. Bein, Schellakowsky, and Schmilewski, 197, 331–32, 437; genealogy of the von Kesslitz family compiled by Andreas Kutschelis in GStAPK, VIII. HA Rep. C no. 295; Leopold von Ledebur, *Adelslexicon der Preussischen Monarchie* (Berlin: Ludwig Rauh, 1854), 1: 426; Johannes Sinapius, *Des Schlesischen Adels, Anderer Theil / Oder Fortsetzung Schlesischer Curiositäten, Darinnen Die Gräflichen, Freyherrlichen und Adelichen Geschlechther / So wohl Schlesischer Extraction, Als auch Die aus andern Königreichen und Ländern in Schlesien kommen / Und entweder darinnen noch floriren, oder bereits ausgangen, In völligem Abrisse dargestellet werden, Nebst einer nöthigen Vorrede und Register* (Leipzig: Michael Rohrlach, 1728), 347–48; Ernst Heinrich Kneschke, *Neues allgemeines Deutsches Adels-Lexikon* (Leipzig: Degener, 1930), 5: 78–79.

37. Sinapius, *Schlesisichen Adels*, 347–48.

38. "Pro Memoria an meine Mandatrium den D. und Capitular Syndicum Detenhoff" (n.d. [1776]), GStAPK, I. HA Rep. 46B no. 211k. Georg Wendt, *Geschichte der Königlichen Ritterakademie zu Liegnitz*, vol. 1: *1708–1840 (Beilage*

zum Programm der Königlichen Ritter-Akademie in Liegnitz) (Liegnitz, 1893), reprinted in Peter Mainka, *Die Erziehung der adligen Jugend in Brandenburg-Preußen: Curriculare Anweisungen Karl Abrahams von Zedlitz und Leipe für die Ritterakademie zu Liegnitz, eine archivalische Studie zur Bildungsgeschichte der Aufklärungszeit* (Würzburg: Verein für Geschichte Schlesiens, 1997), 124.

39. Grünhagen, "Schlesischer Adel," 7.

40. *Glogau im Wandel der Zeiten,* comp. Bein, Schellakowsky, and Schmilewski, 332.

41. *Tabela podatku gruntowego i ludności wsi śląskich z około 1765 roku* [Property tax and population tables for the Silesian towns around 1765], comp. Zbigniew Kwaśny and Jan Wosch, Żródła do Atlasu Historycznego Śląska / Polska Akademia Nauk. Instytut Historii, 1 (Wrocław: Zakład Narodowy im. Ossolińskich, 1975).

42. Ibid., 9, 11. Information on the sale of Salisch and Merzdorf, from "Pro Memoria an meine Mandatrium."

43. *Tabela podatku gruntowego i ludności wsi śląskich z około 1765 roku,* 11–12.

44. "Gesuch des Frhr. von Kesslitz auf Salisch um Konzession zur Tax- und Subhastation einer auf seinem gute Merztdorf befindlichen, in gäntzlichen Verfall geratenen Frei-Gärtner Stelle, 1762," GStAPK, I. HA Rep. 46B 33k14, fasc. 1.

45. My account of Silesia both before and after 1740 relies heavily on Conrads, *Schlesien,* 258–464 and a series of articles in *Kontinuität und Wandel,* ed. Baumgart: Harm Kleuting, "Die politisch-administrative Integration Preußisch-Schlesiens unter Friedrich II.," 41–62; Wilhelm Treue, "Schlesiens Eingliederung in das preußische Wirtschaftssytem," 119–34; Fiegl, "Entwicklung," 135–65; Karl Heinrich Kaufhold, "Friderizianische Agrar-, Siedlungs- und Bauernpolitik," 167–201; and Norbert Conrads, "Politischer Mentalitätswandel von oben: Friedrich II. Weg vom Gewinn Schlesiens zur Gewinnung der Schlesier," 219–36.

46. "An die Glogauische O.A. Regier.," 31 January 1750, GStAPK, I. HA Rep. 46B, no. 306/72e.

47. Norbert Conrads, *Ritterakademien der Frühen Neuzeit: Bildung als Standesprivileg im 16. und 17. Jahrhundert* (Göttingen: Vandenhoeck & Ruprecht, 1982), 15–16.

48. From a plan to improve the education in the Academy from 1743; "Listen derer sich alhier befindenden Academisten," from 1743; "Instruction vor den Director der Ritter-Academie zu Liegnitz, oder demjenigen das Directorium zu führen hat," 3 July 1743, GStAPK, I. HA Rep. 46B no. 306/72e; Ernst Pfudel, *Geschichte der Königl. Ritter-Akademie zu Liegnitz* (reprint; Hofheim/Taunus: Henske-Neumann, 1994 [1908]), 41.

49. Demeter, *Deutsche Offizierkorps,* 77–78.

50. Mainka, *Erziehung,* 124.

51. Conrads, *Schlesien,* 341–42.

52. Wendt, *Geschichte,* 10. Between 1741 and 1810, the Ritterakademie admitted 587 students, about 16–17 annually. Of these, 507 came from Silesia and 80 from elsewhere: 32 "other" Prussians, 31 Poles, and 9 Saxons. Pfudel, *Geschichte,* 13.

53. "An die Glogauische O. A. Regier."

54. Wendt, *Geschichte,* 164; Mainka, *Karl Abraham von Zedlitz,* 398.

55. "Pro Memoria an meine Mandatrium"; Georg Liebe, Em Theuner, and

Ernst Friedländer, *Ältere Universitäts-Matrikeln, aus der Originalhandschrift,* part 1: *Frankfurt an der Oder,* vol. 1: *1649–1811* (Leipzig: Hirzel, 1888), 384; Charles E. McClelland, *State, Society, and University in Germany, 1700–1914* (Cambridge: Cambridge University Press, 1980), 48, 54.

56. Nathaniel William Wraxall, *Memoirs of the Courts of Berlin, Dresden, Warsaw, and Vienna: In the Years 1777, 1778, and 1779* (London: Printed for T. Cadell Jun. and W. Savies, 1799, 1806), 1: 147.

57. GStAPK, "Offiziernomenklatur," IV. HA Preußische Armee, Rep. 1 Geheime Kriegskanzlei, no. 76. The Hubertusburg Peace was signed on 15 February 1763.

58. Philipp von Schröter, *Kurzgefasste Geschichte aller königlichen Preußischen Regimenten, zur Erklärung der illuminirten Abbildungen derselben: Bey dieser vierten Auflage bis ans Ende des Jahres fortgesetzt, und mit der jetzigen Generalität vermehrt* (Nuremberg: Raspische Handlung, 1770), 91; Karl Wilhelm Ernst von Canitz und Dallwitz, *Nachrichten und Betrachtungen über die Thaten und Schicksale der Reuterei in den Feldzügen Friedrichs des II. und in denen neuerer Zeit* (Berlin: E. S. Mittler, 1823–24), 1: 29–140.

59. *Unter der Fahne des Herzogs von Bevern: Jugenderinnerungen des Christian Wilhelm von Prittwitz und Gaffron,* ed. Hans Werner von Hugo and Hans Jessen (Breslau: Wilhelm Gottlieb Korn, 1935), 109–10.

60. Several officers wrote testimonials, including his commanding officers and Prince Heinrich, the commander in chief. Copies in GStAPK, I. HA Rep. 46B no. 211k and also in StAHbg, Senat Cl. VII Lit. Me no. 8 vol. 6 fasc. 7 conv. 1. Frederick's letter, in his own hand, is dated Freiburg 13 November 1762 and given "wegen einer demselben zugestandenen Gratification für dessen Wohlerhalten." Communication to Senat from 8 November 1775, StAHbg, Cl. VIII no. Xa (1775), 283.

61. August Friedrich von Retzow, *Charakteristik der wichtigsten Ereignisse des siebenjährigen Krieges: In Rücksicht auf Ursachen und Wirkungen, von einem Zeitgenossen* (Berlin: Himburgische Buchhandlung, 1802), 2: 91–93; Arnold Schaefer, *Geschichte des siebenjährigen Kriegs* (Berlin: W. Hertz, 1867–74), 2: 294–95.

62. Quoted in Schaefer, *Geschichte,* 2: 314.

63. Prittwitz und Gaffron, *Unter der Fahne,* ed. von Hugo and Jessen, 281–97.

64. Ibid., 287, 290.

65. Michael Morgenbesser, *Geschichte Schlesiens: Ein Handbuch* (Breslau: Joseph Max, 1829), 380–82.

66. Ibid., 386–93.

67. GStAPK, I. HA Rep. 46B no. 211k; on the battle of Freiburg, see Johann Wilhelm von Archenholz, *Geschichte des siebenjährigen Krieges in Deutschland* (1911; reprint, Osnabrück: Biblio, 1982), 506–7.

68. GStAPK, I. HA Rep. 46B no. 211k; Endres, *Adel,* 108; Büsch, *Militärsystem,* 141.

69. On the von Kreckwitz family, see Ekkehart Neumann-Reppert," "Die Familie Kreckwitz" (typescript), GStAPK, Bibliothek. Johann Karl Ferdinand Leopold was Maria Franziska's only surviving brother.

70. Niall Ferguson, *The House of Rothschild: Money's Prophets, 1798–1848* (New York: Viking, 1998), 43–44. I would like to thank Michael Miller for calling my attention to this reference.

71. Gerhard Femmel and Gerald Heres, eds., *Die Gemmen aus Goethes Sammlung* (Leipzig: E. A. Seemann, 1977), 13–14, 26–29; on a nonnoble, nonclerical collector and his collections, see Nuremberg, Stadtarchiv, *Die Kunstsammlung des Paulus Praun: Die Inventare von 1616 und 1719,* comp. Katrin Achilles-Syndram (Nuremberg: Stadtrat, 1994), 77–79, 85–94; Michael North, ed., *Kunstsammlung und Geschmack im 18. Jahrhundert* (Berlin: Arno Spitz, 2002).

72. *ACN* (2 December 1773): 752.

73. Eckart Klessmann, *Geschichte der Stadt Hamburg* (Hamburg: Hoffmann & Campe, 1994), 302–5; Mathias Hattendorff, *Höfische Reglement und Lustbarkeiten: Die Besuche von Caroline Mathilde und Christian VII. in Hamburg und Holstein, 1766–1772* (Hamburg: Kultur, 1999).

74. See, e.g., the projects advanced by Johann Joachim Becher. Pamela H. Smith, *The Business of Alchemy: Science and Culture in the Holy Roman Empire* (Princeton, N.J.: Princeton University Press, 1994).

75. Irgang, Bein, and Neubach, eds., *Schlesien,* 112; Jochmann, "Hamburgische-schlesische Handelsbeziehungen," 222–24.

76. Zimmermann, *Blüthe und Verfall,* 163; Schumann, *Landeshuter Leinenindustrie,* 35.

77. Heinrich [Henrik] Carl von Schimmelmann in *DBA;* Christian Degn, *Die Schimmelmanns im atlantischen Dreieckshandel: Gewinn und Gewissen* (Neumünster: Wachholtz, 1974).

78. GStAPK, I. HA Rep. 46B no. 211k.

79. Zimmermann, *Blüthe und Verfall,* 94–97, 103.

80. Ibid., 106, 141, 163, 167.

81. Statements given on 1 November 1775, StAHbg, Senat Cl. VII Lit. Me no. 8 vol. 6 fasc. 7 conv. 1.

82. GStAPK, I. HA Rep. 46B no. 211k.

83. Statement given on 7 November 1775, StAHbg, Senat Cl. VII Lit. Me no. 8 vol. 6 fasc. 7 conv. 1.

84. "Geschichts-Erzählung."

85. Statement of Hans Andreas Dreyer, 1 November 1775, StAHbg, Senat Cl. VII Lit. Me no. 8 vol. 6 fasc. 7 conv. 1.

86. Statement of Friedrich, baron von Schlabrendorff, 7 November 1775, ibid.

87. Designation of the papers in Kesslitz's possession when arrested, from 21 October 1775, ibid.

88. StAHbg, Senat Cl. VIII no. Xa (1775), p. 267 (Friday, 27 October).

89. Ibid., pp. 319, 327 (Friday, 8 December; Wednesday, 13 December); (1776), pp. 22, 25, 27 (Friday, 19 January; Monday, 22 January; Wednesday, 24 January).

90. Letter dated 6 December 1775, StAHbg, Senat Cl. VII Lit. Me no. 8 vol. 6 fasc. 3.

91. Undated letter listed in the designation of the papers found in Kesslitz's possession when arrested, from 21 October 1775, in StAHbg, Senat Cl. VII Lit. Me no. 8 vol. 6 fasc. 7 conv. 1.

92. From 7 November 1775, StAHbg, Senat Cl. VII Lit. Me no. 8 vol. 6 fasc. 7 conv. 2.

93. *Schlesische Provinzialblätter* 58 (July–December 1813), 376.

CHAPTER 5. *A Woman of Pleasure*

1. I am hardly the first to note the overlap of the worlds of courtesans, imposters, and diplomacy. See Lucien Bély, *Espions et ambassadeurs au temps de Louis XIV* (Paris: Fayard, 1990), esp. 51–208; Alexandre Stroev, *Les Aventuriers des Lumières* (Paris: Presses universitaires de France, 1997), esp. 34–49; Gary Kates, *Monsieur d'Eon Is a Woman: A Tale of Political Intrigue and Sexual Masquerade* (New York: Basic Books, 1995); Philip Mansel, *Prince of Europe: The Life of Charles-Joseph de Ligne (1735–1814)* (London: Weidenfeld & Nicolson, 2003).

2. "Fernweitige summarische Vernehmung Anna Maria Romel[l]ini wegen ihrer Lebensart und des angeb. Grafen Visconti Entleibung," 31 October, 1 November, and 3 November 1775, StAHbg, Senat Cl. VII Lit. Me no. 8 vol. 6 fasc. 7 conv. 1. This lengthy document serves as the principal source of information about her life.

3. Casanova, *History,* 10: 153. Numerous famous courtesans started out as singers and dancers; some had considerable talent, others less. Ibid., 7: 115.

4. On the opera in Parma, see David Kimbell, *Italian Opera* (Cambridge: Cambridge University Press, 1991), 228.

5. Letters (written in French) dated 16 and 25 June 1766 (Augsburg); 12 July 1766 (Frankfurt); and 2 August 1766 (Vienna), StAHbg, Senat Cl. VII Lit. Me no. 8 vol. 6 fasc. 7 conv. 1.

6. The Poniatowski brothers were not elevated to the rank of princes until Stanisław's election in 1764.

7. Jan Nepomucen Poniński was born in 1735 and died in 1782. *PAB; PSB.*

8. Note labeled "No. 6," StAHbg, Senat Cl. VII Lit. Me no. 8 vol. 6 fasc. 7 conv. 1.

9. Osten-Sacken was the Saxon minister plenipotentiary to Russia (from 26 December 1763 to 5 June 1768), *Rep.* 3: 377; dispatches to Dresden, SäHStAD, Geheimes Kabinett, loc. 3037 and 3038 (entry for 11 March 1766, on Courland). In her statement, Romellini said that Poniński was imprisoned for debt. The charges were actually considerably more serious; see Chapter 6.

10. "Fernweitige summarische Vernehmung Anna Maria Romel[l]ini."

11. *Rep.* 3: 361. The secondary literature on Repnin's role in Poland is mostly quite old and in Polish, see, for instance, Aleksander Kraushar, *Książę Repnin i Polska w pierwszem czteroleciu panowania Stanisława Augusta (1764–1768)* (Warsaw: Gebethner i Wolff, 1900); [James Harris], *Diaries and Correspondence of James Harris, First Earl of Malmesbury, containing an Account of his Missions at the Court of Madrid, to Frederick the Great, Catherine the Second, and at the Hague; and of his Special Missions to Berlin, Brunswick, and the French Republic,* 2nd ed. (1845), reprint (New York: AMS Press, 1970), 1: 16–17.

12. This is only a brief and greatly simplified description of a far more complex internal and international situation. Bar was not the only confederation formed against Stanisław August (and by extension, against the Russians). Albert de Broglie, *King's Secret,* 1: 9–23, 183–277; 2: 256, 258–61; Aleksander Gieysztor, Stefan Kieniewicz, Emanuel Rostworowski, Janusz Tazbir, and Henryk Wereszycki, *History of Poland* (Warsaw: Polish Scientific Publishers, 1968), 324–27; Jörg Hoensch, *Geschichte Polens* (Stuttgart: Eugen Ulmer, 1983), 162–65, 252; Jean-Paul Palewski,

Stanislas-August Poniatowski: Dernier roi de Pologne (Paris: Librairie Polonaise, 1946), 104–13; A. Bruce Boswell, "Poland," in *The European Nobility in the Eighteenth Century: Studies of the Nobilities of the Major European States in the Pre-Reform Era* (London: Adam & Charles Black, 1953), 162–63; Ryszard W. Woloszyński, "La Pologne vue par l'Europe au XVIIIe siècle," *Acta Poloniae Historica* 12 (1965): 22–42; Adam Zamoyski, *The Last King of Poland* (London: Phoenix, 1998), 171–72. On de Broglie, see [Stanisław August Poniatowski], *Die Memoiren des letzten Königs von Polen Stanisław August Poniatowski* (Munich: Georg Müller, 1918), 299.

13. Pawelski, *Stanislas-August Poniatowski*, 110. Cross-dressing female spies and couriers were not unusual; see Bély, *Espions*, 177–80.

14. Casanova, *History*, 4: 182–99, 340–41n9; 10: 314–16, 390n52 (elder Manuzzi and imprisonment in Leads); 4: 201, 343n7 (younger Manuzzi); 7: 324n29 (Mocenigo). There were (it seems) at least two Mocenigos who represented the Republic of Venice in Paris, both named Alvise and who served from 1762 to 1768 and 1772 to 1777 (I) and 1768 to 1772 (II). It is not clear which one Casanova means, because there is some confusion about both; see *Rep.* 3 and *ABI*.

15. Note labeled "No. 7," StAHbg, Senat Cl. VII Lit. Me no. 8 vol. 6 fasc. 7 conv. 1.

16. Antonio-Eugenio Visconti (1713–1788) was bishop of Ephesus, and papal nuncio in Poland from 1760 to 1767, and subsequently nuncio in Vienna. He became a cardinal in 1771 (*ABI*); see also the short biographical treatment of him in Andreas Cornaro, Herbert Paulhart, Paul Uiblein, Walter Wagner, and Gerhard Winner, comps., *Der Schriftverkehr zwischen dem päpstlichen Staatssekretariat und dem Nuntius am Kaiserhof Antonio Eugenio Visconti, 1767–1774* (Vienna: Hermann Böhlaus, 1970), xvi–xviii; Charles François, comte de Broglie, *Correspondance secrète du comte de Broglie avec Louis XV (1756–1774)*, ed. Didier Ozanam and Michel Antoine (Paris: C. Klincksieck, 1961), 2: 77n4; Larry Wolff, *The Vatican and Poland in the Age of the Partitions: Diplomatic and Cultural Encounters at the Warsaw Nunciature* (Boulder, Colo.: East European Monographs, 1988), 43–44. See also Chapter 6.

17. Groß was resident and then minister plenipotentiary in Hamburg from 1767 through 1796. *Rep.* 3: 355–56.

18. Heinrich Ernst lived from 1748 to 1817, his father from 1708 to 1766. Rudolf Grieser, *Briefe des Ministers Otto Christian von Lenthe an den Geheimen Kriegsrat August Wilhelm von Schwicheldt (1743–1750)* (Hildesheim: August Lax, 1977), 343.

19. Jonas Ludwig von Heß, *Hamburg topographisch, politisch und historisch beschrieben*, 2nd rev. ed. (Hamburg: J. C. Brüggemann, 1810–11), 1: 427.

20. These testimonies are found in StAHbg, Senat Cl. VII Lit. Me no. 8 vol. 6 fasc. 7 conv. 1. All information about Romellini is taken from them unless otherwise noted.

21. Heß, *Hamburg*, 1: 402, 427, 435, 482.

22. Heinrich [Henrik] Carl von Schimmelmann in *DBA*; Degn, *Schimmelmanns*.

23. "Übersetzung des Briefs der Nina an dem Grafen Visconti à Bergamo, d. dato Hamburg d. 9. August 1775," StAHbg, Cl. VII Lit. Me no. 8 vol. 6 fasc. 7 conv. 2.

24. Ibid.

25. *OED*, s.v. "Gallant" and "libertine"; Johann Christoph Adelung, *Grammatisch-kritisches Wörterbuch*, s.v. *Galant* and *galanterie*. Raoul Vèze's [pseud. Jean Hervez] four-volume *L'Histoire galante du XVIIIe siècle* (Paris: Bibliothèque des curieux, 1924–27) reviews this world for eighteenth-century France, nicely illustrating the overlap of sensuousness, libertinage, power-politics, and diplomacy as does Bèly, *Espions*.

26. Michel Feher, "Libertinisms," in id., ed., *The Libertine Reader: Eroticism and Enlightenment in Eighteenth-Century France* (New York: Zone Books, 1997), 10–15.

27. Poniatowski, *Memoiren*, 69–70.

28. Herbert Stein, *Der galante Roman* (Stuttgart: J. B. Metzler, 1961), 7–8, 38–39; Christian Friedrich Hunold, *Der europäischen Höfe Liebes- und Helden-Geschichte. Faksimiledruck nach der Ausgabe von 1705*, ed. Hans Wagener (Bern: Peter Lang, 1978), 1: 7*–8*, 13*–14* ("Introduction").

29. Karl Ludwig von Pöllnitz, *Das galante Sachsen*, new ed. (Offenbach a/M: n.p., 1735).

30. One example involved a person Romellini knew personally, Marshal Richelieu, whose life was the subject of numerous publications. See, e.g., *Véritable vie privée de Maréchal de Richelieu, contenant ses amours et intriques, et tout ce qui a rapport aux divers rôles qu'a joués cet homme célèbre pendant plus de quatre-vingt ans* (1791), ed. Élisabeth Porquerol (Paris: Gallimard, 1996). See also *Mémoires du maréchal duc de Richelieu, pair de France: Pour servir à l'histoire des cours de Louis XIV, de la régence du duc d'Orléans, de Louis XV, & à celle des quartorze premiéres années du règne du Louis XVI, roi des François, & restaurateur de la liberté* (London: J. de Boffe, 1790–93).

31. Zamoyski, *Last King*; R. Nisbet Bain, *The Last King of Poland and His Contemporaries* (London: Methuen, 1909); Dominique Labarre de Raillicourt, *Richelieu: Le Maréchal libertin* (Paris: Tallandier, 1991).

32. Claude-Carloman de Rulhière, *Anecdotes sur le maréchal de Richelieu* (Paris: Allia, 1993), 9, 53–54; Alex Duval, *La Jeunesse du duc de Richelieu, ou le Lovelace français: Comédie en prose en cinq actes* (Paris: Barba, 1797); Labarre de Raillicourt, *Richelieu*, 7; Raoul Vèze (pseud. Jean Hervez), *La Règence galante* [part of *L'Histoire galante*] (Paris: Bibliothèque des curieux, 1924), 147–212; *Véritable vie privée*; Frederick the Great quoted in Thomas Carlyle, *History of Friedrich II. of Prussia, called Frederick the Great* (London: Chapman & Hall, 1873), 5: 18.

33. Butler, "Paradiplomacy," in Sarkissian, ed., *Studies*.

34. On the "King's Secret," see Butler, "Paradiplomacy," 17–25; Kates, *Monsieur d'Eon*, 63–71, 77–82; Albert de Broglie, *King's Secret*; and esp. Charles François, comte de Broglie, *Correspondance secrète*, ed. Ozanam and Antoine, 1: xi–cxiv. On the Confederation of Bar, see Duchhardt, *Balance of Power*, 374–76. More generally on French policies in and toward Poland in the 1760s, see David Lerer, "La Politique française en Pologne sous Louis XV (1733–1772)" (thesis, University of Toulouse, 1929), 103–57, and John L. Sutton, *The King's Honour and the King's Cardinal: The War of the Polish Succession* (Lexington: University of Kentucky Press, 1980).

35. Exactly how to refer to Poland in this period is a difficult semantic and historical question. One perfectly plausible name is the one I have used here: gentry republic. Other equally common designators include: gentry monarchy, gentry or noble nation, gentry democracy, old-Polish democracy, magnate oligarchy, mixed monarchy, and so on. Almut Bues, *Das Herzogtum Kurland und der Norden der polnisch-lituanischen Adelsrepublik im 16. und 17. Jahrhundert: Möglichkeiten von Integration und Autonomie* (Giessen: litblockin, 2001), 9.

36. Jörg K. Hoensch, *Sozialverfassung und politische Reform: Polen im vorrevolutionären Zeitalter* (Cologne: Böhlau, 1973), 249.

37. Eckhard Buddruss, *Die französische Deutschlandpolitik, 1756–1789* (Mainz: Philip von Zabern, 1995), 39–69, 158–61, 289–97; Lerer, "Politique française en Pologne," 103–57; Woloszyński, "Pologne vue par l'Europe"; Hoensch, *Sozialverfassung*, 251–54; *The Cambridge History of Poland*, ed. W. F. Reddaway et al., vol. 2: *From August II to Pilsudski (1697–1935)* (Cambridge: Cambridge University Press, 1941), 24–88, 112–24, quotation from 112; Renaud Przezdziecki, *Diplomatic Ventures and Adventures: Some Experience of British Envoys at the Court of Poland* (London: Polish Research Centre, 1953), 182–84; Casanova, *History*, 10: 167.

38. Lerer, "Politique française en Pologne," 161–65; Duchhardt, *Balance of Power*, 370–84.

39. Emil Seraphim, *Geschichte Liv-, Est- und Kurlands von der "Aufsegelung" des Landes bis zur Einverleibung in das russische Reich* (Reval: Franz Kluge, 1896), vol. 2, part 2: *Kurland unter den Herzögen*, 606–30.

40. Wolff, *Vatican and Poland*, 17–21, 32–33.

41. Casanova, *History*, 10: 164.

42. Zamoyski, *Last King*, 9, 109, 125, 205, 209–17, 261; Bain, *Last King*, 95, 126; Palewski, *Stanislas-August Poniatowski*, 128–29.

43. Stroev, *Aventuriers des Lumières*, 91–92.

44. Günter Jäckel, ed., *Dresden zur Goethezeit, 1760–1815* (Hanau: Werner Dausien, 1988), 8–10, 16, 30; Erich Haenel and Eugen Kalkschmidt, comps., *Das alte Dresden: Bilder und Dokumente aus zwei Jahrhunderten* (Munich: Franz Hanfstaengl, 1925), 19–25; Böttiger, *Geschichte des Kurstaates*, 2: 661–62, 667.

45. Haenel and Kalkschmidt, *Alte Dresden*, 19–25; Karin Keller, "Saxony: *Rétablissement* and Enlightened Absolutism," *German History* 20 (2002): 309–31.

46. Lynn Hunt, "The Many Bodies of Marie Antoinette: Political Pornography and the Problem of the Feminine in the French Revolution," in id., ed., *Eroticism and the Body Politic* (Baltimore: Johns Hopkins University Press, 1991), 108–30; Darnton, *Forbidden Best-Sellers*, 137–66; on Madame du Pompadeur in the *galant(e)* world, see Raoul Vèze, *Les Maîtresses de Louis XV le bien-aimé* [*L'Histoire galante*] (Paris: Bibliothèque des curieux, 1924), 79–125, and Margaret Crosland, *Madame de Pompadour: Sex, Culture and the Power Game* (Stroud: Sutton, 2000).

47. John H. Elliott and L. W. B. Brockliss, *The World of the Favourite* (New Haven, Conn.: Yale University Press, 1999).

48. Kates, *Monsieur d'Eon*; Bély, *Espions*, 177–80; Poniatowski, *Memoiren*, 314; "Ritter d'Eon in Schlesien," *Schlesische Provinzialblätter* 3 (January–June 1786): 257–62.

49. Helga Thomas, *"Madame, meine teure Geliebte": Die Mätressen der fran-*

zösischen Könige (Vienna: Ueberreuter, 1996), 183–218; Gustav Sichelschmidt, *Friedrich Wilhelm II: Der "Vielgeliebte" und seine galante Zeit* (Berg am See: VGB Verl.-Ges. Berg, 1993), 64, 67.

50. Eduard Vehse, *Geschichte des preußischen Hofs und Adels und der preußischen Diplomatie* (Hamburg: Hoffmann & Campe, 1851), 4: 50–53; Jean-Jacques Olivier and Willy Norbert, *Barbarina Campanini: Eine Geliebte Friedrichs des Großen* (Berlin: Marquardt, 1909), 12–14, 23; Helmut Schnitter, "Die Barbarina—Eine Affäre des Königs," in *Gestalten um Friedrich den Großen: Biographische Skizzen*, ed. id. (Berlin: Preußischer Militär-Verl., 1992), 1: 107–13; Deryck Lynham, *The Chevalier Noverre, Father of Modern Ballet: A Biography* (London: Dance Books, 1972), 17; Ernst Alexander Mügge, *Barbarina: Lustspiel in vier Aufzügen* (Leipzig: P. Reclam jun., [c. 1880]).

51. Natalie Zemon Davis and Arlette Farge, eds., *A History of Women in the West*, vol. 3: *Renaissance and Enlightenment Paradoxes* (Cambridge, Mass.: Belknap Press of Harvard University Press, 1993), 463–64.

52. Roger Duchêne, *Ninon de Lenclos: La Courtisane du Grand Siècle* (Paris: Fayard, 1984); Philippe Erlanger, *Ninon de Lenclos et ses amis* (Paris: Perrin, 1985); Klaus Sasse, "Die Entdeckung der 'courtisane vertueuse' in der französischen Literatur des 18. Jahrhunderts: Réstif de la Bretonne und seine Vorgänger" (diss., University of Hamburg, 1967), esp. 75–83.

53. Barbara Becker-Cantarino, "Von der Prinzipalin zur Künstlerin und Mätresse: Die Schauspielerin im 18. Jahrhundert in Deutschland," in *Die Schauspielerin: Zur Kulturgeschichte der weiblichen Bühnenkunst*, ed. Renate Möhrmann (Frankfurt a/M.: Insel, 1989), 88–89; Klaus Laermann, "Die riskante Person in der moralischen Anstalt: Zur Darstellung der Schauspielerin in deutschen Theaterzeitschriften des späten 18. Jahrhunderts," ibid., 127–53; Davis and Farge, eds., *History of Women*, 3: 469; Casanova, *History*, 3: 193.

54. Roy Porter points out that "pleasure came into its own in the eighteenth century." Obviously, the eighteenth century did not create pleasure or pleasurable pursuits—intellectual or physical—but nonetheless, "it is also important to stress that before the eighteenth century compelling objections were officially raised to the idea that the pleasures of the senses were legitimate, fulfilling and to be encouraged." "Enlightenment and Pleasure," in id. and Marie Mulvey Roberts, eds., *Pleasure in the Eighteenth Century* (London: Macmillan, 1996), 1–2.

55. "Aus so krummen Holze, als woraus der Mensch gemacht ist, kann nichts ganz Gerades gezimmert werden." Immanuel Kant, "Idee zu einer allgemeinen Geschichte in weltbürgerlicher Absicht" (1784).

56. Promemoriums to van der Lepe from 11 March and 1 April 1776, StAHbg, Senat Cl. VII Lit. Me no. 8 vol. 6 fasc. 5.

57. Joachim Whaley, "The German Protestant Enlightenment," in Roy Porter and Mikuláš Teich, eds., *The Enlightenment in National Context* (New York: Cambridge University Press, 1981), 106–17.

58. *Der Patriot nach der Originalausgabe, Hamburg, 1724–1726*, ed. Wolfgang Martens, vol. 4: *Kommentarband* (Berlin: Walter de Gruyter, 1964), 486; Kopitzsch, *Grundzüge*, 260–452.

59. Marion W. Gray, *Productive Men, Reproductive Women: The Agrarian*

Household and the Emergence of Separate Spheres During the German Enlightenment (New York: Berghahn Books, 2000), 158.

60. *Der Biedermann* 8 (23 June 1727); Johann Christoph Gottsched, *Der Biedermann: Faksimiledruck der Original Ausgabe, Leipzig, 1727–1729*, ed. Wolfgang Martens (Stuttgart: J. B. Metzler, 1975), 21*–22* [Nachwort].

61. *Der Patriot* 8 (24 February 1724) and 130 (27 June 1726); *Kommentarband*, ed. Martens, 49–64, 411–13.

62. *Der Patriot* 58 (8 February 1725).

63. Isabel V. Hull, *Sexuality, State, and Civil Society in Germany, 1700–1815* (Ithaca, N.Y.: Cornell University Press, 1996), 236, 252.

64. Ibid., 161.

65. Katherine B. Aaslestad, " 'Sitten und Mode': Fashion, Gender, and Public Identities in Hamburg at the Turn of the Nineteenth Century," in Marion Gray and Ulrike Gleixner, eds., *Formatting Gender: Transitions, Breaks, and Continuity in German-Speaking Europe, 1750–1850* (Ann Arbor: University of Michigan Press, forthcoming); id., " 'No Relationship Aside from Work': Domestic Servants and Prosperous Households in Early Nineteenth-Century Hamburg," in *Wealth and Thrift: Paradoxes of Bürger Culture in Hamburg, 1700–1900*, ed. Frank Hatje and Ann LeBar (Leiden: Brill Academic Publishers, forthcoming).

66. StAHbg, Senat Cl. VIII no. Xa (1776), pp. 174–75, 188 (Monday, 13 May; Friday, 24 May).

67. Ibid., pp. 211–12 (Monday, 17 June; Wednesday, 19 June).

68. Rudolf Joseph, Graf von Colloredo-Mansfeld (1706–88), *Rep.* 3: 64–65, 86, 94.

69. All these letters were written in her own hand and in French. They were dated 16 July, 14 and 21 August 1776, StAHbg, Cl. VII. Lit. Me no. 8 vol. 6 fasc. 3; StAHbg, Senat Cl. VIII no. Xa (1776), pp. 238, 256, 280 (Wednesday, 24 July, Friday, 16 August, and Friday, 23 August); letter from Binder von Kriegelstein to von Colloredo and copy of Romellini's petition, 27 July 1776, HHStAW, Staatskanzlei, Berichte aus Hamburg, fasc. 10.

70. Romellini's petition of 27 July 1776, ibid.

71. Binder von Kriegelstein to Colloredo, 27 July 1776, ibid.

72. From Rotterdam, dated 18 November 1776, StAHbg, Senat Cl. VII Lit. Me no. 8 vol. 6 fasc. 9.

73. Romellini's letter was presented and discussed in the Senat on Wednesday, 27 November, Monday, 2 December, and Wednesday, 4 December 1776, StAHbg, Senat Cl. VIII no. Xa, pp. 342, 345, 348.

CHAPTER 6. *A Real Polish Prince, a Fake Italian Count, and an Authentic Spanish Hidalgo*

1. Dewald, *European Nobility*; Bush, *Rich Noble, Poor Noble*; A. Goodwin, ed., *The European Nobility in the Eighteenth Century: Studies of the Nobilities of the Major European States in the Pre-Reform Era* (London: Adam & Charles Black, 1953), 43–82 (Spain and Lombardy), 154–71 (Poland).

2. Aleksander Gieysztor et al., *History of Poland* (Warsaw: Polish Scientific

Publishers, 1768), 315–19; Jean Fabre, *Stanislas-Auguste Poniatowski et l'Europe des Lumières: Étude de cosmopolitisme,* Publications de la Faculté des lettres de l'université de Strasbourg, fasc. 116 (Paris: Les Belles Lettres, 1952), 125–57; Claude Pasteur, *Le Roi et le prince: Les Poniatowski 1732–1812* (Paris: France-Empire, 1976), 97–100; [Stanisław August], *Memoiren,* xviii–xxv.

3. Fabre, *Stanislas-August Poniatowski,* 152–53; *PSB.* Translations from Polish, here as well as elsewhere, were done by Jolanta Lion.

4. The unfriendly commentator is Jean Fabre, *Stanislas-Poniatowski,* 150. For a more balanced account of the Poniatowski family, see Zamoyski, *Last King,* 27, 89, 123, 210, 237, 256, 263, 401.

5. Casanova, *History,* 6: 11–12, 25, 288n18; 10: 159, 360n40; statement of Philipp Jacob Marechall, 21 November 1775, StAHbg, Senat Cl. VII Lit. Me no. 8 vol. 6 fasc. 7 conv. 2; Saby sent letters to Romellini from Augsburg, Frankfurt, and Vienna, in 1766, Senat Cl. VII Lit. Me no. 8 vol. 6 fasc. 7 conv. 1.

6. Casanova, *History,* 5: 313n48, 6: 11–12, 288n18–21.

7. Ibid., 6: 25.

8. Ibid., 10: 158–59; Zamoyski, *Last King,* 261–62.

9. Karl Ernst, duke of Courland, departed for Venice sometime after Easter (March 30) 1766. Casanova does not mention that Saby or Poniatowski accompanied him. Casanova, *History,* 10: 199.

10. Ibid., 6: 55–56; 10: 90–114; Seraphim, *Geschichte*; Erich Donnert, *Kurland im Ideenbereich der Französischen Revolution: Politische Bewegungen und gesellschaftliche Erneuerungsversuche 1789–1795* (Frankfurt a/M: Peter Lang, 1992), 15–24; A. Taube, "Ernst-Johan von Biron: Hohes Spiel," in *Deutsche Männer des baltischen Ostens* (Berlin: Volk & Reich, 1943), 90–96.

11. Casanova, *History,* 10: 90.

12. *DBA*; Friedrich Wilhlem Barthold, *Die geschichtliche Persönlichkeiten in Jacob Casanova's Memoiren: Beiträge zur Geschichte des achtzehnten Jahrhunderts* (Berlin: Duncker, 1846), 2: 246–49; J. L. Carra, *Mémoires historiques et authentiques sur la Bastille . . . depuis 1475 jusqu'à nos jours, &c* (Paris: J. P. Roux, 1789), 3: 133–52.

13. Casanova, *History,* 7: 45.

14. Taube, "Ernst Johann von Biron."

15. *PAB.*

16. "Fernweitige summarische Vernehmung Anna Maria Romel[l]ini wegen ihrer Lebensart und des angeb. Grafen Visconti Entleibung," 31 October, 1 November, and 3 November 1775, StAHbg, Senat Cl. VII Lit. Me no. 8 vol. 6 fasc. 7 conv. 1; entry of 15 December 1768, StADr, Ratsarchiv, Rathsprotokolle, f. 62 verso.

17. *PSB*; Zamoyski, *Last King,* 25, 84, 155–68; Casanova, *History,* 10: 170–201.

18. Harris, *Diaries and Correspondence,* 1: 10; Zamoyski, *Last King,* 167–69.

19. Harris, *Diaries and Correspondence,* 1: 26.

20. *PSB.*

21. Presented on 20 October 1775, StAHbg, Senat Cl. VII Lit. Me no. 8 vol. 6 fasc. 7 conv. 1.

22. "Fernweitige summarische Vernehmung Anna Maria Romel[l]ini."

23. StAHbg, Senat Cl. VIII no. Xa (1775), pp. 262, 264 (Friday, 20 October and Monday, 23 October).

24. StAHbg, Senat Cl. VIII no. Xa (1775), pp. 267, 290, 293 (Friday, 27 October; Wednesday, 15 November; and Friday, 17 November); "Hof- und Staats Kanzlers Fürsten von Kaunitz Rittberg" to Binder von Kriegelstein, 6 November 1775, StAHbg, Senat Cl. VII Lit. Me no. 8 vol. 6 fasc. 3; *Hamburgischer Correspondent,* Saturday, 18 November 1775.

25. Statement of Johann Christoph Reiss, 22 October 1775, StAHbg, Senat Cl. VII Lit. Me no. 8 vol. 6 fasc. 7 conv. 1.

26. Ibid.

27. Mary Lindemann, "The Wind-Traders: Speculators and Frauds in Northern Europe, 1650–1720," in *Living Dangerously in Medieval and Renaissance Europe,* ed. Barbara Hanawalt (South Bend, Ind.: Notre Dame University Press, forthcoming).

28. A search through the relevant records (in particular, the Ratsprotokolle, the Gerichtsbücher, and Repertorium III, Polizeisachen) in Stadtarchiv Bautzen in November 2002 and a similar search through the Ratsarchiv in Görlitz in September 2003, however, turned up no evidence of Visconti's presence in either place.

29. Statement of Johann Christoph Reiss, 22 October 1775, StAHbg, Senat Cl. VII Lit. Me no. 8 vol. 6 fasc.7 conv. 1.

30. Kesslitz's testimony from 7 and 9 November 1775, StAHbg, Senat Cl. VII Lit. Me no. 8 vol. 6 fasc. 7 conv. 2.

31. Ibid.; "Fernweitige summarische Vernehmung Anna Maria Romel[l]ini"; testimony of Friedrich, baron von Schlabrendoff, 7 November 1775, StAHbg, Senat Cl. VII Lit. Me no. 8 vol. 6 fasc. 7 conv. 1.

32. Statement from 21 November 1775, StAHbg, Senat Cl. VII Lit. Me no. 8 vol. 6 fasc. 7 conv. 2.

33. *Gazette de France,* 27 March 1775; the same report appeared in the *Gazette d'Altona,* 7 April 1775.

34. "Fernweitige summarische Vernehmung Anna Maria Romel[l]ini." Papers found in Visconti's possession after his death support Romellini's statement that his arrival in Hamburg was completely unexpected. A letter dated Braunschweig, 9 October 1775, queried as to why she had not responded to his previous letter. In it, he told her that he had no intention of leaving Braunschweig until he had heard from her. Letter designated no. 11, StAHbg, Senat Cl VII Lit. Me no. 8 vol. 6 fasc. 7 conv. 1.

35. Ibid.; excerpt from letter of Comte Barthy to Senat, 22 November 1775, StAHbg, Senat Cl. VII Lit. Me no. 8 vol. 6 fasc. 3. And again Visconti's papers provide additional evidence. Four letters (designated nos. 3, 4, 5, and 6) were written to Visconti in 1775 while he was being held in the Bergamese fortress. All refer to a court case then under way. However, the man who translated these letters for the Senat (a teacher of Italian named Johann Baptiste Arnoldi) was unable to piece together exactly what was happening. "It appears to involve the confiscation of Visconti's property which a certain Monti [?] had wished to accomplish." For debt? Another letter (no. 7) from one Pietro Arenti reported on a suit going on in Venice and also informed Visconti (still in Bergamo) that no post had arrived for him from Hamburg. StAHbg, Senat Cl VII Lit. Me no. 8 vol. 6 fasc. 7 conv. 1.

36. Elisabeth Ravoux-Rallo, *La Femme à Venise au temps de Casanova* (Paris: Stock/Laurence Pernoud, 1984), 149–59; P. Molmenti, *La Vie privée à Venise depuis l'origine jusqu'à la chute de la république* (Venice: Ferd. Ongania, 1895–97), 2: 32–40, 59–68.

37. Statements of Thomas Brown, 21 or 23 October 1775; Catharina Guido, 23 October 1775, and Heinrich Erdmann, 23 October 1775, StAHbg, Senat Cl. VII Lit. Me no. 8 vol. 6 fasc. 7 conv.1.

38. Statements of Thomas Brown; Johann Gottfried Bruchbach, 28 October 1775; and Friedrich Christopher Holtermann, 31 October 1775, ibid. Philipp Jacob Marechall, who knew Visconti from Dresden, also saw him in what he thought was the uniform of a Russian officer; statement given on 21 November 1775, ibid.

39. "Geschichts-Erzählung."

40. Statement of Hennings, 22 October 1775, StAHbg, Senat Cl. VII Lit. Me no. 8 vol. 6 fasc. 7 conv. 1.

41. "Geschichts-Erzählung," §§ 2, 22, 24–25.

42. Ibid., § 22.

43. Giancarlo Baronti, *Coltelli d'Italia: Rituali di violenza e tradizioni produttive nel mondo populare* (Padua: F. Muzzio, 1986), 19–61; Danielle Boschi, "Homicide and Knife Fighting in Rome, 1845–1914," in *Men and Violence: Gender, Honor, and Rituals in Modern Europe and America*, ed. Peter Spierenburg (Columbus: Ohio State University Press, 1998), 128–29; Pieter Spierenburg, "Knife-Fighting and Popular Codes of Honor in Early Modern Amsterdam," ibid., 107–19. On the violence employed by organized groups of bandits, see Florike Egmond, *Op het verkeerde pad: Georganiseerde misdaad in de Noordelijke Nederlanden, 1650–1800* (Amsterdam: Bert Bakker, 1994), passim.

44. "Defense," § 96.

45. The most original work on the complex character of the adventurer–*chevalier de fortune* is Stroev, *Aventuriers des Lumières*. Stroev limits his study to the last half of the eighteenth century, however, and to adventurers who were men of letters rather than common swindlers which included persons such as d'Eon de Beaumont (1728–1810), Giacomo Casanova (1725–98), Guiseppe Balsami, known as the comte Alessandro Cagliostro (1743–98), and Stepan Zannovich, called Prince Castriotto d'Albanie (1751–86). Stroev admits that his definition applies only to "un nombre restreint de personnalités" (5–6). Also interesting is the somewhat older work of Suzanne Roth, *Aventure et aventuriers au XVIIIe siècle: Essai de sociologie littéraire* (Lille: Service de reproduction des thèses, Université de Lille III, 1980).

46. The most important writing on Casanova is his own: *Mémoires de J. Casanova de Seingalt* in twelve volumes which appeared posthumously between 1826 and 1838. A virtual throng of scholars have fed upon his memoirs, partly because they are so evocative of eighteenth-century life, although we know that many tales of his escapades are exaggerated or deliberately self-promotional. The standard English edition, which I have used here, is Giacomo Casanova, *History of My Life*, trans. and ed. Williard R. Trask (Baltimore: Johns Hopkins University Press, 1997); Stroev, *Aventuriers des Lumières*, 1.

47. Raymond Silva, *Joseph Balsamo, alias Cagliostro* (Montreal: Québec-Amér-

ique, 1976); Jean-Jacques Tatin-Gourier, *Cagliostro et l'affaire du collier: Pamphlets et polémiques* (St. Étienne: Publications de l'Université de Saint-Étienne, 1994); Zamoyski, *Last King*, 263.

48. Theophilus Lucas, *Memoirs of the Lives, Intrigues, and Comical Adventures of the Most Famous Gamesters and Celebrated Sharpers in the Reigns of Charles II., James II., William III., and Queen Anne* (London: Jonas Brown, 1714), 110; Lawrence Lande, *The Rise and Fall of John Law, 1716–1720* (Montreal: Lawrence Lande Foundation for Canadian Historical Research, 1982); Janet Gleeson, *Millionaire: The Philanderer, Gambler, and Duelist Who Invented Modern Finance* (New York: Simon & Schuster, 1999); Kates, *Monsieur d'Eon*; Denyse Dalbian, *Le Comte de Cagliostro* (Paris: Robert Laffont, 1983); Klaus H. Kiefer, ed., *Cagliostro: Dokumente zu Aufklärung und Okkultismus* (Munich: Beck, 1991); Jean Villiers, *Cagliostro: Le Prophète de la Révolution* (Paris: Guy Trédaniel, 1988).

49. Pitaval, *Merkwürdige Rechtsfälle*, 3: 3–102.

50. Pohl, *Beziehungen*, x–xi, 11–13.

51. Ibid., 44, 126–28, 218–27, 303.

52. Ibid., 218; GStAPK, I. HA Rep. 46B no. 211k.

53. William J. Callahan, *Honor, Commerce and Industry in Eighteenth-Century Spain* (Boston: Baker Library, Harvard Graduate School of Business Administration, 1972), 15–17, 32–34. Specifically on Bilbao, see Mercedes Mauleon Isla, *La poblacion de Bilbao en el siglo XVIII* (Valladolid: Universidad de Valladolid, 1961), 5–19. Richard Herr, in *The Eighteenth Century Revolution in Spain* (Princeton, N.J.: Princeton University Press, 1958), 136, identifies the *consulado* as Bilbao's chamber of commerce.

54. *ABEPI*, s.v. "Sanpelayo"; Bush, *Rich Noble, Poor Noble*, 6–7, 14–17, 143.

55. Sanpelayo was probably born in or near Bilbao in 1738; he died on 26 November 1778 in Hamburg at age forty. Johann Martin Lappenberg and Christian Mahlstedt, "Listen der bis 1870 in Hamburg residierenden sowie der Hamburg im Ausland vertretenden Diplomaten und Konsuln," StAHbg, Bibliothek; Pohl, *Beziehungen*, 17–19. Pohl refers to him as "der in Hamburg etablierte Bilbainer" (19).

56. StAHbg, Senat Cl. VIII no. Xa (1768), pp. 1201, 1232, 1238, 1242–43, 1257 (28 November, 5, 7, 9, and 14 December).

57. Pohl, *Beziehungen*, 30–31.

58. StAHbg, Senat Cl. VIII no. Xa (1770), 43, 76, 209, 218 (11, 13, 20 January, and 20 March).

59. See, e.g., the note to this effect from van der Lepe, StAHbg, Senat Cl. VIII no. Xa (1770), p. 521 (7 September).

60. Report of Binder von Kriegelstein to Colloredo, 14 November 1775, in HHStAW, Staatskanzlei, Diplomatische Korrespondenz, Berichte aus Hamburg, fasc. 9, f. 174.

61. Report of Binder von Kriegelstein to Colloredo, 7 February 1776, HHStAW, Reichskanzlei, Berichte aus Hamburg, fasc. 20a.

62. StAHbg, Senat Cl. VIII no. Xa (1769), p. 482 (7 June 1769); (1770), pp. 111–12, 153, 436 (16 February, 9 March, 25 July).

63. StAHbg, Senat Cl. VIII no. Xa (1770), pp. 451–52, 458, 521, 550, 684 (1,

3 August; 7, 21 September; 5, 23 November); ibid., (1771), pp. 130, 156 (8 and 24 April).

64. Ibid. (1769), pp. 456, 476 (31 May and 5 June).

65. "Extractus Protocolli [Senatui?] . . . In Sachen Eleonora Clodine Dispo Klägern contra Sr. Antoinio Sampelajo Beklagter wegen Alimentirung des mit Beklagter erzeugten Kindes auch gegebendes Satisfaction," 12 July 1771, StAHbg, Senat Cl. VII Lit. Me no. 8 vol. 6 fasc. 3; StAHbg, Senat Cl. VIII no. Xa (1771), p. 285 (17 July); ibid. (1774), pp. 107, 124–25 (11 May, 3 and 6 June); ibid. (1775), p. 188 (9 August).

66. For examples, see "Verschiedene mit der Nachtwache entstandene Händel, 1701–1786," Senat Cl. VII Lit. Gd no. 6a.

67. The Hamburg Senat was also concerned about the consular agreement, although it had just (1769) signed an advantageous trade agreement with France. StAHbg, Senat Cl. VIII no. Xa (1769), p. 577 (10 July); Fred-Conrad Huhn, "Die Handelsbeziehungen zwischen Frankreich und Hamburg im 18. Jahrhundert unter besonderer Berücksichtigung der Handelsverträge von 1716 und 1769" (Diss., University of Hamburg, 1952).

68. "Fernweitige summarische Vernehmung Anna Maria Romel[l]ini"; the testimony of the notary Erdmann, StAHbg, Senat Cl. VII Lit. Me no. 8 vol. 6 fasc. 7 conv. 1. See also the letter she sent to the Senat from Rotterdam, StAHbg, Senat Cl. VII Lit. Me no. 8 vol. 6 fasc. 9. My attempts to locate Romellini in the records of the Gemeentearchief Rotterdam in fall 2002 produced no results. Similar letters to Countess von Bentinck (from 9 August 1776) and Binder von Kriegelstein are to be found in HHStAW, Reichskanzlei, Berichte aus Hamburg, fasc. 20a. The letters were written in her own hand and in French (the Senat had translations made), 16 July 1776, 14 and 21 August 1776, StAHbg, Cl. VII Lit Me no. 8 vol. 6 fasc. 3; StAHbg, Senat Cl. VIII no. Xa (1776), pp. 238, 256, 260 (Wednesday, 24 July, Friday, 16 August, and Friday, 23 August); report from Binder von Kriegelstein to von Colloredo and copy of Romellini petition, 27 July 1776, HHStA, Staatskanzlei, Berichte aus Hamburg, fasc. 10. Report from Binder von Kriegelstein to von Colloredo, 21 October 1775, ibid., f. 158.

69. Reports from Binder von Kriegelstein to von Colloredo, 15 June, 17 August 1776, HHStAW, Reichskanzlei, Berichte aus Hamburg, fasc. 20a.

70. Report from Binder von Kriegelstein to von Colloredo, 28 October 1775, in HHStAW, Staatskanzlei, Diplomatische Korrespondenz, Berichte aus Hamburg, fasc. 10, ff. 167–68.

71. Ibid., ff. 174–75.

72. Report from Binder von Kriegelstein to von Colloredo, 25 May 1776, HHStAW, Reichskanzlei, Berichte aus Hamburg, fasc. 20a.

73. Testimony of Catherine Rouget, 22 February 1776, and confrontation between Engauen and Rouget, 4 March 1776, StAHbg, Senat Cl. VII Lit. Me no. 8 vol. 6 fasc. 7 conv. 2.

74. The early twentieth-century Social Democrat Heinrich Laufenberg felt that the Senat was riddled with nepotism and corruption. There are no good historical studies of the important subject of corruption in Hamburg, and the question of whether Hamburg's government was corrupt, or especially corrupt, remains

open. Heinrich Laufenberg, *Geschichte der Arbeiterbewegung in Hamburg, Altona und Umgebung* (Hamburg: Auer, 1911–31), 1: 57; Kopitzsch, *Grundzüge*, 170–77.

75. Report from Binder von Kriegelstein to von Colloredo, 25 May 1776, HHStAW, Reichskanzlei, Berichte aus Hamburg, fasc. 20a.

76. Report from Binder von Kriegelstein to von Colloredo, 27 July 1776, and copy of letter to Countess von Bentinck, ibid.

77. Report from Binder von Kriegelstein to von Colloredo, 17 August 1776, ibid.

78. Report from Binder von Kriegelstein to von Colloredo, 17 August 1776, and copy of Romellini's letter to Countess von Bentinck from 9 August 1776, both ibid.

79. [François Guyard], *Sendschreiben des Kaufmanns Guyard in Hamburg an seine Mitbürger: Als eine Einleitung zu seinen herauszugebenden Mémoires* (n.p. [Hamburg]: n.p., 1767); [Denis Martin], *Vollständige Acten in der seltenen und überaus wichtigen Sache, Denis Martin, wider seinen unwürdigen Schwiegersohn und unwürdige Tochter, Jean François Guyard und Charlotte Guyard gebohrne Martin, in Hamburg, Criminell-Verläumder . . .* (n.p. [Hamburg]: n.p., 1767).

80. The legal *Factum* or *mémoires judiciaires* written by lawyers in civil or criminal cases and then published were a similar form, on which Sarah Maza relied extensively in her *Private Lives and Public Affairs*.

81. Prince Dimitri Alekseyevich Golitsyn, envoy and minister plenipotentiary to France, 1763–68, and to the Netherlands, in the Hague, 1770–82 (on leave 29 May 1775–15 November 1775). He was in the Hague for most of the time that the Kesslitz affair played out in Hamburg. *Rep.* 3: 354, 359, 364.

82. Report from Binder von Kriegelstein to von Colloredo, 29 March 1777, HHStAW, Reichskanzlei, Berichte aus Hamburg, fasc. 20a. Álvaro de Nava, the vizconde de la Herreira, was minister plenipotentiary to the Netherlands from late 1771 through the middle of 1780 (*ABEPI*); on Sanpelayo's recall, *Rep.* 3: 433.

83. "Acta mit dem Spanischen Herrn Consul Urqullen betreffend die Sache Amberg contra Sanpelayo, 1777," StAHbg, Senat Cl. VII Lit. Me no. 8 vol. 6 fasc. 8; ibid., Cl. VIII no. Xa (1776), pp. 174–75, 218 (13 May and 26 June); ibid., (1779), p. 218 (26 June).

Retrospective

1. "Acta betr. die durch den ehemal. Preuß. Lieutenant Herrn Baron von Kesslitz verübte Erstechung des angebl. Grafen Visconti, und was dabei in Ansehung der italienischen Maitresse Romellicini u. des König. Span. Consuls, Herrn San Pelaÿo, vorgekommen, 1775–77," StAHbg, Senat Cl. VII Lit. Me no. 8 vol. 6, fasc. 1–9.

2. Margadant, ed., *New Biography*, 9.

3. E. H. Carr, *What Is History?* (New York: Knopf, 1964), 35.

4. Casanova, *Duel*, 4.

Bibliography

Archival Sources

Archives diplomatiques du Ministère des Affaires étrangères, Correspondance politique (sous-série: Hambourg), Paris, vols. 101 (1775) and 102 (January 1776–December 1777) (ADCP)

Archiwum Panstwowe we Wrocławiu (APW)

Archivum Panstwowe w Zielonej Gorze (AP-Zg)

    5/0 Akta miasta Zielona Gora (Magistrat Grünberg), 1538–1945

Archiwum Panstwowe w Zielonej Gorze, Oddzial w Wilkowie (WAP-Zg)

    374/0 Amtsgericht zu Grünberg, 1608–1940

Geheimes Staatsarchiv, Preußischer Kulturbesitz, Berlin (GStAPK)

    I. HA Rep. 9 Allgemeine Verwaltung

        Z.M. Residenten, Residentursekretäre, Konsuln, Agenten und Postmeister im Niedersächsischen Kreise (Hamburg und Lübeck) 1653–1821

        fasc. 14 Resident Johann Julius Hecht in Hamburg, 1754–1782

        fasc. 16 Agenten Wurmb und Graeve in Hamburg, 1765–1774

        fasc. 17 Konsuln, Agenten und Residentursekretäre in Hamburg, 1766–1800

    I. HA Rep. 46B Schlesien seit 1740

        No. 33k14, fasc. 1 Gesuch des Frhr. von Kesslitz auf Salisch um Konzession zur Tax- und Subhastation einer auf seinem gute Merztdorf befindlichen, in gäntzlichen Verfall geratenen Frei-Gärtner Stelle, 1762

        No. 211k (Kesslitz)

        No. 306/72e Ritterakademie zu Liegnitz, 1741–1804

    I. HA Rep. 50 Beziehungen zu den Reichstädten

        No. 28 (Hamburg) fasc. 88 (1771–1777), 89 (1777–1783)

        No. 28 fasc. 146 Korrespondenz mit der Stadt Hamburg (March 1774–September 1776)

        No. 28 fasc. 147 Korrespondenz mit der Stadt Hamburg (October 1777–March 1783)

No. 28 fasc. 449 Rechtstreit des Hofkommissionars preußischen Denis Martin und seiner Tochter Charlotte Guyard in Hamburg wegen Verläumdung, 1766–1768

I. HA Rep. 81 Hamburg A. Gesandtskorrespondenz mit verschiedenen Fürstlichkeiten und Privatpersonen, 1744–1807

No. 10 Differenzen mit dem Hamburger Magistrat wegen preußischer Werbungen, Einholung von Deserteuren und militärischen Maßnahmen, 1723–1749 et seq.

No. 22 Königliche Reskripte, 1726

No. 27 Desertion eines Quartiermeisters vom Kattschen Regiment, 1727–1728

No. 34 Korrespondenz mit dem Magistrat von Hamburg meist in Privatangelegenheiten, 1728–1806

No. 53 Rekruten- und Werbungssachen, vol. 1: 1735–1738; vol. 2: 1739–1761

No. 67 Königliche Reskripte, 1740

No. 69 betreffend Concepte zu Relationen an den König und die Regierung, 1740–1807

No. 70 (u.a. Königliche Reskripte über Störung des hamburgischen Handels durch die schlesische Affäre . . . 1740–1741)

No. 77 Gesandtskorrepondenz mit verschiedenen Fürstlichkeiten und Privatpersonen, 1744–1807

No. 78 Schmachschriften auf den König von Hamburger Schreibern, 1745

No. 104 (u.a. Schlechte Behandlung preußischer Untertanen seitens des Hamburger Magistrats, January 1761–December 1762)

No. 108 Arrest und Forderungen auf das Vermögen des rüssichen Grafen von Tottleben, 1763–1765

No. 117 Militärdienstgesuche, Werbungen, und Desertionen, 1765, 1768, 1771–1789

No. 122 (u.a. Spanische Werbung, 1768–1771)

No. 133 Gesandschaft zu Hamburg, 1775–1777

I. HA Rep. 96 Geheimes Zivilkabinett, ältere Periode

Nos. 36R, 36S Hecht, preus. geh. Rath und residerender Minister, seine Despeche aus Hamburg, 1752–1786

IV. HA [Preußische Armee] Rep. 1 No. 76 (Offiziernnomenklatur)

VI. HA

K. 483 v. Kesslitz, 1762–1801

VIII. HA

Rep. C No. 295 (Kesslitz genealogy)

XVII. HA Schlesien

Haus-, Hof- und Staatsarchiv, Vienna (HHStAW) (consulted on microfilm in StAHbg, see below)

Reichskanzlei, Berichte aus Hamburg, 1756–1800

Fasc. 20a (January 1770–January 1776, March 1776–December 1777)

Fasc. 20b (January 1778–December 1778)

Staatskanzlei (Ministerium des Äussern)

Diplomatische Korrespondenz, Bericht aus Hamburg

Fasc. 9 (October 1773–1774)

Fasc. 10 (1775–March 1776)

Fasc. 11 (1778–1779)

Niedersächsisches Gesandschaftsarchiv

Fasc. 31 (1776)

Fasc. 32 (1777)

Fasc. 33 (1778, 1779)

Fasc. 34 (1779)

Sächsisches Haupt-Staatsarchiv Dresden (SäHStAD)

II.3.1.03 Geheimes Kabinett

loc. 3037–3038 "des Grafen von Sacken Negotiation in Petersburgh," 1765–1769

loc. 3647 (Graf Poniatowski)

Staatsarchiv Hamburg (StAHbg)

111–1 Senat

Cl. VII Lit. Cc no. 13 vol. 5 fasc. 19

Cl. VII Lit. Gg Pars. 1 no. 3 vols. 1g, 5f

Cl. VII Lit. Gg Pars. 3 no. 4 vol. 6

Cl. VII Lit. Me no. 8 vol. 6 fasc. 1–9

Cl. VII Lit. Me no. 10 vol. 1 fasc. 2, 5

Cl. VIII no. Xa [Senatsprotokolle]

132–5/8 Hanseatischer und Hamburgischer Residentur Madrid

211–1 Reichshofrat

743–4 Österreichisches Staatsarchiv, Abt. Haus-, Hof- und Staatsarchiv. In 741–4 Filmarchiv: Films E Sa 789–791, E Sa 812–814, E Sa 1199, 1200, 2001–2002 (See HHStAW above)

Stadtarchiv Dresden (StADr)

Ratsarchiv, Rathsprotokolle

Staats-und Universitätsbibliothek Hamburg (SUBHbg)

Handschriftensammlung. Cod. Hans. II.

Select Bibliography

Aaslestad, Katherine B. " 'No Relationship Aside from Work': Domestic Servants and Prosperous Households in Early Nineteenth-Century Hamburg." In *Wealth and Thrift: Paradoxes of Bürger Culture in Hamburg, 1700–1900*, ed. Frank Hatje and Ann LeBar. Leiden: Brill Academic Publishers, forthcoming.

———. " 'Sitten und Mode': Fashion, Gender, and Public Identities in Hamburg at the Turn of the Nineteenth Century." In *Formatting Gender: Transitions, Breaks, and Continuity in German-Speaking Europe, 1750–1850*, ed. Marion Gray and Ulrike Gleixner. Ann Arbor: University of Michigan Press, forthcoming.

Adair, E. R. *The Exterritoriality of Ambassadors in the Sixteenth and Seventeenth Centuries*. London: Longmans, Green, 1929.

Adelung, Johann Christoph. *Grammatisch-kritisches Wörterbuch der hochdeutschen Mundart: Mit beständiger Vergleichung der übrigen Mundarten; besonders aber der Oberdeutschen*. 4 vols. Leipzig: Breitkopf, 1793–1801.

Les Affaires étrangères et le corps diplomatique français. Vol. 1: *De l'ancien régime au Second Empire.* Paris: Éditions du centre national de la recherche scientifique, 1984.

Alkemade, G. P. J. van, *Jan Willem, baron van Ripperda: een diplomat-avonturier uit de achttiende eeuw.* Apeldoorn: Semper Agendo, 1968.

Althoff, Frank. *Untersuchungen zum Gleichgewicht der Mächte in der Außenpolitik Friedrichs des Großen nach dem Siebenjährigen Krieg (1763–1786).* Berlin: Duncker & Humblot, 1995.

Anderson, M. S. *The Rise of Modern Diplomacy, 1450–1919.* London: Longman, 1993.

Archenholz, Johann Wilhelm von. *Geschichte des siebenjährigen Krieges in Deutschland.* 1911. Reprint. Osnabrück: Biblio, 1982.

Baasch, Ernst. *Die Handelskammer zu Hamburg, 1665–1915.* 3 vols. Vol. 1: *1665–1814.* Hamburg: Lucas Gräfe & Sillem, 1915.

Bächtold-Stäubli, Hanns, Eduard Hoffmann-Krayer, and Gerhard Lüdtke, eds. *Handwörterbuch des deutschen Aberglaubens.* 10 vols. Berlin: Walter de Gruyter, 1927–42.

Backmann, Sibylle, Hans-Jörg Künast, Sabine Ullmann, and B. Ann Tlusty, eds. *Ehrkonzepte in der Frühen Neuzeit: Identitäten und Abgrenzungen.* Berlin: Akademie, 1998.

Bain, R. Nisbet. *The Last King of Poland and His Contemporaries.* London: Methuen, 1909.

Baronti, Giancarlo. *Coltelli d'Italia: Rituali di violenza e tradizioni produttive nel mondo populare.* Padua: F. Muzzio, 1986.

Barthold, Friedrich Wilhelm. *Die geschichtlichen Persönlichkeiten in Jacob Casanova's Memoiren: Beiträge zur Geschichte des achtzehnten Jahrhunderts.* 2 vols. Berlin: Duncker, 1846.

Basurto Larrañaga, Román. *Comercio y burguesia mercantil de Bilbao en la segunda mitad del siglo XVIII.* Bilbao: Servicio editorial, Universidad del País Vasco, 1983.

Baumgart, Peter, ed., with the assistance of Ulrich Schmilewski. *Kontinuität und Wandel: Schlesien zwischen Österreich und Preußen.* Sigmaringen: Jan Thorbecke, 1990.

Becker-Cantarino, Barbara. "Von der Prinzipalin zur Künstlerin und Mätresse: Die Schauspielerin im 18. Jahrhundert in Deutschland." In *Die Schauspielerin: Zur Kulturgeschichte der weiblichen Bühnenkunst,* ed. Renate Möhrmann, 88–113. Frankfurt a/M: Insel, 1989.

Bély, Lucien. *Espions et ambassadeurs au temps de Louis XIV.* Paris: Fayard, 1990.

Beneke, Otto. "Zur Geschichte des Hamburgischen Consulatswesens." Printed archival report. Staatsarchiv Hamburg.

Berg, W. "Die Barbarina." *Die Grenzboten: Zeitschrift für Politik, Literatur und Kunst* 69, 1 (1910): 25–32, 67–75, 121–29.

Biener, Friedrich August. *Beiträge zu der Geschichte des Inquisitionsprozesses und der Geschworenengerichte.* Leipzig, 1827. Reprint. Aalen: Scientia, 1965.

Billacois, François. *The Duel: Its Rise and Fall in Early Modern France.* Translated and edited by Trista Selous. New Haven, Conn.: Yale University Press, 1990.

Originally published as *Le Duel dans la société française des XVIe–XVIIe siècles: Essai de psychosociologie historique* (Paris: Éditions de l'École des hautes études en sciences sociales, 1986).

Blank, Johann Friedrich, ed. *Sammlung der von E. Hochedlen Rathe der Stadt Hamburg so wol zur Handhabung der Gesetze und Verfassungen als bey besonderen Eräugnisen in Bürger-und Kirchlichen, auch Cammer-, Handlungs- und übrigen Policey-Angelegenheiten und Geschäften vom Anfange des siebenzehnten Jahr-Hunderts bis auf die itzige Zeit ausgegangenen allgemeinen Mandate, bestimmten Befehle und Bescheide, auch beliebten Aufträge und verkündigten Anordnungen.* 6 vols. Hamburg: Piscator, 1763–74.

Bog, Ingomar. "Reichsverfassung und reichsstädtische Gesellschaft: Sozialgeschichtliche Forschungen über reichsständische Residenten in den Freien Städten, insbesondere in Nürnberg." *Jahrbuch für fränkische Landesforschung* 18 (1958): 325–40.

Boguslawski, A[lbrecht] von. *Die Ehre und das Duell.* Berlin: Schall & Grund, 1896.

Bolland, Jürgen. *Senat und Bürgerschaft: Über das Verhältnis zwischen Bürger und Stadt-Regiment im alten Hamburg.* Hamburg: Verein für Hamburgische Geschichte, 1954.

Borcherdt, Albert. *Das lustige alte Hamburg: Scherze, Sitten und Gebräuche unserer Väter.* 2nd ed. Hamburg: F. Dörling, 1890.

Bornhak, Conrad. *Deutsche Verfassungsgeschichte vom westfälischen Frieden an.* Stuttgart: Ferdinand Enke, 1934. Reprint. Aalen: Scientia, 1968.

Boswell, A. Bruce. "Poland." In *The European Nobility in the Eighteenth Century: Studies of the Nobilities of the Major European States in the Pre-Reform Era*, ed. Albert Goodwin, 154–71. London: Adam & Charles Black, 1953.

Böttiger, C. W. *Geschichte des Kurstaates und Königreiches Sachsen.* 2nd. edition, rev. and enlarged by Theodor Flathe. 3 vols. Gotha: Friedrich Andreas Perthes, 1867–73.

Broglie, Albert de. *Le Secret du Roi: Correspondance secrète de Louis XV avec ses agents diplomatiques, 1752–1774.* 2 vols. Paris: Calmann Lévy, 1878–79.

———. *The King's Secret: Being the Secret Correspondence of Louis XV, with his Diplomatic Agents, from 1752 to 1774.* 2 vols. London: Cassell, Petter & Galpin, 1879.

Broglie, Charles François, comte de. *Correspondance secrète du comte de Broglie avec Louis XV (1756–1774).* Edited by Didier Ozanam and Michel Antoine. 2 vols. Paris: C. Klincksieck, 1956–61.

Brunner, Otto. *Adeliges Landleben und europäischer Geist: Leben und Werk Wolf Helmhards von Hohberg, 1612–1688.* Salzburg: Otto Müller, 1949.

Buddruss, Eckhard. *Die französische Deutschlandpolitik, 1756–1789.* Mainz: Philipp von Zabern, 1995.

Buek, Friedrich Georg. *Die hamburgischen Oberalten, ihre bürgerliche Wirksamkeit und ihre Familien.* Hamburg: Perthes, Besser & Mauke, 1857.

Bues, Almut. *Das Herzogtum Kurland und der Norden der polnisch-lituanischen Adelsrepublik im 16. und 17. Jahrhundert: Möglichkeiten von Integration und Autonomie.* Giessen: litblockin, 2001.

Büsch, Otto. *Militärsystem und Sozialleben im alten Preussen 1713–1807: Die Anfänge der sozialen Militärisierung der preußisch-deutschen Gesellschaft.* Berlin: Walter de Gruyter, 1962.

Bush, M. L. *Rich Noble, Poor Noble.* Manchester: Manchester University Press, 1988.

Callahan, William J. *Honor, Commerce and Industry in Eighteenth-Century Spain.* Boston: Baker Library, Harvard Graduate School of Business Administration, 1972.

Canitz und Dallwitz, Karl Wilhelm Ernst von. *Nachrichten und Betrachtungen über Thaten und Schicksale der Reuterei in den Feldzügen Friedrich des II. und in denen neuerer Zeit.* 2 vols. Berlin: E. S. Mittler, 1823–24.

Carlyle, Thomas. *History of Friedrich II. of Prussia, called Frederick the Great.* 10 vols. London: Chapman & Hall, 1873.

Carra, J. L. *Mémoires historiques et authentiques sur la Bastille . . . depuis 1475 jusqu'à nos jours, &c.* Paris: J. P. Roux, 1789.

Casanova, Giacomo, chevalier de Seingalt. *The Duel.* 1780. Translated by J. G. Nichols. London: Hesperus Press, 2003.

———. *History of My Life.* Translated and edited by Willard R. Trask. 12 parts in 6 vols. Baltimore: Johns Hopkins University Press, 1997.

Conrad, Hermann. *Deutsche Rechtsgeschichte.* 2 vols. Karlsruhe: C. F. Müller, 1954–66.

———. "Die verfassungsrechtliche Bedeutung der Reichsstädte im Deutschen Reich (etwa 1500 bis 1806)." *Studium Generale: Zeitschrift für die Einheit der Wissenschaften im Zusammenhang ihrer Begriffsbildungen und Forschungsmethoden* 16 (1963): 493–500.

Conrads, Norbert. *Ritterakademien der Frühen Neuzeit: Bildung als Standesprivileg im 16. und 17. Jahrhundert.* Göttingen: Vandenhoeck & Ruprecht, 1982.

———. *Schlesien.* Deutsche Geschichte im Osten Europas. Berlin: Siedler, 1994.

Cornaro, Andreas, et al., comps. *Der Schriftverkehr zwischen dem Päpstlichen Staatssekretariat und dem Nuntius am Kaiserhof Antonio Eugenio Visconti, 1767–1774.* Vienna: Böhlaus, 1970.

Dalbian, Denyse. *Le Comte de Cagliostro.* Paris: Robert Laffont, 1983.

Darnton, Robert. *The Forbidden Best-Sellers of Pre-Revolutionary France.* New York: Norton, 1995.

Davies, Norman. *God's Playground: A History of Poland.* Vol. 1: *The Origins to 1795.* New York: Columbia University Press, 1982.

Davis, Natalie Zemon. *Fiction in the Archives: Pardon Tales and Their Tellers in Sixteenth-Century France.* Stanford, Calif.: Stanford University Press, 1987.

———. *The Return of Martin Guerre.* Cambridge, Mass.: Harvard University Press, 1983.

Davis, Natalie Zemon, and Arlette Farge, eds. *A History of Women in the West.* Vol. 3: *Renaissance and Enlightenment Paradoxes.* Cambridge, Mass.: Belknap Press of Harvard University Press, 1993.

Degn, Christian. *Die Schimmelmanns im atlantischen Dreieckshandel: Gewinn und Gewissen.* Neumünster: Wachholtz, 1974.

Dekker, Rudolf, ed. *Egodocuments and History: Autobiographical Writing in Its Social Context Since the Middle Ages.* Hilversum: Verloren, 2002.

Demeter, Karl. *Das deutsche Offizierkorps in Gesellschaft und Staat, 1650–1945.* 1930. 4th revised and enlarged ed. Frankfurt a/M: Bernard & Graefe Verl. für Wehrwesen, 1965.

Dewald, Jonathan. *The European Nobility, 1400–1800.* Cambridge: Cambridge University Press, 1996.

Donnert, Erich. *Kurland im Ideenbereich der Französischen Revolution: Politische Bewegungen und gesellschaftliche Erneuerungsversuche 1789–1795.* Frankfurt a/M: Peter Lang, 1992.

Dreyer, Alfred. *Der alte Ratsweinkeller zu Hamburg, 1250–1842.* Hamburg: Hamburgische Bücherei, 1949.

Duchêne, Roger. *Ninon de Lenclos: La Courtisane du Grand Siécle.* Paris: Fayard, 1984.

Duchhardt, Heinz. *Balance of Power und Pentarchie: Internationale Beziehungen 1700–1785.* Paderborn: Ferdinand Schöningh, 1997.

Duffy, Christopher. *The Army of Frederick the Great.* London: David & Charles, 1974.

Duval, Alex. *La Jeunesse du duc de Richelieu, ou le Lovelace français: Comédie en prose en cinq actes.* Paris: Barba, 1797.

Dyhrynfurth, Gertrud. *Ein schlesisches Dorf und Rittergut.* Leipzig: Duncker & Humblot, 1906.

Eakin, Paul John. *How Our Lives Become Stories: Making Selves.* Ithaca, N.Y.: Cornell University Press, 1999.

Ebert-Wiedenfeller, Andreas. *Hamburgisches Kaufmannsrecht im 17. und 18. Jahrhundert: Die Rechtsprechung des Rates und des Reichskammergerichtes.* Frankfurt a/M: Peter Lang, 1992.

Egmond, Florike. *Op het verkeeerde pad: Georganiseerde misdaad in de Noordelijke Nederlanden, 1650–1800.* Amsterdam: Bert Bakker, 1994.

Elias, Norbert. *Über den Prozess der Zivilisation: Soziogenetische und psychogenetische Untersuchungen.* 2 vols. Munich: Francke, 1969.

Elliott, John H., and Laurence W. B. Brockliss, eds. *The World of the Favourite.* New Haven, Conn.: Yale University Press, 1999.

Endres, Rudolf. *Adel in der Frühen Neuzeit.* Munich: R. Oldenbourg, 1993.

Erlanger, Philippe. *Ninon de Lenclos et ses amis.* Paris: Librarie acadèmique Perrin, 1985.

Erler, Adalbert, and Ekkehard Kaufmann, eds. *Handwörterbuch zur deutschen Rechtsgeschichte.* 5 vols. Berlin: Erich Schmidt, 1971.

Evans, Richard J. *Rituals of Retribution: Capital Punishment in Germany, 1600–1987.* Oxford: Oxford University Press, 1996.

Ewald, Martin. *Der Hamburgische Senatsyndicus: Eine verwaltungsgeschichtliche Studie.* Hamburg: Kommissionsverlag Ludwig Appel, 1954.

Fabre, Jean. *Stanislas-Auguste Poniatowski et l'Europe des Lumières: Étude de cosmopolitisme.* Publications de la Faculté des lettres de l'Université de Strasbourg, fasc. 116. Paris: Les Belles Lettres, 1952.

Falke, Jakob von. *Geschichte des fürstlichen Hauses Liechtenstein.* 3 vols. Vienna: W. Braunmüller, 1868–83.

Fechner, Hermann. *Wirtschaftsgeschichte der preußischen Provinz Schlesien in der*

Zeit ihrer provinziellen Selbstständigkeit, 1741–1806. Breslau: S. Schottlaender, 1907.

Feher, Michel, ed. *The Libertine Reader: Eroticism and Enlightenment in Eighteenth-Century France*. New York: Zone Books, 1997.

Fehr, Hans. *Der Zweikampf*. Berlin: Karl Curtius, 1908.

Femmel, Gerhard, and Gerald Heres, eds. *Die Gemmen aus Goethes Sammlung*. Leipzig: E. A. Seemann, 1977.

Ferguson, Niall. *The House of Rothschild: Money's Prophets, 1798–1848*. New York: Viking Press, 1998.

Finder, Ernst. *Hamburgisches Bürgertum in der Vergangenheit*. Hamburg: Friederichsen, de Gruyter, 1930.

Fink, Georg. "Diplomatische Vertretungen der Hanse seit dem 17. Jahrhundert bis zur Auflösung der Hanseatischen Gesandtschaft in Berlin 1920." *Hansische Geschichtsblätter* 56 (1931): 112–55.

Forster, Robert. *Merchants, Landlords, Magistrates: The Dupont Family in Eighteenth-Century France*. Baltimore: Johns Hopkins University Press, 1980.

Frank, Arthur W. *The Wounded Storyteller: Body, Illness, and Ethics*. Chicago: University of Chicago Press, 1995.

Freedman, Jeffrey. *A Poisoned Chalice*. Princeton, N.J.: Princeton University Press, 2002.

Frensdorff, F. "Das Reich und die Hansestädte." *Zeitschrift der Savigny-Stiftung für Rechtsgeschichte* (Germanistische Abteilung) 20 (1899): 115–63.

Fuchs, Ralf-Peter. *Um die Ehre: Westfälische Beleidigungsprozesse vor dem Reichskammergericht, 1525–1805*. Paderborn: Ferdinand Schöningh, 1999.

Gagliardo, John G. *Reich and Nation: The Holy Roman Empire as Idea and Reality, 1763–1806*. Bloomington: Indiana University Press, 1980.

Geheime Nachrichten aus dem Leben einiger der berühmtesten Wucherer, Unterhändler, Rabulisten, Bankerottiers, Geldschneider, und Jugendverführer unserer Zeit. Vienna: n.p., 1798.

Gelderen, Martin van, and Quentin Skinner, eds. *Republicanism: A Shared European Heritage*. 2 vols. Cambridge: Cambridge University Press, 2002.

Geschichte Schlesiens. Edited by Hermann Aubin, Ludwig Petry, Josef Joachim Menzel, Winfried Irgang et al. Vol. 3: *Preußisch-Schlesien, 1740–1945/Österreichisch-Schlesien, 1740–1918/45*. Stuttgart: Jan Thorbecke, 1999.

Gieysztor, Aleksander, et al. *History of Poland*. Warsaw: Polish Scientific Publishers, 1968.

Gleeson, Janet. *Millionaire: The Philanderer, Gambler, and Duelist Who Invented Modern Finance*. New York: Simon & Schuster, 1999.

Glogau im Wandel der Zeiten. Catalog of an exhibition held 3 October–1 December 1992, Muzeum w Głogowie. Compiled by Werner Bein, Johannes Schellakowsky, and Ulrich Schmilewski. Würzburg: Wilhelm Gottlieb Korn, 1992.

Golitschek, Josef von. *Schlesien-Land der Schlösser*. Vol. 1: *Zeugen deutscher Kultur (Bankau bis Moschen)*. Vol. 2: *Das Erbe der Ahnen (Moschen bis Zyrowa)*. Munich: Orbis, 1988.

Goodwin, A., ed. *The European Nobility in the Eighteenth Century: Studies of the*

Nobilities of the Major European States in the Pre-Reform Era. London: Adam & Charles Black, 1953.

——, ed. *The New Cambridge Modern History.* Vol. 8: *The American and French Revolutions, 1763–93.* Cambridge: Cambridge University Press, 1971.

Gottsched, Johann Christoph. *Der Biedermann: Faksimiledruck der Original Ausgabe Leipzig 1727–1729 mit einem Nachwort und Erläuterungen.* Edited by Wolfgang Martens. Stuttgart: J. B. Metzler, 1975.

Gray, Marion. *Productive Men, Reproductive Women: The Agrarian Household and the Emergence of Separate Spheres During the German Enlightenment.* New York: Berghahn Books, 2000.

Grieser, Rudolf. *Briefe des Ministers Otto Christian von Lenthe an den Geheimen Kriegsrat August Wilhelm von Schwicheldt (1743–1750).* Hildesheim: August Lax, 1977.

Griesheim, Christian Ludwig von. *Verbesserte und vermehrte Auflage des Tractats: Die Stadt Hamburg in ihrem politischen, öconomischen und sittlichen Zustände.* Hamburg: Drese, 1760.

Guiard Larrauri, Teófilo. *Historia de la noble villa de Bilbao.* 5 vols. Bilbao: José de Astuy, 1905–12. Reprint. Bilbao: Editorial La Gran Enciclopedia Vasca, 1971–74. Vol. 3: *(1700–1800).*

Grünhagen, Colmar. "Der schlesische Adel vor hundert Jahren im Lichte der öffentlichen Meinung." *ZVGAS* 30 (1896): 1–26.

——. "Schlesien in den letzten Jahrzehnten österreichischer Herrschaft, 1707–1740." *ZVGAS* 15 (1880): 33–62.

——. "Schlesien unmittelbar nach dem Hubertsburger Frieden." *ZVGAS* 25 (1891): 104–23.

Guttandin, Friedhelm. *Das paradoxe Schicksal der Ehre: Zum Wandel der adeligen Ehre und zur Bedeutung vom Duell und Ehre für den monarchischen Zentralstaat.* Berlin: Dietrich Reimer, 1992.

Guyard, François [Franz]. *Sendschreiben des Kaufmanns Guyard in Hamburg an seine Mitbürger: Als eine Einleitung zu seinen herauszugebenden Mémoires.* n.p. [Hamburg]: n.p., 1767.

Haake, Paul. *Kursachsen oder Brandenburg-Preußen? Geschichte eines Wettstreits.* Berlin: Dr. Emil Ebering, 1939.

Haenel, Erich, and Eugen Kalkschmidt, eds. *Das alte Dresden: Bilder und Dokumente aus zwei Jahrhunderten.* Munich: Franz Hanfstaengl, 1923.

Hamburg, Geschichte der Stadt und Ihrer Bewohner. Edited by Werner Jochmann and Hans-Dieter Loose. Vol. 1: *Von den Anfängen bis zur Reichsgründung.* Hamburg: Hoffmann & Campe, 1982.

Hanken, Caroline. *Vom König geküßt: Das Leben der großen Mätressen.* Berlin: Berlin Verl., 1996.

Harris, James. *Diaries and Correspondence of James Harris, First Earl of Malmesbury, Containing an Account of His Missions at the Court of Madrid, to Frederick the Great, Catherine the Second, and at the Hague; of his Special Missions to Berlin, Brunswick, and the French Republic.* 4 vols. 2nd ed. 1845. Reprint. New York: AMS Press, 1970.

Hasche, Theodor. *Kurze Darstellung des Verfahrens im Hamburgischen Nieder-Gerichte.* Hamburg: Nestler, 1802.

Hatje, Frank. *Representationen der Staatsgewalt: Herrschaftstruktur und Selbstdarstellung in Hamburg 1700–1900.* Basel: Helbing & Lichtenhahn, 1997.

Hattendorff, Mathias. *Höfische Reglement und Lustbarkeiten: Die Besuche von Caroline Mathilde und Christian VII. in Hamburg und Holstein, 1766–1772.* Hamburg: Kultur, 1999.

Henderson, W. O. "The Berlin Commercial Crisis of 1763." *EHR* 15 (1962–63): 89–102.

Herr, Richard. *The Eighteenth-Century Revolution in Spain.* Princeton, N.J.: Princeton University Press, 1958.

Heß, Jonas Ludwig von. *Hamburg topographisch, politisch und historisch beschrieben.* 2nd rev. ed. 3 vols. Hamburg: J. C. Brüggemann, 1810–11.

Hoensch, Jörg K. *Geschichte Polens.* Stuttgart: Eugen Ulmer, 1983.

———. *Sozialverfassung und politische Reform: Polen im vorrevolutionären Zeitalter.* Cologne: Böhlau, 1973.

Höfer, Peter. *Deutsch-französische Handelsbeziehungen im 18. Jahrhundert: Die Firma Breton frères in Nantes (1763–1766).* Stuttgart: Klett-Cotta, 1982.

Hoffmann, Gabriele. *Das Haus an der Elbchaussee: Die Godeffroys-Aufstieg und Niedergang einer Dynastie.* Hamburg: Die Hanse, 1998.

Huhn, Fred-Conrad. "Die Handelsbeziehungen unter besonderer Berücksichtigung der Handelsverträge von 1716 und 1769." Diss., University of Hamburg, 1952.

Hull, Isabel V. *Sexuality, State, and Civil Society in Germany, 1700–1815.* Ithaca, N.Y.: Cornell University Press, 1996.

Hunt, Lynn. "The Many Bodies of Marie Antoinette: Political Pornography and the Problem of the Feminine in the French Revolution." In *Eroticism and the Body Politic,* ed. id., 108–30. Baltimore: Johns Hopkins University Press, 1991.

Irgang, Winfried, Werner Bein, and Helmut Neubach. *Schlesien: Geschichte, Kultur und Wirtschaft.* 2nd rev. ed. Cologne: Wissenschaft & Politik, 1998.

Jäckel, Günter, ed. *Dresden zur Goethezeit, 1760–1815.* Hanau: Werner Dausien, 1988.

Jacobi, D(aniel) H(einrich). *Geschichte des Hamburger Niedergerichts.* Hamburg: Nolte, 1866.

Jany, Curt. *Geschichte der Preußischen Armee vom 15. Jahrhundert bis 1914.* 2nd. enlarged edition by Eberhard Jany. 2 vols. Osnabrück: Biblio, 1967.

Jeannin, Pierre, Erich Lüth, and Erich Jahn. *Gekräuselt, gepudert, mit untadeliger Anmut: Hamburg und die französische Revolution.* Hamburg: Christians, 1977.

Jochmann, Werner. "Hamburgisch-schlesische Handelsbeziehungen: Ein Beitrag zur abendländischen Wirtschaftsgeschichte." in *Geschichtliche Landeskunde und Universalgeschichte: Festgabe für Hermann Aubin zum 23. Dezember 1950,* 217–28. Hamburg: "Wihag" Buch-Druckerei, 1950.

Jünger, Johann Friedrich. *Die Entführung: Ein Lustspiel in 3 Aufzügen.* Leipzig: n.p., 1792.

Kates, Gary. *Monsieur d'Eon Is a Woman: A Tale of Political Intrigue and Sexual Masquerade.* New York: Basic Books, 1995.

Keens-Soper, Maurice. "Abraham de Wicquefort und Diplomatic Theory." Discussion Papers 14, Diplomatic Studies Programme, Center for the Study of Diplomacy, 1996.

Kellenbenz, Hermann. "German Aristocratic Entrepreneurship: Economic Activities of the Holstein Nobility in the Sixteenth and Seventeenth Centuries." *Explorations in Entrepreneurial History* 6 (1953): 103–14.

——. *Sephradim an der unteren Elbe: Ihre wirtschaftliche und politische Bedeutung vom Ende des 16. bis zum Beginn des 18. Jahrhunderts.* Wiesbaden: Franz Steiner, 1958.

——. *Unternehmerkräfte im Hamburger Portugal- und Spanienhandel, 1590–1625.* Hamburg: Veröffentlichungen der Wirtschaftlichen Forschungsstelle e.V., 1954.

Keller, Karin. "Saxony: *Rétablissement* and Enlightened Absolutism." *German History* 20 (2002): 309–31.

Kelly, James: *"That Damn'd Thing Called Honour": Dueling in Ireland, 1570–1860.* Cork, Ireland: Cork University Press, 1995.

Kiefer, Klaus H., ed. *Cagliostro: Dokumente zu Aufklärung und Okkultismus.* Munich: Beck, 1991.

Kimbell, David. *Italian Opera.* Cambridge: Cambridge University Press, 1991.

Klefeker, Johann. *Sammlung der Hamburgischen Gesetze und Verfassung in Bürger- und Kirchlichen, auch Cammer-, Handlungs- und übrigen Policey-Angelegenheiten und Geschäften samt historischen Einleitungen.* 12 vols. Hamburg: Piscator, 1765–74.

Klessmann, Eckart. *Geschichte der Stadt Hamburg.* Hamburg: Hoffmann & Campe, 1994.

Klöber und Hellscheborn, Karl Ludwig von. *Von Schlesien, vor und seit dem Jahr MDCCXXXX. . . .* 2 parts. Freiburg: Wilhelm G. Korn, 1788.

Klotz, Ernst Emil. *Die schlesische Gutsherrschaft des ausgehenden 18. Jahrhunderts: Auf Grund der Friderizianischen Urbare und mit besonderer Berücksichtigung der alten Kreise Breslau und Bolkenhain-Landeshut.* Breslau, 1932. Reprint. Aalen: Scientia, 1978.

Knapp, Georg Friedrich. *Grundherrschaft und Rittergut: Vorträge nebst biographischen Beilagen.* Leipzig: Duncker & Humblot, 1897.

Kneschke, Ernst Heinrich. *Neues allgemeines Deutsches Adels-Lexikon.* Leipzig: Degener, 1930.

Koch, Herbert. "Handelsbeziehungen zwischen Hamburg und Jena, 1768–1786." *HGH* 17 (1959): 1–9.

Kopitzsch, Franklin. *Grundzüge einer Sozialgeschichte der Aufklarung in Hamburg und Altona.* 1982. 2nd expanded ed. Hamburg: Verein für Hamburgische Geschichte, 1990.

Kopitzsch, Franklin, and Dirk Brietzke, eds. *Hamburgische Biografie: Personenlexikon.* Vol. 1. Hamburg: Christians, 2001.

Kopitzsch, Franklin, and Daniel Tilgner, eds. *Hamburg Lexikon.* Hamburg: Zeise, 1998.

Krebs, Julius. *Hans Ulrich, Freiherr von Schaffgotsch: Ein Lebensbild aus der Zeit des dreißigjährigen Krieges.* Breslau: Wilhelm Gottlieb Korn, 1890.

Kühl, Heinrich. *Hamburger Rath- und Bürgerschlüsse vom Jahre 1700 bis zum Ende des Jahres 1800.* Hamburg: Bohn, 1803.

Kuhnert, Reinhold P. *Urbanität auf dem Lande, Badereisen nach Pyrmont im 18. Jahrhundert.* Göttingen: Vandenhoeck & Ruprecht, 1984.

Kutzner, Oskar. *Das Landratsamt in Schlesien, 1740–1806: II. Teil, Die Zusammensetzung des Landratsamts*. Doctoral thesis, Königl. Universität Breslau. Breslau: A. Favorke, 1911.

Labarre de Raillicourt, Dominique. *Richelieu: Le Maréchal libertin*. Paris: Tallandier, 1991.

Laermann, Klaus. "Der riskante Person in der moralischen Anstalt: Zur Darstellung der Schauspielerin in deutschen Theaterzeitschriften des späten 18. Jahrhunderts." *Die Schauspielerin: Zur Kulturgeschichte der weiblichen Bühnenkunst*, ed. Renate Möhrmann, 127–53. Frankfurt a/M: Insel, 1989.

Lande, Lawrence. *The Rise and Fall of John Law, 1716–1720*. Montreal: Lawrence Lande Foundation for Canadian Historical Research, 1982.

Langbein, John H. *Prosecuting Crime in the Renaissance: England, Germany, France*. Cambridge, Mass.: Cambridge University Press, 1974.

Lappenberg, Johann Martin. "Listen der in Hamburg residirenden fremden sowie der Hamburg im Ausland vertretenden Diplomaten und Consuln, nebst einer geschichtlichen Einleitung." *ZVHG* 3 (1851): 414–534.

———. "Listen der bis 1870 in Hamburg residierenden sowie der Hamburg im Ausland vertretenden Diplomaten und Konsuln." 2 vols. Typescript. Revised and expanded by Christian Mahlstedt. Hamburg, 1969. Available in the Staatsarchiv Hamburg library.

Laufenberg, Heinrich. *Geschichte der Arbeiterbewegung in Hamburg, Altona und Umgebung*. 2 vols. Hamburg: Auer, 1911–31.

Le Blond, Aubrey. *Charlotte Sophie Countess Bentinck: Her Life and Times*. 2 vols. London: Hutchinson, 1912.

Ledebur, Leopold von. *Adelslexicon der Preussischen Monarchie*. Berlin: Ludwig Rauh, 1854.

Lediard, Thomas (the Elder). *The German Spy: In familiar letters from Munster, Paderborn, Osnabrug, Minden, Bremen, Hamburg, Gluckstadt, Helgoland, Stade, Lubeck, and Rostock. Written by a Gentleman on his Travels, to his Friends in England*. London: J. Mechell, 1738.

Lerer, David. "La Politique française en Pologne sous Louis XV (1733–1772)." Thesis, University of Toulouse, 1929.

Leszczński, Jósef. "La Silésie dans la politique européenne au XVIe–XVIIIe siècles." *Acta Poloniae Historica* 22 (1970): 90–107.

Liebe, Georg, Em Theuner, and Ernst Friedländer. *Ältere Universitäts-Matrikeln, aus der Originalhandschrift*. Part 1: *Frankfurt an der Oder*. Vol 1: 1649–1811. Leipzig: Hirzel, 1888.

Liebel, Helen. "Laissez-faire vs. Mercantilism: The Rise of Hamburg and the Hamburg Bourgeoisie vs. Frederick the Great in the Crisis of 1765." *VSWG* 52 (1965): 207–38.

Lindemann, Mary. "Armen- und Eselbegräbnis in der europäischen Frühneuzeit: Eine Method sozialer Kontrolle?" In *Studien zur Thematik des Todes im 16. Jahrhundert*, ed.Richard Toellner and Paul R. Blum, 125–40. Wolfenbüttel: Herzog August Bibliothek, 1983.

———. *Patriots and Paupers: Hamburg, 1712–1830*. New York: Oxford University Press, 1990.

————. "The Wind-Traders: Speculators and Frauds in Northern Europe, 1650–1720." In *Living Dangerously in Medieval and Renaissance Europe*, ed. Barbara A. Hanawalt. South Bend, Ind.: Notre Dame University Press, forthcoming.

Loewe, Viktor. *Bibliographie der Schlesischen Geschichte*. Breslau: Priebatsch's Buchhandlung, 1927.

[Lossow, Matthias Ludwig von]. *Denkwürdigkeiten zur Charakteristik der preußischen Armee, unter dem großen König Friedrich dem Zweiten: Aus dem Nachlaß eines alten preußischen Offiziers*. Glogau: Carl Heymann, 1826.

Lucas, Theophilus. *Memoirs of the Lives, Intrigues, and Comical Adventures of the Most Famous Gamesters and Celebrated Sharpers in the Reigns of Charles II., James II., William III., and Queen Anne*. London: Jonas Brown, 1714.

Lukowski, Jerzy. *The European Nobility in the Eighteenth Century*. New York: Palgrave Macmillan, 2003.

Lynham, Deryck. *The Chevalier Noverre, Father of Modern Ballet: A Biography*. London: Dance Books, 1972.

McAleer, Kevin. *Dueling: The Cult of Honor in Fin-de-Siècle Germany*. Princeton, N.J.: Princeton University Press, 1994.

McClelland, Charles E. *State, Society, and University in Germany, 1700–1914*. Cambridge: Cambridge University Press, 1980.

Mainka, Peter. *Die Erziehung der adligen Jugend in Brandenburg-Preußen: Curriculare Anweisungen Karl Abrahams von Zedlitz und Leipe für die Ritterakademie zu Liegnitz, eine archivalische Studie zur Bildungsgeschichte der Aufklärungszeit*. Würzburg: Verein für Geschichte Schlesiens, 1997.

————. *Karl Abraham von Zedlitz und Leipe (1731–1793): Ein schlesischer Adliger in Diensten Friedrichs II. und Friedrich Wilhelms II. von Preußen*. Berlin: Duncker & Humblot, 1994.

Mainka, Peter, Johannes Schellakowsky, and Peter A. Süss, eds. *Aspekte des 18. Jahrhunderts: Studien zur Geistes-, Bildungs- und Verwaltungsgeschichte in Franken und Brandenburg-Preußen*. Würzburg: Freunde Mainfränkischer Kunst und Geschichte; Schweinfurt: Historische Verein, 1996.

Mallett, Michael Edward. "The Emergence of Permanent Diplomacy in Renaissance Italy." Discussion Papers 56, Diplomatic Studies Programme, Center for the Study of Diplomacy, 2000.

Mansel, Philip. *Prince of Europe: The Life of Charles-Joseph de Ligne (1735–1814)*. London: Weidenfeld & Nicolson, 2003.

Margadant, Jo Burr, ed. *The New Biography: Performing Femininity in Nineteenth-Century France*. Berkeley: University of California Press, 2000.

Martens, Wolfgang. *Die Botschaft der Tugend: Die Aufklärung im Spiegel der deutschen Moralischen Wochenschriften*. 4 vols. Stuttgart: J. B. Metzler, 1971.

Martin, Denis. *Vollständige Acten in der seltenen und überaus wichtigen Sache, Denis Martin, wieder seinen unwürdigen Schwiegersohn und unwürdige Tochter,* . . . n.p. [Hamburg]: n.p., 1767.

Martin, Laurence W., ed. *Diplomacy in Modern European History*. New York: Macmillan, 1966.

Mascuch, Michael. *Origins of the Individualist Self: Autobiography and Self-Identity in England, 1591–1791*. Stanford, Calif.: Stanford University Press, 1996.

Matsch, Erwin. *Geschichte des Auswärtigen Dienstes von Österreich(-Ungarn), 1720–1920.* Vienna: Böhlau, 1980.

Mauleon Isla, Mercedes. *La poblacion de Bilbao en el siglo XVIII.* Valladolid: Universidad de Valladolid, 1961.

Maza, Sarah. *Private Lives and Public Affairs: The Causes célèbres of Prerevolutionary France.* Berkeley: University of California Press, 1993.

Meinardus, Otto. "Das Gnadengeschenk Friedrich des Großen für den schlesischen Landadel und die Ernennung Carmers zum Justizminister (1768)." *ZVGAS* 44 (1910): 74–109.

Meister, Alois. "Der preussische Residentenstreit in Köln: Ein Versuch zur Einführung des reformierten Gottesdienstes." *Annalen des Historischen Vereins für den Niederrhein* 70 (1901): 1–30.

Miruss, Alexander. *Das europäische Gesandschaftsrecht nebst einem Anhange von dem Gesandschaftsrechte des Deutschen Bundes: Einer Bücherkunde des Gesandschaftsrechts und erläuternden Beilagen.* 2 vols. Leipzig: W. Englemann, 1847.

Mitchell, W. J. T., ed. *On Narrative.* Chicago: University of Chicago Press, 1981.

Mittenzwei, Ingrid. *Preussen nach dem Siebenjährigen Krieg: Auseinandersetzungen zwischen Bürgertum und Staat um die Wirtschaftspolitik.* Berlin: Akademie, 1979.

Möhrmann, Renate. "Die Schauspielerin als literarische Fiktion." In *Die Schauspielerin: Zur Geschichte der weiblichen Bühnenkunst,* ed. id., 154–74. Frankfurt a/M: Insel, 1989.

———, ed. *Die Schauspielerin: Zur Kulturgeschichte der weiblichen Bühnenkunst.* Frankfurt a/M: Insel, 1989.

Molmenti, P. *La Vie privée à Venise depuis l'origine jusqu'à la chute de la république.* 3 vols. Venice: Ferd. Ongania, 1895–97.

Morgenbesser, Michael. *Geschichte Schlesiens: Ein Handbuch.* Breslau: Josef Max, 1829.

Mortier, Roland. *Le "Prince d'Albanie": Un Aventurier au siècle des Lumières.* Paris: Honoré Champion, 2000.

Mügge, Ernst Alexander. *Barbarina: Lustspiel in vier Aufzügen.* Leipzig: P. Reclam jun., [c. 1880].

Mulier, E. O. G. Haitsma. "De affaire Zanovich: Amsterdams-Venetiaanse betrekkingen aan het einde van de achttiende eeuw." *Amstelodamum* 72 (1980): 85–119.

Müller, Klaus. "Diplomatie und Diplomaten im Zeitalter des Prinzen Eugens." In *Prinz Eugen von Savoyen und seine Zeit,* ed. Johannes Kunisch, 45–46. Würzburg: Ploetz Freiburg, 1986.

———. *Das kaiserliche Gesandtschaftswesen im Jahrhundert nach dem Westfälischen Frieden (1648–1740).* Bonn: Ludwig Röhscheide, 1976.

Murphy, Orville T. *Charles Gravier, Comte de Vergennes: French Diplomacy in the Age of Revolution, 1719–1787.* Albany: State University of New York Press, 1982.

Der neue Pitaval: Eine Sammlung der interessantesten Criminalgeschichten aller Länder aus älterer und neuerer Zeit. Edited by J. E. Hitzig, W. Alexis Häring, and Anton Vollert. 60 vols. Leipzig: F. A. Brockhaus, 1845–90.

North, Michael, ed. *Kunstsammlung und Geschmack im 18. Jahrhundert.* Berlin: Arno Spitz, 2002.

Nugent, Thomas. *Travels through Germany . . . with a particular account of the Courts of Mecklenburg, in a series of letters to a friend.* 2 vols. London: Printed for E. and C. Dilly, 1768.

Nuremberg. Stadtarchiv. *Die Kunstsammlung des Paulus Praun: Die Inventare von 1616 und 1719.* Compiled by Katrin Achilles-Syndram. Nuremberg: Stadtrat, 1994.

Olivier, Jean-Jacques, and Willy Norbert. *Barbarina Campanini: Eine Geliebte Friedrichs des Großen.* Berlin: Marquardt, 1909.

Oresko, Robert, G. C. Gibbs, and H. M. Scott, eds. *Royal and Republican Sovereignty in Early Modern Europe: Essays in Memory of Ragnild Hatton.* Cambridge: Cambridge University Press, 1997.

Ortner, Sherry B. *Narrativity in History, Culture, and Lives.* Transformations. CSST Working Paper No. 66 and CRSO Working Paper No. 457. Ann Arbor: University of Michigan, 1991.

Palewski, Jean-Paul. *Stanislas-August Poniatowski; Dernier roi de Pologne.* Paris: Librairie Polonaise, 1946.

Paris an der Alster: Die Französische Revolution in Hamburg. Catalog of exhibition at the Staats- u. Universitätsbibliothek Hamburg "Carl von Ossietzky," 21 April–27 May 1989. Herzberg: Traugott Bautz, 1989.

Pasteur, Claude. *Le Roi et le prince: Les Poniatowski, 1732–1812.* Paris: France-Empire, 1976.

Der Patriot, nach der Originalausgabe, Hamburg, 1724–1726, in drei Textbänden und einem Kommentarband. Edited by Wolfgang Martens. 4 vols. Berlin: Walter de Gruyter, 1964.

Pedlow, Gregory W. *The Survival of the Hessian Nobility, 1770–1870.* Princeton, N.J.: Princeton University Press, 1988.

Peter, Anton. *Das Herzogthum Schlesien.* Vienna: Karl Graeser, 1884.

Pfudel, Ernst. *Die Geschichte der Königl. Ritter-Akademie zu Liegnitz.* 1908. Reprint. Hofheim-Taunus: Henske-Neumann, 1994.

Pitaval, François Gayot de. *Causes célèbres et intéressantes avec les jugements qui les ont decidées.* 24 vols. Paris: Delaune, 1739–70.

———. *Merkwürdige Rechtsfälle als ein Beitrag zur Geschichte der Menschheit: Nach dem Französischen Werk des Pitaval durch merere Verfasser ausgearbeitet und mit einer Vorrede begleitet herausgegeben von Schiller.* 4 parts. Jena: Chris. Heinr. Cuno, 1792–95. Reprint, Frankfurt a/M: Eichborn, 2005.

Pohl, Hans. *Die Beziehungen Hamburgs zu Spanien und dem spanischen Amerika in der Zeit von 1740 bis 1806.* Wiesbaden: Franz Steiner, 1963.

Pöllnitz, Karl Ludwig von. *Das galante Sachsen.* New ed. Offenbach a/M: n.p., 1735.

Poniatowski, Stanisław August. *Die Memoiren des letzten Königs von Polen Stanisław August Poniatowski.* Munich: Georg Müller, 1918.

Porter, Roy, and Marie Mulvey Roberts, eds. *Pleasure in the Eighteenth Century.* New York: New York University Press, 1997.

Postel, Rainer. "Reformation und bürgerliche Mitsprache in Hamburg." *ZVHG* 65 (1979): 1–20.

Prittwitz und Gaffron, Christian Wilhelm von. *Unter der Fahne des Herzogs von*

Bevern: Jugenderinnerungen des Christian Wilhelm von Prittwitz und Gaffron. Edited by Hans Werner von Hugo and Hans Jessen. Breslau: Wilhelm Gottlieb Korn, 1935.

Przezdziecki, Rajnold. *Diplomatic Ventures and Adventures: Some Experiences of British Envoys at the Court of Poland.* London: Polish Research Centre, 1953.

Ramcke, Rainer. *Die Beziehungen zwischen Hamburg und Österreich im 18. Jahrhundert: Kaiserlich-reichsstädtisches Verhältnis im Zeichen von Handels-und Finanzinteressen.* Hamburg: Hans Christians, 1969.

Ravoux-Rallo, Elisabeth. *La Femme au temps de Casanova.* Paris: Stock/Laurence Pernoud, 1984.

Reddaway, W. F., et al. *The Cambridge History of Poland.* Vol. 2: *From August II to Pilsudski (1697–1935).* Cambridge: Cambridge University Press, 1941.

Reincke, Heinrich. *Historisch-politische Betrachtungen über die Reichsunmittelbarkeit der Freien und Hansestadt Hamburg.* Hamburg: Verein für Hamburgische Geschichte, 1952.

Reiner, Hans. *Die Ehre: Kritische Sichtung einer abendländlichen Lebens- und Sittlichkeitsform,* Dortmund: E. S. Mittler & Sohn, 1956.

Reißmann, Martin. *Die hamburgische Kaufmannschaft des 17. Jahrhunderts in sozialgeschichtlicher Sicht.* Hamburg: Hans Christians, 1975.

Retzow, August Friedrich von. *Charakteristik der wichtigsten Ereignisse des siebenjährigen Krieges: In Rücksicht auf Ursachen und Wirkungen, von einem Zeitgenossen.* Berlin: Himburgische Buchhandlung, 1802.

Roepell, Richard. *Polen um die Mitte des 18. Jahrhunderts.* Gotha: Friedrich Andreas Perthes, 1876.

Rohden, Peter R. *Die klassische Diplomatie: Von Kaunitz bis Metternich.* 1939. New ed. Stuttgart: K. F. Koehler, 1972.

Rommerin, Reiner. "Das europäische Staatensystem zwischen Kooperation und Konfrontation, 1739–1856." In *Aufbruch aus dem Ancien régime: Beiträge zur Geschichte des 18. Jahrhunderts,* ed. Helmut Neuhaus, 79–99. Cologne: Böhlau, 1993.

Rosecrance, Richard N. "Diplomacy in the Eighteenth Century." In *Diplomacy in Modern European History,* in Laurence W. Martin, 31–43. New York: Macmillan, 1966.

Rosselli, John. *The Opera Industry in Italy from Cimarosa to Verdi: The Role of the Impresario.* Cambridge: Cambridge University Press, 1984.

Roth, Suzanne. *Aventure et aventuriers au XVIIIe siècle: Essai de sociologie littéraire.* Lille: Service du reproduction des thèses, Université de Lille III, 1980.

Rulhière, Claude-Carloman de. *Anecdotes sur le maréchal de Richelieu.* Paris: Allia, 1993.

Rutland, Barry. *Gender and Narrativity.* Ottawa: Centre for Textual Analysis, Discourse, and Culture, Carlton University Press, 1997.

Sarkissian, Arshag Ohan, ed. *Studies in Diplomatic History and Historiography in Honour of G. P. Gooch.* London: Longmans, 1961.

Sasse, Klaus. "Die Entdeckung der 'courtisane vertueuse' in der französischen Literatur des 18. Jahrhunderts: Réstif de la Bretonne und seine Vorgänger." Diss., University of Hamburg, 1967.

Schaefer, Arnold. *Geschichte des siebenjährigen Kriegs.* 2 vols. Berlin: W. Hertz, 1867–74.

Scharf, Claus. *Katharina II., Deutschland und die Deutschen.* Mainz: Philipp von Zabern, 1995.

Schellenberg. Carl. *Das alte Hamburg: Eine Geschichte der Stadtentwicklung und Baukunst dargestellt in Gemälden, Zeichnungen, Stichen und Photos zeitgenössischer Künstler.* Hamburg: Christians, 1975.

Schmidt, E. *Einführung in die Geschichte der deutschen Strafrechtspflege.* 1947. 3rd. ed. Göttingen: Vandenhoeck & Ruprecht, 1965.

Schnitter, Helmut. "Die Barbarina—Eine Affäre des Königs." In *Gestalten um Friedrich den Großen: Biographische Skizzen,* ed. id., 107–13. Reutlingen: Preußischer Militär-Verl., 1991.

Schramm, Percy Ernst. "Hamburg und die Adelsfrage (bis 1806)." *ZVHG* 55 (1969): 81–93.

———. *Kaufleute zu Haus und über See: Hamburgische Zeugnisse des 17., 18. und 19. Jahrhunderts.* Hamburg: Hoffmann & Campe, 1949.

———. *Neun Generationen: Dreihundert Jahre deutscher "Kulturgeschichte" im Lichte der Schicksale einer Hamburger Bürgerfamilie, 1648–1948.* 2 vols. Göttingen: Vandenhoeck & Ruprecht, 1963–64.

Schreiner, Klaus, and Gerd Schwerhoff. *Verletzte Ehre: Ehrenkonflikte in Gesellschaften des Mittelalters und der Frühen Neuzeit.* Cologne: Böhlau, 1995.

Schroeder, Hans. *Lexikon der hamburgischer Schriftsteller bis zur Gegenwart.* 8 vols. Hamburg: Verein für Hamburgische Geschichte, 1851–83.

Schroeder, Paul W. *The Transformation of European Politics, 1763–1848.* Oxford: Clarendon Press, 1994.

Schröter, Philipp von. *Kurzgefasste Geschichte aller Königlichen Preußischen Regimenter, zur Erklärung der illuminirten Abbildungen derselben: Bey dieser vierten Auflage bis ans Ende des Jahres fortgestzt, und mit der jetzigen Generalität vermehret.* Nuremberg: Raspische Handlung, 1770.

Schück, Carl Eduard. "Die Familie derer von Zedlitz in Schlesien während dreier Jahrhundert." *Rübezahl, der Schlesischen Provinzialblätter* 75 (1871): 59–61.

Schulz, Günter. *Wolfenbütteler Studien zur Aufklärung III.* Wolfenbüttel: Jacobi, 1976.

Schumann, Otto. *Die Landeshuter Leinenindustrie in Vergangenheit und Gegenwart: Ein Beitrag zur Geschichte der schlesischen Textilindustrie.* Jena: Gustav Fischer, 1928.

Schütze, Johann Friedrich. *Hamburgische Theater-Geschichte.* Hamburg: J. P. Treder, 1794.

Scott, H. M. "Prussia's Royal Foreign Minister: Frederick the Great and the Administration of Prussian Diplomacy." In *Royal and Republican Sovereignty in Early Modern Europe: Essays in Memory of Ragnild Hatton,* ed. Robert Oresko, G. C. Gibbs, and H. M. Scott, 500–526. Cambridge: Cambridge University Press, 1997.

Seffrin, R. *Die katholische Bevölkerungsgruppe im Staate Hamburg: Eine historisch-soziologische Untersuchung.* Quakenbrück: Trute, 1938.

Seraphim, Emil. *Geschichte Liv-, Est- und Kurlands von der "Aufsegelung" des*

Landes bis zur Einverleibung in das russiche Reich. Vol. 2, part 1: *Die Provinzial-geschichte bis zur Unterwerfung unter Rußland;* vol. 2, part 2: *Kurland unter den Herzögen.* Reval: Franz Kluge, 1896.

Sheehan, James J. *German History, 1770–1866.* Oxford: Clarendon Press, 1989.

Sichelschmidt, Gustav. *Friedrich Wilhelm II: Der "Vielgeliebte" und seine galante Zeit.* Berg am See: VGB Verl.-Ges. Berg, 1993.

Sieveking, Heinrich. *Georg Heinrich Sieveking: Lebensbild eines Hamburgischen Kauf-manns aus dem Zeitalter der französischen Revolution.* Berlin: Karl Curtius, 1913.

Silva, Raymond. *Joseph Balsamo, alias Cagliostro.* Montreal: Québec-Amérique, 1976.

Sinapius, Johannes. *Des Schlesischen Adels, Anderer Theil/Oder Fortsetzung Schlesischer Curiositäten, Darinnen Die Gräflichen, Freyherrlichen und Ade-lichen Geschlechter/So wohl Schlesischer Extraction, Als auch Die aus andern Königreichen und Ländern in Schlesien kommen/Und entweder darinnen noch floriren, oder bereits ausgangen, In volligem Abrisse dargestellet werden, Nebst einer nöthigen Vorrede und Register.* Leipzig: Michael Rohrlach, 1728.

Sinn, Dieter, and Renate Sinn. *Der Alltag in Preußen.* Frankfurt a/M: Societäts-Verlag, 1991.

Smith, Charlotte. *The Romance of Real Life.* 3 vols. London: T. Cadell, 1787.

Smith, Pamela H. *The Business of Alchemy: Science and Culture in the Holy Ro-man Empire.* Princeton, N.J.: Princeton University Press, 1994.

Soetbeer, Adolph. "Das hamburgische Konsulatwesen." *Zeitschrift des Vereins für deutsche Statistik* 1 (1847): 84–90.

———. *Statistik des hamburgischen Handels. 1839. 1840. 1841.* Hamburg: Hoffmann & Campe, 1842.

———. *Statistik des hamburgischen Handels. 1842. 1843. 1844.* Hamburg: Hoffmann & Campe, 1846.

———. *Über Hamburgs Handel.* Hamburg: Hoffmann & Campe, 1840.

Somers, Margaret R. *Narrativity, Culture, and Causality: Toward a New Episte-mology, or, Where Is Sociology After the New Historic Turn?* Transformations. CSST Working Paper No. 54 and CRSO Working Paper No. 444. Ann Arbor: University of Michigan, 1990.

Somerset, Anne. *The Affair of the Poisons: Murder, Infanticide and Satanism at the Court of Louis XIV.* London: Weidenfeld & Nicolson, 2003.

Spierenburg, Pieter. *Written in Blood: Fatal Attraction in Enlightenment Amster-dam.* Columbus: Ohio State University Press, 2004.

———, ed. *Men and Violence: Gender, Honor, and Rituals in Modern Europe and America.* Columbus: Ohio State University Press, 1998.

Stein-Stegemann, Hans-Konrad, ed. *Findbuch der Reichskammergerichtsakten im Staatsarchiv Hamburg.* 2 vols. Hamburg: Verein für Hamburgische Geschichte, 1993.

Stein, Herbert. *Der galante Roman.* Stuttgart: J. B. Metzler, 1961.

Stroev, Alexandre. *Les Aventuriers des Lumières.* Paris: Presses universitaires de France, 1997.

Strohm, Klauspeter. "*Die Kurländische Frage (1700–1763): Eine Studie zur Mächtepolitik im Ançien Régime.*" Diss., Berlin, 1999.

Stuart, Kathy. *Defiled Trades and Social Outcasts: Honor and Ritual Pollution in Early Modern Germany.* Cambridge: Cambridge University Press, 1999.

Stutzer, Dietmar, with the assistance of Harald Siebenbürger. *Die Verwaltungsgeschichte, die wirtschaftlichen und sozialen Verhältnisse in Oberschlesien und im Fürstentum Troppau-Jägerndorf, 1620–1820, dargestellt am Beispiel der Familie Eichendorff.* Dülmen: Laumann, 1983.

Sutton, John L. *The King's Honor and the King's Cardinal: The War of the Polish Succession.* Lexington: University of Kentucky Press, 1980.

Tabela podatku gruntowego i ludności wsi śląskich z około 1765 roku [Property tax and population tables for the Silesian towns around 1765]. Compiled by Zbigniew Kwaśny and Jan Wosch. Źródła do Atlasu Historycznego Śląska/Polska Akademia Nauk. Instytut Historii, 1. Wrocław: Zakład Narodowy im. Ossolińskich, 1975.

Tatin-Gourier, Jean-Jacques. *Cagliostro et l'affaire du collier: Pamphlets et polémiques.* St. Étienne: Publications de l'Université de Saint-Étienne, 1994.

Taube, A. "Ernst-Johan von Biron: Hohes Spiel." In *Deutsche Männer des baltischen Ostens,* 90–96 Berlin: Volk & Reich, 1943. Reprint. 1984.

Tharau, Friedrich-Karl. *Die geistige Kultur des preußischen Offiziers von 1640 bis 1806.* Mainz: v. Hase & Koehler, 1968.

Thomas, Helga. *"Madame, meine teure Geliebte": Die Mätressen der französischen Könige.* Vienna: Ueberreuter, 1996.

Thompson, James Westfall, and Saul K. Padover. *Secret Diplomacy: Espionage and Cryptography.* 1937. 2nd. ed. New York: Frederick Ungar, 1963.

Tolkemitt, Brigitte. *Der Hamburgische Correspondent: Zur öffentlichen Verbreitung der Aufklärung in Deutschland.* Tübingen: Niemeyer, 1995.

Vehse, Eduard. *Geschichte des preußischen Hofs und Adels und der preußischen Diplomatie.* Vols. 3–4. Hamburg: Hoffmann & Campe, 1851.

Véritable vie privée de maréchal de Richelieu, contenant ses amours et intrigues, et tout ce qui a rapport aux divers rôles qu'a joués cet homme célèbre pendant plus de quatre-vingt ans. 3 vols. Paris: J. P. Roux, 1791. Edited by Élisabeth Porquerol. Paris: Gallimard, 1996.

Vèze, Raoul (pseud. Jean Hervez). *L'Histoire galante du XVIIIe siècle.* 4 vols. Paris: Bibliothèque des curieux, 1924–27.

Villiers, Jean. *Cagliostro: La Prophète de la Révolution.* Paris: Guy Trédaniel, 1988.

Vogel, Walther. "Handelskonjunkturen und Wirtschaftskrisen in ihrer Auswirkung auf den Seehandel der Hansestädte." *HGH* 74 (1956): 50–64.

Voght, Caspar. *Lebensgeschichte.* Hamburg: Alfred Janssen, 1917.

Weber, Matthias, and Carsten Rabe, eds. *Silesiographia: Stand und Perspektiven der historischen Schlesienforschung.* Würzburg: Verein für Geschichte Schlesiens, 1998.

Wechmar, Carl von. *Geschichte des Dorfes und Rittergutes Zedlitz (Kreis Steinau).* Supplement to *ZVGAS,* 12. Breslau: Verfasser, 1874.

Weill, Herman N. "Frederick the Great and His Grand Chancellor Samuel von Cocceji: A Study in the Reform of the Prussian Judical Administration, 1740–1755." Diss., University of Illinois, 1959.

Wendt, Georg. *Geschichte der Königlichen Ritter-Akademie zu Liegnitz.* Part 1: 1708–840. Liegnitz: Oscar Heinze, 1893.

Westphalen, Nicolaus A. *Hamburgs Verfassung und Verwaltung in ihrer allmäh-ligen Entwicklung bis auf die neueste Zeit.* Hamburg: Perthes-Besser & Mauke, 1841.

Whaley, Joachim. "The German Protestant Enlightenment." In *The Enlighten-ment in National Context,* ed. Roy Porter and Mikuláš Teich, 106–17. New York: Cambridge University Press, 1981.

———. *Religious Toleration and Social Change in Hamburg, 1529–1819.* Cambridge: Cambridge University Press, 1985.

White, Hayden. "The Value of Narrativity in the Representation of Reality." In *On Narrative,* ed. W. J. Mitchell, 1–23. Chicago: University of Chicago Press, 1981.

Winter, Otto Friedrich, ed. *Repertorium der diplomatischen Vertreter aller Länder seit dem Westfälischen Frieden* (1648). Vol. 2: *1716–1763,* ed. F. Hausmann. Zurich: Fretz & Wasmuth, 1950. Vol. 3: *1764–1815.* Cologne: Böhlaus, 1965.

Wohlwill, Adolf. *Aus drei Jahrhunderten der Hamburgischen Geschichte (1648–1888).* Hamburg: Lucas Gräfe & Sillem, 1897.

Wolff, Larry. *The Vatican and Poland in the Age of the Partitions: Diplomatic and Cultural Encounters at the Warsaw Nunciature.* Boulder, Colo.: East European Monographs, 1988.

Woloszyński, Ryszard W. "La Pologne vue par l'Europe au XVIIIe siècle." *Acta Poloniae historica* 12 (1965): 22–42.

Wraxall, Nathaniel William. *Memoirs of the Courts of Berlin, Dresden, Warsaw, and Vienna: In the Years 1777, 1778, and 1779.* 2 vols. London: Printed for T. Ca-dell Jun. and W. Savies, 1799, 1806.

Zamoyski, Adam. *The Last King of Poland.* 1992. London: Phoenix, 1998.

Zernack, Klaus. *Preußen-Deutschland-Polen: Aufsätze zur Geschichte der deutsch-polnischen Beziehungen.* Berlin: Duncker & Humblot, 1991.

Ziechmann, Jürgen, ed. *Panorama der Fridericianischen Zeit: Friedrich der Große und seine Epoche. Ein Handbuch.* Bremen: Zeichmann, 1985.

Ziekursch, Johannes. *Hundert Jahre Schlesischer Agrargeschichte: Vom Hubertus-burger Frieden bis zum Abschluss der Bauernbefreiung.* Breslau, 1927. Reprint. Aalen: Scientia, 1978.

Zimmermann, Alfred. *Blüthe und Verfall des Leinengewerbes in Schlesien: Gewerbe- und Handelspolitik dreier Jahrhunderte.* Breslau: Wilhelm Gottlieb Korn, 1885.

Zimmermann, Friedrich. *Neue Chronik von Hamburg vom Entstehen der Stadt bis zum Jahre 1819.* Hamburg: C. E. Hässler, 1820.

Index

abduction, 66–67, 95
academies, 69, 160. *See also*
  Ritterakademie
accusatory (legal) process, 19
actresses, 221
adventurers, 222, 234, 240, 245, 257–59,
  281
Albania, false prince of, 71, 218, 258
Aliens' Contract, 276
Altona, 96, 119
Altranstädter Convention, 143, 162
Amberg (widow), 126–27, 129, 277
Anckelmann, Paridom Friedrich, 26,
  98, 104, 232, 272
Anckelmann family, 26
Anna, tsarina, 216, 240
Apraxin, Stepan Stepanovich, 187
August II ("the Strong," king of
  Poland; Friedrich August I, elector
  of Saxony), 210, 213–14, 216
August III (king of Poland; Friedrich
  August II, elector of Saxony), 184,
  201, 214, 216–17, 235, 237, 244
autobiography, 135–36

Bad Pyrmont, 63
bailiff, 102
balance of power, 78
Ballestrem, Johann Baptist, count von,
  146
ballet, 184

bandits, 256–57
"La Barbarina." *See* Campanini,
  Barbara
Barcker, captain, 188, 190–92, 196–97,
  234, 253
Barry, Madame du (Jeanne Bécu), 220
Barthy, count, 252
Bastille, 241
Bauernschutz, 145
Bautzen, 249
Bentinck, Charlotte Sophie, countess
  von, 72, 73–74, 172, 229, 270, 274
Der Biedermann, 225
Bilbao, 81, 173, 259–62
billiards, 66
bills of exchange, 241, 248
Binder von Kriegelstein, Anton: as
  imperial resident, 63–64, 73, 77, 85,
  86, 91–92, 194; interventions of,
  124–25, 127–29, 246; reports to
  Vienna, 129, 229, 269–78
Biorenberg, Jonas van, 67, 88, 95
Biron, Ernst Johann (duke of Cour-
  land), 216, 240–41
Biron, Karl Ernst. *See* Karl Ernst,
  baron von Treyden
Biron, Peter (duke of Courland), 239–
  40
blood money, 42–43
Blücher, von (gentleman-in-waiting), 74
Bolton, Joachim Friedrich, 1

Borck, von (captain), 98
Bourbon, François-Louis de, 213
Branicki, Jan Klemens, 242–43
Branicki, Ksawary, 243
Brentano, Francesco, 63
Breslau, 14, 145–46, 167
Bretonne, Réstif de la, 137, 281
Brieg, 143, 145
Brinvilliers, marquise de, 66, 258–59
Brockes, Barthold Heinrich, 64
Broglie, Charles François, comte de, 187
Brown, Thomas, 190, 195–97, 253, 255
Bruchbach, Johann Gottfried, 75, 195, 201–3
Buhrbanck, Magdalena Elisabeth and Maria Coecilia, 191, 195
Bürgerlichkeit, 60–62, 70
Bürgermeister, 18, 26, 60
Bürgerschaft, 86–87, 103
Bürgertum, 63
Buttler-Ehrenberg, Gottlob and Carl von, 70
Buvarro, Brentano, 196

Cagliostro, Alessandro, count di (Giuseppe Balsamo), 218, 258
Caledon, Joseph, 195
Calvinists, 86–87, 93
Campanini, Barbara ("La Barbarina"), 220–21
Candide, 70
cardplaying, 66, 75–76, 98, 239
cardsharpers, 75, 239, 257
Carmer, Johann Heinrich von, 153
Carolina. See *Constitutio Criminalis Carolina*
Casanova, Giovanni Giacomo, chevalier de Seingalt: acquaintances of, 69, 71; on actresses, 183–84, 221; as adventurer, 4; on dueling, 44; as imposter, 71, 170, 255, 257, 281; imprisonment in Leads, 188; meets Saby, 237–39; in Warsaw, 217–18
Catai, Caterina, 239
Catherine II, ("the Great"), tsarina, 186, 214–15, 219, 235
Catholics, 85–86, 245–46, 268

cause(s) célèbre(s), 40, 61, 99, 137–38, 279–80
Chamber of Commerce, 126, 262–63
Choiseul, Etienne-François, duc de, 90, 187, 220
civic freedoms (*bürgerliche Freiheiten*), 20, 25
civil strife, 83, 99
Coccejii, Carl Ludwig von, 220
Coccejii, Samuel von, 220
coffeehouses, 69, 74–75, 171–72, 250; Dreyer's, 12–14, 74–75, 176–77, 178
collecting, 168–70
collegial bodies, 19–21, 25, 60–61, 96, 113, 297. *See also* Senat: conflict with collegial bodies
Colloredo, Rudolf Joseph, count von, 229
Comèdie, 75–76
commerce, 125–26
Commerce Deputation, 82
Commonwealth of Poland-Lithuania. *See* Poland
concert européen, 214
Confederation of Bar, 186–87, 216, 243–44, 283
Confederation of Radom, 243
Constitutio Criminalis Carolina, 19, 43–44, 51, 66
consulado, 261
consuls, 269, 271; French, 119; Hanseatic/Hamburg, 79; position in Hamburg, 125–27; privileges of, 263, 269; in Spain, 81, 267; Spanish in Hamburg, 81, 87, 118–19, 121
Conti, Louis-François, prince de, 212
Conty, Antoine de, 81
corruption, 232, 271, 273
cosmopolitan provinicialism, 64
costs (in Kesslitz case), 110, 113, 116–17, 119
Courchetet, Lucien, 92
Courland (duchy), 213–14, 216–17, 239–41
Courland, dukes of, 185–86, 188; Saxon dukes of, 213–15. *See also* Biron, Ernst Johann; Biron, Peter; Karl Ernst, baron von Treyden

courtesans, 221–22, 252–53
courts (European), 18, 65, 67, 72–73
Cropp, Friedrich, 1
cross-dressing, 187
cuirassiers, 164–65
culpability (criminal), 41, 43
Czartoryski family, 214, 234–35

dancers, 221
Davis, Natalie Zemon, 39
debts, 193, 203–4, 241–42, 253
Defoe, Daniel, 182, 281
delictum publicum, 45
Denmark, 83, 98
Destinon, Jean (Johann), 87
Detenhof, Johann Hinrich, 16–17, 26,
    59, 105–8, 111, 116; in Berlin, 106–7,
    110, 112; defense of Kesslitz, 24, 50–
    54
Dewald, Jonathan, 68
Diet (Sejm), 186, 236
diplomacy, 40, 212, 214, 265–66, 279;
    and adventurers, 90; and causes cél-
    èbres, 280; character of, 77–79, 86;
    correspondence in, 101, 129, 229,
    269–78; and criminal cases, 98; and
    Kesslitz affair, 77, 100–102; old
    regime, 89–93, 128; personal, 101;
    principle of reciprocity in, 264–65,
    267; professionalization of, 90;
    quotidian, 77–78, 89, 93, 99, 267;
    "Renaissance," 89; secret, 90, 208,
    212, 258; and sex, 218–20
diplomats, 62–63, 70–71, 73–74, 172,
    280; immunity of, 85–86, 126. *See
    also* residents
dishonorable people, 24
district administrators (*Landräte*),
    145–46, 150–52, 168
Dorner, Martin, 87
drama, 133
Dresden, 166–67, 218–19
Dreyer, Hans Andreas, 74–75, 178
Duchène (Du Chene), 185, 201–2. *See
    also* Romellini, Anna Maria
dueling, 42–49, 75, 97–98, 178, 242,
    244, 256; Casanova on, 44; and
    honor, 48–49; Kant on, 46; language

of, 44; Montesquieu on, 46; prohibi-
    tions of, 41–42, 45–48, 55, 65–66; in
    Prussia, 45–46; punishment of, 47–
    49; as suicide, 52

egodocuments, 135–36, 280
Eichendorff, Joseph von, 147–48
Eimbeck'sches Haus, 1–2, 17, 22, 116,
    230
Elders (Oberalten), 97–98, 114–15
Elias, Norbert, 69
émigrés, 62
Encke, Mincke, 220–21
Engauen, Maria Anna, 12, 195, 206, 273
English common law, 25
Enlightenment, 70, 72, 147, 224–25
Entführung. See abduction
Die Entführung, 66
Eon, Charles de Beaumont, chevalier
    d', 219–20, 258
eques Silesius, 163, 170
Erdmann, Heinrich Christian Georg,
    192, 195, 203–6, 270
espionage, 213, 258. *See also* diplomacy:
    secret

Faber, Hans Jacob (syndic), 85, 97,
    266–67
Fabrice, Joachim Gottlieb, 92
facts, 134
Factum, 10
Familia, 235–36, 243
favorites, 219
Ferdinand I (Holy Roman Emperor),
    141–42
fiction, 38–39, 134, 258–59
Finckenstein, Karl Wilhelm Finck von,
    90, 104, 108–9, 111
Findung, 24
fiscal, 24, 58
fiscal process, 19, 56–57, 102, 108–13
Fiskal. See fiscal
Fonseca, Joseph da, 196, 199
foreigners, 59, 72, 196
Foreign Office (Prussian), 112, 117
France, 89, 119
Frank, Arthur, 135
Frankfurt, 60

Franklin, Benjamin, 73
Frantzen (merchant), 74
Frederick II ("the Great," king of Prussia), 40, 46, 69, 73, 220–21; army officers of, 150–51; character of, 87–88; court of, 209–10; intervention into Kesslitz case, 97–98, 110, 112–13; as military leader, 164; and Poland, 186; protectionist policies, 68, 84–86; and Silesia, 141, 150. *See also* Seven Years' War; Silesian Wars
Frei, von, 208
French Revolution, 89
Friedrich August I, elector of Saxony. *See* August II
Friedrich August II, elector of Saxony. *See* August III
Friedrich I (king in Prussia), 94
Friedrich II. *See* Frederick II
Friedrich Wilhelm (the Great Elector), 45
Friedrich Wilhelm I (king of Prussia), 46, 88
Friedrich Wilhelm II (king of Prussia), 220
Frohn. See jailer-executioner
Frohnerei, 24
Fundatist, 160, 162–63; Kopothsche, 163

galant(e), 201, 208–10, 219, 222, 224, 226
gambling, 70, 74–75, 191, 247, 250
gardens, 69, 171, 172
Gassen-Recht, 22, 102–3
gentleman (as social ideal), 68
Georg Wilhelm (duke of Celle), 210
German dualism, 88
Gevers (swordsmith), 204, 253
Glatz, 167
Glogau, 142, 145, 158, 168
Goethe, Johann Wolfgang, 70, 169
Golgowitz, 158
Golitsyn, Dmitri, prince, 276
Görlitz, 249–50
Görtz "palace," 194
Gottorper Agreement, 83
Gottsched, Johann Christoph, 225

Great Northern War, 80
grec. See cardsharpers
Greiffenberg, 144
Greppi, Jacob, 196
Grimaldi, Jerónimo, marquis de, 77, 82, 90, 121–25, 265, 266, 274
Groß, Fyodor Ivanovich von, 193
Große Johannisstraße, 13
Grund (physician), 17, 26
Guerre, Martin, 137
Guido, Catharina, 195, 253
Gustav III (king of Sweden), 72–73
Guyard incest case, 94, 137, 275–76

Hambourgeoisie, 76
Hamburg: citizens of, 62, 171–72, 223; constitution of, 26, 47; economy, 60–61, 68, 79, 82; ennoblement of citizens, 62–63; as free imperial city, 28, 83; internal tensions within, 47, 61–62; legal system, 18; morality in, 224; as news center, 171; political culture of, 60, 103, 114; relations with France, 88, 124; relations with Holy Roman Empire, 83; relations with Prussia, 84, 87–88, 171; relations with Spain, 79–83, 123–24, 262; religious minorities in, 61–62; as republic, 60, 99, 261–62; society, 60–61, 63–65, 68–69, 72–76; sovereignty of, 28, 58, 98
Hamburgischer Correspondent, 246
Hamburg und Altona, 62
Harris, James, 186, 243
Hecht, Johann Julius von, 107, 264; as resident, 88, 91–101; and Spanish recruitment, 82
Heinrich, prince (Prussia), 106, 111, 166–67, 177–78
Henri III (king of Poland, king of France), 213
Herreira, vicomte de la, 276
Hertzberg, Ewald Friedrich von, 90, 99, 104, 108–9, 111
hetman, 236
hidalgo, 92, 234, 259, 261
Hirschberg, 144
"Historical Narrative," 10, 49–50, 177,

206–7, 245–55. *See also* narrative;
  Sillem, Garlieb
Hofadel. See nobles: types of
Hohberg, Wolf Helmhards von, 70
Holtermann, Friedrich Christoph, 190,
  195, 198
Holy Roman Empire, 82, 84–85
homicide, 18, 21, 28, 40–43. *See also*
  killing
honor: definitions of, 44, 48, 60, 88;
  and dueling, 41, 44, 51–52, 256; Kess-
  litz's, 54–55, 100–106, 109, 115–16; of
  officers, 45, 151
Horst, von der, 81
Houze, Mattheu de Basquiat, baron de
  la: intervention for Kesslitz, 89, 117–
  25, 128; as resident, 62–63, 73, 77, 91–
  92, 172, 260
Hugier, d', 92, 124
Huguenots, 74, 89
Hunold, Christian Friedrich, 210, 281
Hurley, Patrick, 258

identity, 64–65, 136, 245, 280
imperial chapel, 86
imperial resident, 85
imposters, 236, 241, 258–59, 280
imposture, 65, 193, 247
incest, 137
inns (Hamburg), 11, 75, 170
inquisitorial (legal) process, 18, 25
investigations (criminal): general, 21–
  22; procedures, 21, 25, 29, 34, 57, 133;
  special, 22
Italians, 52, 239, 256–57, 259
Ivanov, Charles, 241

Jablonowski, Josef Alexander, prince,
  244
jailer-executioner, 24, 102, 255
Jensen, Christian, 96–97
jeux de commerce. See cardplaying;
  gambling
Josephenine Ritterakademie zu Liegnitz. *See* Ritterakademie
Joseph I (Holy Roman Emperor), 143
Jünger, Johann Friedrich, 66
Jungfernstieg, 75

Jürgensen (physician), 74
jurisdiction, 99, 101
jury trials, 25
justice, 41–42, 44

Kant, Immanuel, 223
Karl Christian of Saxony (duke of
  Courland), 216, 240
Karl Ernst, baron von Treyden (duke
  of Courland), 216, 237, 239–41, 248.
  See also Romellini, Anna Maria
Karl VI (Holy Roman Emperor), 141,
  145
Karl XII (king of Sweden), 143
Kauntiz-Rietberg, Wenzel Anton,
  prince von, 90, 128
Kesslitz, Augustine von (Sister Maria
  Benedicta), 111, 156–58
Kesslitz, Joseph, baron von: after 1776,
  181; autobiography, 159–60, 179; in
  Breslau, 170; and Catholicism, 156;
  character of, 55–56, 58–59, 177–81,
  282; culpability in Visconti's death,
  54–56; death of, 181; defense of, 50–
  54; early life, 159–60; education,
  160–63; fight with Visconti, 16–17,
  31, 33, 48–49, 52–56, 57–59; finances,
  168–69; as gem-dealer, 169–70, 282;
  in Hamburg, 170–72, 176–77;
  imprisonment, 179; and linen trade,
  282; loss of family estate, 168; meets
  Visconti, 170, 249–51; military
  career, 164–66, 177; protects "Moor,"
  282; relationship with parents, 163–
  64, 167–68; and Romellini, 176, 179–
  81; and Sanpelayo, 172–75
Kesslitz, Maria Franziska von (neé
  Kreckwitz), 156
Kesslitz, Maximilian (II) von, 156, 158–
  59
Kesslitz, Maximilian (III) von, 159
Kesslitz family, 151, 154–59
Kettler, Friedrich Wilhelm (duke of
  Courland), 280
killing, 41–43. *See also* dueling;
  homicide
King's Secret, 90, 187, 212–13, 219, 258
Klefeker, Johann, 51–52, 84, 272

knife-fighting, 52–53, 57–58, 256
Köhlern, Catharina Ilsabe, 196
Koschenbahr (general), 97, 106
Kottwitz, baron von, 67, 95–96
Kreckwitz, Johann Karl Ferdinand
  Leopold von, 168
Kreckwitz family, 151, 153, 159
Krohn, baron von, 67
Kyrani (Greek merchant), 247–49

Laclos, Pierre Choderlos de, 212,
  281
Landadel. See nobles: types of
Landeshut, 111, 167, 173
Law, John, 65
Lediard, Thomas, 63–64
legal codes (Hamburg), 22, 41
legal forms (Hamburg), 24–25, 109
Lehwald[t], major von, 164
Lenclos, Ninon de, 221
Lepe, Johann Franz van der, 81, 83,
  120–25, 266–67
Leszcyński, Stanisław, 213–14, 216
Les Liaisons dangereuses, 5, 212
Libellus, 57–58
libertines, 28, 208–12, 219, 223, 257
libertins érudits, 209
liberum veto, 235
Liechtenstein family, 148
Liegnitz, 143
linen, 79–80, 84, 86, 89, 111, 146, 173–
  75, 262
literary theory, 135
Louis, duc de Bourgogne, 201
Louis-Joseph-Xavier, duc de Bour-
  gogne, 237
Louis XV (king of France), 90, 187, 212,
  218, 220
Lower Saxon Circle, 62–63, 91–92
Lutheran clergy, 86–87, 224
luxury, 68, 227–28

Maiden Heinrich, 137
Magnanigo (impresario), 185
manslaughter, 43. See also killing
Manuzzi, Antoine Niccoló, 188
Manuzzi, Giovanni Battista, 188, 247
Marechall, Philipp Jacob, 195, 201, 251

mariage de conscience, 34, 53, 192–94,
  203
Maria-Josepha (of Saxony), 201–2, 212
Maria-Theresa (of Austria), 69, 128,
  145, 164, 209
marriage (clandestine), 95–96
Martin, Denis, 275–76
Marsani ("Massani," Polish subject),
  107–8, 112
Matsen, Nicolaus, 105–6
Mattheson, Johannes, 63–64
Matuschka, count, 220
Matusky, count, 180, 193–94, 205
Mauen, Elisabeth Engel, 95
Mauen, Georg, 67, 95
Mayer, von (general), 167
medical examiners, 1–2, 17, 40
melodrama, 33
memoirs, 136
ménagement, 105, 110
merchants, 47, 60, 63, 68, 126; culture
  of, 65, 262–63; Spanish, 79
Mercy, comte de, 128
minister-plenipotentiary, 92
Mitau, 240
Mitchell, Andrew, 87–88
Mocenigo, Alvise, 188
moderamen inculpatae tutelae. See self-
  defense
Moll Flanders, 182, 259
Montesanto, Jacob Gonsalez, 196
Montmorency-Bouteville, comte de,
  47
Moor, 179
moral weeklies, 63–64, 147
Moritz (of Saxony), 216
Morsan, chevalier de, 66, 137
Münsterberg, 143

narrative, 10, 29, 38–39, 133–36, 138,
  280
Neuer Wall, 11, 13, 75, 194, 277
news, 74
Niedergericht: judges, 20; prerogatives
  of, 20–21, 60, 101, 114–15; procedures, 24–25, 56–57, 100, 103, 108–9,
  113
Niederschlag. See homicide; killing

nightwatch, 16–17, 22, 268
"Ninski." *See* Poniński, Jan
   Nepomucen
nobility, 59–63, 222; pretensions to,
   64–65
nobles: character of, 64–66, 67–68,
   70–71; domestication of, 45; education of, 69, 160–63; financial difficulties, 158; as gentlemen, 45; in
   Hamburg, 27–28, 62–68, 95, 99, 172;
   honor, 44, 102; impostures of, 242;
   lifestyle, 146, 168–69, 170; as officers,
   45; parodies of, 69–71; Polish, 244;
   relations with citizens, 67–68, 71;
   types of, 69, 148, 234–35, 242
Northern System, 78
Nostitz family, 149–51, 159
novels, 136–38, 210, 257, 259, 279

Oberalten. *See* Elders
Obergericht (=Senat), 20, 24
Oels, 143
officers, 66, 94, 150, 152, 160–62
Olbreuse, Elénore Desmier, 210, 220
opera, 63, 69, 74, 75, 172, 184
opera buffa, 239
opium, 53, 257
Oppenheimer, Josef Süss, 242
Ortner, Sherry, 134
Osten, Karl Johann Gustav, von der
   (called Sacken), 186

Panin, Nikita, 78
patriciate, 60
Der Patriot, 64–66, 69–71, 147, 225–
   27
Patriotic Society, 225
patriotism, 225
Peace of Westphalia, 83–84, 143
Pensionisten, 162
Perrine, chevalier de la, 237
Pesne, Antoine, 220
Peter III, tsar, 241
Pfeiffer, Johann, 176
physici. See medical examiners
Piasten, 141–42
Piccolomini, count (Ruggieri Rocco),
   237

Pingel (sugar refiner), 67
Pini, Joseph, 196, 198–99
pirates, 82
pistols, 54, 256, 263
Pitaval, François Gayot de, 137, 182,
   259, 281
pleasure, 68–69, 222, 227
poisoning, 259
Poland: Diet (Sejm), 214–15; as gentry
   republic, 214, 243; internal politics,
   242–43; king, 107 (*see also* Stanisław
   August); nobility of, 234; partitions
   of, 128, 213–14; religious dissidents,
   243; Saxon kings of, 215; after the
   Seven Years' War, 78, 214–15
Pöllnitz, Karl Ludwig von, 210
Pompadour, madame de, 219
Poniatowski, Andrzej, 235–36
Poniatowski, Kazimierz, 235–37
Poniatowski, Michal, 235–36
Poniatowski, "Prince," 185, 203, 211,
   229, 234–35, 237, 239
Poniatowski, Stanisław August. *See*
   Stanisław August
Poniatowski family, 234–37
Poniński, Adam, 217
Poniński, Jan Nepomucen: career,
   242–44; character of, 244; and Con-
   federation of Bar, 187, 242, 244; in
   Dresden, 186, 242–44; opposition to
   Stanisław August, 243; and Polish
   politics, 213, 217; as Romellini's
   lover, 185–86, 188
Poniński family, 234
Poniso, Giacomo, 81, 262–63
Poor Clares' Cloister (Glogau), 111, 156
Potemkin, Gregori, 244
Potocki family, 234
Pour le mérite, 150, 158
praetor, 17, 19–24, 26
Pragmatic Sanction, 145
Presser, Jacques, 135
Prittwitz und Gaffron, Christian
   Wilhelm von, 159, 166
privilegium de non appellando, 85
promenades, 69, 74, 75–76
prosecutor. *See* fiscal
prostitutes, 252–53

Prussia, 84–85, 93–114; General Law Code, 51; officers, 151; subjects in Hamburg, 93–94. *See also* Frederick II; Hamburg: relations with Prussia; Hecht, Johann Julius von

public opinion, 105, 274

Pulcinelli, Caterina, 241

punishments, 22, 56, 109; capital, 42–43

Raab zu Rauenheim, Karl Josef, count, 85

Radziwiłł family, 234

Rathaus, 74

recruiters, 66, 95, 99; Danish, 96–97; Prussian, 88, 93, 98–99, 170–71; Spanish, 82, 262–64, 266–69

Réfugiés, 74

Regiment (surgeon), 17, 26

Reichenbach, Leopold von, 70, 148

Reichenbach family, 70, 148

Reichshofrat (Aulic Council), 25, 85, 88

Reichskammergericht (Imperial Cameral Tribunal), 25, 83, 85

Reiss, Johann Christian, 247

religious toleration, 87

rencontre, 44, 46, 50, 55, 97. *See also* dueling

Repnin, Nikolai Vasilievich, count, 186, 243

republic, 42, 90, 101–2

republicanism, 225, 228

reputation, 44

residents, 87, 89–91, 100

Richelieu, Armand Jean du Plessis, cardinal and duc de, 47

Richelieu, Louis François Armand de Vignerot du Plessis, duc de, 186–87, 211–12

Riecke, Franz, 81

Riga, 240

Ripperda, Jan Willem, baron van, 90

Ritterakademie (Liegnitz), 69, 149, 156, 160–63

Roeder, Friedrich Wilhelm von, 164–65

Rolff, Carl, 96–98, 106, 264

romances, 137, 257

Roman law, 19, 43

Romellini, Anna Maria (Antonina, "Nina"): accusations made by, 229–32, 270, 274, 277; acquaintances of, 195–96; alias of, 203 (*see also* Duchène); in Altona, 228–29, 231, 270, 274, 276; in Amsterdam, 276; appeals to Binder von Kriegelstein, 229–31; appeals to countess von Bentinck, 274–75; appeals to Senat, 231; banished, 228; and Barcker, 190–92; in Bordeaux, 188; at Buhrbancks, 199–200; character of, 59, 207–8, 232, 237; children of, 185–86, 188–89, 194, 270; as dancer, 183; debts, 204; defloration, 185, 235; in Dresden, 188, 200, 213; and duke of Courland, 185, 240–42; early life, 34, 182–84; in the Hague, 228, 274, 276; and Kesslitz, 270; lodgings, 12, 75; miscarries, 198; in Paris, 188, 196, 200, 203; in Rotterdam, 228, 231, 274; and Saby, 183–85, 237–40 (*see also* Saby, Antoine); and Sanpelayo, 36, 192, 194, 205–6, 229–30, 270 (*see also* Sanpelayo, Antoine de); as secret courier, 187–88; sexuality of, 227; testimony of, 35, 183; and Visconti, 33–34, 36, 188–89, 207–8 (*see also* Visconti, Joseph); in Warsaw, 196, 200–201, 203, 207, 213, 239

Romellini, Antonina, 207–8

Roose, Abraham, 195

Rothschild, Mayer Amschel, 169

Rouget, Catherine, 273

rumor, 271, 276, 281

Rzeczpospolita. See Poland

Saby, Antoine (de), 183–88, 201–2, 216, 218, 222, 237–41. *See also* Romellini, Anna Maria

Sagan, 142

Sainte-Croix, sieur Godin, 258–59

Salisch, 153, 158, 163, 168

salons, 69, 72

Sanpelayo, Antoine (Ventura) de: character, 55, 59, 128–29, 205, 267, 269–70, 282; conduct of, 120, 122,

273; conflicts with Senat, 266–69; as
consul, 62–63, 81, 91–92, 120–22,
259–60, 263–65, 273 (*see also* consuls: Spanish in Hamburg); death
of, 127, 277; honor, 117; as merchant,
79, 172–73, 259–61; paternity case
against, 28, 268; prepares to leave
Hamburg, 231; role in Visconti's
death, 3, 12, 36–37, 53, 269; and
Romellini, 75–76, 121, 230, 270 (*see
also* Romellini, Anna Maria); and
Spanish recruitment, 83; violent
temper of, 267, 270; and Visconti,
192
satisfaction, 44
Satisfaktionsfähig, 44–46
Saxony, 213, 218
scandal, 95, 210, 275
Schimmelmann, Heinrich Carl von,
73, 174, 196–97
Schlabrendorff, Ernst Wilhelm von,
164
Schlabrendorff, Friedrich von: duel,
98–99, 179; friendship with Kesslitz,
13, 74, 170–71, 176–78, 250
Schlabrendorff, Gustav Albrecht von
(general), 165
Schlesische Landschaft. See Silesia:
credit organization
Schnittler, Anna Maria, 67
Schuback, Jacob, 85, 118–19, 122, 129
Schuback, Johannes, 85
Schwicheldt, August Wilhelm von, 204
Schwicheldt, Heinrich Ernst von, 204
secretaries (of Senat), 64
seduction, 66
self-defense, 18, 31, 33, 40–41, 43, 48–
59, 100, 108–9, 122
self-fashioning, 136, 280
Sellentin, Friedrich Wilhelm von, 111
Senat: composition of, 9, 18, 26–27,
60–61, 223–24; conflict with collegial bodies, 83, 86–97, 99–100, 103,
279; conflict with Niedergericht, 21,
23, 40, 97, 103, 108–10 (*see also*
Niedergericht); decision in Kesslitz's
case, 114–15; pro-Austrian faction,
85; pro-Prussian faction, 84–85; and

sovereignty, 27–28, 56–57, 87, 97,
105, 113
sepulcrum asininum (Eselbegräbnis), 48
Seven Years' War: battles of, 163–67;
effects on diplomacy, 78, 128, 215,
218; and Hamburg, 68, 84, 86–87;
Kesslitz's participation in, 106, 178
(*see also* Kesslitz, Joseph: military
career); and Silesia, 141, 145, 150
Sheehan, James, 64
Silesia: credit organization (*Schlesische
Landschaft*), 154; economy, 110–11,
143–46, 152–54; Lower, 141–43, 150;
nobility, 141, 144, 146, 147–54, 156,
160; as Prussian territory, 110–11,
157; religion, 142–43; Upper, 143
Silesian Wars, 141, 143, 145–47, 152. *See
also* Seven Years' War
Sillem, Garlieb: charges of bribery
against, 231–32, 272–74; correspondence with van der Lepe, 103–4, 120,
272 (*see also* Lepe, Johann Franz van
der); correspondence with Wever,
103–4, 111, 272 (*see also* Wever,
Jacob); duties as syndic, 18, 23, 25–
27, 101, 272; "Historical Narrative,"
10, 49–53, 177, 245 (*see also* "Historical Narrative"); proposes compromise, 113–14; on Romellini, 206–7
(*see also* Romellini, Anna Maria:
character of)
Singelmann, Engelborg, 103, 137
Singelmann, Jacob, 103
The Sorrows of Young Werther, 70
sovereignty, 79, 82–88, 93, 97, 99–101,
107–8, 117, 126, 267, 279
Spain: court of, 124; and Kesslitz affair,
117–25; trade with Hamburg, 79, 82
species facti, 275–76
The Spectator, 63
Spierenburg, Pieter, 256
Stanisław August (king of Poland):
affair with Catherine the Great, 235;
and Confederation of Bar, 186–87
(*see also* Confederation of Bar);
election of, 215, 235, 243; family, 217
(*see also* Familia; Poniatowski family); mistresses of, 217, 235, 239;

Stanisław August (*continued*)
  opponents of, 213, 217, 235. *See also*
  Poland
Steetz (merchant), 266
Stenglin, Philipp Hinrich, 84
stockjobbers, 65
story-telling, 38–39, 134–35
Struensee, Johann Friedrich, 242
syndics, 9, 17, 26, 57, 64, 90–91, 272
szlachta. See Poland: nobility of

The Tatler, 63
testimony: character of, 133–34; collec-
  tion of, 22, 26–27
theater, 30–38, 69, 74, 75, 172
Thonus, 189–90, 208, 234. *See also*
  Romellini, Anna Maria
Tillot, Guillaume de, 184
Tomatis, Carlo, 239
Tom Jones, 259
torture, 23
Totschlag. See killing
Treaty of Hubertusburg, 167. *See also*
  Seven Years' War
true crime, 136–38, 257, 279, 281
truth, 134
Turkish (Polish) War, 187

universities, 68, 160, 161, 163
Urfehde, 100, 115–17, 129, 179–80
Urqullu, Manuel d', 126–27, 277

venereal disease, 192, 205, 270
Verführung. See seduction
Vergennes, Charles Gravier, count de,
  73, 90, 124–25
Der Vernünfftler, 63
violence, 41, 59–60
virtues (civic), 65–66, 224
Visconti, Antonio Eugenio, 189, 246
Visconti, Joseph: arrangement with
  Barcker, 191; attacks Kesslitz, 15,
  30–31, 33, 52–53, 57–58; attacks
  Romellini, 15; attacks Sanpelayo, 15–
  16; autopsy, 1–3, 27, 110, 245; in
  Bergamo, 252; in Breslau, 194, 247–
  49; at Brown's, 190–91, 197–98;
  burial of, 27; character of, 31, 34–37,
  54–56, 58–59, 189, 195, 245, 253–54,
  282; as con-man, 247–49; death of,
  16, 27, 36, 54; debts, 193, 203–4, 253;
  in Dresden, 251; as imposter, 4, 65,
  193, 197, 246, 249–51, 254–55; in
  Italy, 4, 35, 251; as knife-fighter, 13,
  16, 52–53, 118, 256–57; life history,
  244–59; manservants of, 250, 254;
  and opera singer, 250–53; parentage,
  246; returns to Hamburg, 192–93;
  and Romellini, 32, 245; travels of,
  192–93, 251; in Venice, 194; violent
  disposition of, 191, 193, 204, 253–57;
  wounds, 2–3, 53–54
Visconti family, 206, 234, 246
visum repertum. See Visconti, Joseph:
  autopsy
Voght, Caspar, 62, 72–74
Voght, Caspar (father), 74, 118–19
Volkmann, Peter Dietrich, 17
Voltaire, 70
Vorführung, 24, 103–4, 109, 114. *See also*
  Niedergericht: procedures

Warnery auf Langendorf, Carl Eman-
  uel von, 158
War of the Austrian Succession. *See*
  Silesian Wars
War of the Polish Succession, 214
War of the Spanish Succession, 80
Warsaw, 217–18, 223
Wechmar, Ludwig Anton von, 150
Wedde, 96
Wedel, Karl Heinrich von (general),
  165
Wentzhardt, Johann Heinrich, 67
Wentzhardt scandal, 67
Wessel, Teodor, 243
Wever, Jacob, 92, 97, 107, 112, 116. *See
  also* Sillem, Garlieb: correspondence
  with Wever
White, Hayden, 135
Wicquefort, Abraham, 90
Wiedau, Johann Carl von, 237
Winserbaum, 22
witnesses, 22–23, 195–96
Wobersnow, Moritz Franz Kasimir
  von (general), 164, 165–66

Wolff, Christian, 227
Woltersdorff (merchant), 69, 176
women, 75, 225–227
Wraxall, Nathaniel, 164
Wurmb, Friedrich Christoph, 173

Zannovitch, Stiépan (Annibale). *See* Albania, false prince of
Zedlitz, Carl Abraham von, 149
Zedlitz family, 148–49
Zweikampf. See dueling